Land Reform in the British and Irish Isles since 1800

Scotland's Land
Series editor: Professor Annie Tindley

Editorial Advisory Board
Dr Calum MacLeod, University of Edinburgh
Dr Malcolm Combe, University of Aberdeen
Dr Iain Robertson, University of the Highlands and Islands
Professor Terence Dooley, Maynooth University
Professor Ewen A. Cameron, University of Edinburgh
Dr John MacAskill, University of Edinburgh

This series presents the latest scholarly work to academic and public readers on Scotland's land issues. Predominantly focusing on the history of Scotland's economic, political, and social and cultural relationships to land, landscape, country houses and landed estates, it also brings in cutting-edge approaches to explore new methodologies and perspectives around this politically contentious but stimulating issue. As an interdisciplinary series, it necessarily contains a wide range of approaches, including history, law, economics and economic history, philosophy, environment/landscape studies and human/cultural geography. The aim of the series is to bring together and publish the best work on land issues across a wide range of disciplines for a diverse set of audiences.

Published titles

The Land Agent: 1700–1920
Annie Tindley, Lowri Ann Rees and Ciarán Reilly (eds)

Scotland's Foreshore: Public Rights, Private Rights and the Crown, 1840–2017
John MacAskill

Land Reform in Scotland: History, Law and Policy
Malcolm Combe, Jayne Glass and Annie Tindley (eds)

Land Reform in the British and Irish Isles since 1800
Shaun Evans, Tony McCarthy and Annie Tindley (eds)

edinburghuniversitypress.com/series/slf

Land Reform in the British and Irish Isles since 1800

Edited by Shaun Evans, Tony McCarthy
and Annie Tindley

EDINBURGH
University Press

Edinburgh University Press is one of the leading university presses in the UK. We publish academic books and journals in our selected subject areas across the humanities and social sciences, combining cutting-edge scholarship with high editorial and production values to produce academic works of lasting importance. For more information visit our website: edinburghuniversitypress.com

© editorial matter and organisation Shaun Evans, Tony McCarthy and Annie Tindley, 2022
© the chapters their several authors, 2022

Edinburgh University Press Ltd
The Tun – Holyrood Road
12 (2f) Jackson's Entry
Edinburgh EH8 8PJ

Typeset in 10.5/13pt Sabon by
Cheshire Typesetting Ltd, Cuddington, Cheshire

A CIP record for this book is available from the British Library

ISBN 978 1 4744 8768 9 (hardback)
ISBN 978 1 4744 8770 2 (webready PDF)
ISBN 978 1 4744 8771 9 (epub)

The right of Shaun Evans, Tony McCarthy and Annie Tindley to be identified as editors of this work has been asserted in accordance with the Copyright, Designs and Patents Act 1988 and the Copyright and Related Rights Regulations 2003 (SI No. 2498).

Contents

List of Figures and Tables	vii
Acknowledgements	ix
Notes on the Contributors	x
Introduction: Land Reform, Estates and Society *Shaun Evans, Tony McCarthy and Annie Tindley*	1

Part I Tenants, Landowners and Estate Management

1. Culmaily, a Model of Improvement: Reform, Resistance and Rationalisation in South-eastern Sutherland — 27
Duncan Simpson

2. 'An overwhelming tide of disappointments and vexation': A Case Study of Reform in Estate Management on the Island of Lewis, 1817–1837 — 48
Finlay McKichan

3. Public Interest or Profit? The Management of the Crown-owned Foreshore, 1866–2019 — 71
John MacAskill

Part II Agitation and Agendas of Reform

4. 'Not a bashful man': Dr Gavin Brown Clark and Land Nationalisation — 95
Ewen A. Cameron

5. The Rhetoric and Politics of Land Redistribution in Southern Ireland, 1919–1923: National and Local Perspectives — 113
Terence Dooley

6 The Liberties of the Land: Preserving the Commons in England in the Later Nineteenth and Early Twentieth Centuries 136
Ben Cowell

Part III Legislation and its Impacts

7 The Introduction of the 'Gregory Clause' and Ireland's Great Famine 157
Ciarán Reilly

8 Small Landholdings and Society: The Legacy of Small Landholder Legislation in the South-west of Scotland, 1911–Present Day 172
Micky Gibbard

9 The Case for Separate Agricultural Legislation for Wales 190
John Gwilym Owen and Nerys Llewelyn Jones

10 'The price of our loyalty?' Ulster Landlords, Tenants and the Northern Ireland Land Act of 1925 211
Olwen Purdue

Part IV Landowner Responses

11 Landed Responses to Land Reform in Scotland and Ireland, c. 1860–1903 237
Annie Tindley

12 'The battle of the Welsh nation against landlordism': The Response of the North Wales Property Defence Association to the Welsh Land Question, c. 1886–1896 259
Shaun Evans

13 Under Pressure? The Cawdor Estates and their Responses to Agricultural Depression, Land Reform and Land Crisis 285
John E. Davies

14 From Landlord to Rentier: The Wealth Management Practices of Irish Landlords, 1903–1933 303
Tony McCarthy

Index 327

Figures and Tables

FIGURES

2.1	Abandoned crofts at Garenin, Lewis	54
6.1	View of Runnymede from Coopers Hill with a distant view of Windsor Castle	137
6.2	Magna Carta memorial vandalism, July 1932	148
14.1	Advertisement for War Loan stock from *Daily Mail*, 26 June 1915	312

TABLES

2.1	Lewis parishes: number of tenancies at different rent levels, 1823 and 1831	59
10.1	Number of landlords owning estates of 2,500 acres and above in the six counties of the north of Ireland, 1876	213
10.2	Land remaining on twenty-five sample estates after 1925	226
13.1	Stackpole Court Estate: income and expenditure	293
13.2	Golden Grove Estate: income and expenditure	293
13.3	Cawdor Castle Estate: income and expenditure	294
14.1	Bellew Estate: initial estimate of sales proceeds, 1904	306
14.2	Bellew Estate: estimated rental versus investment income, 1904	306
14.3	Sample sovereign bond prices on 12 January 1910	309
14.4	Realised rates of return on quoted railway securities, 1870–1913	309
14.5	Leinster Estate application of sales proceeds at July 1905	316
14.6	Breakdown of Clonbrock portfolio by investment category at 12 May 1917	317
14.7	Coolgreany Estate trust investment portfolio, December 1904	317
14.8	Estimated surplus of annual investment income over net rental income for four estates, 1904–18	319

14.9 Leinster Estate quoted securities portfolio at 8 February 1922 320
14.10 Value of securities on the London Stock Exchange, 1853–1920 322

Acknowledgements

The genesis of this volume can be traced to a post-conference dinner in Maynooth, Co. Kildare in June 2018. As so often happens at such dinners, the conversation became a compare-and- contrast exercise, with the participants exchanging views on various topics of mutual interest, with much of the conversation focused on the landed gentry, landed estates and by extension the issue of land reform. What made this conversation particularly interesting was the presence of historians from all jurisdictions and nations of Great Britain and Ireland. It quickly became clear that there were gaps in our knowledge of landed histories and that such voids impeded a better understanding of our respective historical narratives. As a consequence, a collaboration between the Centre for the Study of Historic Irish Houses and Estates (Maynooth University), the Centre for Scotland's Land Futures (University of Dundee, University of Stirling and University of the Highlands and Islands) and The Institute for the Study of Welsh Estates (Bangor University) came into being and this volume is the eventual result. Our first acknowledgement is therefore to those three vibrant research centres for supporting the development of this project and the collaboration between the contributors. We would like to acknowledge especially the Institute for the Study of Welsh Estates, which hosted a workshop bringing together many of the contributors at Bangor University in 2017.

The contributors have identified areas which had previously remained underexplored and overall this volume makes the case that land reform issues, far from being a remnant confined to the nineteenth- and early twentieth-century historiography, are very much alive and pertinent as the United Kingdom becomes more devolved and a post-Brexit world becomes a reality. Many of the contributions to this volume illustrate this point in action and our second acknowledgement is to those, our contributors, who took up the challenge with great enthusiasm and have seen the volume to completion despite the added and unexpected pressures of a global pandemic and national lockdowns.

Lastly, the editors would like to thank the anonymous reviewers for their extremely helpful critiques and the team at Edinburgh University Press.

Notes on the Contributors

Ewen A. Cameron is the Sir William Fraser Professor of Scottish History at the University of Edinburgh. He has long-standing interests in the history of land legislation in Scotland and has published widely on the subject from the nineteenth century to the present day.

Ben Cowell's PhD at the University of Nottingham (1998) was on the landscape history of late eighteenth- and early nineteenth-century estates in England. His subsequent published work includes a history of the heritage movement, *The Heritage Obsession* (2008), a biography of the theorist of the Picturesque, Uvedale Price (with Charles Watkins, 2012) and *Landscapes of the National Trust* (with Stephen Daniels and Lucy Veale, 2015). He has co-edited (with Elizabeth Baigent) a volume of essays on the life and work of Octavia Hill (2016) and wrote a biography of another of the founders of the National Trust, Sir Robert Hunter, reissued in *The Three Founders* (2020) to mark the Trust's 125th anniversary. He is the Director General of Historic Houses, which represents over 1,500 of the UK's finest and most significant historic houses, castles and gardens, all independently owned.

John E. Davies is a retired county archivist of Carmarthenshire, since when, as an independent scholar, he has continued to research the history of landed estates, particularly those of Wales. He has recently published *The Changing Fortunes of a British Aristocratic Family: The Campbells of Cawdor and their Welsh estates, 1689–1976* (2019).

Terence Dooley is Professor of History at Maynooth University, where he is also Founder and Director of the Centre for the Study of Historic Irish Houses and Estates. He has published extensively on the history of country houses and landed estates, as well as the Irish revolutionary period. His latest monograph is *The Irish Revolution 1912–23: Monaghan* (2017).

Shaun Evans is Director of the Institute for the Study of Welsh Estates (ISWE), a research centre based at Bangor University to enhance both academic and public understanding of country houses and landed estates in Wales. This includes a portfolio of projects focusing on the historical impacts and influences of these places, especially in relation to the histories and cultures of Wales, its landscapes, identities and global connections, and a sustained effort to make use of this knowledge in the spheres of heritage interpretation, cultural tourism, the rural economy, built environment and visitor experience. His own research focuses on gentry culture and landed estates in Wales, 1500–1900. He is also Chair of the North East Wales Heritage Forum.

Micky Gibbard is a rural historian with interests in land and improvement from the eighteenth century to the present day. His doctoral thesis was completed in 2019 and gave new perspectives on the planned village movement in eighteenth-century Scotland. His work focuses on community history and he has worked on various heritage projects including Written in the Landscape (Argyll and Bute Council, 2018) and Cheltenham Diaspora (Cotswold Centre for History and Heritage, 2019). He has previously worked at the universities of Dundee, Gloucestershire and Newcastle.

Nerys Llewelyn Jones is the founder and Managing Partner of Agri Advisor Legal LLP, which was established on her home farm in Pumsaint, Carmarthenshire in 2011. She is an experienced agricultural solicitor who also has first-hand knowledge of the farming industry. She is a Fellow of the Agricultural Law Association and an Accredited Mediator. She has two young sons and farms a sheep farm in conjunction with her husband.

John MacAskill is a retired lawyer and the author of *We Have Won the Land: The Story of the Purchase of the North Lochinver Estate by the Assynt Crofters' Trust* (1999); *The Highland Destitution of 1837: Government Aid and Public Subscription* (2013); and *Scotland's Foreshore: Public Rights, Private Rights and the Crown, 1840–2017* (Edinburgh University Press, 2018).

Tony McCarthy is a PhD graduate of the Department of History, Maynooth University. He is a qualified accountant and stockbroker and holds an MBA from University College Dublin. He is author of *The Shaws of Terenure, A Nineteenth-century Dublin Merchant Family* (2010). He is currently working on a book on George Wyndham's time in Ireland.

Finlay McKichan is a retired Senior Lecturer in the Education School of the University of Aberdeen. His recent publications are a monograph, *Lord Seaforth: Highland Landowner, Caribbean Governor* (Edinburgh University Press, 2018), which was shortlisted for the Saltire Society History Book of the Year award in 2019, and chapters in *The Land Agent 1700–1920* (Edinburgh University Press, 2018) and *The Mackenzie Moment and Imperial History* (2019). He is writing a biographical monograph on Lord Seaforth's daughter and heir Mary, whose life reflects Highland, British and imperial issues and the role of elite women of ability.

John Gwilym Owen is Senior Lecturer in Law at Bangor University and was elected a Fellow of the Royal Historical Society in 2019. He qualified as a solicitor in 1981 and as a solicitor advocate in 1999. During his thirty years in practice he specialised in property litigation and agricultural law before becoming a full-time lecturer in law at Bangor University in 2011. He holds an MA in jurisprudence from Oxford University (1978) and was awarded a PhD by publication in September 2017 and appointed a Senior Lecturer in 2018. He teaches Property Law, Roman Law and English Legal History through both English and Welsh.

Olwen Purdue is a Professor in History at Queen's University Belfast. She specialises in the social and economic history of nineteenth- and twentieth-century Ireland. Her research focuses on poverty, welfare and public health in the industrial city and on the history of landed estates in the north of Ireland from the end of the Famine until the onset of the Northern Troubles. She is founder and Director of the Centre for Public History, and of the MA in Public History at QUB.

Ciarán Reilly is based at the Centre for the Study of Historic Irish Houses and Estates, Maynooth University and is a historian of nineteenth- and twentieth-century Irish history.

Duncan Simpson is a recent MLitt graduate from the University of the Highlands and Islands. He is the son of a Highland sheep farmer, the descendant of cleared Sutherland tenants and currently works as a guide interpreting the Highlands' past and present for visitors to the region.

Annie Tindley is Professor of British and Irish Rural History at Newcastle University. Her research interests revolve around the interrogation of the aristocratic and landed classes, landed estates and their management from the mid-eighteenth to mid-twentieth centuries, in the Scottish, Irish, British and imperial contexts. In 2015 she established and became the first Director of the Centre for Scotland's Land Futures, an interinstitutional and interdisciplinary research centre, and is the series editor for the book series 'Scotland's Land' published by Edinburgh University Press.

Introduction: Land Reform, Estates and Society

Shaun Evans, Tony McCarthy and Annie Tindley

[Our aim is] to organise co-operation between the Scottish, Welsh and Irish parties in Parliament and in the Country, with a respect not only to the common general objects of Home Rule, and a thorough-going settlement of the Land Question, but with respect also to the special questions more urgently demanding solution in the Highlands, in Wales, and in Ireland respectively. (*Keltic League*, 1886)

What is the most neglected issue in British politics? I would say land. Literally and metaphorically, land underlies our lives [. . .] yet for 70 years this crucial issue has scarcely featured in political discussions. (George Monbiot, 2019)

LAND REFORM HAS BEEN and still is a live political issue in the British and Irish isles. It is one of the political constants in the modern period, although as the opening quotations demonstrate, there has traditionally been an imbalance of intensity between Scotland, Ireland and Wales, where land reform centred on the nature and conditions of tenure, protections and land redistribution, and England, where it has been more diffuse, feeding into a multitude of debates including on enclosure, commons, game, housing and conservation. The historiography of land reform has been well served by individual nation-based studies, but – with some notable exceptions – significantly less so by comparative or transnational work.[1] This volume goes some way towards addressing this lacuna. It is also enhanced by contributions from authors whose professional expertise and life experiences lie outside the traditional domain of academic historians. Cases in point are the contributions from J. Gwilym Owen, a lecturer in property law, and Nerys Llewelyn Jones, a practising solicitor, who trace the case for separate agricultural legislation for Wales; from John MacAskill, a retired lawyer who now applies his legal expertise to the complex history and contemporary controversies of the foreshore; and from Tony McCarthy, a professional stockbroker of many years' standing, whose chapter sheds light on the hitherto unexamined financial fortunes and trajectories of Irish landlords who sold their estates under the 1903 Wyndham Land Act.

The essays included here interrogate the drivers behind, opposition to and impacts of land reform across the nineteenth and early twentieth centuries, and reflect on the legacies of such programmes up to the present day. Building on a rich body of work addressing the land question in different localities across Britain, Ireland and the British Empire, this book presents original case studies which interconnect to contextualise experiences of reform in order to draw out commonalities and connections but also highlight the distinctive nature of land issues and reform programmes in particular nations and regions.[2] In this context the contributions to the volume illustrate a multiplicity of relationships and connections between high politics and local experiences. Duncan Simpson addresses this issue in his chapter, which examines the impact of the 'improvement' agenda on rural Scotland in the early nineteenth century, a case study of the complexities – practical and ideological – of competing visions for the future and purpose of land. Ciarán Reilly's chapter on the Gregory clause details how the application of the doctrine of *laissez faire* had such devastating consequences for Irish smallholders during the Great Famine period. Finlay McKichan's case study of the attempts to restructure the Mackenzie estate on the Isle of Lewis shows how efforts were thwarted by the British government's decision to reduce tariffs on kelp and salt during the 1820s.

The 'four nations' framework, which invites a consideration of comparisons and contrasts, is critical to the new perspectives the volume provides on land reform. The development of devolution across the United Kingdom from the late 1990s has provided significant impetus for the advancement of 'four nations' approaches to the study of British and Irish histories and identities. Such studies partially exist as a response to the Anglo-centric character of some earlier works on 'British' history, but also as a framework for expanding the significance of separate national historiographies, recognising the composite nature of the British State and the points of shared and distinctive experience which served to connect and differentiate nations and regions across the British and Irish isles (or Atlantic archipelago).[3] Nowhere is this more starkly illustrated than in the fortunes of landlords in post-partitioned Ireland. Olwen Purdue's chapter highlights the relatively benign treatment of Northern Irish landlords under the Northern Ireland Land Act 1925 compared to the bleak prospects facing their counterparts in the newly created Free State, who had to deal with a multiplicity of challenges and threats, as evidenced in Terence Dooley's chapter addressing the rhetoric and politics of land redistribution in Southern Ireland.[4] The importance of a cross-British and Irish perspective is not one imposed by historians alone: as indicated by the quotation opening this introduction, contemporaries could be just as exercised by the linkage and opportunities for collaborating on land questions, as Ewen Cameron's contribution on Dr Gavin Clark demonstrates. Clark was a political radical, MP and committed rambler, who – not unlike Michael Davitt in the Irish context – saw clearly the links between the land questions of Scotland, Ireland, Wales and England.

In our initial vision for this volume we set out to balance perspectives from the four jurisdictions. The final manifestation draws special attention to land reform movements and their connections to wider political and cultural contexts within Ireland, Scotland and Wales. One of the challenges of this collaboration has been the relative paucity of studies which directly tackle legislative land reform programmes from an English perspective. Land reform movements in England lacked the explicitly national emphasis which tended to characterise such debates elsewhere in Britain and Ireland. In England, land reform campaigns took different forms, particularly around flashpoints of enclosure, changing rights and access to common lands, agricultural mechanisation, the game laws and smallholdings.[5] As Ben Cowell's chapter on preserving the commons in England brings out, this was not a purely nineteenth-century development but one with resonances right up to the present day. This relative geographical imbalance is therefore one we hope to see rectified in future work.

LAND, ESTATES AND SOCIETY

At the beginning of the nineteenth century the majority of cultivated land in the British and Irish isles formed part of a patchwork of landed estates – varying in size, character and composition – in the ownership of families who derived much of their social status from their relationship with land. This situation was being reinforced by a wave of parliamentary acts allowing for the enclosure and cultivation of wastes and commons.[6] The landed estate was an essential factor in determining the social, economic and political position of the squirearchy, gentry, aristocracy and nobility, collectively forming the landed elite.[7] Within this group there was considerable volatility and mobility: though some families succeeded in transferring their landed interest through a succession of generations, occasionally over hundreds of years, this longevity was never guaranteed. Estates often changed hands, were broken up, amalgamated with other holdings and passed into new ownership through inheritance, marriage or purchase, a process which accelerated as profits from industrialisation and manufacturing were used to acquire country seats and their associated landed status.[8] Additionally, as demonstrated by John E. Davies' contribution to this volume, estate ownership very often transcended national boundaries, with some families owning land in two (sometimes more) of the four nations. This was particularly the case in Ireland, which had experienced waves of plantation from England, Wales and Scotland, resulting by the nineteenth century in a transnational landed elite – the Anglo-Irish – in Ireland.[9] Nowhere was the land question more pronounced. The perceived alien nature of the landed class made it a perfect battleground for the expression of deeper nationalist sentiments. In that context the politicisation of land by both separatist campaigners and successive British governments meant that it was a central theme of political, social and economic life across the late nineteenth and early twentieth centuries.[10] Despite these instabilities and challenges, the overarching structure of society conditioned by the operation of the landed estate appeared deeply embedded and secure at the beginning of the 1800s.

The proprietorship and power of landowners was physically etched in the landscape, most notably through the appearance of the country house and its associated parkland and designed landscape.[11] Agriculture was usually the primary land use, with tenanted farms and farmland occupying much of the countryside, with the ways and means of that agricultural activity increasingly dictated by landowners through the application of 'improving' leases and tenancy agreements.[12] However, an estate might also incorporate industrial works such as mining or quarrying, ports and docks, in addition to woodlands and forests, spaces used and designed for sport and leisure, villages and urban settlements, and a range of religious and educational buildings.[13] Outside the major urban centres, these landscapes provided the setting for the lives and experiences of most individuals and communities who lived, worked and operated within and across their bounds. Although the historiography of the nineteenth century is dominated by the rise of industrialisation and urbanisation, the rural and agricultural world maintained a significant proportion of the population, especially in Ireland.[14] The influence of a landed estate on people's lives could be profound. People and, more particularly, relations between people were critical to the functioning of the landed estate. The most important of these was the hierarchical bond between tenant and landowner, often mediated through a land agent, factor or steward.[15] Landowner–tenant relations are fundamental to understanding the programmes of land reform, agitation and legislation which emerged across the period, and form a core theme in this book.[16] This relationship was not only about paying and receiving rent, it was the cornerstone of estate management and land use, most clearly expressed through agricultural improvement, which transformed the appearance and use of the countryside across the eighteenth and nineteenth centuries. It also underpinned the operation of rural society, shaping social roles and expectations. For landowners it prescribed paternalistic ideas of duty and responsibility to the community, which went hand in hand with concepts of leadership, governance and gentility; and for tenants a sense of obligation and deference, to be expressed and performed in a range of social and political scenarios. Although traditionally ascribed to individual or familial landowners, these paternalistic approaches and hierarchical structures were and are just as relevant to institutional and charitable landowners such as the National Trust, as this volume demonstrates.

Land, then, was not just something that was owned, inherited and fashioned by its proprietors; it was also lived on and experienced, underlying all human activity.[17] Critical to this understanding are the perspectives and experiences of women: of female landowners, elite women and women of all social and economic status who lived and worked on landed estates. This perspective has until recently often been neglected by historians and, despite the efforts of the editorial team, is disappointingly not addressed directly within the framework of this volume. This is a potentially very rich area of study, as highlighted by the works of historians, historical geographers and literary scholars such as Briony McDonagh, Ruth Larson, K. D. Reynolds and others.[18] Because of its centrality to everyday life, the way land was managed and used – and especially changes to the same – could have profound social as well as economic consequences. Changes in landownership and inheritance, rent raises, new tenancy agreements, policies on agricultural practice and improvement, industrial development and game management could all affect lived experience. This book also recognises the agency of individuals in the landscape and their willingness to act, contest, negotiate, protest and compromise to defend and uphold their interests in land. The private management of land on a commercial basis had long had the potential to degenerate into a cause of rural discontent. As Richard Hoyle reminds us with reference to the sixteenth-century source material, individual case studies focusing on animosity and division between tenants and landowners can have a tendency to mask relations that were habitually characterised by partnership, mutual understanding and harmony.[19] However, discord and discontent could be especially prevalent when the process of estate building or management involved the disregard or misuse of established custom and the eradication of other people's rights or access to land, and was often accentuated during periods of economic or agricultural depression. A classic example of this were the Highland Clearances, the label given by historians to the events running from the 1780s to the 1860s and roughly mapping across the transition to a recognisably modern framework of the region's economy and society. The Clearances were led by landowner policies of restructuring tenancies and economic activities wholesale, in the process destabilising and removing tens of thousands of people from their traditional tenancies, leading to decades of controversy and conflict.[20] Indeed, much of Scottish land reform from the 1880s was predicated on the principle of righting the historical wrong of the Clearances, an approach which has only loosened its grip in the twenty-first century.[21] Overall, though, rural protest tended to be localised and limited in scope and duration except in Ireland, where there was very much a national movement related to land in evidence, as the Land League, the subsequent land war and the Plan of Campaign all showed, and which drove British government policy in Ireland.[22] However, and notwithstanding the fears that emanated from the French Revolution, the landed estate seemed remarkably secure well into the nineteenth century, with little threat to its status as the prevailing institute for managing the countryside.

The owners of these estates – the gentry, squirarchy, aristocracy and nobility – collectively formed the national polity for most of the period covered by this volume. They had a tight hold on parliamentary representation in the Commons and dominated the House of Lords. Their hands gripped all the levers of local government, justice and administration and provided the personnel for the religious, military and legal apparatus of state.[23] Many had estates, interests and family connections which straddled Wales, Scotland, Ireland, England and further afield, notably in the West Indies, and, irrespective of the location of their main power base, shared certain common interests and cultures.[24] They were central to the constitution and operation of the United Kingdom, which following the 1800 Acts of Union incorporated the Kingdom of Ireland, until the establishment of the Irish Free State in 1922.[25] Land had always been closely entwined with concepts of territory, property, place and identity. It was often a central component of the imagined national communities being forged across eighteenth- and nineteenth-century Europe.[26] In this respect, land could be politically, as well as socially, charged and imbued with profound cultural meaning. This is clearly reflected in the songs and anthems which developed to embody national character: the 'green valley, or towering crag' of *Amhrán na bhFiann*; 'mountains green' and 'pleasant pastures' of 'England's Green and Pleasant Land'; 'wee bit hill and glen' of *Flower of Scotland*; and the complete second verse of Wales' *Hen Wlad Fy Nhadau*. As such, the essays in this volume reflect on the extent to which the politics of land contributed to and defined the development of national agendas and identities across and within Britain and Ireland.

The programmes of reform and legislation analysed in this book contributed to an undermining of the traditional operation and status of the landed estate and its owners. The chronological focus is weighted towards the late nineteenth and early twentieth centuries, but with considerations of earlier contexts and later legacies, sometimes extending into the present day. Land reform movements were part of and drew inspiration and leadership from wider social, political and economic transformations, especially industrialisation, urbanisation, political democratisation and changes in the constitutional make-up of the United Kingdom. All of these fed into the changing status of the landed estate and its traditional owning class, characterised famously by David Cannadine as 'decline and fall'.[27] Cannadine, F. M. L. Thompson and others have traced the declining power of the landed and aristocratic classes in nearly all aspects of their operations: financial, territorial, political and social. A society changing its orientation from rural and agricultural to urban and industrial, the breaking of aristocratic monopolies over political power and financial ruin led to many estates being sold or reduced particularly from the 1890s to the 1930s, a process facilitated by land reform legislation in Scotland and England but one which was more market-driven in England and Wales.[28] Does this mean that land reform has been a success? In Scotland and, to a lesser extent, in Wales and England, it is still a live political issue, with debate over community landownership and new legislation in 2016 in Scotland; and in England and Wales a lively debate focusing on land use, climate crisis and public access to land. As the contributions to this book show, land reform is a process not an event, and one which reflects the variety of competing perspectives and interests based in land.

SCOTLAND

In Scotland, land reform has a relatively long pedigree, particularly when non-state reform is considered. Landowners and their managers instituted waves of tenancy reforms and economic restructuring on Scottish estates from the seventeenth century, a process which accelerated in the eighteenth century.[29] One of the main drivers of this process was the impact of the Jacobite Risings, the last of which was defeated in 1746. The British government took a broad view on the prevention of a further outbreak of rebellion, and as well as measures of military repression, established the Forfeited Estates Commission. This body was tasked with managing the thirteen landed estates forfeited to the Crown as a result of their owners' commitment to the Jacobite cause and included some of the largest estates in the country. The Commission turned this task into a mission to demonstrate the patent benefits of modernisation (economic, political and social), introducing agricultural reform, rural industrial diversification, employment schemes and planned towns and villages.[30] Their work was a forerunner to the wider Agricultural Revolution, with the Enlightenment as its intellectual engine, which rolled out across the country, led by landowners, rather than the state.[31] The historiography focuses on these processes of improvement and agricultural revolution and their impact, not least in the link between tenancy restructuring and the introduction of commercial sheep farming and the Clearances. Estates and their owners have been the focus of attention for historians firstly in terms of the introduction and development of capitalism in Scotland and its relation to the growing imperial footprint of the United Kingdom from 1707, and secondly, in relation to their estate management and treatment of their many small tenants who faced eviction to make room for the new world order. The story changes rapidly from around the 1830s, however: from being in the economic vanguard, Scottish landed estates are seen to fossilise in the face of multiple challenges: poor economic performance, ruinous debt and financial management, tenant agitation and, eventually, state interference.[32]

The first legislative land reform came not for Scotland as a whole but the Highlands and Islands (the 'crofting counties') in 1886, after nearly a decade of sustained tenant agitation which, to some extent, reflected the Irish Land War.[33] The 1886 Crofters Holdings (Scotland) Act was the first in Scotland to actively rework land tenure by introducing basic protections for tenants, rights that were extended to the rest of rural Scotland in 1911 and then consolidated in the 1919 Land Settlement Act.[34] While the historiography of Scottish land has focused on the Clearances and the Highlands, Micky Gibbard's chapter on small landholdings in the south-west of Scotland highlights that the Scottish lowlands have also been shaped through legislative reform, particularly in the twentieth century.[35] The pursuit of greater economic efficiency and social equity via the redistribution of property rights is a common theme of land reform in other countries.³⁶ In Scotland, however, land reform legislation has placed the concept of community at its core, although definitions of community have shifted over the past 135 years. Liberal politicians and thinkers of the late nineteenth century defined the Scottish Highlands (in a strikingly similar way to rural India) as being structured around historical 'village communities' and the Crofters Holdings (Scotland) Act 1886 set out a historical and structural definition of crofting which was built around a historicist ideal of the communal.³⁷ The twenty-first-century version of this approach can be found in the 2003 and 2016 Land Reform Acts and the 2015 Community Empowerment Act, which provide a framework for collective (or community) landownership. Legislation in Scotland was deeply influenced by and in turn influenced legislation in Ireland, India and non-imperial territories such as Tsarist Russia.³⁸

ENGLAND

One place with which there was not a great deal of overlap was England. Here, there were a number of controversial flashpoints around which debate flared: enclosure of common lands, the game laws, rural poverty and housing and taxation reform. Liberals and radicals fought in a long tradition against the pernicious evils of 'landlordism' and Conservatives fought back strongly, recognising this as part of a wider social shift against their traditional monopoly of economic and political power.³⁹ It was in England that one of the most important texts in the history of land reform in Britain and Ireland was published: John Bateman's *The Great Landowners of Britain and Ireland* appeared in 1876 and from that date to this acted as a kind of Doomsday Book for land reformers. And it was also in England, forty years before Bateman, that the Swing Riots and then the Chartist movement turned radical political opinion to the land as a fundamental aspect of their approach to property ownership and inequalities. The Land Plan, developed by Fergus O'Connor, by 1847–8 had over 70,000 subscribers: it proposed the reappropriation of land – especially 'waste' land in parks, policies and landscaped grounds – from Old Corruption and the aristocracy to a free market in land to promote its productive use, underpinned by radical taxation regimes to maintain the balance and prevent the build-up of class monopolies again.⁴⁰ These themes were echoed in the Anti-Corn Law agitation and again much later by David Lloyd George in 1913–14 in his Land Campaign. In between were the major rural agitations in Ireland, Scotland and Wales and sitting behind those, the continuing impact of a long depression in agriculture. Despite the great movements of the Chartists, Gladstonian liberalism and Lloyd George's People's Budget and Land Campaign, as Matthew Cragoe and Paul Readman have argued, there was to be 'no heroic political climax' to the land question in England.[41] They note that the land question faded away in the twentieth century, and this might be argued for England where it has instead become embedded in debate around public access, taxation, housing crises and the role of charitable landowners such as the National Trust. They point out that the land question as a specific political movement has been folded into wider political questions in the historiography, meaning it is less visible to historians than it was to contemporaries. But as this volume shows, the picture for Scotland, Ireland and Wales is very different.

WALES

On 13 September 1892, Gladstone delivered a public speech on 'Justice to Wales' at Cwm-llan on the slopes of Snowdon.[42] He had just formed his fourth government, a minority, aided by the return of thirty-one Liberal members from the thirty-four Welsh seats. The speech, delivered in a highly symbolic cultural landscape, was arguably the most momentous occasion of the Welsh Land Question, which had arisen as a central issue in Welsh politics in the 1880s.[43] Gladstone's speech recognised, from the ultimate position of political authority, a distinctively Welsh national agenda, reaffirmed many of the messages and arguments about Welsh society that figures such as Tom Ellis and Thomas Gee had been advocating over the previous decade, and importantly, set the wheels in motion for the appointment of a Royal Commission on Land in Wales.[44] This Commission was a massive three-year investigation into Welsh life, centred on the role of estates and the nature of landowner–tenant relations. Its recommendations were not implemented: unlike Ireland and the crofting areas of Scotland, Wales was not to have its own land reform legislation by the turn of the twentieth century. But within a generation the picture of Welsh society captured by the *Report* of the Commission had been transformed with the mass break-up and sale of landed estates and country houses across the early twentieth century.[45] The purchase of farms, primarily by former tenants, coupled with the diminished social and political influence of landowners, signified a major transformation in society, which in large part delivered the changes earlier demanded by the proponents of the Welsh land reform movement.

Despite the occasionally violent rhetoric of *Y Faner* and other radical Welsh papers, the land reform movement in Wales was overwhelmingly peaceful in nature. The two most prominent examples of mass rural protest in nineteenth-century Wales were the Rebecca Riots of 1839–43 (largely confined to the south-west) and Tithe War of c. 1886–95 (largely confined to the north-east).[46] Landowner–tenant relations featured only as a secondary concern in both of these movements. Local reactions to the enclosure of common land, examples of individual tenant grievance and injustice, and the reputation of some land agents and gamekeepers suggest a degree of discontent and disharmony on Welsh estates, which could be exacerbated by poverty and during periods of agricultural depression. The works of Samuel Roberts (1800–85) provide the clearest articulation of such tensions. Numerous of his complaints were echoed in the evidence submitted to the Royal Commission, though it found no evidence of endemic landowner tyranny (as alleged by some radicals). Similarly, the public statements of attachment and affiliation addressed by tenants to their landowners on occasions such as coming-of-age and marriage celebrations, rent-day dinners and as gratitude for rent abatements during periods of depression, present a very different picture of relations in the Welsh countryside. Certainly, unlike Ireland and Scotland, in Wales there were no mass clearances nor tenant evictions: the closest Wales came to a *cause célèbre* was the targeted political evictions on some estates owned by Tory landowners in the aftermath of the 1859 and 1868 elections, which fuelled the cause of Welsh land reformers across the late nineteenth century.[47]

The land reform movement in Wales was tied to the political goals of radical nonconformity, a powerful vision for the future of the Welsh nation that was reliant on the disestablishment of the Anglican church and dismantling of the landed estate. In this respect the ownership, management and occupancy of land emerged as a key feature in the Welsh reform agenda. The narratives of tenant injustice and oppression espoused from the 1860s onwards formed part of a larger effort to paint landlords as uniformly Tory, Anglican and anglicised, and therefore as unsuitable representatives and leaders of the caricature of the Welsh-speaking, politically radical and nonconformist '*gwerin*' society over whom they had long held sway. This movement achieved success across many spheres, heralded by historians as a 'rebirth' and 'reawakening' which redefined modern Wales.[48] Furthermore, the political narrative of an anglicised and alien landowning class was absorbed as a pervading theme in the twentieth-century historiography of Wales, underpinned by the new academic and cultural institutions created as part of the triumphs of national revival.[49] The propaganda generated about landowners as part of the late nineteenth-century Welsh land reform movement has exerted a significant influence on the interpretation and understanding of Wales' entire post-medieval history, aligning with both the nationalist and socialist sensibilities which tended to characterise twentieth-century Welsh historiography. The centrality of the gentry versus *gwerin* narrative is epitomised by David Williams, one of the most influential historians of the twentieth century, who concluded that of all 'the factors which have influenced the growth and development of the Welsh nation [. . .] the most important is the anglicisation of the gentry'.[50] Virtually every key work on the history of Wales published across the twentieth century featured aspects of an interpretation which delineated that ever since the Tudor 'Acts of Union' an increasingly anglicised and alien gentry had constituted a negative force in Welsh life, a historiographical feature which demonstrates the pervading influence radical nonconformity exerted on Welsh consciousness.

David W. Howell's *Land and People* and his other research on aspects of Welsh rural and agricultural history provide a framework for understanding the operation of estates and landowner–tenant relations in modern Wales. Focused studies on gentry culture and estates by J. Gwynfor Jones, Philip Jenkins, R. J. Moore-Colyer, Matthew Cragoe and others have also contributed to a reassessment of social and cultural relations in the history of the Welsh countryside.[51] Nevertheless, the convincing conclusions of these works, which do not always mesh comfortably with established interpretations of Welsh history, have often struggled to be absorbed into the broader Welsh historiographical tradition, which for many people still has a role in determining, or at least bolstering, Wales' status and image as a nation. In this respect, the land reform movement continues to exert an influence on how Wales – its history, culture, identity and future – is conceived.

IRELAND

Land and its attendant struggles have occupied a central theme in the Irish historical narrative of the second half of the nineteenth century. The convergence of the land question with that of the national one gave rise to a powerful force for political change. The emergence of land as a battleground at that time gives rise to an obvious question: why had it not been prominent in the first sixty years of the century? Why, flush from victory following his Catholic Emancipation crusade, was it not embraced by The Liberator Daniel O'Connell and why, despite the influential writings of James Fintan Lalor, was it an irrelevancy in the risings of the Young Irelanders (1848) and the Fenians (1867)? It was not as if land or landlord–tenant relations had not attracted attention in earlier decades.⁵² Land agitation in the closing decades of the eighteenth century and sporadically in the opening years of the nineteenth, through the actions of clandestine groups such as the Peep O day boys, the Catholic Defenders and the Whiteboy movements, had achieved prominence, albeit based on a more localised and *ad hoc* basis than the agitation of the 1870s and 1880s. In terms of practicality, land could hardly have possessed less utility and therefore been of less consequence to tenants in the early nineteenth century than in its latter part. Why then did it achieve such prominence?

As with most great social movements, the answer consists in an alignment of people, events and circumstances at a given time. The presence of a number of prominent individuals who saw the land struggle as a means of delivering on their political aspirations was critical. Michael Davitt, on his release from prison in December 1877, saw the land struggle as a means of tapping into an anti-British sentiment and the best way of delivering on his aspiration for an independent Ireland.⁵³ Charles Stewart Parnell, on the other hand, saw land as a means of delivering on his and his party's ambitions for repeal of the Act of Union and the granting of Home Rule.⁵⁴ These two charismatic individuals were to find uncommonly common ground and became the personification of the land reform movement from 1879 to 1890. The land reform movement thrived in the straitened economic circumstances occasioned by the poor harvests of 1879 and 1880 and the onset of a decline in agriculture brought about by the opening up of markets in the new world as a cheap source of agricultural produce.⁵⁵ Alongside these developments, the political landscape was changing in Britain and the omnipotence of land as a source of power was in decline. Against such a background, beleaguered and financially vulnerable Irish landlords no longer presented an image of invincibility and were seen as fair game by opponents.⁵⁶

Irish landlords in the 1880s were faced with a perfect storm in terms of tenant unrest and defiance, a worsening economic environment and a political establishment that had little sympathy with their plight, intent on placating tenant agitation in what would transpire to be a vain attempt to kill the demand for Home Rule.⁵⁷ Thus, landlords became sacrificial lambs on the altar of political expediency. Their property rights were gradually eroded through a series of land acts from 1870 onwards which introduced the concepts of dual ownership, compensation for tenant improvements, judicial rent reviews and fixity of tenures. These regulatory acts were followed by a number of state-funded land purchase acts before a veritable final solution was introduced with the Wyndham Act of 1903 and its follow-on, the Birrell Act of 1909, which provided the majority of landlords with a somewhat dignified and financially viable exit. While the new Free State 1923 Land Act would finally bring the shutters down, the 1903 and 1909 acts did effectively resolve the issue of landownership and brought an end to agrarian landlordism in Ireland once and for all.[58] As the contributions of Dooley and Purdue highlight, the fortunes of landlords in the two parts of the island of Ireland differed greatly. In Southern Ireland, despite some mild attempts by the Free State government to accommodate the former landed gentry, they were to become virtually extinct and mere historical artefacts within a few years. In the North, however, the situation was different in that while economically they lost their pre-eminence, they were to maintain significant political influence and position up until the 1970s, with many of their scions such as Basil Brooke, Terence O'Neill and James Chichester-Clark becoming prime ministers of Northern Ireland. This highlights once again the striking historical differences in the nature and outcomes of land reform across the British and Irish isles.

LANDLORD RESPONSES

Historiography has tended to understate or in many cases ignore the formalised responses of landlords to the demands from agitators, reformers and tenants for fundamental land reforms. Tenant-based movements, particularly the Irish Land League or the Plan of Campaign, which precipitated significant agitation and anti-landlord hostility and resulted in forceful and coercive political responses, have occupied a central place in historical narratives, but how landlords responded has received less attention.[59] The contributions of Annie Tindley, Shaun Evans and John E. Davies are attempts to redress this deficit. There is a composite of reasons for the lack of focus by historians on this response, including that up to the advent of land agitation movements in the 1860s landed response could be said to have been built into the organs of central and local government, which were to all intents and purposes controlled by landowning gentry, reducing the need for specific associated actions. The changing political landscape evolving from the growth in urban politics, an expanding franchise, nascent globalisation, the emergence of a powerful albeit obsequious middle class and philosophical challenges from intellectuals such as John Stuart Mill and Henry George to the very essence of a narrowly based landownership system, meant that the old land-based social order – Britain and Ireland's *ancien régime* – was inexorably changing.⁶⁰

Not surprisingly, it was in Ireland that the landlord response was most evident in the face of concerted, virulent and well-organised tenant rights movements. The formation of the Irish National Land League in 1879 brought organisation and structure to various tenant rights entities. Its foundation saw a serious escalation in agrarian agitation and violence targeted at landlords, their families and their estates. This development, along with the Plan of Campaign (1886–91), meant that the period from 1879 to 1891 saw rent strikes, boycott campaigns and violence against both people and livestock, inculcating a sense of fear and terror among the landed class. Sporadic counteractive coercive measures introduced by successive British governments provided only occasional respite. Against such a background it was not surprising that landlords sought to organise resistance movements. Between 1879 and 1887, eight landlord defence associations were established.⁶¹ Some of these organisations, such as the Irish Land Committee (1879) and the Irish Legal and Patriotic Union (1885), focused more on the dissemination of pro-landlord information and what would today be described as lobbying activities. Others provided direct practical support, such as the Land Corporation of Ireland (1882), a quasi-mortgage company which provided loans to landlords in financial distress due to tenant agitation on their estates. The two most prominent organisations, however, were the Emergency Committee of the Orange Institution (1879) and the Property Defence Association (1880). Both organisations could be said to be 'physical force' in terms of their confrontational nature in protecting estates targeted by the Land League and providing emergency labour to harvest crops, milk cows and repair estate boundaries. Such measures generated great enmity on the estates where they were deployed but ensured at least the short-term survival of the landlords affected. While ultimately these organisations did not prevent the eventual abolition of the landlord system, they did certainly delay its demise and secured a more financially beneficial settlement for their membership.

Similar in some ways to the fear of contagion that emanated from the French Revolution, landlords, particularly in Wales and Scotland, feared that the Irish experience would spread across the Irish Sea.⁶² The appearance of Michael Davitt at meetings in Wales, where he teamed up with E. Pan Jones, and in Scotland, where he worked closely with John Ferguson, added to the sense of foreboding. Welsh land reform movements in the 1880s, like those in Ireland, sought to align themselves with the national question through links with the *Cymru Fydd* movement and attempts to disestablish the Anglican Church. While never to occupy the same space in the national psyche or become a mass movement as in Ireland, Welsh landlords feared greatly Irish contagion. The formation of the North Wales Property Defence Association in 1886 sponsored by two of the Welsh landed grandees, lords Harlech and Penrhyn, signified a structured response to the threat posed by the emergent Welsh Land League. An all-Wales landlord defence association never materialised and it was not until 1893 that a South Wales Property Defence Association was established under the auspices of Viscount Emlyn, Earl Cawdor and the Earl of Dunraven, who was to play a prominent role in Irish land politics in the early years of the twentieth century. Neither organisation needed to engage in 'physical force' interventions in support of their members. Their activities were largely confined to defending landlord claims in newspapers, publishing pamphlets and making submissions to various parliamentary commissions of enquiry.

As John MacAskill's chapter highlights, landlord combinations were not unknown in Scotland, though here the response to the land reform movements of the late nineteenth century was less coordinated than in either Ireland or Wales. The lack of coordination did not, however, mean that landlords were unconcerned or indifferent to attempts at land reform. Landed elites such as the dukes of Sutherland and Argyll were very involved both personally and through their land agents in defending the rights of landowners.[63] Unlike the other three nations of the British Isles, the demand for land reform in England tended not to come from the tenantry but from middle-class radicals such as Richard Cobden and James Edwin Thorold Rogers and the American political economist Henry George, whose demands were of a more ideological than practical nature.[64] The absence of a mass land reform movement in England was perhaps due to the historical and cultural acceptance of the landlord–tenant relationship and its underlying contract-based nature. While local disagreements existed from time to time around such issues as game and tenant rights, the relationship between landlords and their tenants was devoid of the rancour found in Scotland, to a lesser extent than in Wales and certainly less than the outright hostility experienced in Ireland.

In 2019 George Monbiot lamented the lack of interest shown by the political classes in land as a political issue in the UK, but if this is examined historically and broken down into its constituent jurisdictions, a more nuanced and active picture can be discerned, one where politicians built careers on land issues.[65] Though sometimes labelled differently – social housing versus right to buy, energy policies, private property versus common good, or the controversies of the Poll Tax of the 1980s – all raised the ghosts of the land campaigns of the past: land in politics has stubbornly survived. As demonstrated by this volume, debates about land historically had an important part to play in determining the political configuration of the British and Irish isles. Land was used as a central ingredient in campaigns to highlight the distinct national characteristics and needs of Ireland, Scotland and Wales *vis-à-vis* England. The essays in this volume highlight that land in all its manifestations is a complex and multifaceted issue subject to global, national, local and even individual and personal influences. The inheritance of an estate by an incapable, incompetent or disinterested landowner, or the management of an overly zealous agent, could have significant local consequences. Technological changes, the Industrial Revolution, the emergence of new political philosophies and the gradual democratisation of the political landscape, the vagaries of the weather, the exigencies of human nature, plus the geographical and geological nature of landholdings, have all had a profound effect on land and the relationship between landowners and their tenantry. These, coupled with the declining place of agriculture in the economic profile of most leading nations, an expanding urban-based electorate and an ever more hostile media meant that the traditional landlord-centred hegemony was in decline. The essays also highlight the almost perfect correlation between economic conditions and the state of landowner–tenant relationships, exemplified by the impacts of existential shocks to the system such as the ending of the Napoleonic Wars and the advent of the great agricultural depression in the late 1870s.

The outcome of the 2016 Brexit Referendum, its emergent consequences and implementation have once again refocused a spotlight on the make-up of the UK and its relationship with the Republic of Ireland. Moves by the UK to segregate itself from the political and economic frameworks of the European Union – and away from an identification with Europe – have not only energised the Irish Border as a political feature, but also laid bare political differences across and between the nations of an increasingly dis-United Kingdom. Since the late 1990s the devolution process has provided degrees of increasing self-government to national parliaments and assemblies in Northern Ireland, Scotland and Wales, with the West Lothian Question and implementation of English votes for English laws (EVEL) to the UK House of Commons also highlighting the position of England in the UK's constitutional settlement. Despite the result of the 2014 Scottish Independence Referendum, the continued electoral success of the SNP means that the future make-up and break-up of the UK is likely to remain high on the political agenda. As both the UK and Ireland's relationship with the EU evolves, the impact of macro political change in the coming years on land and agriculture will come into sharper focus.[66] The UK's departure from the EU Common Agricultural Policy is provoking intense debate on the policy framework and vision for post-Brexit agriculture and land use across the nations of the UK. This focus on the future of the countryside and rural economies is meshing with the wider environmental and sustainability agenda, including issues of food production and consumption, woodland management, well-being, rewilding, the resilience of rural communities and socio-political debates on housing policy, planning and landownership. The Scottish government established a Scottish Land Commission in 2017 and the UK and Welsh governments have both recently undertaken reviews into the future of designated landscapes within their jurisdictions. Similarly, the cultural significance of land and landscape, and its centrality to concepts of identity and belonging, continue to find clear expressions. The recent award of UNESCO World Heritage Status to the English Lake District and the Slate Landscapes of Gwynedd are cases in point. So too the contemporary prominence of political graffiti in Wales focused on the 1965 flooding of Tryweryn Valley to create a reservoir for Liverpool City Council. Land has re-emerged as a significant political issue.

While throwing light on neglected aspects of land history and exposing and addressing various lacunae, this volume also identifies areas for further study and research, including opportunities for understanding of historical contexts and perspectives to inform future agendas on the environment, land use, management and sustainability. The nature of transnational influences at both tenant and landlord organisational level both between and within Britain, Ireland and other international spheres is likely to provide a rich vein of knowledge. Similarly, an expansion both in terms of scope and timeline of research into the family finances of landowners who sold their estates either privately or, as in Ireland, under the land legislation will provide a suitable bookend to the study of the landlord class in Britain and Ireland. In Wales, the full corpus of evidence submitted to the Royal Commission on Land is crying out for comprehensive analysis. The volume also highlights potential for an exploration of the multilingual cultures characterising life on landed estates across the British and Irish isles, and the articulation of desired reforms. Given the direct correlation identified in this volume between economic circumstance and the changing temperature of landlord–tenant relationships, this is an area that would benefit greatly from further exploration and interpretation. We hope that the cooperation evinced in this volume through the pooling of case studies can provide a foundation for future collaboration and analysis of land issues into the future.

NOTES

1. Most prominently, M. Cragoe and P. Readman (eds), *The Land Question in Britain, 1750–1950* (Basingstoke, 2010) and D. W. Howell, 'The land question in nineteenth-century Wales, Ireland and Scotland: a comparative study', *Agricultural History Review*, 61:1 (2013).
2. For example, P. Bull, *Land, Politics and Nationalism: A Study of the Irish Land Question* (Dublin, 1996); N. E. Wright (ed.), *Despotic Dominion: Property Rights in British Settler Societies* (Vancouver, 2004); C. A. Bayly, S. Beckhert, M. Connolly, I. Hoffmeyr, W. Kozol and P. Seed, 'AHR conversation: on transnational history', *American Historical Review*, 111:5 (2006); C. Dewey, 'Celtic agrarian legislation and the celtic revival: historicist implications of Gladstone's Irish and Scottish Land Acts', *Past and Present*, 64 (1974); E. A. Cameron, 'Communication or separation? Reactions to Irish land agitation and legislation in the Highlands of Scotland, c. 1870–1910', *English Historical Review*, 120:487 (2005); D. W. Howell, *Land and People in Nineteenth-Century Wales* (London, 1977).
3. See N. Lloyd-Jones and M. M. Scull, 'A new plea for an old subject? Four nations history for the modern period', in N. Lloyd-Jones and M. M. Scull (eds), *Four Nations Approaches to Modern 'British' History: A (Dis)United Kingdom?* (London, 2018), pp. 3–31.
4. See also T. Dooley, *The Decline of the Big House in Ireland: A Study of Irish Landed Families, 1860–1960* (Dublin, 2001); O. Purdue, *The Big House in the North of Ireland: Land, Power and Social Elites, 1878–1960* (Dublin, 2009).
5. A. Howkins, 'Diggers to Dongas: the land in English radicalism, 1649–2000', *History Workshop Journal*, 54 (Autumn 2002); D. Wall, *The Commons in History: Culture, Conflict, and Ecology* (Cambridge and London, 2014); J. M. Neeson, *Commoners: Common Right, Enclosure and Social Change in England, 1700–1820* (Cambridge, 1993).
6. P. Linebaugh, *Stop Thief! The Commons, Enclosures and Resistance* (Oakland, CA, 2014); J. R. Wordie, 'The chronology of English enclosure, 1500–1914', *The Economic History Review*, 36:4 (1983), pp. 483–505.
7. D. Cannadine, *The Decline and Fall of the British Aristocracy* (London, 1990); F. M. L. Thompson, 'English landed society in the twentieth century: I, Property: Collapse and survival', *Transactions of the Royal Historical Society*, 5th series, 40 (1990); J. V. Beckett, *The Aristocracy in England 1660–1914* (Oxford, 1986); T. Williamson and L. Bellamy,

Property and Landscape: A Social History of Land Ownership and the English Countryside (London, 1987).

8. F. M. L. Thompson, 'English landed society in the twentieth century: II: New poor and new rich', *Transactions of the Royal Historical Society*, 6th series, 1 (1991); L. Stone and J. C. F. Stone, *An Open Elite? England 1540–1880* (Oxford, 1984); P. Jenkins, 'The creation of an "Ancient Gentry": Glamorgan 1760–1840', *Welsh History Review*, 12:1 (June 1984), pp. 29–49.

9. Cannadine, *Decline and Fall*, pp. 1–23. For early Welsh involvement in the colonisation of Ireland, see R. Morgan, *The Welsh and the Shaping of Early Modern Ireland, 1558–1641* (Woodbridge, 2014).

10. T. Dooley, 'Landlords and the land question, 1879–1909', in C. King (ed.), *Famine, Land and Culture in Ireland* (Dublin, 2001).

11. J. Finch and K. Giles (eds), *Estate Landscapes: Design, Improvement and Power in the Post-Medieval Landscape* (Woodbridge, 2007); T. Williamson, *Polite Landscapes: Gardens and Society in Eighteenth-Century England* (Baltimore, MD, 1995).

12. R. W. Hoyle (ed.), *Custom, Improvement and the Landscape in Early Modern Britain* (Oxford, 2011); S. Wade-Martins, *Farmers, Landlords and Landscapes: Rural Britain, 1720 to 1870* (Oxford, 2004); T. Williamson, *The Transformation of Rural England: Farming and the Landscape 1700–1870* (Exeter, 2002); S. Daniels and S. Seymour, 'Landscape design and the idea of improvement', in R. A. Dodgshon and R. A. Butlin (eds), *An Historical Geography of England and Wales* (London, 1990), pp. 487–520.

13. For example, A. Adonis, 'The survival of the great estates: Henry 4th Earl of Carnarvon and his dispositions in the 1880s', *Historical Research*, 64 (1991).

14. Cannadine, *Decline and Fall*, pp. 391–406; E. Richards, *The Leviathan of Wealth: The Sutherland Fortune in the Industrial Revolution* (London, 1973).

15. For the role of the land agent, see L. A. Rees, C. Reilly and A. Tindley (eds), *The Land Agent, 1700–1920* (Edinburgh, 2018).

16. See, for example, W. E. Vaughan, *Landlords and Tenants in Mid-Victorian Ireland* (Oxford, 1994); W. H. Crawford, 'Landlord–tenant relations in Ulster, 1609–1820', *Irish Economic and Social History*, 2 (1975); W. E. Vaughan, 'Landlord and tenant relations in Ireland between the famine and the land war, 1850–1878', in L .M. Cullen and T. C. Smout (eds), *Comparative Aspects of Scottish and Irish Economic and Social History, 1600–1900* (Edinburgh, 1977); Howell, *Land and People*. For earlier perspectives focusing on England, see J. Whittle (ed.), *Landlords and Tenants in Britain, 1440–1660: Tawney's Agrarian Problem Revisited* (Woodbridge, 2013).

17. N. Whyte, *Inhabiting the Landscape: Place, Custom and Memory, 1500–1800* (Oxford, 2009); N. Whyte, 'Senses of place, senses of time:

Landscape history from a British perspective', *Landscape Research*, 40:8 (2015), pp. 925–38.
18. See, for instance, K. D. Reynolds, *Aristocratic Women and Political Society in Victorian Britain* (Oxford, 1998); H. Worthen, B. McDonagh and A. Capern, 'Gender, property and succession in the early modern English aristocracy: the case of Martha Janes and her illegitimate children', *Women's History Review* (2019), pp. 1–20; R. M. Larsen, 'Sisterly guidance: elite women, sorority and the life cycle, 1770–1860', in T. Dooley, M. O'Riordan and C. Ridgway (eds), *Women and the Country House in Ireland and Britain* (Dublin: Four Courts Press, 2018); B. McDonagh, *Elite Women and the Agricultural Landscape, 1700–1830* (London, 2016); A. L. Capern, B. McDonagh and J. Aston (eds), *Women and Land, 1500–1900* (Woodbridge, 2019).
19. R. Hoyle, 'Lords, tenants and tenant right in the sixteenth century', *Northern History*, 20 (1984), p. 38.
20. J. Hunter, 'The Politics of Highland land reform, 1873–1895', *Scottish Historical Review*, 53 (1974); E. Richards, *The Highland Clearances: People, Landlords and Rural Turmoil* (Edinburgh, new edn, 2008); J. Hunter, *The Making of the Crofting Community* (Edinburgh, 1976).
21. See, for example, Dewey, 'Celtic agrarian legislation and the celtic revival'.
22. P. Bull, *Land, Politics and Nationalism: A Study of the Irish Land Question* (Dublin, 1996); A. G. Newby, *Ireland, Radicalism and the Scottish Highlands, c. 1870–1912* (Edinburgh, 2007).
23. Cannadine, *Decline and Fall*, pp. 1–23.
24. See, for example, F. Mckichan, *Lord Seaforth: Highland Landowner, Caribbean Governor* (Edinburgh: Edinburgh University Press, 2018).
25. For a perspective on the Anglo-Irish Union from the landed position, see J. Bew, *Castlereagh: Enlightenment, War and Tyranny* (London, 2011).
26. E. Frie and J. Neuheiser, 'Introduction: noble ways and democratic means', *Journal of Modern European History*, 11:4 (2013); R. Gibson and M. Blinkhorn (eds), *Landownership and Power in Modern Europe* (London, 1991).
27. Cannadine, *Decline and Fall*, pp. 1–23.
28. J. Davies, 'The end of the great estates and the rise of freehold farming in Wales', *Welsh History Review*, 7:2 (December 1974), pp. 186–212; F. M. L. Thompson, 'english landed society in the twentieth century: IV: Prestige without power?', *Transactions of the Royal Historical Society*, 6th series, 3 (1993).
29. See, for example, P. Jones, *Agricultural Enlightenment: Knowledge, Technology, and Nature 1750–1840* (Oxford, 2016); E. J. Hobsbawm, 'Scottish reformers of the eighteenth century and capitalist agriculture', in E. J. Hobsbawm (ed.), *Peasants in History: Essays in Honour of Daniel Thorner, vol. 3* (Calcutta, 1981), pp. 3–29; H. Cheape, 'For the

betterment of mankind: Scotland, the Enlightenment and the Agricultural Revolution', *Folk Life-Journal of Ethnological Studies*, 40:1 (2001), pp. 7–24; N. Davidson, 'The Scottish path to capitalist agriculture 3: The Enlightenment as the theory and practice of improvement', *Journal of Agrarian Change*, 5:1 (2005), pp. 1–72.
30. T. M. Devine, *The Transformation of Rural Scotland: Social Change and the Agrarian Economy, 1660–1815* (Edinburgh, 1994).
31. For example, B. Bonnyman, *The Third Duke of Buccleuch and Adam Smith: Estate Management and Improvement in Enlightenment Scotland* (Edinburgh, 2014).
32. F. A. Jonsson, *Enlightenment's Frontier: The Scottish Highlands and the Origins of Environmentalism* (New Haven, CT, 2013); C. Kidd, 'Eighteenth-Century Scotland and the three unions', in T. C. Smout (ed.), *Anglo-Scottish Relations from 1603–1900* (Oxford, 2005), p. 185; B. Bonnyman, 'Agrarian patriotism and the landed interest: The Scottish "Society of Improvers in the Knowledge of Agriculture", 1723–1746', in K. Stapelbroek and J. Marjanen (eds), *The Rise of Economic Societies in the Eighteenth Century: Patriotic Reform in Europe and North America* (Houndsmills, 2012), pp. 27–32.
33. Hunter, *Making of the Crofting Community*; E. A. Cameron, 'Politics, ideology and the Highland land issue', *Scottish Historical Review*, 72 (1993).
34. E. A. Cameron, *Land for the People? The British Government and the Scottish Highlands, c. 1880–1925* (East Linton, 1996).
35. R. Anthony, *Herds and Hinds: Farm Labour in Lowland Scotland, 1900–1939* (East Linton, 1997).
36. B. Slee, K. Blackstock, K. Brown, R. Dilley, P. Cook, J. Grieve and A. Moxey, *Monitoring and Evaluating the Effects of Land Reform on Rural Scotland – A Scoping Study and Impact Assessment* (Edinburgh, 2008).
37. C. Dewey, 'Images of the village community: A study in Anglo-Indian ideology', *Modern Asian Studies*, 6 (1972); E. D. Steele, 'Ireland and the empire: imperial precedents for Gladstone's first Irish Land Act', *Historical Journal*, 11:1 (1968).
38. Cameron, *Land for the People*; B. Crosbie, *Irish Imperial Networks: Migration, Social Communication and Exchange in Nineteenth-century India* (Cambridge, 2012).
39. I. Packer, *Lloyd George, Liberalism and the Land: The Land Issue and Party Politics in England, 1906–1914* (London, 2001); Cragoe and Readman, *Land Question*, p. 1; E. F. Biagini, *Liberty, Retrenchment and Reform: Popular Liberalism in the Age of Gladstone, 1860–1880* (Cambridge, 1992).
40. J. Bateman, *The Great Landowners of Great Britain and Ireland* (London, 1876); Cragoe and Readman, *Land Question*, pp. 4, 57–73.
41. Cragoe and Readman, *Land Question*, p. 15; A. Taylor, *Lords of Misrule:*

Hostility to Aristocracy in Late Nineteenth and Early Twentieth Century Britain (Basingstoke, 2004).
42. See C. J. Williams, 'Gladstone, Lloyd George and the Gladstone Rock', *Caernarvonshire Historical Society Transactions*, 60 (1999), pp. 55–75.
43. M. Cragoe, '"A contemptible mimic of the Irish": The land question in Victorian Wales', in M. Cragoe and P. Readman (eds), *The Land Question in Britain, 1750–1950* (Basingstoke, 2010), pp. 92–108; J. Graham Jones, 'Michael Davitt, David Lloyd George and T. E. Ellis: The Welsh experience, 1886', *Welsh History Review*, 18:3 (1997), pp. 450–82.
44. J. Graham Jones, 'Select Committee or Royal Commission? Wales and "The Welsh Land Question", 1892', *Welsh History Review*, 17:2 (December 1994), pp. 205–29; K. O. Morgan, *Wales in British Politics, 1868–1922* (Oxford, 1991), pp. 1–27; M. Cragoe, *Culture, Politics and National Identity in Wales, 1832–1886* (Oxford, 2004), pp. 142–72; Howell, *Land and People*.
45. J. Davies, 'The end of the great estates and the rise of freehold farming in Wales', *Welsh History Review*, 7:2 (December 1974), pp. 186–212.
46. D. J. V. Jones, *Rebecca's Children: A study of Rural Society, Crime and Protest* (Oxford, 1989), pp. 45–98; M. Cragoe, "A contemptible mimic of the Irish", pp. 92–108.
47. M. Cragoe, 'The anatomy of an eviction campaign: the General Election of 1868 in Wales and its aftermath', *Rural History*, 9 (1998), pp. 177–93; I. Gwynedd Jones, 'Merioneth politics in mid-nineteenth century: the politics of a rural economy', *Journal of the Merioneth Historical and Record Society*, 5 (1965–8), pp. 273–334.
48. Summarised in K. O. Morgan, *Rebirth of a Nation: A History of Modern Wales 1880–1980* (Cardiff, 1981).
49. M. Cragoe, *Culture, Politics and National Identity in Wales, 1832–1886* (Oxford, 2004), pp. 142–72.
50. D. Williams, *A History of Modern Wales* (London, 1950), p. 269.
51. For example, M. Cragoe, *An Anglican Aristocracy: The Moral Economy of the Landed Estate in Carmarthenshire, 1832–1895* (Oxford, 1996); D. W. Howell, *Patriarchs and Parasites: The Gentry of South-West Wales in the Eighteenth Century* (Cardiff, 1986); P. Jenkins, *The Making of a Ruling Class: the Glamorgan Gentry 1649–1790* (Cambridge, 1983); J. Gwynfor Jones, *The Welsh Gentry, 1536–1640: Images of Status, Honour and Authority* (Cardiff, 1998).
52. S. Clark and J. S. Donnelly (eds), *Irish Peasants: Violence and Political Unrest, 1780–1914* (Manchester, 1983); J. S. Donnelly, *The Land and the People of Nineteenth Century Cork* (London, 1975); P. Bull, *Land, Politics and Nationalism: A Study of the Irish Land Question* (Dublin, 1996); K. T. Hoppen, 'Landlords, society and electoral politics in mid-nineteenth century Ireland', *Past and Present*, 75 (1977).
53. M. Davitt, *The Fall of Feudalism in Ireland* (London, 1904).

54. A. Jackson, *Home Rule: An Irish history, 1800–2000* (Oxford, 2004); P. Bew, *Enigma: A New Life of Charles Stewart Parnell* (London, 2011).
55. L. P. Curtis, 'The Anglo-Irish predicament', *Twentieth Century Studies*, 4 (1970).
56. P. Bew, *Conflict and Conciliation in Ireland, 1890–1910: Parnellites and Radical Agrarians* (Oxford, 1987); K. T. Hoppen, *Governing Hibernia: British Politicians and Ireland, 1800–1921* (Oxford, 2016).
57. A. Gailey, *Ireland and the death of Kindness: The Experience of Constructive Unionism, 1890–1905* (Cork, 1987).
58. L. P. Curtis, 'Landlord responses to the Irish Land War, 1879–1887', *Eire/Ireland*, 38 (2003).
59. With some exceptions: L. P. Curtis, *Coercion and Conciliation in Ireland, 1880–92: A Study in Conservative Unionism* (Princeton, NJ, 1963).
60. J. S. Mill, *England and Ireland* (London, 1868); E. D. Steele, *Irish Land and British Politics: Tenant-right and Nationality, 1865–1870* (Cambridge, 1974); E. F. Biagini, *Liberty, Retrenchment and Reform: Popular Liberalism in the Age of Gladstone, 1860–1880* (Cambridge, 1992).
61. L. P. Curtis, 'Landlord responses to the Irish Land War, 1879–1887' *Eire/Ireland, Journal of Irish Studies*, Fall-Winter (2003), p. 178.
62. A. G. Newby, '"Scotia Major and Scotia Minor": Ireland and the birth of the Scottish land agitation, 1878–1882', *Irish Economic and Social History*, 31 (2004).
63. For example, 8th Duke of Argyll, 'A model land law: A reply to Arthur Williams MP', *Fortnightly Review*, 41 (1887); J. W. Mason, 'The Duke of Argyll and the land question in late nineteenth century Britain', *Victorian Studies*, 21 (1978).
64. For example, H. George, *The Irish Land Question* (1881).
65. For example, in Scotland, A. Wightman, *Who Owns Scotland* (Edinburgh, 1996); R. Callander, *How Scotland is Owned* (Edinburgh, 1998).
66. See, for example, C. Ray, 'Neo-endogenous rural development in the EU', in P. Cloke, T. Marsden and P. Mooney (eds), *Handbook of Rural Studies* (London, 2006), pp. 278–91.

PART I

Tenants, Landowners and Estate Management

1

Culmaily, a Model of Improvement: Reform, Resistance and Rationalisation in South-eastern Sutherland

Duncan Simpson

INTRODUCTION

CULMAILY FARM WAS AT the heart of the early nineteenth-century attempt to transform land use on the Sutherland estate, one of the leading improving operations of the period in Britain. This chapter will consider whether what was attempted there matched the objectives expressed at the outset, as a case study of non-legislative land reform. A particular focus will be the influence of models of improvement imported from other parts of Britain in the project's planning and implementation. The 'revolutionary' model of agriculture has been overstated at times, and perhaps over-employed for narrative convenience. It is now generally accepted that the role of 'Great Men' as pioneers and innovators in agriculture has been exaggerated, but there is still some explanatory power to that myth, and this chapter will explore some of the mechanisms which fuelled it in the case of Sutherland.[1] The rarity of first-hand experience of farming in multiple areas of Britain at this time allowed false impressions to be created about the relative advancement of agriculture. Recent research concluded that the most significant changes in productivity in England occurred considerably later than formerly believed, well after the middle of the eighteenth century and in many cases into the nineteenth.[2] Similar investigation of Scottish agriculture placed the productivity increases in the lowlands firmly in the last quarter of the eighteenth century.[3] Investigation of the agriculture of the Highlands at the same period found a willingness to innovate and adapt among the tenantry but concluded that until the closing decades of the eighteenth century there was more risk than advantage in this.[4]

The ideological context to improvement in Scotland has also been recently examined.[5] The focus in this chapter in that regard is on state-sponsored attempts to create 'colonies' in the Highlands and Islands during the eighteenth century, and the connections between those eighteenth-century attempts at reform, and the non-legislative changes pursued by the Sutherland estate in the early decades of the nineteenth century. Recent developments in the historiography have sought to counter a perceived 'Highland Exceptionalism', holding that the focus on Highland Clearance has obscured the less-investigated lowland dispossessions, considered to be of the same character by those writers.[6] Within Sutherland, there has been an equivalent historiographical focus on clearance for sheep farming from the 'Highland' interior to the coastal region.[7] To some extent that can be misleading, as the story of Culmaily set out here will demonstrate. In the wider economic context, the Sutherland estate was not unique in its strategies, and the same economic and ideological drivers operated on other aristocratic estates in Scotland at this time as they responded to new opportunities. Sutherland's prominence in the historical narrative is arguably the unintended consequence of the estate's attempts to control that very narrative.

VISIONS OF IMPROVEMENT

The transformation of Culmaily has been described as 'emblematic of improvement' by James Hunter in his recent study of Sutherland. It was a central theme in the defence of the estate's reform vision written by James Loch, in control of that strategy from 1815.[8] That publication also constituted a defence of the men who delivered those changes, estate Commissioner William Young and the notorious land-agent, farmer and arch-evangelist of improvement Patrick Sellar. It is necessary to consider the actions of those individuals in depth, as they wielded an extraordinary power over the lives of the people of the region. Behind those men, and the figureheads of her husband and son, stood the Countess of Sutherland, and the ultimate say and responsibility for what was done in Sutherland was hers.

Patrick Sellar's dual role as factor and farmer, together with his pungent proclamations, have made him an enduringly controversial symbol. His activities have been the focus of an in-depth historical biography.[9] He became the focus of resistance to the estate's policies, and was tried in Inverness for culpable homicide as the management abandoned persuasion for force.[10] His agricultural activities have been less examined and so will be the focus of this chapter. William Young was a critical figure in the initial planning, and some consideration of his previous projects helps situate the Sutherland developments in a wider context of regional development. James Loch was not involved in the projects in Sutherland until 1815, when he was brought in prior to Sellar's trial to manage damage limitation. Culmaily makes a good case study for the wider model of improvement and reform attempted in Sutherland because the thought process behind it is available to us in remarkable detail, alongside the publicly expressed justifications.[11] While this presents the risk of being deaf to other perspectives, the voice of the tenantry makes itself heard in the letters written over their heads, revealing their attempts at resistance as well as the estate managers' misgivings and admissions of failure. Contrasting those internal communications with the apologia published for public consumption at a later date, those elements which the estate was most keen to exaggerate or diminish become apparent.

The strategy proposed by Young for Culmaily and Morvich was a pilot of his grand design for the whole estate. An industrial hub at Culmaily was intended to demonstrate the estate's intention to retain and employ the people displaced by agricultural reform. Flax would be grown on the tidal flats at Morvich and floated to Culmaily, where there would be a milling and processing centre producing linen. The intention was to retain the population in situ, where they would be rehoused and reskilled. In the opinion of the late Eric Richards, who researched the estate's development programme in great detail, the 'demonstration effect' of this pilot scheme was understood to be crucial to the success of the whole project.[12] In light of that, it seems surprising that their attempt to establish flax cultivation as a major endeavour appears to have made practically no headway.

An earlier attempt to manufacture linen from flax at Spinningdale on the Dornoch Firth had met with final defeat in 1807, when the factory operation there was not rebuilt after a fire. Assessments of the reasons for that specific failure echo the conclusion of wider studies of flax cultivation in rural Scotland. While the factory had found willing hands, they were not prepared or able to undertake factory work on a full-time basis. There were two factors which contributed to that. First, the demands of seasonal labour on their own land, and second, a well-established pattern of temporary migration to work seasonally in other areas at higher wages. According to the 1812 *General Agricultural Survey of Sutherland*, the Spinningdale concern failed because the Highlanders were not prepared to work at Glasgow wages.[13]

Mill-dressed flax at the standard then processed was also considered poorer than that which had been worked by hand. There continued to be a successful distributed industry in Caithness and Sutherland encouraged and facilitated by Aberdeen-based linen manufacturers who supplied the raw materials via the existing ports of Wick and Brora, which were then spun into lint thread within the home. This trade was considered an important lifeline during periods when food crops were poor and was described in a 1799 report as the chief employment of the women in Caithness, Sutherland and Ross.[14] However, Young insisted that the pursuit of the greater 'sweets of manufacture' was paramount to the estate's interests, and that meant control of the process right through to the end product.[15] There are several references in Young and Sellar's letters from 1810 highlighting the need for urgency to make the most of those opportunities, and plans submitted for the new settlements proposed stressed 'the necessity of having a flax mill ready in Golspie that autumn'.[16] In the end, a mill was indeed constructed there in 1814 for that purpose, but seems to have coincided with the end of flax processing in Sutherland, rather than its intensification. There never was a flax 'experiment' at Morvich or Culmaily. It might be observed that the 1810 letters in which Young and Sellar insisted on the necessity of flax milling 'for the employment and maintainance [sic] of the people' clearly had the principal aim of persuading the estate to remove sitting tenants, who were portrayed as the obstacle to those developments. Once they had full control, they appear to have lost interest in flax entirely.

Their tone regarding the inhabitants changed rapidly as well. The originally expressed intent was to settle 'as many of the population who choose . . . in neat cottages at the bottom of the farm'.[17] That amnesty was swiftly limited to those 'best adapted to be useful on the farm'.[18] The factor at that time still understood that to mean 'the bulk of the small tenants', and that they would be accommodated upon Culmaily and Morvich.[19] In the final analysis, only around thirty people were retained on a temporary basis from a population of more than two hundred and fifty, and few of those were kept on after the initial groundworks were complete. The designated resettlement location intended for the majority was an uninhabited area of muir land at Achavandra behind the farm of Skelbo, where Young proposed to found a village.[20] Following a day trip around the district, he designated the hill beyond as 'improvable', declaring that 'wheat would flourish there, upon the very moors'. He believed that Skelbo would make an ideal fishing port, being 'at a suitable distance from Dunrobin', the ducal seat. When eventually surveyed by engineers, it was dismissed as being too close to the sandbanks, but by then Achavandra had been designated 'a village', and attempts to colonise the area would persist despite its unsuitability.

Young had rejected another site suggested by the estate at Wester Garty because the soil there was 'too good for lotters'. Similarly, when

Stafford interpreted his intention for the Culmaily people to mean the existing arable land at Skelbo, and signalled his willingness to make that available, Young insisted that they had to be placed onto muir ground in order to 'extend their industry'.[21] A few months later, he mentioned the regretful 'unpleasantness' of dispossessing them before other holdings had been chalked out for them, remarking in the context of a hastily arranged clearance, 'we had too much of that on Culmaily'.[22]

OPPONENTS OF IMPROVEMENT

The clearance of Culmaily does not appear to have been a single dramatic event. The estate records from Young's factorship show a summons of removal naming fifty-six heads of families, raised in February 1808 but not passed to the Sheriff officer until March 1809. The delays were partly due to resistance on the part of a local tacksman, Colonel Sandy Sutherland. The interpretation of his behaviour supplied by Adam credited his behaviour to 'stubbornness', and characterised him as 'old, obstinate and reluctant to move or accept new ideas'. The negotiations to remove him were described as 'tedious', echoing the extreme impatience expressed by Young and Sellar. As a man in his seventies, he was regarded by them as the actualisation of the 'old ways', time-wasting when it was his fate to be swept aside. Another interpretation might be that his rearguard action provided valuable time for those in the line of advance to assess their options, time which by Young's own admission was not adequately granted in the later clearances which provoked much greater resistance, and led to extreme measures from the management.[23]

While Colonel Sutherland occupied and obstructed the core of the land at Culmaily, the full force of improvement was held back for a season or two. When he finally retreated to Braegrudie, at the head of Strathbrora, a sizeable proportion of the people from Culmaily went with him. More went to Kinnauld and Rhemusaig, where the Murrays who had worked the mill at Salach built a new one between those two townships. Some left Sutherland altogether, and found small farms in Caithness. Others moved to the comparatively unreconstructed areas around Rogart and Lairg. For a substantial number, that was to be a staging post for later emigration to the Americas or Australasia.[24] None were reported to have accepted lots at Achavandra, despite Sellar's claim that the former inhabitants were 'exerting every nerve in the cultivation of their sea-side lots'.[25]

In 1819 the estate came for Sandy Sutherland again, by then in his late seventies. Both their words and their tactics had hardened considerably by that time. Sellar's replacement, Francis Suther, wrote that 'the colonel is a decided enemy to improvements conducive to strip the interior of the country of its population', and that he was behind 'an intention to resist the removings in Strathbrora'. This resistance took the form of the people quietly rebuilding the houses after the evicting parties had moved on, and so Suther ordered the timbers and thatches burned, much to James Loch's horror from the public relations perspective.[26] Despite lots being available at Achavandra, the people chose instead Caithness or America.[27] Colonel Sandy would not be moved. His gravestone in Rogart reads: 'He was affectionate to his relatives, kind to the poor and loyal to his King and Country. He lived to do good and died regretted by all who knew him. He died at Braegrudie in this parish the residence of his ancestors.' The antagonistic nature of these operations seems far removed from what had been promised by William Young in the original improvement prospectus.

Young's employment as estate Commissioner was the reward for bold developments in Moray, where he had risked limited capital to carry out land reclamation schemes. His claim at Inverugie was to have 'settled near three hundred souls on a spot which was perfectly barren'. The model of labour Young deployed, mobilising landless 'lotters' to bring waste land into cultivation in exchange for advantageous leases, was arguably the key innovation which he brought to the region. The Countess believed he had created a settlement 'out of a desert'.[28] Though abandoned while storms continued to drive sand inland, the *Old Statistical Account* entry for Duffus parish reveals the land to have previously been 'a rich cultivated soil', with 'but little depth of sand on top'. Once the sand had 'ceased to blow', the land could be brought back into cultivation simply by turning the sand down and the soil up with plough or spade. The anonymous 'Friend to Improvement' who contributed the entry for the parish of Duffus not only had an impressive insight into Young's previous projects, but also presented a detailed prospectus for one which he was promulgating. Young was evangelical about the draining of Spynie Loch, which he believed to conceal thousands of acres of 'very rich ground'. In the *Old Statistical Account* this was described enthusiastically as 'very practicable', and something which would be 'deemed easy in other countries'.[29]

Young had supplied the model for the Spynie plan previous to his occupation of Inverugie, draining the smaller Loch of Cotts while tenant of Inchbroom around 1800. This was successful, but much dubiety was expressed by contemporaries regarding the economic outcome, which he insisted had been profitable despite costing more than a thousand pounds. A finely wrought piece of puffery was despatched to the *Farmer's Magazine* lauding the achievement, signed by an anonymous admirer, one 'T.T.'.[30] In 1807 a certain Thomas Telford produced a blueprint for the draining of Spynie, which was then executed by William Hughes between 1808 and 1812. The eventual cost was reckoned at £12,740, inflated by years of legal feuding among the landowners who had backed the scheme. The disunity was chiefly due to the disappointing and uneven quality of land reclaimed. Thunderstorms in 1829 led to severe flooding, and during this 'Muckle Spate' the River Lossie burst through the canal, destroying all the sluices, and the sea claimed all of the land once more. The *New Statistical Account* of 1845 lamented the failure of the 'golden hopes' cherished for the project, and cast a somewhat jaundiced eye upon 'the projectors' responsible for raising them so high.[31]

IMPROVEMENT AND ITS SUPPORTERS

The term 'projectors' has been employed in several periods of British history. In connection with Scotland, it was used most prominently by the writer and government agent Daniel Defoe, who referred to the turbulent period around the time of the Treaty of Union as 'The Age of Projectors'.[32] The aftermath of the unsuccessful Jacobite risings brought opportunities for entrepreneurs in the Highlands. The Forfeited Estates Commission had financial reparation as their stated mission, with the involvement of projectors from England giving a colonial character to their operations, particularly those of the buccaneering York Buildings Company. Alongside the drive to develop manufacturing and exploit natural resources, the creation of new villages was considered a powerful tool of advancing civilisation. The Annexed Estates Board had a clearer goal of pacification, and its aim of a 'loyal well policed colony' was more explicitly stated.[33] Through the writings of Lord Kames and the other commissioners, the goal of agricultural reform came to be strongly associated with the Board's civilising purpose. Kames was a powerful advocate of the 'Enlightenment' doctrine of progress, which divided humanity into distinct stages of development. This philosophy encouraged the dismantling of pastoral and agrarian communities in the drive to reach the desired end state of commercial society. However, a cross-purpose given the near-constant state of war during the lifetime of the Board was the requirement to settle soldiers in such a way as to maintain the supply of recruits. In the end, the funds available were very limited and the frustrated Kames declared the sums expended to be no more use than 'water poured upon the ground'.[34]

Ironically, a significant sum was available to the Annexed Estates Board at the point of its dissolution, the resuming owners having to pay the incumbent debts previously honoured by the Crown. Spotting the opportunity, the Highland Agricultural Society was brought into being, appropriating capital for the purchase of a fine South Bridge townhouse in Edinburgh with a large meeting room and accommodation for Board members. With the Countess of Sutherland and the Duke of Argyll as founding members, this was a vehicle for landlords to express their enthusiasm for agricultural reform. Their initial goals included an enquiry into the condition of the people of the Highlands, and a nod to 'the preservation of the Gaelic Language', but those were soon abandoned as being a distraction from the chief object of establishing commercial society in the Highlands.[35]

While the idea of military colonies was transplanted to North America, leading to many soldiers settling there, most officers returned to the Highlands and the half-pay list was a significant component of the Highland economy from the 1770s onwards. Many Highland units being temporary, the region received a disproportionate amount, even considering its high military engagement.[36] The final analysis on whether this strengthened or weakened the sinews of society is less plain, though it could be argued it was a catalyst for change.[37] It is the contention of Andrew Mackillop in his study of military recruitment that the traditional tacksman class was profoundly undermined across the Highlands at this period because returning soldiers had to be granted lots, bypassing and breaking down the old sub-lettings. Much of the tacksman's power and responsibility was diminished as he was no longer necessary to recruitment or letting. In Sutherland, those bargains were made directly and on paper, but with enough of an overtone of the old obligations to lead to rancour when the letter was later observed instead of the spirit. The 'half-pay, half-gentlemen', as Loch sneeringly called these demobilised officers, came to be considered a dangerous enemy by the Sutherland estate. They were believed to have little enthusiasm for improvement, even those who were fair farmers. Loch described the dangers of having given the 'rudiments of education' to the officers, allowing their influence over the 'ignorant and credulous' people. He judged that the Highlander was no longer required as a soldier, due to the 'industrial refuse of the cities and the Irish being more cheaply obtained'.[38]

One man born in the Highlands who was dedicated to improvement was Sir John Sinclair of Lybster. As a landed gentleman he had of course been given the 'rudiments of education' at Edinburgh and Oxford. He became the first chair of the Board of Agriculture, fulfilling the wish of Lord Kames, who believed that it would achieve much more than previous colonial efforts with 'but a small share of the sums bestowed on raising colonies in America'.[39] He used that position to embed the ideology of agricultural revolution at the heart of the county surveys which were carried out across Britain. This opportunity was seized by those improvers with an eye to their own advancement, and the surveys had a certain 'advertorial' quality as a result. For Sutherland, the author was Captain John Henderson, a half-pay officer. He was also factor on Sinclair's Caithness estate, and married to a cousin of Sir John. Henderson's survey was undertaken in 1807, the year when the 'Great Sheep Run' was being established in Sutherland. He found the potential of Morvich and Culmaily obvious, and with draining and embanking more could be added to the already existing 700 acre strip of arable across the farms there. He did not mention the need to move any townships in order to accomplish that, though he envisaged the need to build further villages in order to prevent emigration. He adjudged the south-east coast 'or arable district' of Sutherland to be 'a warm, kindly soil, capable of raising excellent green crops as well as corn'. He commented sympathetically on the fledgling rotation which the small tenants had adopted there, 'having observed that a better crop of oats followed one of potatoes'.[40]

The final publication incorporated an appendix written in 1811, after Henderson carried out a second survey 'at the desire of the President of the Board of Agriculture'. Towards the conclusion of the 1807 report, there were several footnotes added deferring to 'a gentleman from Moray'. Appended was a lengthy interview with William Young, and a glowing assessment of the changes at Culmaily implemented by that 'intelligent farmer' Patrick Sellar, who had discovered that the soil there would grow 'turnips, barley and wheat – unlimed', and that the wet meadow ground was 'immensely productive'.[41] The reprinted 1815 edition was padded out with several other documents, one of which was written by a previous Sutherland factor, Hugh Rose, in 1791. Rose was an advocate of improving the native breed of sheep and strongly against large-scale clearance for sheep in place of mixed agriculture, contrasting the 'lasting and permanent good' of gradually improved cultivation with the 'fleeting and uncertain benefits' of industrial bounties. His key recommendations were that such an extensive and varied estate should never be managed by one factor alone, and that factors must be restrained from trading in stock on their own account.

The procession of factors subsequent to Rose seem to have been broadly in agreement, but in 1807 the estate embarked on its first reckless venture. The scale of their 'Great Sheep Run' was immense, and unmeasured at the time, with the remark that 'obstacles and difficulties' had prevented any detailed survey or plan. Those unspecified obstacles broke one factor, a retired colonel from Argyll, David Campbell. The aftermath would break the Edinburgh lawyer Cosmo Falconer who replaced him. Falconer's letters give some illumination regarding the nature of those difficulties. The people displaced had been offered lots at Achavandra moor. Falconer reported that 'none of them would accept of that offer'. With little conviction he reported the eventual negotiation of 'a tolerable accommodation for the whole', with many remaining temporarily upon 'places set to proper tenants'.[42] The majority expelled went to Upper Strathnaver, but others to unspecified locations within Golspie and Dornoch parishes. It seems likely that the townships around Culmaily were swelled by some of these refugees. At the same time, those townships had their resilience greatly reduced through the loss of their traditional summer grazings. Among the papers of David Campbell, there is a list of twenty-five shielings annexed to the sheep run, associated with townships in Farr, Lairg, Rogart and Golspie parishes.[43]

The winter of 1807 was an exceptionally harsh one, with early and 'uncommon severe frosts', which 'blasted the woods', destroyed the harvest and 'reduced the greater part of the tenants to a low extreme'.[44] For those cleared this came at the worst possible time, while they were trying to establish a new foothold on the land. Those who had to adjust to the loss of shielings would have been similarly off balance. Change reduced resilience in other ways. The sudden introduction of imported sheep in huge numbers presaged an outbreak of scab and rot so severe that it killed the majority of the native sheep and goats over the winter of 1807, 'as if to make way for a new order of things'.[45] According to Falconer's 1808 situation reports, the parishes of Golspie and Rogart suffered most severely in the subsequent famine, whereas more northerly areas later characterised as 'the interior', while under pressure were largely able to cope using their own resources. He admitted that the scarcity in food in Golspie parish was chiefly attributable to the home farms of Dunrobin and Rhives having been allowed to 'dwindle to nothing in terms of agriculture'.[46] By the reckoning of the *Old Statistical Account*, that was around a thousand acres of the best ground in the parish. The baseline from which Young and Sellar began their assessment of the people's condition and abilities was thus desperately and artificially low.

CULMAILY – A COMPLEX STORY

The name Culmaily is now applied only to the present farm, but the scope of the name has varied considerably from 1275, when it covered the whole parish. By the 1799 *Old Statistical Account* Culmaily was considered 'a village'.[47] While the settlement pattern at Culmaily was very long established, that did not imply stasis, but rather dynamic survival capability.[48] The notion that the township represented something pre-historic was one which was bandied around as much by the improvers as by those lamenting its loss. That idea often went hand in hand with the classification of the inhabitants as 'subsistence farmers', rooted in place and dependent upon meagre arable crops for survival. In fact, the precarious balance of climate and seasons made them necessarily flexible in their approach to securing food supplies. Loss of that diversity exacerbated the difficulties they had always faced in keeping the wolf from the door.

Loch's 1820 *Account* presented the miserable harvests of 1808 and 1816 as though they were unquestionably the outcome of poor husbandry on the part of the small tenants. There is a case at least as strong ascribing the severity of those episodes to the sudden loss of their shielings and the consequent diminishing of resilience, combined with the unfavourable climatic conditions which struck at this moment of vulnerability. In the *Account* Loch declared that harsh growing conditions in 1816 had brought 'two thousand persons' down from 'distant parts of the estate', who had 'settled in those places without leave' and 'had no title to remain where they were'.[49] This total likely included many of those Falconer had permitted to 'remain temporarily' in 1809. The estate's charity was extended to them on the proviso that they accept 'cottages on the sea-shore' and 'be encouraged to improve the land'. The 'sea-side' destination offered to them was of course the previously rejected Achavandra muir, where Sellar reported 'a great population gathering thither, and getting forward with the culture of the wastes'. He speculated that if they were successful, the land won from the moor would then 'by 1836 be put into the regular farms, and the present possessors drawn away into some town or village'.[50] They did not succeed. Loch submitted a report to the Royal Highland and Agricultural Society of Scotland in 1843, which touched upon that quarter of the estate. His theme was 'the advantages of planting waste lands', and he described the areas which the estate had put under trees, including Skelbo plantation, covering the fields of the old townships there 'formerly arable, on a gravel or clay bottom', and Harriet plantation, on Achavandra muir where 'The prevailing rock is gneiss . . . the soil a poor thin peat.' Loch's report was awarded a Gold Premium by the Society in the category of Agricultural Improvement.[51]

The account of the preceding state of the land which Loch finally published in 1820 was substantially prepared by him in the weeks leading up to Patrick Sellar's 1816 trial. In the event, he delayed publication due to the Stafford family's fears that it would lead to a paper war. Appended was a report by Sellar of his farming activities there and at Morvich in Strathfleet, which stated that he had found Culmaily 'in the greatest possible state of Barrenness'. Loch too described Culmaily as 'barren waste', which Sellar's efforts had 'rendered arable'.[52] Tales grow taller in the telling and the legend of Sellar's deeds at Culmaily was no exception. According to the agricultural reports of the 1880s, 'by him the greater part of it was reclaimed'.[53] The parish history too records that 'the greater part of the area' was 'swampy land', and talks of Sellar 'draining the moss', as though it had been blanket bog.[54] Sellar himself claimed in 1820 a comparatively modest increase in cultivated ground of 100 acres at Culmaily, and 60 acres at nearby Morvich.[55] In his 1840 Farm Report, he stated that he had 'more than four hundred and fifty acres of tillage land' between his two lowland farms, of which he had converted 'full two hundred and fifty acres' from 'moor, moss and pasture'.[56] His employment of the word 'pasture' there seems rather significant.

Initially at Culmaily, Sellar tried an intensive four-course rotation which used fodder and grazing crops instead of allowing the ground to lie fallow. This system is referred to in Loch's 1820 report as 'The Norfolk Rotation', after its popularisation in England by Coke of Holkham and 'Turnip' Townshend. Those gentlemen have been credited with the invention of this system, which Townshend is understood to have observed in the Low Countries where he was ambassador for several years.[57] In the aftermath of Sellar's trial, although James Loch built the myth of Culmaily, he admitted that what had worked in Norfolk had been far from an unqualified success in Sutherland. Sellar tried to capitalise on the high price of wheat initially, but came close to exhausting the soil by 'attempting to raise more corn than the soil was calculated to bear'.[58] The challenging growing conditions in the 'summerless' year 1816 almost broke Sellar, but his crops survived, which he ascribed to his pioneering use of enriching bonemeal, imported via Moray ports from the battlefields of Europe.[59] By 1820 Culmaily and Morvich were on a six-year rotation with three years grass, and Sellar was 'sowing up to grass' on both farms as quickly as possible as there was 'no profit at present in growing corn in Sutherland'.[60] A detailed study of Sutherland farming has concluded that claims regarding the 'high state of cultivation' at this period were exaggerated, and that the 'arable' farms were 'entirely subservient to the more extensive pastoral system'.[61]

Loch considered there to be a 'misapprehension' existing regarding the 'comparative merits of Scotch and English husbandry, and the state of improvement to be met with in the two parts of the island'. Believing the English countryside to have 'the stamp of the most perfect civilisation which the world ever witnessed', he was horrified when Young, on visiting the Stafford estates in Shropshire, recommended the 'total eradication of the present tenants, and the introduction of Scotch farmers'.[62] Ironically though, Loch's stewardship of those same estates saw him reduce that 'tenantry of 200 years standing' to the extent where he became simply 'that ruthless Scot' to the local historians.[63]

Sellar would earn still greater infamy once he perceived the value of Culmaily's pasture land as a hub for sheep farming on an industrial scale. This development connected Sutherland closely with the border regions between England and Scotland, and particularly with Northumberland. Gabriel Reed was a key figure. His father was one of the consortium behind a 1794 sheep run created at Armadale on the north coast of Sutherland. The Reed family had occupied the hills around Troughend Hall for more than 900 years, but Gabriel married the daughter of Mackay of Bighouse. His connections to the wool buyers in Yorkshire were understood to be invaluable to the estate. He told the Countess in 1820 that Sutherland would soon be 'the richest county in England'.[64] There were elements reminiscent of a kin-based network structure in the way that the sheep farms expanded. Reed's brother Ralph became head shepherd for Adam Atkinson and Anthony Marshall when they took on the thousand-acre 'Great Sheep Run'. Reed was their cautioner and doubtless had a hand in bringing them north. Atkinson made his capital as a soldier in the Bengal Army, building the mansion of Lorbottle Hall on his return to England. His son-in-law Marshall had the sheep farming expertise required. Their time in Sutherland was not an unqualified success. The 'Great Sheep Run' was ill thought out, with little appropriate wintering. While they succeeded in managing some of the ground for what was still considered 'a pittance of rent', they could not stock the whole of the hill grazings. They were unprepared for the worst extremes of the hill country and retreated after losing fully half of their stock in 1828, writing to Loch to report their 'utter and irretrievable ruin' if they continued with their operations.[65]

On his retreat to Northumberland, Atkinson was adjudged to have overstepped his bounds in resettling eight hundred sheep upon Rothbury

Common. To the indignation of the freeholders, he built 'a line of wall' to give his claim more solidity. Finding against him, the jury asserted their opinion 'that the wall should be taken down'.[66] As well as serving as a reminder of the universality of the land question, this does raise some interesting questions about the extent of traffic between the Northumberland and Sutherland components of Atkinson's international operations.

The firm of Morton and Culley took a lease of Invershin in 1814, when Atkinson and Marshall backed out of their arrangement. The Culley brothers were considered the 'Great Men' of Northumberland sheep farming, credited with the creation of the Border Leicester, one of the most successful improved breeds. It has been suggested that their skill as writers and publicists was key to that claim, aimed at establishing them as the leading authority on sheep breeding.[67] They themselves were notably wary of placing theory and received opinions over experience. In 1771 the brothers undertook a tour through Moray and into Sutherland, early in their farming career in Northumberland. Their observations on the state of field agriculture in Moray at this time do not suggest that it was particularly advanced, with the use of 'maslin' being sown an indication of near-exhausted soil; mixing grains of different character together in hopes of getting a crop of any kind. Their descriptions of 'despicable habitations and wretched inhabitants' are typical of travellers' tales about the Highlands at this time. Elsewhere in their journals this is put into some context by their reflections on the state of agriculture in Northumberland upon their arrival. They could relate to some of the classic images of Highland poverty on a personal level, recalling their first winter in the Cheviot hills, when they were reduced to feeding the cows on straw from their own thatch.[68] At this time they established their key relationship with Lockhart-Ross at Balnagowan, Easter Ross, which led to Cheviots being introduced onto that estate in 1777, and to the firm's long association with farms in Ross-shire and Sutherland, maintained until 1829.[69]

One technique which brought the Culleys arable success and reputation was the controlled flooding of fields in autumn and winter. This is a technique generally understood to have been learned from George Boswell in Dorset, when the brothers sent one of their men there in 1787. Reading Matthew's journal of their travels in 1771, he describes witnessing this practice in several parts of the north-east coast. It is plain from the detail with which it was recorded and his close questioning that Culley had not observed or considered it before, and it was clearly something of a light-bulb moment. The *County Survey* for Northumberland, however, claimed that the brothers had introduced this practice to the county in 1767, though it was then said to be 'twenty years before it was adopted by another other'.⁷⁰ It is perhaps worth noting that the co-author of that survey was George Culley. The *Old Statistical Account* for the Highland district of Stratherrick recorded that flooding before planting was well understood by the people there to 'ameliorate vegetation' and result in 'a redundant crop of corn', and a 'most exuberant crop of natural hay and pasturage'.⁷¹

While he considered himself a well-read farmer, Sellar himself travelled little outside Scotland. According to Eric Richard's research, he did not visit England until 1828, when he is known to have been in Northumberland. He found that a melancholy exercise, the sheep farmers of his acquaintance 'dead, failed or gone' and their flocks 'sadly dilapidated'. The demise of the sheep trade in the place which he considered one of the cradles of its birth must have been a shock.⁷² It was not such a surprise to the Culleys, with their much wider experience of markets. Matthew Jr wrote to Sellar at the close of his lease at Balnagowan that their 'little fortunes' had been built up on 'the un-natural heights to which prices had been forced'.⁷³

Sellar's words travelled much further than he did. The Farm Report he authored was syndicated via such publications as *The Farmer's Monthly Visitor* to lonely agriculturists in New Hampshire. The editor was 'charmed with the idea that some obscure corner of a country surrounded by rough mountains and forests, under the hand of industry has been made to produce the means of living to man and beast'.⁷⁴ *Burke's British Husbandry*, on the other hand, helpfully relocated Sellar's farms to Cumberland, then a less obscure locale. England was declared to be 'the bravest and most generous nation on earth' within Sellar's piece, which may have confused the issue of the author's nationality, and possibly led to his being employed to light the fire in New Hampshire. One aspect of the phenomenon of the 'Great Man' of Agriculture is the weight which their name gave, and to some extent still gives, to an opinion. Eric Richards quoted the opinions of Matthew Culley in 1771 as those of an 'expert breeder', but he was a young man then, and had only been in arable farming for a few years. The agricultural journalist James MacDonald, surveying the changes in 1845, declared that the Countess had consulted 'two Agricultural Experts' before embarking upon the project. At the time in question Sellar had never farmed on his own account at all. Young revealed his own opinion of his colleague when he wrote privately to Stafford in 1811. Proposing to despatch him to Assynt, he stated that Sellar was 'no agriculturist', and would be best placed in a situation where 'abilities in that way are not wanted'.[75]

CONCLUSIONS

By about 1820, in the assessment of Eric Richards all of the estate's attempts at industrial development were loss-making, and already on course to abandonment.[76] What remained would have the key characteristics of a colonial economy, what would now be termed 'under-development', where the needs of Sutherland were subordinated to the needs of the 'mother country', and justified largely from that perspective. Loch's account attempted to cast that as a virtue, declaring that the estate would feed the 'greater towns of the south', and 'support the population of our West-Indian Colonies'.[77] This echoed Sellar's declaration that providence itself had intended the interior of Sutherland to 'grow wool and mutton for the employment and maintenance and enrichment of industrious people living in countries suited to manufacture'.[78]

While it might seem absurd to discuss under-development when enormous sums had undoubtedly been expended, the immediate result of that expenditure was a congested population, crammed onto poor agricultural land with no alternative industry. High expenditure could be tolerated or even expected where improvement had been brought about, but there were profound issues with how the money had been spent in Sutherland. Loch, upon taking the reins of management in 1815, acknowledged that the improvements carried out had almost exclusively benefited those from outwith the county, particularly where employment opportunities were concerned.[79] Privately, he concurred with his confidant, James Grant, that the large coastal farms seemed designed 'rather to impress the natives with an idea that improvement is beyond their attainment than to hold out any encouragement to them to attempt it'.[80]

All Young's developments in Sutherland relied heavily upon the importation of skilled labour, often as temporary migrants. Colliers came from Wales, Strathclyde and Staffordshire, fishermen from Moray, Aberdeenshire and Berwick, and dykers from Northumberland. Fishing developed into a major employer in the region in the medium term, but the initial pattern set the course of ownership. While the port of Helmsdale was outwardly successful, the Elgin fish-curer operating there in 1823 reported that only 58 of 142 boats landing there were from Sutherland. The others were Moray- or Wick-owned. By 1828 only 44 out of 131 were local boats. Another dealer in 1844 reckoned Loch's claim that 50,000 barrels of herring had been cured there was not only exaggerated by around 25,000 barrels, but that only 7,000 of the total were caught by Sutherland boats.[81]

In agriculture, the direction of travel was the same. The sheep runs which utilised the coastal farms as fodder stations simply did not require many hands, and those were predominantly from outwith the region. In 1840 Sellar stated that he possessed his vast farms by 'eighteen south-country families', and that 'five scores of South Country families' had been imported into Sutherland through his farming activities. While his farm records were reportedly destroyed upon his death by his sons at his own request, the census returns for Culmaily and Morvich mid-century confirm that the workforce was substantially born outwith Sutherland, with the best-paid positions of responsibility being held by men from Moray and the Borders.

Historian and arch-provocateur Michael Fry succeeded in attracting some fierce public criticism for his use of the phrase 'land reform' in relation to the measures undertaken in Sutherland in his 2006 volume *Wild Scots*.[82] There is a case to be made that the original objective was a reforming one, but the undermining of that intent began almost as soon as the ink was dry on Sellar and Young's thirty-year leases. Sellar sought to characterise the clearances as an act of mercy, rescuing people from land fit only for 'the beasts of the field'.[83] That sermon falls flat when considering the expulsion of a long-established population from the most viable soil upon the estate, onto land which was fundamentally unimproveable. Young's failure to appreciate that becoming a 'lotter' on such challenging ground was a very different proposition put to those being evicted than to those who had elected to take such a gamble was a significant factor in the growing resistance to the estate's plans. Abandonment of the flax-processing plan at Culmaily punctured the principal justification for its clearance, and once Sellar was free of the bonds of his estate responsibilities he was able to use Culmaily as a lever to enrich himself by transforming it into a hub for commercial sheep farming on an industrial scale. That change represented a reversal of what was promised and claimed in terms of agriculture from intensive arable cultivation to grazing and fodder. Culmaily is an instructive example, representing a less visible form of clearance than those traditionally associated with Sutherland and demonstrating that the estate narrative about clearance from 'the interior' to 'the coast' misrepresents both the previous and the new settlement pattern.

NOTES

1. M. Overton, *Agricultural Revolution in England: The Transformation of the Agrarian Economy 1500–1850* (Cambridge, 1996).
2. G. Mingay, 'Review of *Agricultural Revolution in England: The Transformation of the Agrarian Economy 1500–1850*', reviews.history.ac.uk/review/12 [last accessed 20 July 2020].
3. T. Devine, *The Transformation of Rural Scotland: Social Change and the Agrarian Economy, 1660–1815* (Edinburgh, 1994), p. 165.
4. I. Mowat, *Easter Ross 1750–1850: The Double Frontier* (Edinburgh, 1981).
5. B. Bonnyman, 'Agricultural enlightenment, land ownership and Scotland's culture of improvement, 1700–1820', in M. Combe, J. Glass and A. Tindley (eds), *Land Reform in Scotland: History, Law and Policy* (Edinburgh, 2020).
6. P. Aitchison and A. Cassell, *The Lowland Clearances: Scotland's Silent Revolution 1760–1830* (Edinburgh, 2003); T. Devine, *The Scottish Clearances: A History of the Dispossessed 1600–1900* (London, 2018).
7. R. Houston, 'The Clearances in South East Sutherland', in J. Baldwin (ed.), *Firthlands of Ross and Sutherland* (Edinburgh, 1986) focuses on other estates. J. Hunter, *Set Adrift Upon the World: The Sutherland Clearances* (Edinburgh, 2015) does comment on this, p. 357.
8. J. Loch, *An Account of the Improvements on the Estates of the Marquess of Stafford* (London, 1820).
9. E. Richards, *Patrick Sellar and the Highland Clearances: Homicide, Eviction and the Price of Progress* (Edinburgh, 1999).
10. J. G. Leith, *The Man Who Went to Farr* (Edinburgh, 2010) transcribes evidence not presented at the trial, most damningly the full statements of the sheriff officers under Sellar's command.
11. R. J. Adam, *Papers on Sutherland Estate Management, 1802–1816* (Edinburgh, 1972).
12. E. Richards, 'The prospect of economic growth in Sutherland at the time of the Clearances, 1809 to 1813', *Scottish Historical Review*, 49 (1970), pp. 154–71.
13. J. Henderson, *General View of the Agriculture of the County of Sutherland* (Inverness, 1812), p. 13.
14. *Transactions of the Highland and Agricultural Society of Scotland*, Vol. 1, 1799.
15. Young and Sellar to Marchioness of Stafford, 20 September 1809, in Adam, *Papers on Sutherland Estate Management Vol. 9*, p. 99.
16. Young to Stafford, 21 October 1810, in Adam, *Papers on Sutherland Estate Management Vol. 8*, p. 38.
17. Young and Sellar to Stafford, 5 July 1809, in Adam, *Papers on Sutherland Estate Management Vol. 9*, p. 91.

18. Young and Sellar to Stafford, 3 August 1809, in Adam, *Papers on Sutherland Estate Management Vol. 9*, p. 93.
19. Falconer to Earl Gower, 4 September 1809, in Adam, *Papers on Sutherland Estate Management Vol. 9*, p. 96.
20. Richards, 'Prospect of economic growth in Sutherland', pp. 154–71.
21. Young to Earl Gower, 21 September 1809, in Adam, *Papers on Sutherland Estate Management Vol. 9*, p. 101.
22. Young to Earl Gower, 30 April 1810, in Adam, *Papers on Sutherland Estate Management Vol. 8* 'Introduction', p. xlv.
23. Young to Loch, 8 December 1815, in Adam, *Papers on Sutherland Estate Management Vol. 9*, p. 266.
24. These movements have been reconstructed by descendants and shared via subscription sites such as ancestry.co.uk and non-commercial heritage groups such as the cosuthpeople mailing list.
25. *The Farmer's Magazine*, Vol. 21 (Edinburgh, 1820), p. 435.
26. Staffordshire County Record Office [hereafter SCRO], Sutherland Estates Papers, D593/K/1/3/7, F. Suther to James Loch, 29 April 1819.
27. Hunter, *Set Adrift Upon the World*, p. 279.
28. E. Richards, *Leviathan of Wealth: The Sutherland Fortune in the Industrial Revolution* (London, 1973), p. 172.
29. Duffus, County of Elgin, *Old Statistical Account*, Vol. VIII, 1793, p. 391.
30. *The Farmer's Magazine*, Vol. 3 (Edinburgh, 1802), p. 319.
31. Duffus, County of Elgin, *New Statistical Account*, Vol. XIII, 1845.
32. D. Defoe, *An Essay upon Projects* (London, 1697).
33. National Library of Scotland, Minto Papers, Ms 11009, f. 30.
34. A. Mackillop, *More Fruitful than the Soil: Army, Empire and the Scottish Highlands, 1715–1815* (East Linton, 2000), pp. 82–6.
35. *Transactions of the Highland and Agricultural Society of Scotland*, Vol. I (Edinburgh, 1799); *Transactions of the Highland and Agricultural Society of Scotland*, Fourth Series, Vol. IX (Edinburgh, 1877).
36. M. Dziennik, *The Fatal Land: War, Empire, and the Highland Soldier in British America* (New Haven, CT, 2015), p. 180.
37. S. Nenadic, 'The impact of the military profession on Highland gentry families, c. 1730–1830', *Scottish Historical Review*, 85 (2006), pp. 75–99.
38. Loch, *An Account*, p. 150.
39. H. Home, *The Gentleman Farmer* (Edinburgh, 1776), p. 391.
40. J. Henderson, *General View of the Agriculture of the County of Sutherland* (Inverness, 1812).
41. Ibid., p. 151.
42. Falconer to Earl Gower, 4 September 1809, in Adam, *Papers on Sutherland Estate Management Vol. 9*, p. 96.
43. Adam, *Papers on Sutherland Estate Management Vol. 9*, p. 95.
44. D. Sage, 'Hints regarding the state of the parish of Kildonan', in Henderson,

General View of the Agriculture of the County of Sutherland (London, 1815), p. 174.
45. J. MacDonald, 'On the agriculture of the county of Sutherland', *Transactions of the Highland and Agricultural Society of Scotland*, Vol. XII (Edinburgh, 1845).
46. Adam, *Papers on Sutherland Estate Management Vol. 8*, p. 12.
47. Golspie, County of Sutherland, *Old Statistical Account*, Vol. IX, 1793.
48. R. Dodgshon, *No Stone Unturned: A History of Farming, Landscape and Environment in the Scottish Highlands and Islands* (Edinburgh, 2015) argues persuasively that the Highland landscape was 'always in the making', p. 118.
49. Loch, *An Account*, p. 81.
50. Richards, *Leviathan of Wealth*, p. 200.
51. *Transactions of the Highland and Agricultural Society of Scotland* (Edinburgh, 1847), p. 36.
52. Loch, *An Account*, p. 17.
53. Macdonald, 'On the agriculture of the county of Sutherland', pp. 1–90.
54. M. Grant, *Golspie's story* (Golspie, 1983).
55. Loch, *An Account*, p. 67.
56. P. Sellar, 'Reports of select farms', *The Farmer's Register Vol. 8* (Petersburg, VA, 1840), p. 66.
57. Overton, *Agricultural Revolution in England*.
58. Loch, *An Account*, p. 18.
59. *The Gentleman's Magazine*, Vol. 92 (London, 1822), p. 461 describes this trade in detail, human bone having been identified by Sir John Sinclair as particularly effective. He recommended a bounty for vessels engaged in this trade in 'The Code of Agriculture'.
60. Loch, *An Account*, p. 67.
61. S. Wade-Martins, 'A century of farms and farming on the Sutherland Estate, 1790–1890', *Review of Scottish Culture*, No. 10 (1997), pp. 41–2.
62. Richards, *Patrick Sellar and the Highland Clearances*, p. 178.
63. D. C. Cox, J. R. Edwards, R. C. Hill, A. J. Kettle, R. Perren, T. Rowley and P. A. Stamper, *A History of the County of Shropshire: volume 4, Agriculture*, G. C. Baugh and C. R. Elrington (eds) (London, 1989).
64. SCRO, D593/6579/9, Lady Stafford to Lord Stafford, 3 October 1820.
65. SCRO, D593/K/1/3/17, Atkinson and Marshall to Loch, 4 August 1829.
66. E. Mackenzie, *An Historical, Topographical, and Descriptive View of the County of Northumberland* (Berwick, 1825), p. 46.
67. R. A. Trow-Smith, *History of British Livestock Husbandry, 1700–1900* (London, 1959), p. 273.
68. A. Orde (ed.), *Travel Journals and Letters, 1765–1798, M. and G. Culley* (Oxford, 2002), p. 288.
69. M. Bangor-Jones, 'Sheep farming in Sutherland in the eighteenth century', *Agricultural History Review*, 50:2 (2002), pp. 181–202.

70. D. J. Rowe, 'The Culleys, Northumberland farmers, 1767–1813', *Agricultural History Review*, 19:2 (1971), pp. 156–74.
71. Boleskine and Abertarff, County of Inverness, *Old Statistical Account*, Vol. XX, 1798.
72. Richards, *Patrick Sellar and the Highland Clearances*, p. 265; Richards is of the opinion that this was Sellar's first visit, suggesting travel references in his 1815 report were invented.
73. National Records of Scotland, GD129/2/90, Matthew Culley to Sellar, 26 November 1827 (Matthew was George's son).
74. *The Farmer's Monthly Visitor*, Vol. 1 (Concord, 1839).
75. Young to Stafford, 29 November 1810, in Adam, *Papers on Sutherland Estate Management Vol. 9*, p. 131.
76. E. Richards, 'The prospect of economic growth in Sutherland at the time of the Clearances, 1809 to 1813', *Scottish Historical Review*, 49 (1970), pp. 154–71.
77. Loch, *An Account*, p. 67.
78. Cited by Eric Richards in *A History of the Highland Clearances* (London, 1985), II, p. 371.
79. Loch to William Mackenzie, 23 October 1816, in Adam, *Papers on Sutherland Estate Management Vol. 9*, p. 302.
80. Grant to Loch, 23 October 1816, in Adam, *Papers on Sutherland Estate Management*, p. 290.
81. Hansard's Debates, third Series, Vol. 72 (London, 1845), p. 1452.
82. A. Mackintosh, *The Land*, 1 (2006), pp. 7–10 cites Fry in this regard, as does R. Gibson, *Scottish Affairs*, 61 (2007).
83. Sellar, cited by Eric Richards in *A History of the Highland Clearances* (London, 1985), II, p. 371.

2

'An overwhelming tide of disappointments and vexation': A Case Study of Reform in Estate Management on the Island of Lewis, 1817–1837

Finlay McKichan

INTRODUCTION

ON 21 MAY 1817, Mary Elizabeth Frederica Mackenzie (1783–1862), proprietor since the death of her father Lord Seaforth in 1815 of the Seaforth estates in Lewis and Wester and Easter Ross, married James Alexander Stewart of Glasserton (1784–1843), a Wigtownshire landowner who was subsequently known as Stewart Mackenzie of Seaforth. Lord Seaforth had been in many respects a man of principle, who felt a real concern for his small tenants.[1] Mary and James were evangelical Christians. They encouraged a religious revival in Lewis in the 1820s and additional churches were built at Knock and Cross, to which they presented evangelical ministers. The minister of Uig wrote that 'one and all of us cease not to praise God that we are in this island blessed with rulers who have pious interest and the good of souls at heart'.[2] James presented himself as being different to proprietors who were 'without even semblance of benevolent and human feeling' towards the poor inhabitants of their Hebridean estates.[3] On the other hand, James Hunter suggests that, having failed to find finance for large-scale emigration, he consolidated and extended sheep farming all over the southern part of Lewis, moving those evicted to crofts in the northern part of the island with little concern for their viability.[4] Eric Richards described the development schemes in Lewis in the 1820s as failures, followed by evictions and rationalisation. In his view, Lewis became 'a watchword for poverty and squalor and vulnerability'.[5] Donald Macdonald, the historian of Lewis, argued that Stewart Mackenzie's 'imaginative ideas for increasing his rapidly diminishing income were not matched by his power of accomplishment'.[6] A contemporary view is given by Joseph Mitchell, the chief engineer of the Highland Roads and Bridges Commission. While he heard inhabitants of the Seaforth lands complaining of the 'folly and unkindness' of the Stewart Mackenzies, he believed from working with them that 'no two people were more anxious for the welfare of their tenants or more earnest for the redemption of the heavy burdens on their estates'.[7]

How far were the principles of the Stewart Mackenzies reflected in their role as proprietors? In this chapter an examination will be made of their management of the island of Lewis, the largest part of their estate, between their marriage and their departure from Britain in 1837 for James to become Governor of Ceylon. The introductory section discusses the economic and social position of the island at the time of their marriage, the debt position they inherited and their initial plans to develop Lewis. Although these did not necessarily appear beneficial to people on Lewis, it will be argued that they represented a landowner-led programme of land reform. This case study illustrates, it is believed, that land reform was not sought only by campaigners or implemented by statute. Subsequent sections of the chapter discuss and assess the plans of the Stewart Mackenzies for fisheries, the Stornoway distillery and for tenancies and sheep farming. It is then argued that by the 1830s Stewart Mackenzie, disillusioned, was disengaging himself from active management of the island. Conclusions are reached on why he ultimately gave up hope that he personally could reform the economy and society of Lewis or thereby solve his debt problem.

At the time of the Stewart Mackenzies' marriage the income of the Lewis estate was diminishing. The principal source of cash of tenant farmers was cattle. Cattle prices had been high during the Napoleonic Wars to meet demand from the army and navy, but dropped from about £6 for a three-year-old in 1810 to about £3 10s. by the 1830s. The consequence, as Malcolm Gray put it, was that tenants passed the deficiency to what had always been the residual item of expense – the rent.[8] Stewart Mackenzie complained in 1823 that 'all rentals since 1814 have been a mere form'.[9] At least equally serious was the drop in kelp prices. Kelping involved the laborious collecting and burning of seaweed to produce an alkaline extract used in the manufacture of soap and glass. Kelp had been protected from the superior Spanish barilla by import duties and by wartime restrictions on trade. Post-war conditions reduced Lewis kelp profits from £8,484 in 1808 to £2,221 in 1815.[10] Nevertheless, until the early 1820s the best-quality kelp often secured about £10 per ton compared to £16 at the peak in 1808.[11] The serious decline of the kelp industry began in the 1820s, when it suffered from tariff reform, the result of *laissez-faire* ideas on economics becoming accepted orthodoxy. In 1822 the import duty on barilla was reduced from £11 to £5 5s. per ton. The most damaging reform came in 1824 with the complete removal of salt duties. The Leblanc process enabled the manufacture of soda from salt, thus providing a viable alternative to kelp. John MacAskill has described this as 'a critical blow to the kelp industry'.[12] The price of best Lewis kelp (from Lochs and Uig) was now £5 per ton and from Stornoway only £3 per ton.[13] Stewart Mackenzie's view was that the good name of Lewis kelp would find it a market as long as there was any demand, and it survived at a lower level for some time. The proceeds were £1,506 in 1828, £1,267 in 1829 and £1,207 in 1830.[14]

Stewart Mackenzie's principal problem when he began to consider the future of Lewis lay in population increase. The Census returns show the population of the island as 9,168 in 1801, 12,231 in 1821, 14,541 in 1831 and 17,037 in 1841.[15] Between 1801 and 1841, the population of the western seaboard and the islands as a whole increased by 53 per cent and that of Lewis by 85.3 per cent.[16] The concern was that while the numbers increased, the means of subsistence for them was declining. Stewart Mackenzie's initial opinion of Lewis was unfavourable and his first proposals were dramatic and with major potential consequences for its people. In 1819 he sought government assistance to finance colonial emigration, observing that:

> If it becomes necessary for me, as I fear it will do, to carry through a measure of dispossessing a population overgrown, and daily becoming more burdensome, to pave the way for the grand improvement of mutton in lieu of man, the numbers almost appal me ... 5000 souls and upward may be spared from this island and the Seaforth mainland estates.[17]

This sounds like a classic proposal for mass emigration, clearance and sheep farming, and is the starting point for Hunter's criticism of the Stewart Mackenzies.[18] Since the late eighteenth century, many Highland proprietors had used competitive bidding for leases as a means of creating large-scale farms, often sheep farms tenanted by outsiders. Small tenants were 'cleared' to less eligible lands on the estates or, after the ending of the wartime demand for military recruits, encouraged to emigrate to the lowlands or to the colonies. These were the main tools available to landowners to restructure (they argued, to 'improve') their estates.[19] The government quickly replied that it could not finance emigration on the scale suggested by Stewart Mackenzie, but other aspects of the proposal remained on the table.[20] An adviser's report in 1820 suggested that:

> The population of Lewis is nearly 12,000, but if it should be put under sheep, 2,000 would be sufficient including fishing and kelp. However, motives stronger than of a pecuniary nature may guide the conduct of the proprietors,

who may not be disposed rashly to break ties of affection which unite 10,000 people to their place of nativity. Improvable lands should be allotted to industrious small tenants, who may not only render lands now raising corn doubly or triply productive, but may also bring into culture heretofore uncultivated lands. The whole northern part of the island is favourable to this plan ... Small tenants will be placed within reach of fishing grounds ... grounds peculiarly fitted for sheep pasture should be so arranged that present occupiers remove to settlements to be laid out for them.[21]

This report reflects the tensions facing Highland proprietors, especially clan chiefs, in contemplating the introduction of large-scale sheep farms. The prospect of a very large increase in rent was a strong 'motive of a pecuniary nature'. However, Mrs Stewart Mackenzie had inherited from Lord Seaforth the chiefship of the Clan Mackenzie and Lewis had been part of the Seaforth estate for two hundred years. The 'ties of affection' were not only between the people and their birthplace. Lord Seaforth had tried to maintain the traditional role of a chief as protector of his people, with damaging consequences for his level of debt, estimated at his death in 1815 at £163,399.[22] Although there is a hint in this report that maximising financial benefit might not be the only motivation, it seems clear that Stewart Mackenzie's initially poor impression of Lewis and his wish to clear Lord Seaforth's debts were the decisive factors at this point. He proposed in early 1823 a scheme of mass clearance to take place at Whitsunday. Letters exist from tenants objecting to the short notice and asking for information on where their new lands were to be.[23] Robert Brown, a senior adviser, argued that it would cause disturbances and public attention and frighten investors. The sort of investors advisers had in mind were sheep farmers, fish merchants and even land purchasers. Putting poor people on uncultivated moors, Brown believed, would turn them into paupers, whose relief the estate would have to pay. There was not capital to establish a thousand families in fishing villages and supply tackle and boats. The changes, if necessary, should be done gradually. Stewart Mackenzie unhappily acceded, complaining that he feared the consequences of indecision 'much more than moderate decisive steps'.[24]

By the summer of 1823, Stewart Mackenzie appeared to be even more disenchanted with Lewis. He complained to a government minister of 'the evils produced by high priced kelp for twenty years past, viz. growth of population beyond the means of a barren soil (or rather barren rocks) to support'.[25] He wrote to Patrick Cockburn, estate accountant, 'Mrs S. M. will apply to the House of Lords [i.e. the Court of Session] for permission to sell Lewis'. In 1817, to placate creditors, a private Act of

Parliament had been obtained authorising a cumbersome sale process to repay debts, initiated by petition to the Court.[26] He thought its sale would clear their debts and commented that 'Lewis was not worth an attempt to retain as where would be means to bring it forward? ... There is little capital among the tacksmen.'[27] A tacksman was a large farmer, often with many sub-tenants and sometimes the descendant of several generations who had held this land.[28] The testimony of the estate officials to the Court was not encouraging. Arrears of rent since 1815 totalled £16,569 and were now increasing more rapidly. To reflect the general fall in prices, rents should be reduced by 25–30 per cent. The Court's decision was that the three Lewis parishes of Lochs, Uig and Barvas should be advertised, and they were sold by auction in the Parliament House, Edinburgh on 2 March 1825.[29]

The astonishing outcome was that 'The Three Parishes' were purchased by Stewart Mackenzie for £161,600, about £25,000 more than the valuation of £136,378. Why did he do it? The bidding was brisk and the preceding offer only £500 less.[30] All of the sum realised except £1,670 was used in payment of Lord Seaforth's debts, and there is evidence that Mrs Stewart Mackenzie (his daughter) had pressed for this.[31] The effect of the repurchase was to clear these lands of the entail on them and to enable them, it was hoped, to be used as security for more easily obtained and cheaper loans.[32] The intention was to pay for the repurchase by raising a loan of £125,000 (secured from the Bank of Scotland in June) and to sell Stewart Mackenzie's Ayrshire estate of Muirkirk, for which a buyer was not found until 1830.[33] In 1827 he admitted that the repurchase had been a mistake, but claimed Lord Seaforth's debts had made it necessary to have a *bona fide* sale. The effect had been to largely transfer these debts to him, but he thought that rewards might still be looked for.[34] It was certainly followed by serious attempts to develop the economy of Lewis, a land reform programme which will be analysed in the following sections. However, there was no immediate improvement in his finances. On the contrary, by 1829 Stewart Mackenzie's debts and other obligations totalled £229,000.[35] A new trust had to be set up to pacify the pressing demands of creditors (including the Bank of Scotland), which the estate accountant Patrick Cockburn blamed on the repurchase.[36]

FISHERIES

By the end of the eighteenth century there were already signs of commercial white fisheries on Lewis.[37] Fishery historians have argued that such fishing was encouraged by the growing demand in Scotland's expanding towns and cities. It was also assisted from 1821 by a government bounty of 4s. per cwt. on fish cured to an adequate standard and by the repeal of salt duties in 1824.[38] From 1822 to 1828, the bounty paid for cod and ling cured on Lewis averaged the substantial sum of £1,045 per annum.[39] The combination of this and the need to maximise income after the repurchase encouraged Stewart Mackenzie to enter the fishery business on his own account. By 1827 he was ordering oars and canvas and offering inducements for fish curers of capital to set up on Lewis.[40] He admitted that his fishermen had not yet 'skill in or capital for decked smacks nor [were] expert enough yet to salt and cure in the best manner'. However, he assured curers that London decked boats got large catches of cod off the west coast. It was clearly this type of year-round fishery in which he was most interested, rather than the seasonal and more uncertain herring trade.[41] One of the tasks given to the factor (the estate manager) in 1828 was to promote the fishing in Ness in the far north of Lewis.[42]

Stewart Mackenzie's promotion of Lewis fisheries was not only intended as a reform in the way he derived income from the island. It was also designed to provide employment for those who were already fishermen or who might take it up. This may not have been welcomed by former agricultural tenants moved to the coast, but there were successes. In 1829 the factor reported that tenants in Stornoway Parish who fished were gradually getting out of debt, and that district became the major white fishing centre on the island.[43] In 1837 the newly created parish of Knock (on the Eye Peninsula) was reckoned to be in 'better circumstances than the rest of the island, chiefly from the natives being engaged in fishing'.[44] However, there were problems, which explain why the fisheries programme did not overall deliver the anticipated results. In 1830 the bounty on cod and ling was abolished, another result of free trade doctrine.[45] A petition was presented, ostensibly by the Lewis cod and ling fishermen, but repeating the sort of language Stewart Mackenzie used. It described fishing as 'the true source of wealth and employment for natives of these barren shores' and argued that without the bounty 'they must either starve or reluctantly quit their native country'.[46] This confirms that the fisheries programme was seen as a reform with the potential to create and maintain livings for the islanders. Stewart Mackenzie wrote in very similar terms to a trustee, arguing that the impetus given to fishing should not be checked, at least for a few years.[47] Another problem was that the results of fishing were not as predictable as had been hoped. William McGregor, a Lewis

Figure 2.1 Abandoned crofts at Garenin, Lewis; some of Stewart Mackenzie's lotters were placed on terrain like this in the hope of cropping hitherto uncultivated land.

tenant and estate adviser, reported that there was good fishing throughout the island in 1832. There were more boats in Ness than formerly and fishing had started at Carloway in Uig.[48] However, a year later it was reported that the almost total failure of fishing in 1833 due to bad weather had prevented curers advancing rent money to tenants in Point.[49] Another issue was that the Stornoway merchants McIver and Morrison controlled the marketing of fish on the island, thus limiting the prices catchers could achieve. Alexander Stewart, the former Lewis factor, complained that they 'have monopolised fisheries ... and all young traders are put down.'[50]

A further problem was that the fishery plans were impeded by a lack of suitable piers. By the 1830s, Stewart Mackenzie was campaigning to obtain government funds for that purpose. Plans were submitted to the Fisheries Board for possible sites in 1833, but it was not until 1835 that preliminary approval was given for the only two piers agreed by the Board that year.[51] An issue was how much the estate would contribute to the cost, estimated to be £3,446. The Board asked for one-third of the contract price, to which the trustees ultimately agreed after at first pleading poverty.[52] It was not until 1837, shortly before the Stewart Mackenzies left for Ceylon, that the piers were completed. The factor

Thomas Knox noted that when this was achieved, 'as many more as possible must be crowded onto their neighbourhood that the advantages of the piers to fishermen may be made available'.[53] This confirms that the estate wished to move small tenants to lots of a size which would oblige them to make part of their living from fishing. Although seen by the proprietors as a reform process, it was a very paternalistic one, which explains the complaints of 'unkindness' heard by Joseph Mitchell. That one of the piers was to be at Calicott, near the Ness of Lewis, implies that people were moved north to fish. However, the other pier was at Carnish in Uig, which does not indicate that parish was intended to be depopulated, as suggested by Hunter.[54] Indeed, T. M. Devine has calculated that in the decade 1831–41 net emigration from Uig was only 1 per cent.[55]

Robert Graham, who visited Lewis in 1837 to report on destitution, suggested that Uig could be made a good cod fishing station, but that the people would need to be furnished with tackle, good boats and a few expert fishermen from the East Coast to share their skills.[56] This was not a ringing endorsement of Stewart Mackenzie's promotion of fisheries, although it was a crucial element in his plan and he had devoted considerable energy to it. When he left for Ceylon in 1837, he included 'to encourage fishing' in the suggestions he made for the island's management.[57] However, a Fisheries Board inspector, visiting Lewis in 1843, criticised the cod and ling fishery. It suffered from 'wretched boats', lack of direct communication to London, unsatisfactory curing methods and consequent low prices.[58] Clearly shortage of capital (notwithstanding the new piers) and distance from markets inhibited the development of the fisheries, as it will be argued they did for other aspects of Stewart Mackenzie's plans for Lewis.

STORNOWAY DISTILLERY

Illegal distilling of whisky had been common and profitable in the Highlands and Islands for decades before the 1820s. After 1815, declining cattle and kelp prices gave the trade an added incentive in order to pay rents. This has been described as 'the golden age' of whisky smuggling.[59] Devine has argued that the Excise Act of 1823 'substantially eroded the illicit producer's cost advantage over his licensed rival'. Permission to distil could be purchased for a uniform charge of £10. The duty on each gallon distilled was reduced by more than half. A drawback (amounting to about a half of the new reduced spirits duty) was given on malt used in distillation. The Act made it economically possible to distil whisky solely from malted barley, which gave a product of superior quality, rather than by using grain or a mixture of the two.[60] However, this business model depended on maintaining a sufficient supply of malted barley.

Stewart Mackenzie enthusiastically welcomed the 1823 Excise Act, and stated that he wished to drive out illicit distillation, which he described as a 'demoralising system'.[61] James Loch claimed that one of the motives for the Sutherland Clearances was to remove the demoralising effect of illicit distilling and thus, it was hoped, improve the people morally as well as economically.[62] German and Adamson have argued that landowners deliberately denigrated the small-scale illicit producers to secure a statute to drive them out of business and obtain a new income flow for themselves.[63] Contrary to the advice of Robert Brown, who clearly doubted the viability of a distillery at Stornoway, Stewart Mackenzie was keen to take advantage of the 1823 Act as soon as the repurchase of the island was completed.[64] In November 1825 he ordered two copper stills, to hold 600 and 400 gallons, and two copper boilers, which were shipped to Lewis in April 1826.[65] By 1827, with the distillery not yet operational, total costs including inputs for the first year of operation were estimated to be £11,643.[66] German and Adamson argue that the annual capacity of 54,000 gallons was (as with a similar enterprise of Lord Lovat's at Beauly) unrealistically high.[67] However, there were other problems. Production was delayed, costs increased and revenue reduced by what Macdonald described as Stewart Mackenzie's poor 'power of accomplishment'.[68] The manager Bulloch reported in November 1826 the malt barn, granary and kiln were still to be roofed and the waterwheel built.[69] The opening date was now postponed till late autumn 1827 at the earliest.[70] Henry Armstrong, the still manufacturer, wrote pained letters, pointing out that the identical plant at Prestonpans had been working with entire satisfaction for sixteen months and enquiring when his workmen could at last come to Stornoway to fit up the equipment.[71] That payment of his outstanding account, £1,180, was not arranged until early 1828 suggests that the delay was at least in part financial.[72] By 1829, with the distillery still not in operation, the estate's debt position (as has been seen) necessitated the creation of a new trust. One adviser described the distillery, with notable understatement, as an 'unfortunate concern'.[73] Another estimated that Stewart Mackenzie's speculations on Lewis had cost him £100,000 and raised the question of whether the island should be sold.[74] While the distillery was a business speculation, it was also intended to provide a market for locally grown quality barley and thus contribute to improving the island's agriculture.

When it finally opened in April 1829, the distillery had not (as hoped) been leased by a commercial operator, but was run by a company controlled by the landowners.[75] German and Adamson suggest that a major reason for its failure was the use of a mixture of imported raw barley and malted local bear (a primitive barley), presumably because in the event insufficient malted barley could be obtained on Lewis, and in consequence a lower price was obtained. A further problem was (as with the fishery enterprise) distance from the major markets in the Central Belt. In Campbeltown, not unlike Stornoway but much nearer Glasgow, twenty-seven distilleries were opened between 1823 and 1827.[76] A Glasgow firm considered taking a share in the Stornoway distillery, but only if there was a weekly steamboat to Glasgow.[77] From 1832 it was leased to the Morrison brothers (partners in the monopolistic Stornoway fish merchants).[78] Under the terms of their 1834 lease the estate was to put the distillery in working condition (the top floor having fallen in), advance two-thirds of the money to carry it on, and guarantee the Morrisons against any loss.[79] Thus, as with the fisheries, the lack of any alternative entrepreneurs on Lewis put the proprietor at the mercy of the Stornoway merchants. The distillery closed within twelve years of its formation.[80]

TENANCIES AND SHEEP FARMING

An important part of Stewart Mackenzie's plans for tenurial change was the replacement of multiple tenant holdings (worked in common) by individual crofts, a process known at the time as 'lotting', greatly accelerating its limited introduction under Lord Seaforth.[81] Sometimes this involved dividing the existing township lands into separate lots (known subsequently as crofts). Sometimes people were moved to new land and given separate crofts there. Hunter has described this as being either a means of reducing a family's land to oblige them to supplement their income with kelping or fishing (a recipe, he argues, for catastrophe) or of clearing their land for sheep farms.[82] Gray has pointed out that the stated intention of lotting was to 'allow a man the full fruit of initiative and thus release a reserve of energy'.[83] The 1820 Lewis plan envisaged lotters achieving grain yields of six to eight seeds instead of the current three to four, and growing grasses and turnips for cattle feed.[84] Gray admits that frequently this was not the happy result.

It is evident that a programme of lotting began in 1823 and continued through the 1820s, twenty years after the 5th Duke of Argyll's much more expensive lotting scheme on Tiree.[85] It is less clear whether the stated intentions of the estate were actually carried out and whether the lotting of particular townships involved removals.[86] There is evidence that managerial resources did not match the proprietor's aspirations. In one of the earlier lotting schemes, at South Shawbost, the factor James Adam had to point out how much detailed work was required. He only had time to make a quick examination of the ground. A surveyor would have to be employed, then about a dozen men would be needed to mark off and prepare the ground. All this, and the necessary warnings to the tenants, would take three months.[87] Stewart Mackenzie regularly stated his wish that the lotted tenants should be given leases to encourage them to improve the land, clearly an exercise in land reform. For example, soon after the programme began, he asked for it to be halted unless the tenants could be given a lease of five or seven years.[88] However, McGregor complained as late as 1837 that small tenants could not be expected to improve without a lease, which he believed factors opposed to maintain their authority.[89] The proprietor himself blamed his factors for the failure, but it may be that they did not have the finance, time, administrative ability or support staff for the task.[90]

As elsewhere in the Highlands, failure to prepare new lots could be a serious problem.[91] In March 1827 Adam reported that he had 'put the Aird of Tong tenants in possession of their new lots and with few exceptions they seem satisfied'.[92] However, eleven months later an adviser, Alexander Craig, visited and complained that they 'had been forced into new allotments without matters being previously arranged for their moving'. The people were up to their knees in mud to reach their houses and, it was said, deaths had resulted from the unwholesome situation, worse than he had seen in Donegal. If more people were to be brought into the Point district, the road must be completed to avoid the Aird of Tong experience.[93] A serious problem appears here, as so often on Lewis, to have been a lack of development capital. At the Aird of Tong the lotters had clearly been removed from their original townships. However, at North Shawbost in 1827, Stewart Mackenzie instructed that, while the more promising tenants should have larger lots, the remaining ones should have some land 'according to their circumstances'.[94] This was part of a larger lotting scheme for the Carloway district of Barvas, a parish with an unusual number of townships of multiple tenants (as opposed to sub-tenants of a tacksman).[95] Thereafter these were turned into smaller tenancies.[96] There is less evidence of lotting in the 1830s, suggesting that the scheme had been hindered by the difficulties outlined above and, as will be argued later, a loss of enthusiasm by the proprietor.

Table 2.1 Lewis parishes: number of tenancies at different rent levels, 1823 and 1831 (NRS, GD46/1/128/2, GD46/1/339).

Rent Levels	Uig 1823	Uig 1831	Barvas 1823	Barvas 1831	Stornoway Rural 1823	Stornoway Rural 1831	Lochs 1823	Lochs 1831
Below £20	1	10	Nil	3	Nil	3	Nil	3
£20–49	10	21	1	9	5	11	19	19
£50–99	7	12	7	12	3	11	10	14
£100–199	13	5	13	6	6	4	8	5
£200–299	1	1	2	Nil	1	Nil	Nil	Nil
£300–399	1	Nil	Nil	Nil	2	1	1	1
TOTAL	33	49	23	30	17	30	38	42

GRAND TOTAL OF TENANCIES 1823: 111; 1831: 151

As shown above, Hunter has argued that Stewart Mackenzie consolidated and extended sheep farming all over the southern part of Lewis. Macdonald states that there were wholesale evictions to make way for sheep farms.[97] However, Devine has argued that 'one of the most extensive and best documented series of removals' took place in Lewis between 1851 and 1855, that is, after the island changed hands.[98] Some evidence that the extent of clearances for sheep by the Stewart Mackenzies has been exaggerated is given by the rentals for 1823 and 1831, the only ones extant for Lewis in this period.[99]

Table 2.1 shows the number of tenancies at different rent levels in the three parishes and the rural part of Stornoway Parish. The first sheep farm on the island had been at Valimos in Southern Lochs in 1802, rented at £317.[100] In 1823 four farms on Lewis were rented at £300 or over and thus equivalent to the 1802 Valimos farm. By 1831 this had been reduced to two, although at £251 the Lineshadder and Crossbost farm in Uig approached that level. There is evidence that none of these three large farms in 1831 was purely a sheep ranch. Dr Donald Macaulay of Lineshadder and Crossbost and Lewis McIver of Gress and Back were the two largest cattle dealers on the island, indeed accused of being monopolists of that trade.[101] Clearly cattle breeding was a major function of their farms. However, there had been clearances to make way for sheep on Lineshadder, for example at Kirkibost on the island of Great Bernera, from which people were moved to Little Bernera.[102] The most noted Lewis sheep farm was Park. In 1825 the separate holdings in South Lochs tenanted by the Stewart family were combined into one holding at £300 rent, clearances certainly being involved.[103] However, in

1833 one of the family wrote to Stewart Mackenzie that Park had a full cattle stock and fewer black-faced sheep than the proprietor thought.[104] Other sheep farms on Lewis appear to have been smaller and, perhaps for that reason, marginally profitable. For example, Alexander McRae, tenant of the Scaliscro farm in Uig (running 700–800 sheep at £35 rent) complained in 1833 of its small size, ruinous farmhouse and neighbours who destroyed his grass with their cattle.[105] Knox argued that a better tenant should be sought.[106]

The estate continued to seek substantial sheep farmers. Uig was reckoned to be the most promising area. In 1825 Stewart Mackenzie advised one of the trustees that the southern part of Uig was 'the first part of the island you will have to put into large lots of pasture'.[107] However, six years later exactly the same thing was being proposed, this time by Stewart the factor.[108] The problem appears to have been that substantial sheep graziers were unwilling to come to Lewis. In 1826 Stewart Mackenzie complained that 'the difficulty to get tenantry is very great indeed to that distant quarter'.[109] In 1831 the trustees instructed the factor to make the best bargain he could with the Stewarts for Park Farm so that it should not become vacant.[110] In 1833 Knox wished that the Laidlaws (the mainland factor and his sheep-farming brother) would visit Lewis and tell their friends in the south about its prospects. It may be that the nature of the Lewis terrain was unattractive to such men. Another problem was the remoteness of Lewis from the main markets. Knox argued that, if there could be a 300 ton steamboat to Glasgow, he had 'no doubt we shall see men of substance come to look at the lands, who will give their fair value'.[111]

Table 2.1 illustrates what was in effect an alternative policy. In all parishes except Lochs, the number of tenancies below £100 increased substantially between 1823 and 1831 and those between £100 and £199 dropped. The reason was given by Knox in 1833. Sub-tenants of Knock should be given leases of seven or nine years 'as small tenants can pay more than one tenant'.[112] Sub-tenants were often converted into tenants. In 1833 the factor referred to the proprietor an application for Loch Shell which 'includes sub tenants, diametrically opposed to your system', and his successor referred in 1834 to 'the evils of the subletting system'.[113] McGregor explained that 'tacksmen in Barvas cannot change from the old practice of farming and are getting poor ... small tenants ... can pay better as they work their own lots with little expenses'.[114] Another reason for encouraging smaller farmers was to grow barley for the island's distilleries.[115] As early as 1826, Stewart Mackenzie noted that the old tenants were reduced from constantly accumulating arrears.[116] There were improving tacksmen, such as Lewis McIver. In 1831 he was allowed to renew his lease for Gress and Upper Coll with their sub-tenants (presumably his labour force) in order, the trustees argued, to retain 'the capital, industry and example of such men'.[117] However, in 1835 they unwillingly deferred to Stewart Mackenzie's view that McIver's Back farm should be let to the sub- tenants, as he had promised.[118] It should be pointed out that at least until the 1831 rental the 'small tenants' were mainly the holders of what by Lewis standards were medium-sized arable and cattle farms. Uig was exceptional in having ten tenants paying below £20 in 1831. A more substantial exception was Point, which in 1829 was said to have about three hundred tenants, clearly fishermen.[119] In conclusion, Table 2.1 illustrates a significant change in the structure of the estate in favour of small tenants (some of whom had previously been sub-tenants) at the expense of tacksmen. The plan was not fully implemented, for example in the granting of leases. However, there was a clear intention to benefit smaller tenants as well as to increase rental income.

DISENGAGEMENT

In the mid- and late 1820s, when the Stewart Mackenzies spent long periods in Lewis, there were energetic efforts to develop fisheries, distilleries and lotting. By the end of the decade, with poor financial results and pressing debts, his trustees and advisers felt the need to take control. Craig argued for an end to 'problematical schemes of improvement' and to interference with the trustees in management.[120] Cockburn reported that creditors would insist on management being totally in other hands.[121] The new trust deed was executed on 31 March 1829, Cockburn and William Mackenzie being the trustees.[122] Mackenzie was advised, 'you must find employment for Seaforth for his active mind cannot be idle, a seat in the House would be suitable'.[123] In 1831 he did indeed become MP for Ross-shire, after which he secured posts on the Board of Control for India and held his seat until 1837.[124] It would appear that, with the proprietor in London, much estate business was now transacted between the factor and the trustees in Edinburgh. Factors sent frequent reports to him and his view on estate matters could still be decisive, as in the letting of Back to sub-tenants in 1835. However, McGregor's view was that now 'factors and trustees work together and resent interference'.[125]

That Stewart Mackenzie's debts at the end of 1836 were still over £144,000, only £20,000 less than at Lord Seaforth's death, must have been very discouraging.[126] His belief that the improvement of Lewis could restore his fortunes was finally undermined by what Devine has described as 'a classic subsistence crisis reminiscent of pre-industrial times'.[127] There were cold springs and late harvests in 1835 and 1836. In April 1836 Knox lamented 'continued wet, cold and stormy weather ... very unpropitious for getting seed into the ground'. Potatoes had been planted but subsequently rotted.[128] McGregor estimated that about seven hundred cattle had been lost in the north of Lewis in early 1836.[129] By early 1837 there was a desperate shortage of food and seed throughout the North-west Highlands. Robert Graham, a Whig politician and heir to estates in Perthshire, was commissioned to tour the distressed districts and send reports to the Home Office.[130]

Graham's extended letter from Stornoway was, as MacAskill has pointed out, distilled from what he learned of the fundamental issues which had given rise to these conditions.[131] It was also in effect a report on Stewart Mackenzie's stewardship of the island. The state of destitution was very great (though not so high as on Skye), varying from half the population of Stornoway Parish to almost everyone in Lochs and Barvas. This was notwithstanding, thanks to Knox, the most uniform arrangements Graham had seen for distributing charitable supplies (from Glasgow). Destitution to some extent was inevitable on Lewis, he stated, because of excessive population. Lots had been laid out to support four or five people but, due to sub-division, were supporting three times that number. Graham estimated that the population exceeded by a third the island's powers of subsistence. The only people 'better circumstanced' were the fishermen of Knock. Fishing might be extended in Uig and Lochs, but only if tackle and good boats were supplied and expert fishermen brought in as trainers. This illustrated the poor state of economic development in Lewis. In the emergency of 1836–7, the trustees were concerned about the affordability of Stewart Mackenzie's requests for seed bear to be sent by the estate, but Knox subsequently claimed that considerable relief had been given in seed corn and meal to relieve want.[132]

EMIGRATION

After government refused to finance emigration on the scale Stewart Mackenzie proposed, he was by 1822 protesting that he would not encourage an individual of good character to emigrate.[133] Hunter correctly suggests that, having failed to find finance for large-scale emigration, he moved on to other strategies to address the problems of Lewis.¹³⁴ A search of the *British Newspaper Index* has shown no reports of mass emigration from the island before the departure of the Stewart Mackenzies for Ceylon in 1837, but several thereafter under the Seaforth trustees and Sir James Matheson.¹³⁵ Nor has any reference to such a scheme been found in the estate correspondence. It seems clear that no significant amount of estate-sponsored emigration took place in this period. It simply could not be afforded. Richards argued that Lewis 'became a watchword for poverty', and it is thus not surprising that there was a demand for the means to emigrate. In 1837 Graham was present at a demonstration of around a thousand people 'of the poorest denomination' at Seaforth Lodge expressing their wish to emigrate if they had the means. A deputation from Uig stated that a hundred families would go if means were provided.¹³⁶ Large-scale emigration could not be afforded by proprietor or people.

CONCLUSION

By the time Graham arrived in Stornoway, the Stewart Mackenzies knew that their future, at least for a few years, lay far from Lewis. On 10 July 1837, he was commissioned as Governor of Ceylon and, after the long voyage from Britain, they arrived there on 6 November.¹³⁷ He sent his final instructions to Knox from Edinburgh on 6 June and was never to return to the island or to its management.¹³⁸ It can be no coincidence that he chose to become a colonial governor during the third successive year of harvest failure and destitution, and with his debts still as high as ever. After all his efforts, admittedly less intensive since he became an MP, he appears to have finally given up hope that he personally could reform the economy and society of Lewis or thereby solve his debt problem. On their marriage in 1817, Brown advised that the Stewart Mackenzies' Wester Ross estates should be sold, they should draw income from Lewis and live at Glasserton, his Wigtownshire estate, thus abandoning Brahan near Dingwall, the Seaforth seat for two hundred years. Mary later argued that 'had we done this boldly we had been rich and at ease ... as it is the best years of life are spent in fruitless struggle against an overwhelming tide of disappointments and vexation'. They had not followed Brown's advice because 'you must feel what a clamour and outcry would have been against us'.¹³⁹ Mixed motives had, as with her father Lord Seaforth, resulted in confused decision making.¹⁴⁰ Devine has argued (accurately for the Stewart Mackenzies) that many Highland landlords in these years 'refused to exploit their economic opportunities to the full and settled instead for a muddled response of partial clearance, inaction, indirect and direct subsidy to the people who lived on their estates, and desultory attempts to sponsor assisted emigration'.[141] In Lewis these were accentuated by poor entrepreneurial skills and project management and by shortage of development capital.

NOTES

1. F. McKichan, *Lord Seaforth: Highland Landowner, Caribbean Governor* (Edinburgh, 2018), pp. 20–2.
2. D. Macdonald, *Lewis: A History of the Island* (Edinburgh, 1978), p. 112; Edinburgh, National Records of Scotland [hereafter NRS], GD46/17/78, A. Macleod to J. A. S. Mackenzie, 11 May 1829.
3. NRS, GD46/17/44, J. A. S. Mackenzie to J. Gladstone, 11 June 1823.
4. J. Hunter, *The Making of the Crofting Community* (Edinburgh, 2018 edn), pp. 85–6.
5. E. Richards, *The Highland Clearances: People, Landlords and Rural Turmoil* (Edinburgh, 2013 edn), pp. 243–4.
6. Macdonald, *Lewis*, p. 37.
7. J. Mitchell, *Reminiscences of My Life in the Highlands* (Newton Abbot, 1971 reprint), I, pp. 240–1.
8. M. Gray, *The Highland Economy 1750–1850* (Edinburgh, 1957), pp. 155, 181–3.
9. NRS, GD46/17/44, J. A. S. Mackenzie to P. Cockburn, 9 June 1823.
10. McKichan, *Lord Seaforth*, pp. 242–5, 270.
11. NRS, GD46/17/45, Account of sales of kelp shipped from Lewis 1816; GD46/17/52, Sales of Lewis kelp 1819; GD46/17/55, Account sales of Lewis kelp, 16 and 19 September 1820.
12. J. MacAskill, 'The Highland kelp proprietors and their struggle over the salt and barilla duties, 1817–1831', *Journal of Scottish Historical Studies* [hereafter *JSHS*], Vol. 26, 2006, pp. 60–7.
13. NRS, GD46/1/128, Memorial and abstract in the sale of Lewis, 1824.
14. NRS, GD46/17/41, J. A. S. Mackenzie to A. Mosman, 2 October 1827; GD46/1/334/1 and 21, State of returns from Seaforth Trust estates 1828, 1829, 1830.
15. Macdonald, *Lewis*, p. 129; *Encyclopedia Britannica*, 8th edn, 1857, quoted www.facebook.com/UigHistoricalSociety [accessed 29 September 2019].
16. T. M. Devine, *Clearance and Improvement: Land, Power and People in Scotland, 1700–1900* (Edinburgh, 2006), p. 18.
17. NRS, GD46/17/53, J. A. S. Mackenzie to H. Goulburn, 27 July 1819.
18. Hunter, *Making of Crofting Community*, p. 83.
19. There is a huge literature on the Highland Clearances, most recently

T. M. Devine, *The Scottish Clearances: A History of the Dispossessed* (London, 2018).
20. NRS, GD46/17/53, H. Goulburn to J. A. S. Mackenzie, 16 August 1819.
21. NRS, GD46/17/55, Observations after examining the North part of Lewis, October 1820.
22. McKichan, *Lord Seaforth*, pp. 271-2; NRS, GD46/1/26, Abstract of deed of entail on lands and estate of Seaforth.
23. See, for example, NRS, GD46/1/293 (Kearnhove tenants, 11 February 1823), /294 (Ardentroime tenants, 12 February 1823).
24. NRS, GD46/17/63, R. Brown to P. Cockburn, 19 February 1823; NRS, GD46/17/44, J. A. S. Mackenzie to P. Cockburn, 9 June 1823.
25. NRS, GD46/17/44, J. A. S. Mackenzie to C. Grant, 4 July 1823.
26. 57 Geo III, cap.23, pp. 408-10.
27. NRS, GD46/17/44, J. A. S. Mackenzie to P. Cockburn, 9 June 1823.
28. McKichan, *Lord Seaforth*, pp. 25-6; NRS, GD46/1/128/2, Lewis Rental 1823.
29. NRS, GD46/1/128, Memorial and abstract of sale of Lewis.
30. NRS, GD46/17/67, Proposal for a loan over part of Island of Lewis, 4 March 1825.
31. NRS, GD46/17/77, P. Cockburn to J. A. S. Mackenzie, 12 January 1829.
32. NRS, GD46/17/67, P. Cockburn to A. Mitchell, 19 March 1825.
33. NRS, GD46/17/67, A. Mundell to J. A. S. Mackenzie, 25 March 1825; GD46/17/68, bond of relief J. A. S. Mackenzie to P. Cockburn, 23 June 1825; GD46/1/334/1, State of net returns from estates of Seaforth, 1828-30.
34. NRS, GD46/17/41, J. A. S. Mackenzie to A. Young, 26 September 1827.
35. NRS, GD46/17/77/14, Memo by J. A. S. Mackenzie re: debts, 7 January 1829.
36. NRS, GD46/17/77/39 and 40, P. Cockburn to J. A. S. Mackenzie, 12 and 13 January 1829.
37. J. R. Coull, *The Sea Fisheries of Scotland: A Historical Biography* (Edinburgh, 2003 edn), p. 86; Gray, *The Highland Economy*, pp. 114-15, 123.
38. J. R. Coull, A. Fenton and K .Veitch (eds), *Scottish Life and Society: Boats, Fishing and the Sea* (Edinburgh, 2008), p. 262.
39. NRS, GD46/13/148/1, J. Mackenzie to J. A. S. Mackenzie, 11 October 1828.
40. NRS, GD46/17/71, J. Adam to J. A. S. Mackenzie, 15 May 1826; 46/17/41, J. A. S. Mackenzie to J. Outram, 28 February 1827.
41. NRS, GD46/17/72, J. A. S. Mackenzie, circular, 23 March 1827.
42. NRS, GD46/17/76/196, A. Stewart to Mrs Stewart Mackenzie, 2 April 1828.
43. NRS, GD46/17/79, T. Knox to J. A. S. Mackenzie, 14 April 1829.

44. London, The National Archives [TNA], T1/4201, R. Graham to F. Maule, 14 April 1837.
45. Coull et al., *Boats, Fishing and the Sea*, p. 262; Coull, *Sea Fisheries of Scotland*, p. 106.
46. NRS, GD46/13/148/2, Petition of Lewis fishermen occupied in catching and drying cod and ling fish, n.d. but clearly 1829, received by Charles Grant MP, 29 May 1829 [NRS, GD46/17/78].
47. NRS, GD271/48/57, J. A. S. Mackenzie to W. Mackenzie, 24 April 1829. I am indebted to Malcolm Bangor-Jones for drawing my attention to this series.
48. NRS, GD46/1/537, W. McGregor to Mrs Stewart Mackenzie, 27 March 1833.
49. NRS, GD46/1/539, J. Knox to Mrs Stewart Mackenzie, 26 February 1834.
50. NRS, GD46/1/530/31, A. Stewart to J. A. S. Mackenzie, 11 February 1835.
51. NRS, GD46/13/63, J. A. S. Mackenzie to J. Dunsmure, Fisheries Board, 13 October 1833; NRS, GD46/13/94/4, J. Dunsmure to J. A. S. Mackenzie, 30 January 1835.
52. NRS, GD46/13/94/1, J. Dunsmure to J. A. S. Mackenzie, 18 February 1835; GD46/1/198, T. Mansfield to J. A. S. Mackenzie, 10 March 1835; GD46/1/198, T. Mansfield to J. A. S. Mackenzie, 27 May 1835.
53. NRS, AF7/12, Board of Fisheries – Harbours General Account; NRS, GD46/1/539, T. Knox to J. A. S. Mackenzie, 5 September 1835.
54. Hunter, *Making of Crofting Community*, p. 86.
55. T. M. Devine, *The Great Highland Famine: Hunger, Emigration and the Scottish Highlands in the Nineteenth Century* (Edinburgh, 1988), p. 70.
56. TNA, T1/4201, R. Graham to F. Maule, 14 April 1837.
57. NRS, GD46/1/89, J. A. S. Mackenzie to T. Knox, 6 June 1837.
58. NRS, AF5/1/86-9, Fisheries Board of Scotland Inspector's Report, 11 September 1843.
59. I. R. Mowat, *Easter Ross 1750–1850: The Double Frontier* (Edinburgh, 1981), pp. 61–2.
60. T. M. Devine, 'The rise and fall of illicit whisky-making in Northern Scotland, c. 1780–1840', *Scottish Historical Review*, 54 (1975), pp. 173–4.
61. NRS, GD46/17/44, J. A. S. Mackenzie to C. Grant, 4 July 1823; NRS, GD46/17/69, J. A. S. Mackenzie to P. Cockburn, 19 August and to J. C. Herries, 14 November 1825.
62. J. Loch, *An Account of the Improvements on the Estates of the Marquess of Stafford* (London, 1820).
63. K. German and G. Adamson, 'Distilling in the Cabrach, c. 1800–1850: The illicit origins of the Scotch whisky industry', *JSHS*, 39:2 (2019), p. 151.

64. Referred to in NRS, GD46/17/69, J. A. S. Mackenzie to P. Cockburn, 20 September 1825.
65. NRS, GD46/13/118, J. A. S. Mackenzie to H. Armstrong, 12 November 1825.
66. NRS, GD46/17/41, J. A. S. Mackenzie to R. Brown, 2 April 1827; GD46/13/120/4, Estimate of expenditure, November 1826.
67. German and Adamson, 'Distilling in the Cabrach', p. 156.
68. Macdonald, *Lewis*, p. 37.
69. NRS, GD46/13/120/2, Estimate of joinery and millright work for completing the distillery, November 1826; /3, J. A. S. Mackenzie, Memo for Mr Bulloch, 6 November 1826.
70. NRS, GD46/17/69, J. A. S. Mackenzie to J. Bulloch, 19 December 1826.
71. NRS, GD46/13/119/4, H. Armstrong to J. A. S. Mackenzie, 24 March 1827; /3, H. Armstrong to J. Adam, 5 July 1827.
72. NRS, GD46/13/119/2, H. Armstrong to J. A. S. Mackenzie, 16 January 1828.
73. NRS, GD46/1/155, A. Craig memo re: affairs of JASM, 11 December 1828.
74. NRS, GD46/17/79, P. Cockburn to Lord Mackenzie, 21 January 1829.
75. NRS, GD46/17/79, Notes on commencement of work, Stornoway Distillery, n.d. but apparently early 1829.
76. German and Adamson, 'Distilling in the Cabrach', pp. 156–7, 162–3.
77. NRS, GD46/1/530, A. Stewart to Mrs Stewart Mackenzie, 4 November 1831.
78. NRS, GD46/13/123, Memo by J. A. S. Mackenzie on the terms of offer by Mr Morrison for lease of Stornoway Distillery, 3 March 1832.
79. NRS, GD46/13/124/2–3, W. and R. Morrison to T. Mansfield, 13 August 1834.
80. German and Adamson, 'Distilling in the Cabrach', p. 156.
81. McKichan, *Lord Seaforth*, p. 43.
82. Hunter, *Making of Crofting Community*, p. 68.
83. Gray, *The Highland Economy*, pp. 78–9.
84. NRS, GD46/17/55, Observations after examining North part of Lewis, October 1820.
85. E. R. Cregeen (ed. A. Tindley), 'The creation of crofting townships in Tiree', *JSHS*, 35:2 (2015), pp. 183–6; Cregeen, *Argyll Estate Instructions 1771–1805* (Edinburgh, 1964), pp. 73, 78.
86. J. Randall, *The Historic Shielings of Pairc* (Laxay, Isle of Lewis, 2017), p. 8.
87. NRS, GD46/17/64, J. Adam to J. A. S. Mackenzie, 18 October 1823.
88. NRS, GD46/17/44, J. A. S. Mackenzie to J. Adam, 18 April 1823.
89. NRS, GD46/1/545, W. McGregor to Mrs Stewart Mackenzie, 10 June 1837.

90. NRS, GD46/1/538, Memo by Seaforth for Mr Mansfield, 18 September 1833.
91. For example, in Sutherland: Richards, *The Highland Clearances* (2013 edn), pp. 179, 181; T. M. Devine, *The Scottish Clearances: A History of the Dispossessed* (London, 2018), p. 227.
92. NRS, GD46/17/74, J. Adam to J. A. S. Mackenzie, 21 March 1827.
93. NRS, GD46/17/76, A. Craig to J. A. S. Mackenzie, 29 February 1828.
94. NRS, GD46/17/41, J. A. S. Mackenzie to J. Adam, 28 March 1827.
95. NRS, GD46/1/128/2, Lewis Rental 1823.
96. TNA, T1/4201, R. Graham to F. Maule, 14 April 1837.
97. Macdonald, *Lewis*, p. 160.
98. Devine, *The Scottish Clearances*, p. 235.
99. NRS, GD46/1/128/2, Rental of Lewis 1823, GD46/1/339, rental of Lewis 1831.
100. NRS, GD46/20/4/1/16, Rental of Lewis 1803; McKichan, *Lord Seaforth*, pp. 36–7.
101. NRS, GD46/1/539, T. Knox to J. A. S. Mackenzie, 20 November 1833.
102. NRS, GD46/17/68/518, Precognition of Archibald McCallum, 13 December 1826.
103. NRS, GD46/1/128/2, Lewis rental 1823, GD46/17/69, J. A. S. Mackenzie to A. Stewart, tenant in Valimos, 8 October 1825; NRS, GD46/13/118, J. A. S. Mackenzie to H. Armstrong, 12 November 1825; J. B. Caird et al., *Park – A Geographical Study of a Lewis Crofting District* (Glasgow, 1958), p. 9; www.uhi.ac.uk/en/t4-media/one-web/university/research/centre-for-history/napier/napier-commission-vol-2.pdf, pp. 1139–40, Q. 17386–8, testimony 1883 of George Mackenzie, cleared to Laxay c. 1828 [accessed 18 September 2019].
104. NRS, GD46/1/316, A. Stewart to J. A. S. Mackenzie, 11 December 1833.
105. NRS, GD46/1/315, A. McRae to J. A. S. Mackenzie, 9 December 1833.
106. NRS, GD46/1/539, T. Knox to J. A. S. Mackenzie, 18 December 1833.
107. NRS, GD46/17/68, J. A. S. Mackenzie to P. Cockburn, 20 September 1825.
108. NRS, GD46/1/530, A. Stewart to J. A. S. Mackenzie, n.d. but apparently June 1831.
109. NRS, GD46/17/69, J. A. S. Mackenzie to P. Cockburn, 26 October 1826.
110. NRS, GD46/1/157, Excerpts from Stewart Mackenzie Trustees Minutes re: letting of farms, 26 April 1831.
111. NRS, GD46/1/539, T. Knox to J. A. S. Mackenzie, 18 December 1833.
112. NRS, GD46/1/539, T. Knox to J. A. S. Mackenzie, 24 December 1833.
113. NRS, GD46/1/530/4, A. Stewart to J. A. S. Mackenzie, 25 April 1833; and GD46/1/539, J. Knox to J. A. S. Mackenzie, 1 February 1834.
114. NRS, GD46/1/537, W. McGregor to Mrs Stewart Mackenzie, 27 March 1833.
115. NRS, GD46/1/530, A. Stewart to J. A. S. Mackenzie, 9 May 1833.

116. NRS, GD46/17/69, J. A. S. Mackenzie to P. Cockburn, 26 October 1826.
117. NRS, GD46/1/15, Minutes of Seaforth Trustees, 8, 12 and 13 March 1831.
118. NRS, GD46/1/197, W. Mackenzie to J. A. S Mackenzie, 1 April 1835.
119. NRS GD46/17/79, T. Knox to J. A. S. Mackenzie, 13 April 1829.
120. NRS, GD46/1/155, A. Craig memo, 16 October 1828.
121. NRS, GD46/17/77/39, P. Cockburn to J. A. S. Mackenzie, 13 January 1829.
122. NRS, GD461/157, Minutes of Seaforth Trustees, 2 June 1829.
123. NRS, GD271/48/69, J. Gillanders to W. Mackenzie, 29 April 1829.
124. T. F. Henderson, revised by K. D. Reynolds, 'Mackenzie, Mary Elizabeth Frederica Stewart Mackenzie, Lady Hood (1783–1862)', *Oxford Dictionary of National Biography* (Oxford, 2004), www.oxforddnb.com, article no. 26521 [accessed 4 September 2019].
125. NRS, GD46/1/537, W. McGregor to Mrs Stewart Mackenzie, 30 July 1833.
126. NRS, GD46/1/89, State of debts under Seaforth Trust deed, 31 December 1836.
127. Devine, *Great Highland Famine*, p. 27.
128. NRS, GD46/1/323/4 and 6, T. Knox to J. A. S. Mackenzie, 20 and 21 April 1836.
129. NRS, GD46/323/7, T. Knox to J. A. S. Mackenzie, 4 May 1836.
130. J. MacAskill (ed.), *The Highland Destitution of 1837: Government Aid and Public Subscription* (Edinburgh, 2012), pp. xiv–xv, xxiv.
131. TNA, T1/4201, R. Graham to F. Maule, 14 April 1837; J. MacAskill, 'The Highland destitution of 1837', paper given at the Scottish History Society AGM, 2 March 2013, pp. 12–13. I am indebted to Neil Bruce for drawing this to my attention.
132. NRS, GD46/1/198, T. Mansfield to J. A. S. Mackenzie, 13 and 14 May 1836; *First Report from Select Committee on Emigration, Scotland*, Parliamentary Papers 1841, VI, p. 176, Q.2237.
133. NRS, GD46/17/59, J. A. S. Mackenzie to N. Varsittart, 21 September 1822.
134. Hunter, *Making of Crofting Community*, pp. 85–6.
135. British Newspaper Archive, www.britishnewspaperarchive.co.uk [accessed 10 December 2019]; J. I. Little, *Crofters and Habitants: Settler Society, Economy and Culture in a Quebec Township, 1848–1881* (Montreal, 1991), p. 16.
136. Richards, *The Highland Clearances*, p. 243; TNA, T1/4201, R. Graham to F. Maule, 14 April 1837.
137. TNA, C055/79, f.1, Commission and Instructions 10 July 1837, CO54/156, f. 470, J. A. S. Mackenzie to Lord Glenelg, 11 November 1837.
138. NRS, GD46/1/89, J. A. S. Mackenzie to T. Knox, 6 June 1837.

139. NRS, GD46/17/80/137, to Lord Mackenzie, apparently from Mrs Stewart Mackenzie, n.d.
140. McKichan, *Lord Seaforth*, pp. 38–9.
141. Devine, *The Scottish Clearances*, pp. 248–9.

3

Public Interest or Profit? The Management of the Crown-owned Foreshore, 1866–2019

John MacAskill

INTRODUCTION

THIS CHAPTER IS FIRMLY rooted in, and examines, issues at the heart of this book: issues of land ownership, land management and use, governance and policy, albeit the issues focused on here are a particular part of the land – the foreshore[1] – and on a particular aspect of policy – the management of the foreshore as part of the assets of the Crown, or 'Crown assets'. The examples recounted demonstrate the part that an understanding of history can play in informing the decisions of policymakers and the consequences of a lack of such understanding. As Lord Bingham said in a comment on the anti-historicist approach of the eminent constitutional lawyer A. V. Dicey, paraphrasing words in Walter Scott's *Guy Mannering*: 'A lawyer without history . . . is a mechanic, and probably not a very good mechanic at that.'[2] A sentiment that might usefully apply to legislators and policymakers as well as to lawyers.

But what are these 'Crown assets'? The distinction between property owned by the sovereign in a personal capacity and owned by the sovereign in a representative or public capacity as head of state is well recognised, and the assets with which we are concerned in this chapter are the latter. Collectively they are known as the 'Crown estate'. Their origins date back to 1760, when George III surrendered the revenues from Crown lands to parliament in return for support by the civil list.[3] Ownership of all these assets has always been in the Crown, and the Office of Woods and Forests was responsible for the management of all the Crown estate in England, Wales and Ireland from 1829 and in Scotland from 1833.[4] That was until 1866, when responsibility for the foreshore, seabed and the bed of public rivers became during the years 1866 to 1947 successively that of the Board of Trade, the Minister of Shipping and then the Minister of Transport, while all the rest of the Crown estate remained the responsibility of the Office of Woods.⁵ Today, The Crown Estate, or Crown Estate Commissioners, in London is responsible for managing all the Crown assets in England, Wales and Northern Ireland, and in Scotland the Scottish Crown Estate in Edinburgh has since 2017 been responsible.⁶ As we shall note later, the bifurcation of ownership and management that was left in the wake of the 1998 devolution settlement in Scotland, when property belonging to the sovereign in right of the Crown was devolved to the Scottish Parliament but management of the property was reserved to the Westminster Parliament, left an anomalous situation that was only corrected with the devolution of management responsibility to the Scottish Parliament in 2017. The anomaly remains for Wales and Northern Ireland. The assets that are managed by the Scottish Crown Estate consist of a diverse portfolio of property rights and interests, including management rights to the seabed, the bed of public rivers, leasing for offshore wind farms, the rights to wild salmon fishing and naturally occurring gold and silver, and rights over urban and rural property and just under half the foreshore around Scotland.⁷ The Crown Estate has responsibility for a similar portfolio of assets and it is no surprise that among the most significant are the seabed and around half the foreshore around England, Wales and Northern Ireland.⁸

Before turning to our consideration of the history of the management of the Crown-owned foreshore since 1866, it is important to set the foreshore in its proper context. It is, self-evidently, a piece of land quite unlike the other Crown assets (apart from the seabed) and it has a distinct public interest dimension recognised by certain common law public rights that exist over the foreshore, whether as a Crown asset or in private ownership. In Scotland, there are public rights of navigation, fishing and recreation.⁹ In England and Wales the common law rights of the public are rather more restricted – there are rights of navigation and fishing but no common law right of general recreation on the foreshore.¹⁰ But in neither Scotland nor England and Wales is the extent of the public interest dimension in the foreshore as advanced as it is in the United States with its 'public trust doctrine', a doctrine that, paradoxically, has its roots in the English common law. At its most basic, the public trust doctrine asserts that possession of the foreshore must be used in the public interest; that it should be held, protected and regulated for the common use and benefit.¹¹

THE PERIOD 1866 TO 1958

We now turn to consider the history of the management of the Crown-owned foreshore since 1866. The theme that will flow through what follows is that there has been a conflict between public interest and profit; the provisions of the law, on the one hand, that the pecuniary interest in the foreshore should be taken as its most important interest, and the requirements, on the other hand, of the broader public interest given the singular characteristics of the foreshore with its public interest dimension mentioned above.

Responsibility for the management of the bulk of the Crown-owned foreshore, seabed and the bed of public rivers was transferred in 1866 from the Office of Woods to the Board of Trade. Management of the foreshore dealt with by lease by the Office of Woods before the end of 1866, the foreshore in front of government property above the high-water mark, and mines and minerals under the foreshore were all excluded from the transfer and remained with the Office of Woods. The principal reason given for the transfer was a desire to unite responsibility for management with the protection of navigation – the Board had, in 1862, taken this responsibility from the Admiralty. But there was another very important and more far-reaching reason that marked a distinct change of policy, as explained by Thomas Farrer the permanent secretary to the Board: the Board was to be 'empowered to deal with the foreshore with a view to the public interests generally', as compared with what the sole duty of the Office of Woods had been – 'to treat the foreshore as property'.[12] The Office of Woods explained in a report to the Treasury that it had been their duty under the Land Revenue Acts 'to exercise the rights of the Crown so as to realise the greatest amount of revenue that can legitimately be obtained'.[13] Sections 28 and 34 of the 1829 Act provided the legal basis for this duty, sections that Farrer was to explain in 1866 had:

> been purposely framed so as to prevent [the Office of Woods] parting with land at less than its value ... and it is obvious that according to the spirit of [the legislation] the rent or consideration ought to represent the full value.[14]

Furthermore, it had been the Treasury's opinion that there was no 'general principle that can be applied to the management of Crown property below the line of high water mark, different from that which applies to property above this line'.[15] Farrer recognised that as a result of this change of policy it was not improbable that the revenue to be derived from dealings would be less than hitherto.[16] The Crown Lands

Bill that was to effect the transfer was drafted very carefully so as to include powers for the Board of Trade that allowed it to deal with the foreshore in the broad public interest and so that the Board should not be obliged as the 1829 Act required to realise the greatest amount of revenue. The Bill gave the Board the power to sell or lease the foreshore and an unrestricted power to grant licences, all on such terms as it thought fit.[17] Unfortunately, the clauses that gave these powers were removed when the Bill was debated in the House of Lords and a simple clause inserted that gave to the Board only the powers and authorities that the Office of Woods had had – in effect replicating the duty imposed by the 1829 Act, thus leaving the Board with powers over the foreshore under the Crown Lands Act 1866 that conflicted with the new policy: powers that required dealings with the Crown-owned foreshore to realise the greatest amount of revenue.[18]

After the 1866 Act was passed, Farrer wrote a memorandum explaining how the Board would manage its new responsibilities.[19] The memorandum is an important and significant document in the history of the management of the Crown-owned foreshore and was still being cited as providing 'excellent guidance' nearly a hundred years after it was written.[20] Farrer wrote that 'A great deal of the prejudice which exists upon this subject has arisen from the fact that the Office of Woods has been bound to get the best possible price; and it is not unnaturally alleged that they have been ready to sacrifice important public rights if they could only get high prices.' He went on to say that it was a 'fatally erroneous assumption that the pecuniary interest of the public in the foreshore [was] its most important interest'.[21] Farrer was at pains to point out in the memorandum that the Board would struggle to fulfil the broad public interest responsibilities that it had been intended the Board should have, because the 1866 Act had not given the Board the discretionary powers the Board needed to enable it properly to manage the foreshore having regard to the public interest generally. In a key passage of his memorandum, Farrer described the public interest dimension of the foreshore with words that might be seen as articulating something close to the idea of a public trust doctrine for the foreshore:

> In a country crowded as England [sic] is, where the preservation of every open space is of the highest importance for the public health and enjoyment; in a maritime country, where facilities for navigation, for fishing, boating, beaching, landing, and shipping are essential to our trade and to the well-being of our maritime population – it is of the greatest moment that the control of the public and of the Government over the bed of the sea and over the strip of common which lies between land and open sea should

be preserved, so that it may be used for the furtherance of the important interests above referred to, and so that nothing may be done with it which is inconsistent with those interests. To sell [it] to private persons because a high price is offered, without reference to these interests would be ... absurd, [and] we must be prepared to forego in many cases the prices which, if we were private landowners, we might insist on demanding.[22]

Farrer said that sooner or later there would have to be legislative change to enable the Board properly to fulfil its public interest responsibilities.[23]

A Royal Commission was appointed in 1906 to inquire into and report on questions affecting coast erosion. One of its terms of reference was to consider 'whether any alteration in the law is desirable as regards the management and control of the foreshore'.[24] It reported in 1911 that the split of the responsibility for management of the foreshore between the Office of Woods and the Board of Trade was 'unscientific, unnecessary, and a source of inconvenience to the public, particularly in view of the fact that the two Departments pursue different policies in their dealings with the foreshore' – 'in the public interest and not with the object of realising a revenue from it' by the Board of Trade, while 'the Office of Woods consider they are bound by the [1829 Act] which contains stringent provisions preventing them from parting with any property for less than full value'. The Royal Commission recommended that:

> provision should be made for the administration of the foreshore by one Department in the public interest, and that for this purpose a transfer of such foreshore as remains under the control of the [Office of Woods] should be made to the Board of Trade which has now under its management in the public interest, the greater part of the foreshores of the United Kingdom which are Crown property.[25]

Strangely, however, the Royal Commission made no recommendations that the defective management powers that Farrer had written of in 1866 should be amended.

In 1927 the Office of Woods (renamed in 1924 as the Commissioners of Crown Lands[26]) became a body corporate under the name of the Commissioners of Crown Lands, and the powers of sale and leasing in the 1829 Act (the spirit of which, if not the letter, Farrer had explained in 1866 required rent or consideration to represent full value) were replaced by provisions in the Crown Lands Act 1927[27] that expressly provided sales could only be made for the best consideration in money, and leases for the best rent, that could reasonably be obtained, provisions which applied to all the Crown estate assets; again, there was no proposal to amend the defective powers so far as the management of the foreshore by the Board of Trade was concerned, which was, of course, subject to the provisions of the 1927 Act.[28] The recommendation by the Royal Commission in 1911 that the management of all the foreshore should be united in the Board in the public interest was to have been given effect by the Coast Protection Bill of 1929, and the Bill also included a provision that would have remedied with retrospective effect the defective management powers, giving the Board the discretionary powers that Farrer had wanted; but the Bill failed to pass the House of Commons.[29]

The Board's responsibility for management of Crown foreshore, seabed and the bed of public rivers passed in 1939 to the Minister of Shipping at the outbreak of war,[30] and in 1941 to the Minister of War Transport,[31] who became the Minister of Transport in 1946, and in that year consideration was given to yet another transfer of responsibility to the Commissioners of Crown Lands (who of course had responsibility for the management of the parts of the foreshore excluded from the 1866 transfer, and all the other assets of the Crown estate).[32] On 1 April 1947 the Commissioners assumed responsibility on an agency basis,[33] and legislative effect was given to the transfer in the Coast Protection Act 1949.[34] The reunification of the management of Crown foreshore that had been recommended by the Royal Commission in 1911 was thus, finally, achieved but not crucially as had been recommended as a reunification in the Board of Trade, but back to where it had been before 1866. Furthermore, the discretionary management powers that had been in the Coast Protection Bill of 1929 were not included in the 1949 Act.[35] When the decision was taken to reunite the management of all the foreshore in the Commissioners of Crown Lands it seems that issues of policy were not uppermost in the minds of those who took the decision. Papers by the joint secretaries of the Machinery of Government Committee at the Cabinet Office and the permanent secretary to the Ministry of Transport make it plain that the decision was taken to 'simplify administration'; the foreshore did not 'fit conveniently into the [Ministry of Transport's] organisation'. It was said that 'the historical reasons' behind the transfer in 1866 'had lost their force during the present century'. But the historical reasons were not explained; the Cabinet paper said only that the foreshore 'had been removed from the [Office of Woods] in 1866 in the interest of navigation'.[36] But no mention was made of the significance of the public interest that had been Farrer's guiding principle and that had been re-emphasised by the Royal Commission in 1911. It is difficult to escape the conclusion that the decision taken was not informed by a proper understanding of the public interest dimension of the foreshore and why it was that the original decision had been taken in 1866 to transfer management of the foreshore to the Board of Trade. The consequences of this would become apparent, as we shall see, in 1958.

The Commissioners of Crown Lands were the subject of an inquiry in 1955 into their activities, from which major reforms resulted.[37] The resulting Crown Estate Act 1956 established a new board of Commissioners under the name of the Crown Estate Commissioners and the remaining part of the reform, including the powers of management, was brought about in the Crown Estate Act 1961, which we will return to.[38] Despite Farrer's gloomy view of the legislative regime under which the Board of Trade had to operate, it does appear that up to 1958 the Board and its successors, including surprisingly the Crown Estate Commissioners, had all managed to work within the legislative framework 'and had [yet] satisfied the requirements of the public interest' because, it was observed, 'no rigorous policy of getting the best return' had, despite the apparently clear terms of the legislation, been followed by the Board or indeed the Commissioners.[39] The Royal Commission had reported, in 1911, that the Board had been content to demand only small sums as consideration money or as rent under a lease and that sometimes they issued a licence on payment of a nominal acknowledgement;[40] and a Board official commented in 1958 that: 'It is clear that the [Board] used "licences" as a means of escaping from the "best rent duty" attaching to a lease or the "best price duty" attaching to a sale.'[41] But as Farrer had noted in 1866, the Board had no express power to grant licences.[42]

THE MILFORD HAVEN DISPUTE – 1958 TO 1960

This relative calm was, however, disturbed in 1958 as the consequences of the reunification of the management of all the foreshore in the Commissioners of Crown Lands in 1949 became apparent. The flashpoint concerned the foreshore at Milford Haven, Wales where BP asked for some 4 acres of foreshore and seabed on which to build their jetties, and rights of dredging and other works over some further 20 acres. During the consideration of BP's request it became clear, as a memorandum produced by the Ministry of Transport stated, that 'the Commissioners, in contrast to their predecessors, [were] pursuing a rigorous policy of getting the best revenue from the Crown foreshores and seabed and [were] using Milford Haven as the first major exercise of their policy'.[43] The memorandum went on that 'there is the inherent conflict between the broad public interest and a rigorous policy of getting the best revenue', and that while it was well understood that a

> strict interpretation of the statutes under which they [worked] would preclude the Crown Estate Commissioners from any policy which does not bring them in the best rent they can get ... it must be borne in mind ... that predecessors of the present Commissioners as managers of the foreshore and seabed, including the Board of Trade, had worked within a similar statutory authority or legal framework and have yet satisfied the requirements of the public interest.[44]

The dispute between BP and the Commissioners was considered at high levels within the civil service and the notes and memoranda produced are a rich archive of material that confirms and lays bare the inherent conflict that Farrer had written of in 1866 but had remained beneath the surface throughout the Board's benign interpretation of its statutory duties under the Crown Lands legislation. The documents reveal that the effect of the reunification in 1949 of management of all the foreshore in the Commissioners (the old Office of Woods) had been to aggravate the conflict because the importance of the public interest that had been the policy of the Board of Trade and its departmental successors had been lost in favour of the policy of the Commissioners of raising the greatest revenue.

The principal issue identified was that the Crown had a virtual monopoly of the foreshore and the seabed and an absolute monopoly at Milford Haven. It was considered that

> the public interest is touched in any circumstances of substantial monopoly exploitation, and the actions of the Crown Estate Commissioners administering as they do the monopoly of that amphibious strip of foreshore and seabed that stands between the land and the deep sea across which all our seaborne trade must pass, are no exception. It is on this count therefore that the policies of the Crown Estate Commissioners at Milford Haven must be examined.[45]

The view of the Ministry of Transport, which had previously had responsibility for the foreshore, was that 'the market value in the circumstances of the foreshore and seabed [represented] exploitation of a necessity in which there is a virtual monopoly [and that it was] a well-established principle that necessity should not be exploited for profit'.[46] At a Cabinet Office meeting in November 1958 chaired by Sir Norman Brook, there was general agreement that 'the present policy of the Commissioners ... was not, in relation to the foreshore, compatible with the public interest'; and at a later meeting in October 1960 the distinct public interest dimension of the foreshore was recognised as being critical:

> it remained fundamentally illogical to equate the foreshore and seabed with, e.g. Windsor Park or Carlton House Terrace. The latter were properly parts of a landed estate, which should be administered by reference to the ordinary criteria of sound and profitable estate management. The foreshore and seabed, however, fell in a wholly different category and should be administered primarily by reference to the public interest.[47]

A Board of Trade note expressed a similar sentiment and also stressed the point about the monopoly:

> getting the best rent or price for ordinary Crown lands (which are very much like any other property and in respect of which the Crown Estate is by no means in a monopoly position) is a very different matter from exploiting the foreshores and seabed which are not in the nature of private property and in which the Crown Estate has a virtual monopoly.[48]

There were discussions between the various officials as to what should and could be done. The Commissioners argued that any suggestion that they might, after the passing of the Coast Protection Act 1949 confirming the transfer of responsibility to them, have been permitted to manage the foreshore according to principles that were different from the relevant provisions of the Crown Lands Acts, was fundamentally wrong.[49] But the Board's riposte to this was that

> it may well have been an oversight that the ... foreshore [was] returned to the Crown Estate Commissioners in 1949 without any special provision being made to ensure that the Commissioners would continue the policy of the Board of Trade and later the Ministry of Transport of administering the foreshore ... in the general public interest rather than primarily as a source of revenue.

Indeed, the Board went further and suggested that had it been suspected, at the time of the Coast Protection Act 1949, 'that the policy of the last century would be reversed ... the provisions of Part III of the Coast Protection Act 1949 might have been very different'.[50]

What, however, was to be done to deal with these unruly Commissioners who, it was said, 'do not seem willing or able to pursue a policy in the broad public interest'?[51] The recommendation was that the management of the foreshore and seabed should be transferred to a government department 'with an appropriate amendment to the [1927 Act] to remove any duty to get the highest price or rent ... so as to enable the policy which had been successfully followed for the past century in respect of the disposal of foreshores ... to be continued'. In other words, what the Crown Lands Bill of 1866 had originally provided. And in November 1958 it was decided that responsibility for management should be transferred back to the Minister of Transport.[52]

There then followed, over the next twelve months or so, discussions over the practicalities of the proposed transfer to the Minister of Transport and the terms on which the transfer would be made. There were also, crucially, discussions with the Commissioners about the possibility of involving the district valuer in negotiations for foreshore transactions.[53] In October 1960, Brook convened another meeting of the permanent secretaries at the Cabinet Office. He recalled the agreement that had been reached in November 1958 that ministers should be advised to approve the transfer of responsibilities from the Commissioners to the Minister of Transport. But he now suggested that this conclusion should be reconsidered, a move that seemed to be driven mainly by the fact that over the time since the proposal was first mooted, the Commissioners now appeared to be prepared to exercise their functions with respect to the foreshore with greater moderation than they had originally shown; they were prepared to employ the district valuer in assessing the consideration and, most importantly, they were prepared to exclude any element of monopoly value in negotiating the consideration they would ask for. In these circumstances it was, Brook recorded, 'open to question whether it would be expedient for the Government to introduce legislation to transfer the administrative responsibility for the foreshore and seabed to the Minister of Transport'.[54]

And in the event the Commissioners gave express undertakings to involve the district valuer, who was instructed to ignore the element of monopoly value.[55] The strong words of the various departmental officials who had exposed the consequences of the reunification of the management of all the foreshore in the Commissioners of Crown Lands in 1949 came to nothing, and the proposal to transfer responsibility for the foreshore and seabed to the Minister of Transport with an appropriate amendment to the 1927 Act was, rather lamely, heard of no more.

THE CROWN LANDS ACT 1961

Shortly after the Milford Haven dispute was settled, the 1961 Act, that was the second stage of the reforms recommended by the 1955 inquiry, was passed. The Act replaced the best consideration and best rent provisions of the 1927 Act with a provision that sales or leases could only be made for the best consideration in money or money's worth which could reasonably be obtained. The only concession to the Milford Haven dispute was the inclusion of a requirement that the duty to obtain the best consideration or rent should 'exclude any element of monopoly value attributable to the extent of the Crown's ownership of comparable land', a shortened formula from the express undertakings given by the Commissioners over Milford Haven and, moreover, one that applied to all the Crown estate assets and not just the foreshore and the seabed.[56] The 1961 Act did not contain any provisions relating to the foreshore or seabed along the lines discussed during the Milford Haven dispute; indeed, the Treasury Solicitor had advised that it would be undesirable to do so.[57]

There was one other change made by the 1961 Act. The 1955 inquiry had reported that the general duties of the Commissioners were unwritten and undefined, and in particular the Commissioners were not specifically required to take active steps to preserve the value of the estate. The inquiry had said:

> it can be inferred ... that the Commissioners are to act generally as trustees ... and it is tacitly understood that it is the [Commissioners'] duty to preserve and increase the value of the properties entrusted to their charge to meet the obligations of a good landowner, and subject to these duties to obtain the maximum revenue for the sovereign

and had recommended that these duties should be written into statute.[58] The 1961 Act duly imposed, in slightly different words, a new duty on the Commissioners, 'while maintaining the Crown estate as an estate in land ... to maintain and enhance its value and the return from it, but with due regard to the requirements of good management'.[59]

The 1961 Act did not address the inherent conflict between public interest and profit that Farrer had written of in 1866 and that was exposed over the Milford Haven dispute, and the conflict was to surface again in the context of discussions over whether the management of the Crown estate assets in Scotland should be devolved to the Scottish Parliament and, if so, on what terms. But now the conflict was seen to apply to the management of all the Crown estate assets and not just the foreshore.

MANAGEMENT OF SCOTLAND'S CROWN ASSETS IS DEVOLVED

The devolution settlement outlined in the Scotland Act 1998 left in its wake, as we have noted, an anomaly over the ownership of the Crown estate and its management.[60] Property belonging to the sovereign in right of the Crown and the public rights held by the Crown in trust for the public were not reserved matters, but the management of Scotland's Crown estate assets was reserved to the Westminster Parliament, a split that was criticised in the debate on the Bill that became the 1998 Act when a long-standing dissatisfaction with the operation in Scotland of the commissioners who ran The Crown Estate was made clear.[61] Roseanna Cunningham said that 'it is generally felt that the [Crown Estate] Commissioners constitute one of the most secretive and unaccountable bodies in Scotland', and that 'in many areas the Crown Estate Commissioners act as a direct barrier to economic development in Scotland with their interference in foreshore development in particular ...'[62] The anomaly was more colourfully described by the land reform campaigner and MSP Andy Wightman in these terms:

> The property rights and interests of the Crown Estate are a form of public land which are defined by Scots law, situated in Scotland but administered by what is, in effect, a commercial property company based in London. In many ways, it is no different from the many absentee landowners in Scotland with whom the only contact people have is a demand for rent.[63]

A report in 2006 by the six local authorities covering the Highlands and Islands, Highlands and Islands Enterprise and the Convention of Scottish Local Authorities noted that there had long been criticisms of the Crown Estate Commissioners' approach to managing the Scottish Crown estate assets, in particular the adverse impact of the seabed and foreshore charges introduced by the Crown Estate Commissioners on public sector and community interests in the Highlands and Islands. There was, the report noted, a stark contrast between the Crown Estate Commissioners' approach to generate revenue from the resource and the ways in which the public interest in the Crown's ownership of the seabed and foreshore could be managed to complement the Scottish Executive's policies designed to support rural, coastal and island communities and the public interest more generally.[64]

In 2009 the report of the Commission on Scottish Devolution – the Calman Report – was published, in which it was acknowledged that the Commission had received evidence calling for the Crown Estate Commissioners' Scottish responsibilities to be devolved 'to enable the Crown Estate to be made more accountable and to help ensure that its Scottish assets are managed in Scotland's interests' and noting that it had been argued that 'the current management of the Crown Estate focuses too narrowly on securing revenue'. Nevertheless, the Calman Report did not recommend devolution.[65]

Then in 2012 came a report by the House of Commons Scottish Affairs Committee on the Crown Estate in Scotland. The Committee noted that many of its witnesses reasserted the findings of the 2006 report that the Crown Estate Commissioners were largely driven by the pursuit of revenue, with very little regard to other public benefits. One witness in particular captured the conflict that has been the theme of this chapter. He said:

> The Crown Estate works within a commercial mandate, seeks a commercial return on [its assets], but in doing so wishes to act as a good corporate citizen delivering business objectives in the wider public interest . . . that is a very difficult set of issues to weigh up by a body that is a public body . . . Under the terms of the legislation they have a difficult task to pull off – of being commercial while working in the public interest all at the same time.[66]

The Committee noted that the Treasury had

> encountered circumstances where the extent of [the Commissioners'] emphasis on revenue generation appeared to prevent [them] taking full account of potential wider public interests.[67]

Speaking of the seabed, the Committee said that it was 'a publicly owned national asset, which requires proper multiple objective management in the public interest to benefit the people of Scotland and its coastal communities'.[68] Words that recall what Thomas Farrer had said in his 1866 memorandum, and that apply with equal force to the foreshore. The Committee heard evidence that the Commissioners did not believe that 'the 1961 Act allowed them to act in the wider public interest in a non-specific way'.[69]

In November 2014 the Smith Commission proposed that 'Responsibility for the management of the Crown estate's economic assets in Scotland, and the revenue generated from those assets [should be] transferred to the Scottish Parliament' and that responsibility for the management of these assets should be further devolved to local authorities;[70] legislative effect was given to this proposal in section 36 of the Scotland Act 2016.[71] An interim body corporate was set up by the Scottish government in February 2017 to manage the Scottish Crown estate assets and the responsibility for the management of those assets was transferred to this body on 1 April 2017.[72]

THE SCOTTISH CROWN ESTATE ACT 2019

On 15 January 2019 the Scottish Crown Estate Act 2019 received the Royal Assent.[73] The 2019 Act provides that the body that had been formed to manage the Scottish Crown estate assets be named 'Crown Estate Scotland' and provides for the management of the assets. The most important provisions in the context of this chapter are the disapplication of the 1961 Act[74] and the imposition of a duty under section 7 requiring the manager of the Scottish Crown estate assets to maintain and seek to enhance the value of the relevant estate assets and the income arising from them,[75] and in complying with this duty the manager must act in the way best calculated to further the achievement of sustainable development in Scotland,[76] and must seek to manage the assets in a way that is likely to contribute to the promotion or the improvement in Scotland of economic development, regeneration, social well-being and environmental well-being.[77] The intention behind these words was to make it explicit that 'wider factors – the economic, social and environmental benefits that can arise from decision making – can properly be taken into account', rather than being limited to the 1961 Act principle of 'good management', an expression that had never been defined.[78] Section 8 gives the manager power to do anything on behalf of the Crown in respect of an asset that the Crown could do as owner of the asset. There is a duty under section 11, on transfers of ownership and grants of leases and of any other rights in or over the assets, not to make any of the transactions for a consideration of less than market value, but the 2019 Act introduces an important qualification.[79] A transaction may be made for less than market value (including for no consideration) if the manager of the asset is satisfied the relevant transaction is likely to contribute to the promotion or the improvement in Scotland of economic development, regeneration, social well-being, environmental well-being or sustainable development, provided the manager in deciding to make a transaction for less than market value has regard to the likely effect of such a transaction on the value of the Scottish Crown estate assets as a whole.[80] Paragraphs 50 and 52 of the Scottish Crown Estate Strategic Management Plan, March 2020, offer an interpretation of what these words mean: the manager must be able to 'demonstrate that wider benefits of equivalent scale will be delivered' and 'should consider – and demonstrate – that the non-monetary benefits which will accrue as a result of a transaction for less than market value are equal to or greater than the income or capital foregone by the transaction. The prospect of achieving these wider benefits should be equally as certain as the financial benefits foregone to realise these benefits.'[81] The specific wording about disregarding the monopoly position that was contained in the 1961 Act is replaced by a provision that requires an assumption to be made that, on the day of the relevant transaction, some other person is offering to make an equivalent transaction in relation to a similar asset.[82] The manager of the Scottish Crown estate assets also has an overriding duty under the Scotland Act 1998 to continue to manage the assets on behalf of the Crown and to maintain them as an estate in land or as estates in land managed separately.[83] Finally, we should note that under section 10 the transfer of ownership of an asset that is, or includes, a portion of the seabed – defined as the bed and subsoil of the sea – can only be made with the consent of Scottish Ministers. While on the face of it the foreshore would not seem to be subject to this provision because it is not part of the sea or the bed of the sea,[84] the incorporation into this provision of the definitions of the 'Scottish marine area' and 'the sea' from the Marine (Scotland) Act 2010 means that the foreshore is indeed included within section 10.[85]

When the Scottish government consulted in 2017 about the long-term management of the devolved assets, it posed a fundamental question that seemed to address the public policy/profit conflict:

> whether the estate should continue being managed on a primarily commercial basis, or whether there is a case for a wider set of considerations to be taken into account ... [and that] wider socioeconomic benefits, including community benefits [could] be taken into account.[86]

So, how has the 2019 Act answered this fundamental question, and how should we assess the Act in the context of the theme that has run through this chapter? Will the Act allow the foreshore (and, indeed, all the other Scottish Crown estate assets) to be managed with the broad public interest in mind and not, as Thomas Farrer put it in 1871, simply 'as a matter of £. s. d.'?[87]

We should note first that the Act does not address the singular characteristics of the foreshore as a unique part of the Scottish Crown estate assets; there is nothing in the Act that addresses the 1960 Cabinet Office conclusion that it was fundamentally illogical to equate the foreshore with the other Crown estate assets: the Act does not differentiate the foreshore, with its distinct public interest dimension, from the other Scottish Crown assets.[88] And the spectre of the reduction of Scotland's annual block grant by the estimated net revenues that the Scottish Crown estate earns may cast its shadow, as the minister who opened the Stage 1 debate on the Bill said: 'Whoever manages the assets clearly has to maintain and seek to enhance their value and the income arising from them, otherwise Scotland will be out of pocket.'[89] But on the plus side the lead committee for the Bill did confirm its support in the Stage 1 debate for the intention of the Bill 'to move beyond a focus on profitability and to encompass other factors', an intention that is reflected in the provisions of the 2019 Act, provisions that apply to all the Scottish Crown estate and not just the foreshore.[90] The 1961 Act, which has been seen to impose constraints on acting in the wider public interest because of its focus on treating the Crown assets primarily as a source of revenue, has been cast aside and replaced with provisions that aim at enabling, indeed requiring, managers to seek to manage the assets in a way that contributes to the promotion of socio-economic, environmental and community factors, factors that suggest the wider public interest is to be taken account of. All this suggests that the Scottish Parliament has taken notice of the criticism that led to the pressure for devolution of the management of the Scottish assets of The Crown Estate; that it has answered the fundamental question posed by the consultation exercise by agreeing that management should no longer be on a primarily commercial basis; and that in doing so it has moved towards a resolution of the conflict between public interest and profit that has been the theme of this chapter.[91] While the 2019 Act does not give the discretionary powers in relation to the foreshore that Thomas Farrer had wanted in 1866, he might, nonetheless, be satisfied that there does not appear any longer to be an assumption being made, at least for Scotland, 'that the pecuniary interest of the public in the foreshore is its most important interest'.[92]

NOTES

1. The land that lies between, in England, Wales and Northern Ireland, the high-water mark of medium high tides and the low-water mark of such tides (or possibly of the lowest astronomical tide – Lynn Shellfish Ltd v. Loose [2016] UKSC 14 at para. 64), and in Scotland between the high- and low-water marks of ordinary spring tides.
2. T. Bingham, *Lives of the Law – Selected Essays and Speeches 2000–2010* (Oxford, 2011), p. 44.
3. See R. B. Pugh, *The Crown Estate – An Historical Essay* (London, 1960); Report of the Crown Estate Working Group, 2006, Annex 1; Parliamentary Papers [hereafter 'PP'] 1955–56 Report of the Committee on Crown Lands, June 1951 Cmd. 9483 [hereafter 'Cmd. 9483']; M. E. Deans, 'The Crown Estate Commissioners: Their role and responsibilities in respect of the foreshore and seabed around Scotland', *Journal of Energy and Resources Law*, 4:3 (1986); A. Wightman, *The Poor Had No Lawyers* (Edinburgh,

2010), pp. 138–43. The revenues from the Crown lands in Scotland were not surrendered until 1830 – 1 Will. IV c. 25, section 2.
4. Crown Lands Act 1829 [hereafter the '1829 Act'] and the Crown Lands (Scotland) Act 1832 and 1833.
5. The criterion of a public river in Scotland was, until 1877, navigability but thereafter became tidality as it has always been in England and Wales.
6. The Crown Estate Transfer Scheme 2017, SI 2017/524 [hereafter 'SI 2017/524'].
7. https://www.crownestatescotland.com/what-we-do [last accessed 14 October 2019]. The word 'seabed' can, as we shall see later – perhaps confusingly, be used to include the foreshore.
8. https://www.thecrownestate.co.uk/en-gb/our-business/2019-annual-report/ [last accessed 14 October 2019].
9. J. MacAskill, *Scotland's Foreshore – Public Rights, Private Rights and the Crown, 1840–2017* (Edinburgh, 2018), pp. 234–7.
10. R (on the application of Newhaven Port and Properties) v. East Sussex CC [2015] UKSC 7, see J. Robbie, 'Finding common ground', in *Conveyancer and Property Lawyer*, 6 (2016), pp. 487–96; Scottish Law Commission Discussion Paper, No. 113, April 2001, paras. 51–8. There are also certain statutory public rights: Land Reform (Scotland) Act 2003, Countryside and Rights of Way Act 2000 and Marine and Coastal Access Act 2009.
11. J. L. Sax, 'The Public Trust Doctrine in Natural Resource Law: Effective judicial intervention', in *Michigan Law Review*, 68 (1969), pp. 471–566; c.f. J. L. Huffman, 'Speaking inconvenient truths – A History of the Public Trust Doctrine', in *Duke Environmental Law and Policy Forum*, 1 (2007), pp. 1–102; A. R. Oakes, 'Judicial resources and the Public Trust Doctrine: A powerful tool of environmental protection', in *Transnational Environmental Law*, 7:3 (2018), pp. 469–89.
12. It is also clear that the contest over rights of ownership over the foreshore in Scotland between the Crown and private proprietors played an important part in this decision: see MacAskill, *Scotland's Foreshore*, pp. 63–4. PP 1866 LX Return of Correspondence between the Treasury and the Board of Trade as to the transfer of the Management of the Crown in Tidal Lands [hereafter 'PP 1866 LX'], pp. 1–2.
13. Ibid., p. 4.
14. Section 28 said that leases were to be at a Rack Rent and section 34 required a sale to be 'for such sum or sums of money as to the [Commissioners] shall appear a sufficient consideration'. PP 1867/68 LVII Copy of Memorandum as to Board of Trade's Dealings with Foreshore and Bed of the Sea [hereafter the 'Farrer Memorandum'], pp. 7–8.
15. PP 1866 LX, p. 4.
16. Ibid., p. 2.
17. Clauses 8, 9 and 10 of the Crown Lands Bill 1866, PP 1866 Bills and Acts, Bill Number 98.

18. Section 8. [Hereafter the '1866 Act'.] The reason for, and background to, the amendment of the Bill in the House of Lords is outwith the scope of this chapter but is explored fully in MacAskill, *Scotland's Foreshore*, pp. 63–73.
19. The Farrer Memorandum; see MacAskill, *Scotland's Foreshore*, pp. 73–80.
20. TNA:PRO, BT 243/95 Note for meeting with Sir Norman Brook, 11 October 1960.
21. The Farrer Memorandum, p. 6.
22. Ibid., pp. 6–7. See Arnold v. Munday (1821) 6 NLJ 1, one of the earliest of the cases in the United States on the public trust doctrine: 'the land on which water ebbs and flows [should] be held, protected and regulated for the common use and benefit'.
23. The Farrer Memorandum, p. 8.
24. PP 1907 XXXIV Royal Commission Vol. 3 (Part 1) Cd. 3683, p. iv.
25. PP 1911 XIV Royal Commission Vol. 1 (Part 1) Cd. 5708 paras. 23 and 24; something that was also to be recommended by the Committee on Crown and Government Lands in 1922 (PP 1922 Interim and Final Reports of the Committee on Government and Crown Lands, Cmd. 1689, p. 19).
26. By the Forestry (Title of Commissioners of Woods) Order 1924, SI 1924/1370.
27. Hereafter the '1927 Act'.
28. Sections 3 and 5, which replicated the Settled Land Act 1925 provisions for trust property – as the Report of the Committee on Crown Lands was to say in 1955, 'it can be inferred from the Crown Lands Acts ... that the Commissioners are to act generally as trustees' (Cmd. 9483, p. 7); Parliamentary Debates [hereafter 'PD'] Fifth Series Vol. 204 House of Commons column 1302 (30 March 1927). Section 10 of the 1927 Act also introduced certain exceptions to the 'best consideration and best rent' requirement, again replicating the Settled Land Act 1925.
29. PP 1929/30 I, Bills and Acts, Bill Number 19, clauses 1 and 2.
30. The Minister of Shipping (Transfer of Functions) Order 1939, SI 1939/1470.
31. The Ministers of the Crown (Minister of War Transport) Order 1941, SI 1941/654.
32. TNA:PRO, T 227/1096 Cabinet. Machinery of Government Committee, Coast Protection and the Management of Crown Foreshore, Treasury Report, May 1946; TNA:PRO, MT 45/117 Memorandum for the Official Committee on the Machinery of Government – Crown Foreshore and Coast Erosion, June 1946.
33. PD Fifth Series Vol. 436 House of Commons Written Answers column 150 (25 April 1947).
34. Sections 37–40.
35. Although, as we shall see, the Board later thought that this might have been an oversight: TNA:PRO, BT 243/95 Crown Estate and the Foreshores and Seabed, p. 2.

36. TNA:PRO, T/227/1096 Cabinet: Machinery of Government Committee – Coast Protection and the Management of Crown Foreshore, 29 May 1946; Crown Foreshore: Meeting at the Treasury, 9 April 1946.
37. Cmd. 9483.
38. Hereafter the '1961 Act'.
39. TNA:PRO, BT 243/95 Memorandum by Ports Division, Ministry of Transport and Civil Aviation, Foreshores and Seabed and the Crown Estate, 10 April 1958, p. 1.
40. PP 1911 XIV Royal Commission, Vol. 3 (Part 1), Cd. 5708, para. 23.
41. TNA:PRO, BT 243/95 Foreshore and Seabed, Memorandum by the Crown Estate Commissioners, 15 May 1958, p. 7.
42. The Farrer Memorandum, p. 7.
43. TNA:PRO, BT 243/95 Memorandum by Ports Division, Ministry of Transport and Civil Aviation, Foreshores and Seabed and the Crown Estate, 10 April 1958, p. 2.
44. Ibid., pp. 1, 6.
45. Ibid., p. 2.
46. TNA:PRO, BT 243/95 Foreshore and Seabed, Note agreed between the Ministers of Transport, Power and Housing and Local Government and the G.P.O., 1959, pp. 2, 3.
47. TNA:PRO, BT 243/95 Cabinet – Foreshore and Seabed, record of meeting 10 November 1958; TNA:PRO, BT 243/95 Foreshore and Seabed, record of meetings at the Cabinet Office on 12 and 18 October 1960, p. 3.
48. TNA:PRO, BT 243/95 Crown Estate and the Foreshores and Seabed, p. 1.
49. TNA:PRO, BT 243/95 Foreshore and Seabed. Memorandum by the Crown Estate Commissioners, 15 May 1958, p. 9.
50. TNA:PRO, BT 243/95 Crown Estate and the Foreshores and Seabed, p. 2. Part III of the 1949 Act contained the provisions relating to the transfer of management of the foreshore.
51. TNA:PRO, BT 243/95 Crown Estate and the Foreshores and Seabed, p. 2.
52. Ibid.
53. TNA:PRO, BT 243/95 Letter Edwards to Sharp, 20 October 1960.
54. TNA:PRO, BT 243/95 Foreshore and Seabed, record of meeting at the Cabinet Office, 26 October 1960.
55. TNA:PRO, BT 243/95 Instruction to District Valuers.
56. Section 3(1). Sections 3(6) and 4 also preserved, and extended, the exceptions from the 'best consideration and best rent' requirement that had been in the 1927 Act. Section 3(1) was also a relaxation of the 1927 Act requirement that for leases a 'best rent' should be obtained because 'best rent' had been interpreted to mean that a lease could not allow for rent reviews – PD Fifth Series Vol. 643 House of Commons column 1819 (6 July 1961). There was considerable reluctance on the part of the Commissioners to have the wording of these undertakings written into the Bill – TNA:PRO, TS 58/538, Crown Estate and the Foreshore and Seabed, para. 6.

57. TNA:PRO, TS 58/538, Crown Estate Bill, further Notes for the Chancellor of the Exchequer for Legislative Committee, 31 January 1961, para. 3.
58. Cmd. 9483, pp. 7, 20.
59. Section 1(3) 1961 Act. See PD Fifth Series Vol. 643 House of Commons columns 1760–88 (6 July 1961) and PD Fifth Series Vol. 233 House of Lords columns 1054–9 (26 July 1961).
60. Hereafter the '1998 Act'.
61. Scotland Act 1998, schedule 5, paras. 1, 2(3) and 3(1). In relation to Wales, property owned by the sovereign in right of the Crown is not a reserved matter (paragraph 3(1) of schedule 7A to the Government of Wales Act 2006), but the management of The Crown Estate in Wales is (paragraph 1 of schedule 7A). In relation to Northern Ireland, the management of The Crown Estate in Northern Ireland remains the responsibility of the Westminster Parliament (paragraph 1 of schedule 2 to the Northern Ireland Act 1998) but paragraphs 2 and 5 of schedule 3 provide that property owned by the sovereign in right of the Crown including, specifically, the seabed and foreshore is reserved to the Westminster Parliament but the Northern Ireland Assembly can legislate in relation to it with the consent of the secretary of state.
62. PD Sixth Series Vol. 309 House of Commons columns 907–13 (30 March 1998) and Vol. 312 House of Commons columns 806–13 (19 May 1998).
63. Wightman, *The Poor Had No Lawyers*, p. 140.
64. Report of the Crown Estate Working Group, 2006, pp. 89–91.
65. Calman Commission on Scottish Devolution Final Report June 2009, pp. 179–81.
66. House of Commons Scottish Affairs Committee – The Crown Estate in Scotland – Seventh Report of Session 2010–12, HC 1117 [hereafter 'HC 1117'], at p. 27.
67. Ibid., p. 26.
68. Ibid., p. 28.
69. House of Commons Scottish Affairs Committee – The Crown Estate in Scotland – Fifth Report of Session 2013–14, HC 889, p. 11.
70. Report of the Smith Commission for further devolution of powers to the Scottish Parliament, 27 November 2014, paras. 32 to 35 p. 16. PP 2014–15 Scotland in the United Kingdom: An enduring Settlement, Cmnd. 8990, para. 5.5.
71. Hereafter the '2016 Act'.
72. The Crown Estate Scotland (Interim Management) Order 2017, SSI 2017/36 and The Crown Estate Transfer Scheme 2017, SI 2017/524. Section 90B(3) of the 2016 Act and excludes from the transfer property held by a limited partnership.
73. Hereafter the '2019 Act'.
74. The 1961 Act was made applicable to the Scottish Crown estate by virtue

of section 36(7) of the 2016 Act and disapplied under the provisions of section 36(8) by paragraph 1 of schedule 2 to the 2019 Act.
75. Section 7(1). A requirement that replicates section 1(3) of the 1961 Act but with the subtle difference that it is a duty to 'seek' to enhance.
76. Section 7(2)(a).
77. Section 7(2)(b).
78. Scottish Parliament Official Report: Environment, Climate Change and Land Reform Committee 20 February 2018, column 2. HC 1117, pp. 25–8.
79. Section 11(1).
80. Section 11(2) and (3); section 12 defines market value, a definition that is based on the RICS Valuation – Global Standards 2017, Red Book. But the wording in the 1961 Act as to best consideration and monopoly is still used in paragraphs 15 and 25 of schedule 4 to SI 2017/524.
81. https://www.gov.scot/publications/first-strategic-management-plan-scottish-crown-estate/ [last accessed 7 September 2020]. Section 22 of the 2019 Act required Scottish Ministers to prepare such a plan.
82. Section 12(1)(e).
83. Section 90B(5) and (8) – provisions that are matters reserved to the Westminster Parliament and thus unalterable by the Scottish Parliament (section 36(4), 2016 Act). This duty reflects section 1(3) of the 1961 Act but without a requirement to have due regard to the requirements of good management.
84. In paragraphs 12 and 15 of schedule 1 to SI 2017/524 (that lists the Scottish assets that are part of the Crown estate), the seabed and the foreshore are shown as separate assets.
85. The Scottish Crown Estate Guidance note on seabed ownership does not on the face of it appear to apply to the foreshore https://www.crownestatescotland.com/maps-and-publications (last accessed 14 October 2019). And rather oddly, the foreshore is not taken to be part of the seabed for the purposes of the regulation-making powers in section 42 of the 2019 Act.
86. Crown Estate – A Consultation on the Long-Term Management of the Crown Estate in Scotland, 2017, p. 18.
87. TNA:PRO, MT 10/130, Minute, 27 November 1871, THF.
88. A radical suggestion that the Crown's ownership of the foreshore should be abolished was rejected (Scottish Parliament Official Report Meeting of the Parliament, 19 June 2018, column 52).
89. Ibid., column 41.
90. Ibid., column 43.
91. Albeit that it is not apparent that the parliamentarians responsible for the 2019 Act were aware of the history recounted in this chapter (with one notable exception: Scottish Parliament Official Report Environment, Climate Change and Land Reform Committee 18 September 2018, column 5).
92. The Farrer Memorandum, p. 6.

PART II

Agitation and Agendas of Reform

4

'Not a bashful man':[1]
Dr Gavin Brown Clark and Land Nationalisation

Ewen A. Cameron

THE LAND QUESTION WAS a prominent issue on the political agenda in Great Britain and Ireland in the 1880s. In the Scottish Highlands, one of the most notable political manifestations was the election in 1885 and 1886 of a group of so-called 'Crofter MPs', sometimes even called a Crofters' Party. Since the 1950s they have attracted attention from historians, essentially because their election was one of the few examples of the newly enfranchised using their votes to elect politicians other than Liberal and Conservative MPs, mostly the former in Scotland. Their moment on the stage was brief, as they were quite quickly absorbed by the Liberal party, although one – Charles Fraser-Mackintosh – became a Liberal Unionist in 1886. The electoral cycle turned against them by 1895. In the words of one historian, the party 'died young'.[2] The established narrative pays very little attention to their political ideas and their intellectual and ideological place in wider debates. In some cases this is because they had few original ideas or made no real contribution to wider political debate.[3] The figure who was exceptional in almost all these respects was the MP for Caithness, Dr Gavin Brown Clark. He remained an MP until his defeat by Leicester Harmsworth in a remarkable contest in 1900.[4] He was involved in a series of radical causes – temperance, the peace movement, anti-imperialism, socialism, republicanism, Scottish Home Rule, secularism – in Britain and Ireland from the 1860s until the aftermath of the Great War. His last electoral campaign was as a Labour candidate in Glasgow Cathcart at the general election of 1918.[5] On his death in 1930, Thomas Johnston wrote, aptly, that he was 'a friend and counsellor to every group of his countrymen who raised a standard for a Scottish or socialist cause' and that he 'had a restless finger in every pie of trouble for the existing order in two hemispheres'.[6]

The purpose of this essay will be to look at Clark's career and to shed light on some of the ideas that figured in the debates on the land question in Britain and Ireland in the late nineteenth century. There is a wider biographical project to be pursued connecting his ideas on land to his strident anti-imperialism and the 'Pro-Boer' views that were used against him to such telling effect by Harmsworth in 1900.[7] My principal focus here will be on his consistent advocacy of land nationalisation.[8] After the provision of biographical details the essay will look at some of the key influences on Clark's political formation, examine some of his contributions on land-related issues and conclude with a focus on his place in the movement for the nationalisation of land.

Clark was born in Kilmarnock in 1846 of lower-middle-class parentage. He is said to have run away to sea in the early 1860s but returned to Glasgow in the later years of that decade. He then studied medicine in Glasgow, Edinburgh and London, qualifying in 1874. He practised medicine in London in the 1870s and was involved in a host of radical organisations and causes. He was involved in the protest against the Turkish massacres of Bulgarians in 1876 and the formation of the National Liberal Federation in 1877, and edited the temperance publication *The Good Templar* in the 1870s. As will be discussed below, he was a member of the International Working Men's Association (The 'First International') in London in the early 1870s. Following his second marriage in 1879 (he had been widowed in 1876), he travelled widely and came to prominence as a supporter of the Boer Republics during the first Boer War. He is said to have been present at the Boer Camp at Majuba Hill in 1881. This was the beginning of his Pro-Boer activity, work that brought him prominence and obloquy in equal measure. From 1881 to 1891 he was Consul General of the South African Republic. In 1884 he was selected as the Crofter candidate for Caithness after a period as President of the London Highland Land Law Reform Association from 1882.[9] He represented Caithness from 1885 until his defeat in 1900. In the later part of his career he was active in the peace movement and in organisations interested in the welfare of prisoners of war and refugees. His anti-imperialism was evident in his involvement in organisations for Indian independence as well as his South African work.[10] His membership of the International in the 1860s was no youthful flirtation with left-wing politics: throughout his career he can be found in the (Social) Democratic Federation, the Fabian Society, the Scottish Labour Party (as one its founders) and the Labour party, culminating in his candidacy in 1918.[11] The challenge with a career like Clark's is to find some themes that can help us to place him amid this diverse hyperactivity. This essay will pick out his consistent advocacy of land nationalisation as one strand of his work that can help us to understand his position and the context in which he operated. There is a tendency sometimes to separate the land movements in Britain and Ireland into their national contexts; this is reasonable as there is particularity in each case, but many of the activists crossed the national boundaries and many of the ideas that they advocated – such as land nationalisation – were potentially universal in their application. The connections to wider social movements was also a theme that connects politicians like Clark and, for example, Michael Davitt and the Welsh land nationalisers, as well as Alfred Russel Wallace and Helen Taylor.[12]

Clark left no substantial body of correspondence, although he crops up in a range of collections and there is a significant corpus of material, particularly publications and speeches, in the public domain. One of the most interesting sources is his serialised autobiography – 'Rambling Recollections of an Agitator' – published in the *Forward* in 1910. This was a carefully curated account of his career. It is a skilful narrative that situates the author in the centre of the maelstrom of radical movements in the late-Victorian period.[13] It also places Clark in a classic radical and intellectual genealogy. As we noted, Clark was born in the industrial town of Kilmarnock in 1846 and in the first instalment of his recollections he recalls his father's involvement in the Chartist movement in that town.[14] This article reads like a *Who's Who* of mid-century radical politics. It establishes connections with leading Chartists and early Socialist agitators, such as Robert Buchanan and Lloyd Jones, but he gives the greatest emphasis to his inspiration by the ideas of the utopian Socialist Robert Owen.

> I still believe with Owen than 'man's character is made for him and not by him', that 'circumstances make character', that you can grow potatoes if you have the proper soil and that most of the evils of society are the necessary result of the bad conditions which we allow to exist.[15]

This was an explicit counter to the prevailing religious ideas of the day in Scotland, although they were already changing by the 1860s.[16] Clark was attracted to Owenism by its suspicion of organised religion and by its emphasis on non-violence – a key theme in his later career – as well as its veneration of utopian views of the value of the small self-sustaining community 'as the ideal form of social organisation'.[17] Clark was not alone among late-Victorian land nationalisers in being influenced by Robert Owen. Alfred Russel Wallace was exposed to Owenite ideas at the earliest stages of his political development in London in 1837.[18] Wallace emphasised the same point as Clark – the effect of the environment on the individual – in his thoughts on the influence of Owen. Owen was again influential in turning Wallace away from individualist views towards socialism in the late 1880s and 1890s.[19] He placed himself firmly in the secular milieu of mid-century socialism, drawing on the ideas of Thomas Paine and Robert Owen, which he discovered through the activities of the Eclectic Society. Clark was also active in the loose group of radicals of both an older and younger generation known as the Democratic Society.[20] This explicit attempt to link his political development to this period and context was strengthened in the second article of the series, which emphasised the role of Ernest Jones in his political development.[21]

Jones was a key figure in the development of radical politics in the nineteenth century. He was a prominent Chartist in the 1840s and a prolific journalist, poet and lawyer. In this last capacity he was involved in defence of the Manchester martyrs in 1867. Jones was an influence on Clark's general politics as he was a key figure in the sustenance of working-class politics in the period following the collapse of the Chartist movement, when, as John Saville has noted, 'there no longer existed an independent political movement of working people'.[22] This was a crucial period in Clark's political formation. Jones was a familiar figure in Scotland in the 1850s and 1860s, and in his journalism and public speeches he constantly emphasised the importance of the land question, the breaking up of the great estates and the pernicious influence of the aristocracy. Jones argued for a form of land nationalisation and the creation of smallholdings of around two acres, which, along with the development of waste and fallow land, would provide for the entire body of surplus labour that he saw as a natural product of the capitalist system. He advocated these views in a tour of Scotland in 1867.[23] It was during this tour that he participated in the famous set-piece debate in Edinburgh on the subject of 'democracy' with Professor John Stuart Blackie.[24]

This was a very different set of influences to those that worked on the other Crofter MPs. In most cases they came to the Highland land question from a position that saw the grievances of the crofters as being particular and exceptional. They were steeped in political questions around the Gaelic language. It is true that Donald MacFarlane, MP for Argyll, had been an MP for an Irish constituency but he was hardly in the vanguard of social politics and, in any case, the Irish MPs elected in 1880 in support of the cause of Irish Home Rule were often very socially conservative. Angus Sutherland, MP for Sutherland, was the Crofter MP who was closest to Clark in his views on land nationalisation and the connections between the Highland land question and wider social issues. Sutherland had been active in radical circles in Glasgow in the 1870s and sought to push these ideas in his campaigns in his native county in the 1880s.²⁵ Thereafter, however, his career diverged from Clark's as he became President of the Scottish Fishery Board and the Scottish Congested Districts Board, and served on a host of other official bodies. By contrast, to the end of his career, Clark saw the vicissitudes of the Highlands as part of a general social problem, rather than an exceptional grievance.

The Chartist background was important because of that movement's emphasis on the land question. The Chartist Land Plan has been identified as a form of proto-nationalisation of the land. The ignominious failure of the Plan should not detract from the importance of a broad attack on the landed classes as a key feature of Chartism.²⁶ Clark's memoirs indicate exposure to these currents of thought. Land reform was central to the conception of democracy advocated by Ernest Jones, popular with Scottish audiences. Indeed, in the aftermath of one visit to Glasgow by Jones, Clark recalled that a land nationalisation society was formed.²⁷ Clark called this a 'democratic movement' but admitted that it was not very successful:

> We found it difficult to make the people in the towns understand how seriously the land question affected them. Nor was it easy to get at the agricultural population and when we came in touch with them, we found that the farmers were only interested in getting their rents reduced at the end of their leases: while, as in the towns, it was only the question of hours and wages which raised the labourers in the country.²⁸

It was this visit of Jones to Glasgow that stimulated the next level of Clark's engagement with the land question. Initially, he argued that landlords should be bought out, at their own valuation, by local authorities at twenty-six years' purchase. He then accepted some of Alfred Russel Wallace's ideas about stopping the inheritance of landed wealth and rights, before becoming 'more inclined to support Henry George's proposal of progressive taxation till the full annual value be obtained'.²⁹ This is a useful point because Henry George was very important to the debate on the land question in Britain in the late nineteenth century. The distinctions between Georgite 'land restoration' and 'land nationalisation' will be developed in the final section of the essay but it is important to note here what Clark has to say about his role, probably exaggerated, in the popularisation of Henry George's book *Progress and Poverty* in Britain. While Clark may not have been as significant in helping to develop the enormous influence that George and his publications had in

Britain and Ireland in the early 1880s, it is significant that he plays this up in his recollections. George argued for a form of land nationalisation through taxation rather than expropriation or confiscation. He argued that the full economic rent of the unimproved value of land should be taxed, thereby destroying the essence of private landownership by attacking the 'unearned increment' that was enjoyed by landowners who did not make any investment in their land and profited from the rising tide of values generated by the efforts of others. Clark was not an apostle of Georgite views, however, being opposed to the way in which his ideas would have led, effectively, to the expropriation of landlords.[30] This became a key point in the discussion of land nationalisation in the 1880s and led Clark in a new direction. He recalled that at the very time that George's ideas were becoming popular in Britain in 1880 and 1881, he came under the influence of the other leading figure in the debate over land ownership – Alfred Russel Wallace. Clark, like so many others, had read Wallace's initial publications on the subject and then his 1882 book, *Land Nationalisation*.[31] Although George was a popular speaker in the industrial areas of Scotland and made several tours in the Highlands, it cannot be said that the ideas of land restoration or nationalisation were very popular with the crofters, who were mostly interested in more moderate schemes of land reform that would secure the basics of security of tenure. Georgite acolytes were very active in the Highlands and their politics served as a connection between the rather limited, in an ideological sense, crofters' movement and the wider politics of the land question. George's ideas also stimulated a debate in print with the Duke of Argyll, who argued that landed wealth was the product of investment, as in other forms of business. This was part of a political and intellectual reaction to socialistic ideas that seemed to threaten individualist principles.[32]

A significant moment for Clark was his move to London and his involvement in the International Workingmen's Association, or First International. As Clark recalled in 1910, the organisation was founded in London in 1864 and, although Marx was involved, the International was not Marxist.[33] In his view, the key figures 'derived their political and economic ideas from Adam Smith, Thompson [an Owenite], John Stuart Mill, Carlyle, Ruskin, Maurice and Kingsley, and not from any German source'. In a number of publications about the International he emphasised this point, and the importance of the land question:

> Then, as now, the Lords of the land and money monopolised the Government and the legislature, and used their influence to maintain the natural monopoly

of land and the artificial monopoly of capital, by means of which the labourer is deprived of the full and just reward of his toil.³⁴

For Clark, despite his criticisms of the British trade unionists in the International as conservative and opportunist, it was advanced European influences that led to its break-up. In his recollections, sectarian though they are, Clark touches on an important point about the 1860s, which began to see a recovery of advanced politics after the failure of the revolutionary moment of 1848 – the rise of debates about democracy and egalitarianism stimulated by the Italian unification movement, the Polish uprising and, above all in the Scottish context, the American Civil War. The war is now seen as a conflict about slavery and abolition but that was not how it seemed to all contemporaries. Many, including Clark, saw issues about the role of the state and democracy in the war and its legacy. Clark emphasised Lincoln's 'Government of the people, by the people, for the people' as an ideal 'definition of democracy' and of the 'function of government', and even more important was his 'object of government, which was to secure to each labourer the whole produce of his labour, or as nearly as possible'.³⁵

Clark's presence in London in the early 1870s, as a medical student and then establishing himself in private practice, was important in his political development. London was a centre for political refugees from Europe, of whom Marx was the most famous, although he was relatively unknown at the time of the formation of the International. This gave Clark access to a wide range of political thinking on questions – such as land, labour, empire, revolution, peace and war – of a general nature, as well as more particular causes that touched on these, such as the Irish question and the 'Bulgarian horrors'.³⁶

Clark did, however, develop an interest in the Crofters and the Highland land question prior to his candidature for Caithness in 1885. In his 1882 pamphlet on land nationalisation he remarked on the 'atrocities' which took place during the Clearances, and argued that they were 'equal to any perpetrated by the Russians in Poland, the Austrians in Italy, or the Turks in Bulgaria . . .' In a further pamphlet in 1885 he condemned the Napier Commission as a landlord-dominated body and its conclusions as 'unsatisfactory'.³⁷ Clark had spent his summer holidays in the Highlands for many years and in his lectures on land nationalisation he had often alluded to the Highland Clearances, but it was not until the Battle of the Braes in 1882 and the formation of the Highland Land Law Reform Association that he became actively involved as a member of the executive committee of the new organisation.³⁸ Clark's interest in the

Highland land question stemmed from his belief that conditions in the north of Scotland were symptomatic of the flaws and injustices which stemmed from the land laws. In this belief his views were closer to John Murdoch than Charles Fraser-Mackintosh or Alexander Mackenzie, who came to the Highland land question from an engagement with Highland history and a supposition that the Highland land question was unique and self-contained: they were not so well placed or widely connected within the broader radical movement to make the connections to other issues, and throughout their careers demonstrated much more socially conservative positions.[39]

Clark was well informed about the Irish land question at an early stage and took a favourable attitude to the programme of the Land League. In 1881 he had visited Ireland as part of a deputation sent by the Social Democratic Federation. He remarked that 'the land system of Ireland was a disgrace to our system of civilisation'; but, he argued in a speech in Dublin, conditions in the West Highlands were 'as bad, if not rather worse than in the west of Ireland'. He went on to make the point that 'the formation of great sporting tracts for the amusement of the idle rich' added an extra dimension to the Highland land question. Clark concluded that he 'was glad to say that in the Island of Skye the people had begun to rebel against the evils under which they were suffering'.[40]

The influences that worked to develop Clark's mature political stance can be seen by a close reading of his recollections and other sources. There is no doubt that he carefully constructed this account to place himself in a virtuous political lineage that would meet with the approval of the skilled industrial workers who formed the main readership of the *Forward*. Nevertheless, despite possible slight embellishments, such as the depth of his personal connection with Henry George, the general direction of travel was clear and was borne out by his political actions on anti-imperialism and federal Home Rule as well as his consistent advocacy of land nationalisation, which will be the theme of the final section of this essay.

Clark became aware of the writings of Alfred Russel Wallace, the British naturalist, in the early 1880s. His awareness of the work of Wallace goes back to the early 1870s. While a medical student in Glasgow, he contacted Wallace to ask for details on biological subjects and they were still in touch, debating the vaccination question, on which he agreed with Wallace, in 1898.[41] Nevertheless, it was the land question which brought Clark into the circle surrounding Wallace and his fellow land nationalisers.[42] Clark was certainly part of this group. He can be found at the early meetings of the Land Nationalisation Society, which was formed in the aftermath of Wallace's early publications on the question. At a conference of the Society in January 1882, he moved a resolution

> That private property in land secures to a class what rightly should belong to the community and be appropriated to the relief of state burdens, namely, the inherent value or economic rent of land which is caused by population, wealth, and civilisation, and cannot be increased or diminished by the action of any individual landlord or tenant.[43]

This was a concise summary of Wallace's views, which argued that a wide range of social ills could be traced back to the private ownership of land and suggested that, in contrast to reform of tenure or free trade in land, nationalisation would provide a solution. The state would become the owner of the land and would lease the land back to tenants, who would have the freedom to invest in the land through the incentive of ownership of their improvements.[44] This section will assess Clark's ideas on the subject and then consider where he fitted into the contemporary literature on the subject.

His views were those of a conventional follower of Wallace. His principal publications on the subject were his pamphlets of 1882 and 1918, which were strikingly similar in tone and content, despite the long gap between their publication dates. His 1882 pamphlet was a product of the fact that the land question was becoming more widely discussed beyond small coteries of radicals because of the widespread distress in Ireland and Highland Scotland. The overall effects of the agricultural depression had bankrupted farmers and taken large acreages out of cultivation.[45] He covered the history of Scotland, where he deprecated the shift from productive cultivation to sport, and Ireland, whose 'history ... is also a record of landlord misrule, of terrible cruelty and inhumanity, or grinding tyranny and oppression'.[46] He did not neglect England, although he admitted that its history was less atrocious, but pointed out that its small tenants were coerced on account of their political and religious views and their farming was 'fettered with stupid rules'.[47] His view, like that of Wallace and other land nationalisers, was that 'the land, the air, and the water no man has created' therefore could not be subject to legitimate claims of ownership.[48] His solution was similar to that of Wallace, in that he called for the resumption of the possession of the land by the state for the 'use and enjoyment' of the people. This would be facilitated by legislation to establish a process of land valuation. This would allow a rental value to be established, to be paid to the current owner, less a land tax, by the state in the form of an annuity, thus converting public to private ownership and, crucially, perpetuating 'no injustice . . . to any living being'.[49] This 'compensation' was a distinguishing feature of the schemes of Wallace and his supporters. The overall results would not only be greater cultivation[50] and an end to eviction of the small tenantry but would amount to a panacea for the litany of social ills that was often listed by land nationalisers:

> We would ultimately be able to pay off our national debt and defray all our local and national expenses from the income derived from the land . . . a large proportion of our crime and pauperism would soon disappear. The moral and physical degeneration caused by overcrowding would cease, our fever dens would give place to comfortable homes and the mass of the people would be elevated to a higher and better position – physically, intellectually and morally.[51]

Although slightly more prominent in his later work, the effect of land nationalisation on the health of the urban population was an important point for Clark:

> We must depend more upon our home market. The hygienic and sanitary conditions of our towns will tend to improve, but the invigorating strains from the country will still be needed to mitigate the deteriorating influences of city life.[52]

The Great War had shown the need for increased domestic food production, and the debates in the Edwardian period over the condition of the urban population and the revivifying effects of rural repopulation influenced Clark, as they had many other land reformers.

Clark's views highlight a number of themes that were prominent in the literature on land nationalisation and the critical responses to it. The idea of theft, or at least illegitimate encroachment on former rights, was central to the case for land nationalisation. Wallace was clear about this, arguing that the land system was one of 'modified feudalism', in which customary rights had been eroded and landlords constituted a 'vast and injurious . . . despotism'.[53] Even quite moderate land nationalisers used the language of grievance and theft in arguing that the increased economic value of land had provided an incentive for the 'strong and unscrupulous' to become 'desirous of appropriating it'.[54] The fundamental argument of this strand of thinking was that, essentially, the land belonged to the people, a common phrase in the pamphlet literature and one used by land nationalisers in the Wallace and, for our purposes, Clark tradition as well as Georgites. George himself had argued this case in Book VII of *Progress and Poverty*, in which he went as far as putting the results of private land ownership in the same category as chattel slavery.⁵⁵ Just as the concept of human beings as property was illegitimate and offensive, so was the ownership of land. The fundamental building block of the case for land nationalisation was that the land was the result of economic activity such as investment, and therefore, it could not be truly owned.⁵⁶ In arguing this point, and in the title of his 1918 pamphlet, Clark was certainly in the mainstream of the land nationalisation movement.

Although it appears to be a technical question, the issue of whether landowners should be compensated was central to the distinction between land nationalisers and land restorers. Clark, as we have seen, was clear on this point.⁵⁷ This issue was an important one for Wallace, as he wanted to avoid the accusation of confiscation and to nationalise the land in the least disruptive manner. His preferred device was a terminable annuity for a set number of lives, thereby avoiding a sudden cessation of income to an individual at a given point, as would be the case if the annuity was terminated after a number of years, and not granting a perpetual benefit, thereby undermining the whole process of nationalisation.⁵⁸ While there were occasional voices on the left who argued that there was no ground for compensation because land ownership was 'evil' in its effect, the more common argument came from the right that, compensation or not, land nationalisation was communistic and would undermine individual responsibility.⁵⁹ These attacks produced a constant refrain by land nationalisers that their ideas were just, fair and reasonable, and compensation was crucial to this claim. The issue was tackled by a tract produced by the Land Nationalisation Society. This argued that compensation was not a recognition of the moral right to ownership but was to account for the loss of investment that the existing system provided the landowner with an expectation of a return.⁶⁰ The desire to avoid spoliation and the sense of 'punishing' the current landlord class was, for land nationalisers, a reason to compensate and an attempt to occupy the ethical high ground in the debate: 'the landlords of the present day did not found the system of private property in land, and should not be punished . . . as if they had'.⁶¹

The issue of compensation was also important for the ground it put between the land nationalisers and the Georgite land restorers. The former argued that the single tax would induce landlords to sell plots of land and, thereby, multiply the number of landowners, which would play into the hands of Conservative supporters of peasant proprietorship. This was an important point and a development of it was that land values taxation would, essentially, leave land in the hands of the owners.⁶² For other land nationalisers the single tax solution would take too long and 'smacks of confiscation', thereby eroding the justice of the case for state ownership.[63]

A final point to touch on is the extent to which land nationalisation was seen as a panacea and a solution to a host of social ills, as Clark argued repeatedly in his publications. In some cases land nationalisers went beyond this to suggest that their programme would usher in a state of moral improvement and 'friendly cooperation', as well as stimulating economic activity by bringing more land into cultivation, a key argument of Clark's.[64] One subtly dissenting voice was Clark's friend, Helen Taylor, who argued that land nationalisation would not 'be a security against political corruption' or a 'cure for all political, moral, and social evils', which would have to wait for a 'general raising of the moral standard of human life', but that morally, economically, socially and politically it would do more to these ends than any other measure and it would remove a 'fundamental source of inequality . . . oppression and demoralisation'.[65]

Clark lived to see two minority Labour governments and also to observe the expansion of state ownership of land, not least through the work of the Board of Agriculture for Scotland in the aftermath of the Great War. This, however, did not constitute the realisation of his many pleas for the nationalisation of land. He is not a well-known figure today, even as land reform has come back onto the political agenda in Scotland, although in a manner much more moderate than he argued for over a century ago. He was an intensely controversial figure during his political career and his parliamentary service ended amid the hostility of the Caithness contest in the Khaki election of 1900 and accusations of unpatriotic activity.[66] In many ways, Clark was a maverick: he was distinctive among the Crofter MPs, he was regarded as extreme even among the 'Pro-Boers' and not much respected by his political opponents; Churchill called for him to be 'boarded and lodged at the public expense'.[67] One area where he was a key figure and very much in the mainstream, however, was in his advocacy of land nationalisation, an idea that crossed the boundaries of the nations of the United Kingdom in the late-Victorian period. It was also an idea that crossed political boundaries. That land nationalisation was not an exclusively Socialist idea in the Victorian period, but its longer-term influence was on the labour movement.[68] While Clark himself was not an especially influential figure, land nationalisation was also an idea which remained important to the left of the labour movement and central to their frequent disappointment with the performance on this issue during their periods of government, even from 1945 to 1951.[69]

Understanding the land nationalisation movement of the late nineteenth century, and the early nineteenth-century influences on it, is important for left-wing politics in the twentieth century.

NOTES

1. *Scotsman*, 6 September 1886, p. 4.
2. T. C. Smout, *A Century of the Scottish People, 1830–1950* (London, 1950), p. 253.
3. D. W. Crowley, 'The "Crofters" Party, 1885–92', *Scottish Historical Review*, 35 (1956), pp. 110–26; James Hunter, 'The politics of Highland land reform, 1873–95', *Scottish Historical Review*, 53 (1974), pp. 45–68; Ewen A. Cameron, *The Life and Times of Fraser-Mackintosh* (Aberdeen, 2000), pp. 206–17; Donald Meek, 'The Catholic knight of crofting: Sir Donald Horne MacFarlane, MP for Argyll, 1885–86, 1892–95', *Transactions of the Gaelic Society of Inverness*, 58 (1992–4), pp. 70–122; J. P. D. Dunbabin, 'Electoral reforms and their outcome in the United Kingdom 1865–1900', in Terence Richard Gourvish and Alan O'Day (eds), *Later Victorian Britain* (Basingstoke, 1988), pp. 93–126.
4. *Caithness Courier*, 12 October 1900; *John O'Groat Journal*, 12 October 1900; *Daily Mail*, 10, 12 October 1900; *Manchester Guardian*, 5, 12 October 1900; *Edinburgh Evening News*, 10, 12 October 1900.
5. *Forward*, 30 November, 21 December 1918.
6. Thomas Johnston, 'Dr G. B. Clark: The passing of a pioneer', *Forward*, 12 July 1930; for other obituaries, see *British Medical Journal*, 19 July 1930, pp. 126–7; *The Lancet*, 19 July 1930, p. 168.
7. Clark features prominently in Arthur Davey, *The British Pro Boers, 1877–1902* (Cape Town, 1978).
8. G. B. Clark, *A Plea for the Nationalisation of Land* (Glasgow, 1882); G. B. Clark, *The Land and the People: A Plea for Nationalisation* (Manchester, 1918).
9. He can also be found at meetings of the London Inverness-shire Association, *Scotsman*, 18 May 1882, p. 6.
10. Clark, 'Recollections', *Forward*, 27 August 1910.
11. Ewen A. Cameron, 'Clark, Gavin Brown (1846–1930), politician', *Oxford Dictionary of National Biography*, https://doiorg.ezproxy.is.ed.ac.uk/10.1093/ref:odnb/47107; W. J. de Kock (ed.), *Dictionary of South African Biography* (Cape Town, 1968), i, p. 168; M. Espinasse, 'Gavin Brown Clark', in J. M. Bellamy and J. Saville (eds), *Dictionary of Labour Biography* (London, 1981), iv, pp. 59–61.
12. For attempts to deal with the land question across these national boundaries, see J. P. D. Dunbabin, *Rural Discontent in 19th Century Britain* (London, 1974); Matthew Cragoe and Paul A. Readman (eds), *The Land Question in Britain, 1750–1950* (Basingstoke, 2010); David W. Howell,

'The Land Question in nineteenth-century Wales, Ireland and Scotland: A comparative study', *Agricultural History Review*, 61 (2013), pp. 83–110; Ewen A. Cameron, 'Communication or separation? Reactions to Irish land agitation and legislation in the Highlands of Scotland, c. 1870–1910', *English Historical Review*, 120 (2005), pp. 633–66.

13. Themes relating to the Highlands are prominent in six of the eighteen articles that constitute the 'Rambling recollections': 13, 20 August, 1, 8, 22 October, 26 November 1910.
14. Kilmarnock was a noted centre of Chartism: W. Hamish Fraser, *Chartism in Scotland* (Pontypool, 2010), pp. 40, 53, 60, 62–3.
15. Clark 'Recollections', *Forward*, 11 June 1910, p. 1.
16. Donald J. Withrington, 'From godly commonwealth to Christian state, c. 1850–c. 1920', in J. Kirk (ed.), *The Scottish Churches and the Union Parliament, 1707–1999* (Edinburgh, 2001), pp. 103–24; Donald J. Withrington, 'The churches in Scotland, c. 1870–1900: Towards a new social conscience', *Records of the Scottish Church History Society*, 19 (1975–7), pp. 155–68; Stewart J. Brown, 'Reform, reconstruction, reaction: The social vision of Scottish presbyterianism, c. 1830–c. 1930', *Scottish Journal of Theology*, 44 (1991), pp. 489–517.
17. Gregory Claeys, *Citizens and Saints: Politics and Anti-politics in Early British Socialism* (Cambridge, 1989), p. 12.
18. Alfred Russel Wallace, *My Life: A Record of Events and Opinions* (London, 1905), i, pp. 87–105.
19. David Stack, 'Out of "the limbo of 'unpractical politics'"': The origins and essence of Wallace's advocacy of land nationalization', and Gregory Claeys, 'Wallace and Owenism', both in Charles H. Smith and George Beccaloni (eds), *Natural Selection and Beyond: The Intellectual Legacy of Alfred Russel Wallace* (Oxford, 2008), pp. 279–304; Greta Jones, 'Alfred Russel Wallace, Robert Owen and the theory of natural selection', *British Journal for the History of Science*, 35 (2002), pp. 73–96.
20. Elaine W. McFarland, *John Ferguson 1836–1906: Irish Issues in Scottish Politics* (East Linton, 2003), p. 30.
21. Clark, 'Recollections', *Forward*, 18 June 1910.
22. John Saville, 'Jones, Ernest Charles (1819–69), radical and writer', *ODNB*, https://doi-org.ezproxy.is.ed.ac.uk/10.1093/ref:odnb/15000.
23. Miles Taylor, *Ernest Jones, Chartism and the Romance of Politics 1819–1869* (Oxford, 2003), pp. 141–6, 232–4.
24. Clark, 'Recollections', *Forward*, 18 June 1910; on the democracy debate, see Taylor, *Jones*, pp. 222–6; Stuart Wallace, *John Stuart Blackie: Scottish Scholar and Patriot* (Edinburgh, 2006), pp. 235–6.
25. Andrew G. Newby, *Ireland, Radicalism and the Scottish Highlands, c. 1870–1912* (Edinburgh, 2007), p. 31; Ewen A. Cameron, 'Sutherland, Angus (1848–1922), politician', *ODNB*, https://doi-org.ezproxy.is.ed.ac.uk/10.1093/ref:odnb/58136.

26. Malcolm Chase, 'Chartism and the land: "The mighty people's question"', in Cragoe and Readman (eds), *The Land Question in Britain, 1750–1950*, pp. 57–73; Malcolm Chase, '"Wholesome object lessons": The Chartist land plan in retrospect', *English Historical Review*, 118 (2003), pp. 59–85.
27. Clark, 'Recollections', *Forward*, 18 June 1910.
28. Ibid.
29. Ibid.
30. *Scotsman*, 21 February 1884, p. 7; 12 September 1885, p. 8.
31. Clark, 'Recollections', *Forward*, 13 August 1910; Wallace, *My Life*, ii, p. 240.
32. Duke of Argyll, 'The Prophet of San Francisco', *Nineteenth Century*, 15 (1884), pp. 553–5; Henry George, 'The "reduction to iniquity"', *Nineteenth Century*, 16 (1884), pp. 134–55. I have explored this territory in two essays: '"It was not a crofter question, it was more gigantic": political networks in the Scottish Highlands in the 1880s', in Michel Byrne and Sheila Kidd (eds), *Liontan Lionmhor: Local, National and Global Gaelic Networks from the 18th to the 20th Century* (Glasgow, 2019), pp. 175–200; and 'Poverty, protest and politics: Perceptions of the Scottish Highlands in the 1880s', in D. Broun and M. Macgregor (eds), *Miorun Mor nan Gall, The Great Ill-Will of the Lowlander: Lowland Perceptions of the Scottish Highlands* (Glasgow, 2009), pp. 218–48. Duke of Argyll, 'Land reformers', *Contemporary Review*, 48 (1885), pp. 470–9; Argyll, *The Unseen Foundations of Society: An Examination of the Fallacies and Failures of Economic Science due to Neglected Elements* (London, 1893); J. W. Mason, 'Political economy and the response to socialism in Britain, 1870–1914', *Historical Journal*, 23 (1980), pp. 565–87; J. W. Mason, 'The Duke of Argyll and the land question in late nineteenth-century Britain', *Victorian Studies*, 21 (1978), pp. 149–70; Kirsteen M. Mulhern, 'The intellectual duke: George Douglas Campbell, eighth Duke of Argyll, 1823–1900', unpublished PhD thesis (University of Edinburgh, 2006), pp. 190–232. For Georgite activity in the Highlands, see Andrew G. Newby, 'Edward McHugh, the National Land League of Great Britain and the "Crofters' War", 1879–1882', *Scottish Historical Review*, 82 (2003), pp. 74–91; for George's tours, see Charles Albro Barker, *Henry George* (New York, 1955), pp. 411–12.
33. Clark, 'Recollections', *Forward*, 2 July 1910.
34. G. B. Clark, 'The International: Recollections', *Socialist Review*, July–September 1914, p. 251.
35. Clark, 'Recollections', *Forward*, 2 July 1910.
36. Fabrice Bensimon, 'The IWMA and its precursors in London, c. 1830–1860', in Fabrice Bensimon, Quentin Deluermoz and Jeanne Moisand (eds), *'Arise Ye Wretched of the Earth': The First International in a Global Perspective* (Leiden, 2018), pp. 21–38; see also in the same collection, Gregory Claeys, 'Professor Beesly, Positivism and the International: The Patriotism

Question', pp. 332–42, and Detlev Mares, 'Little Local Difficulties? The General Council of the IWMA as an Arena for British Radical Politics', pp. 39–53. Margot C. Finn, *After Chartism: Class and Nation in English Radical Politics, 1848–1874* (Cambridge, 1993), pp. 227–34.
37. Clark, *Plea*, p. 9; G. B. Clark, *The Highland Land Question* (London, 1885), p. 3.
38. Clark, 'Recollections', *Forward*, 13 August 1910.
39. James Hunter (ed.), *For the People's Cause: From the Writings of John Murdoch, Highland and Irish Land Reformer* (Edinburgh, 1986); Cameron, *Fraser-Mackintosh*, pp. 205–17; Ben Thomas, '"The Clach": Alexander Mackenzie and the Land Question in the late-nineteenth century Highlands and Islands', *Northern Scotland*, 8 (2017), pp. 68–86.
40. Clark, 'Recollections', *Forward*, 16 July 1910, 13 August 1910; see also Clark, *Plea*, p. 12.
41. British Library, Add Ms 56435, f. 210, Clark to Wallace, 6 February 1871; Add Ms 56440, f. 327, Clark to Wallace, 16 March 1898. The earlier letter also discusses spiritualism, a believer in which Clark seems to have been.
42. For a good account of this, see Janet Smith, 'Helen Taylor's work for land nationalisation in Great Britain and Ireland 1879–1907: Women's political agency in the British Victorian land movement', *Women's History Review*, 27 (2018), pp. 778–98.
43. *Report of the Land Nationalisation Society, 1881/3* (London, 1883), p. 9; *The Radical*, 24 June 1882, 1 July 1882. Clark was also prominent in the Land Reform Union, a body with a broader canopy, covering land nationalisers as well as those interested in the reform of tenure: *Christian Socialist*, June 1883, p. 10 and Supplement, pp. i–iv.
44. Alfred Russel Wallace, *Land Nationalisation, Its Necessity and its Aims: Being a Comparison of the System of Landlord and Tenant with that of Occupying Ownership in their Influence on the Well-Being of the People* (London, 1882), pp. 175–233.
45. Clark, *Plea*, p. 5.
46. Ibid., pp. 8–9; the iniquity of sport was one of his most common themes: Clark, *Land and the People*, p. 7; Clark, 'Recollections', *Forward*, 1 October 1910; Clark, *The Land Question in Scotland* (Glasgow, 1911); Clark, 'The land problem in the Highlands', *Nineteenth Century and After*, 76 (1914), p. 136.
47. Clark, *Plea*, p. 16.
48. Ibid., p. 28.
49. Ibid., p. 34.
50. He returned to this theme in 1918: Clark, *Land and the People*, pp. 2, 4.
51. Clark, *Plea*, pp. 39–40.
52. Clark, *Land and the People*, p. 8.
53. Wallace, *Land Nationalisation*, pp. 29–30.
54. Alfred McDonnell, *Landlords' Rights and Englishmen's Wrongs: Being*

a Reply to a Pamphlet by Samuel Smith Erroneously entitled 'The Nationalisation of the Land' (London, 1883), p. 3.
55. Henry George, *Progress and Poverty: An Inquiry in the Cause of Industrial Depressions, and of Increase of Want with Increase of Wealth – The Remedy*, Book VII, chapter 2; see also the views of an author from the English Land Restoration League, a Georgite body, John Sketchley, *Land – Common Property* (London, 1881).
56. Arthur Arnold, *The Land and the People* (Manchester, 1887), pp. 3–4; Charles Wicksteed, *Our Mother Earth: A Short Statement of the Case for Land Nationalisation* (London, 1892), pp. 2, 17–18.
57. Clark, *Plea*, p. 34.
58. Wallace, *Land Nationalisation*, pp. 197–200; Wallace, *Note on Compensation to Landlords*, LNS Tract, No xvi, 1888, in which he defended the device of the terminable annuity.
59. *Justice*, 11 November 1884; A. Boyle, *The Right of the State to Control All Monopolies of Necessary Articles* (London, 1888), p. 8; Henry Fawcett, *State Socialism and the Nationalisation of the Land* (London, 1883), p. 24; Lord Bramwell, *Nationalisation of Land: A Review of Mr Henry George's 'Progress and Poverty'* (London, 1883), published by the Liberty and Property Defence League, an organisation which attacked all forms of state intervention, including the provision of seats for shop girls: see Edward Bristow, 'The Liberty and Property Defence League and individualism', *Historical Journal*, 18 (1975), pp. 761–89; J. C. Spence, *Property in Land: A Defence of Individual Ownership* (London, 1897), also published by the LPDL; Isaac B. Cooke, *'Progress and Poverty': A Reply to Mr Henry George* (Liverpool, 1884); Samuel Smith, *The Nationalisation of the Land* (London, 1884).
60. *The Ethics of Compensation (to Dispossessed Landlords)*, LNS Tract, No. xxxii, June 1890.
61. Joseph Hyder, *The Crux of the Land Question: Compensation to Landlords* (London, 1899), p. 5, published by the LNS. Hyder noted that landlords could not be held solely responsible for the system when 'the great mass of unthinking landless people who send a majority of landlords and friends of landlords to parliament at every chance they get'.
62. Hyder, *Crux*, pp. 9–10; see also his *The Curse of Landlordism and How to Remove it* (London, 1897); Henry W. Ley, *Land Nationalisation: Who Shows the Way?: Henry George, Thomas Spence, Thomas Paine or Alfred Russell Wallace?* (London, 1888): since Ley had been Secretary of the LNS in the 1880s, the answer to his question was obvious; Charles Wicksteed, *The Land for the People: How to Obtain It and How to Manage It* (London, 1885).
63. A. J. Ogilvy, *Land Nationalisation* (Manchester, 1890), p. 17.
64. Ibid., p. 36; John Vivian, *Land Monopoly and Its Evils* (Truro, 1891), pp. 15–16.

65. Helen Taylor, *Nationalisation of the Land*, LNS Tract, No. xix, 1887.
66. Paul A. Readman, 'The Conservative Party, patriotism, and British politics: The case of the General Election of 1900', *Journal of British Studies*, 40 (2001), pp. 107–45.
67. *Manchester Guardian*, 29 July 1901, p. 7.
68. Paul Readman, *Land and Nation in England, Patriotism, National Identity and the Politics of Land, 1880–1914* (Woodbridge, 2008), pp. 126–9.
69. Claire V. J. Griffiths, *Labour and the Countryside: The Politics of Rural Britain, 1918–1939* (Oxford, 2007), pp. 230–2; Kevin Manton, 'The Labour Party and the Land Question, 1919–51', *Historical Research*, 79 (2006), pp. 247–69; Michael Tichelar, 'Socialists, Labour and the land: The response of the Labour Party to the Land Campaign of Lloyd George before the First World War', *Twentieth Century British History*, 8 (1997), pp. 127–44; Michael Tichelar, 'The Labour Party and land reform in the inter-war period', *Rural History*, 13 (2002), pp. 85–101; Michael Tichelar, 'The conflict over property rights during the Second World War: The Labour Party's abandonment of land nationalization', *Twentieth Century British History*, 14 (2003), pp. 165–88; Michael Tichelar, 'The Labour Party, agricultural policy and the retreat from rural land nationalisation during the Second World War', *Agricultural History Review*, 51 (2003), pp. 209–25.

5

The Rhetoric and Politics of Land Redistribution in Southern Ireland,* 1919–1923: National and Local Perspectives

Terence Dooley

INTRODUCTION

ERNIE O'MALLEY (1897–1957), REVOLUTIONARY, politician, intellectual and writer, was born in the rural county of Mayo, raised in Dublin city, and during the War of Independence came to understand what access to land meant to the country people he moved among as an IRA organiser. In his highly praised memoir of the conflict, *On another man's wound* (1936), described as 'the outstanding literary achievement of the Anglo-Irish War' and 'perhaps the finest account that has ever been written about that period',[1] he articulated his sense of that importance:

> There was a strange passionate love of the land amongst the people. Material possessions were low or gone, the arts were a broken tradition, the ideal of beauty had gone into the soil and the physical body. Their eyes had long dwelt on the form, colour and structure of the landscape. It had become personal; its praise had been sung by joyous or despairing poets, and had been felt by the people. An old soil well-loved had given much to them, and they had put much into it. They clung to this last treasure and solace with imagination and with physical senses.[2]

The ordinary IRA volunteer, with a very basic education, drawn from a small farmer or landless labourer background, might have struggled to grasp all of O'Malley's intellectual eloquence, but the same volunteer would have fully understood the need to cling to the land, which was predicated upon the simple fact that in a non-industrial society, access to land was, for the many, the only form of livelihood, and a conduit for social respectability.

Thus, at the outbreak of the War of Independence in 1919, the landscape continued to whisper historical grievances that O'Malley could sense as he wandered through the countryside: 'There is a hunger for the soil, an elemental feeling that even the stranger or the foreigner can sense.'³ What he witnessed throughout Ireland – 'a hunger' for the land in Donegal; vivid 'memories of the bitter land war' in Clare; and, everywhere, that the countryman 'was sympathetic enough where a land revolution was concerned' – was no mere figment of his literary imagination; it was the reason why the War of Independence and Civil War period, 1919–23, had an agrarian dimension.⁴

The dramatic transfer of land ownership from landlord to tenant under various Irish land acts between 1870 and 1909 had not been the panacea to Ireland's land problems that many scholars have argued; the most pertinent issue was not 'peasant proprietorship' but farm viability. Moreover, the landless demanded access because they believed there was enough to go around, if equitably redistributed.⁵ The *Report of the Proceedings of the Irish Convention* published in 1918 might have been taken as cautionary advice.⁶ Basing its findings on Irish Land Commission statistics, the Convention showed that there were still 101,000 pending purchase cases covering an area of 3.3 million acres valued at £23.9 million, so not even land transfer had been completed by the beginning of the War of Independence. There were also 2.6 million acres that would remain unaffected by existing land legislation, namely demesne and untenanted lands (extensive swathes of which were let on the conacre system, or eleven-month system, rented at market value by the landlord each year to graziers). This accounted for around 25 per cent of the total agricultural land of Ireland and 36 per cent of the total valuation.⁷ There were 57,476 farmers of between 100 and 200 acres; 23,159 of between 200 and 500 acres; and 1,967 of 500 or more acres.⁸ The First World War had been exceptionally good to these large farmers: from the beginning of agricultural depression in the late 1870s up to 1914, the prices of Irish agricultural produce had remained stable, but there was an explosion in prices from 1914 to 1920.⁹ In any social revolution, these large farmers might feel under the same pressure as landlords who retained untenanted lands and demesnes, particularly if they were paying heed to what was happening across Europe from 1917.¹⁰ Most especially when one considers that the land acts had not addressed the inequalities of the Irish land system. When the Land Commission decided on a standard size for a farm to support a family, it set it at 23 acres of mixed land (or £20 valuation). It is very difficult to estimate with certainty the number of farms below that size in Ireland in 1919 because official government statistical returns up to then divided farms into categories of 10–15 acres, 15–30 acres and so on. (And, of course, farm size is not as dependable a gauge to viability as valuation, which determines land quality and, by extension, productivity.) However, if holdings below 30 acres are taken as a rough benchmark of viability in 1917, 65 per cent of the total number of farms in Ireland were below that acreage. Moreover, there were 226,468 farms below 15 acres and 112,787 below 5 acres.[11]

From 1917, 'land redistribution' was regenerated as a political catch-cry of revolutionaries, and, for a time, played a role in transforming Sinn Féin into a mass popular movement. The simple ideology promoted the dispossession of those who in the past had stood against Irish independence, or, regardless of politics, against the division of grasslands. Redistribution simultaneously promised farm viability, access to lands for the landless and agricultural labourers and revenge against the colonial usurpers or the graziers, and held out hope of a better way of life without having to leave Ireland. There was absolutely nothing new in this. During the Great Famine (1845–51), James Fintan Lalor, arguably the first agrarian radical, contended that as the conquest of Ireland had been political and economic, its undoing had to adopt a similar dual approach: economic freedom could only come with a revolutionary redistribution of Irish land.[12] The Young Irelanders gave publicity to his ideologies in the *Nation* in 1848; the Fenians supported, albeit tentatively, the principle of redistribution before their uprising in 1867.[13] The year before, Isaac Butt, who does not come readily to mind as a radical agrarianist, angrily propounded that 'The whole system of landed property is regarded by the great mass of the people as an alien institution, all its rights are looked upon as enforced by conquest, and maintained only by a foreign force.'[14] During the Land War of the 1880s, nationalist rhetoric, as espoused from Land League platforms, juxtaposed the 're-conquest' of the land of Ireland with national independence.[15] At the same time, the constitutional Irish Parliamentary Party under Charles Stewart Parnell was prepared to come together with agrarian radicals under Michael Davitt and separatists under John Devoy in the New Departure of 1878, that gave precedence to 'vigorous agitation of land question on basis of peasant proprietary' over Home Rule, and the party's grassroots organization, the United Irish League, continued the campaign for redistribution from the late nineteenth century, especially in the years after the passing of the 1903 Land Act.[16] Perhaps Devoy summed up best of all the relationship between land and revolution:

> The struggle with the English invaders had been as much a fight for land as for political supremacy, and, therefore, every uprising of the people after

the conquest partook largely of an agrarian character. The hope of driving back to England, or to perdition, the foreigner who played the rural tyrant and made their lives miserable, had as much to do with stimulating the Irish farmer and agricultural labourer to participation in revolutionary conspiracies, as any idea of the benefits to be derived from national self-government.[17]

Thus, in 1917–19, Sinn Féin propagandists such as Laurence Ginnell were ploughing old furrows when they traversed the country reinvigorating 'The land for the people campaign', advocating that 'the true remedy for the land problem' would only come with 'sovereign independence alone', and urging the young landless men to demand 'the distribution of these [grazier] lands as reparation for the past, for the general good of the country, for historical and other reasons transcending the cash value of the land'.[18] This type of rhetoric appealed to the aspirations of a young rural generation who began to consider that Irish independence might offer them a better quality of life. This was all happening simultaneously with other developments during and after the Great War – the conscription crisis, the shutdown of emigration, the closure of seasonal labour outlets in England and Scotland, the rise in the cost of living, continued rationing, demobilisation, the increase in unemployment, exploitation of the markets by greedy merchants, and the rise of the labour movement. The leading labour historian, Emmet O'Connor, has shown how widespread radicalism was at this time; 'Bolshevism', he argued, 'was a powerful inspiration.'[19] Kevin O'Shiel lived through the last land war and later recalled 'The astonishing intensification of deep, national feeling amongst the people, due to Sinn Féin propaganda . . . [which produced] a resultant determination, especially among the younger elements, to live at home at all costs, and on the land, if at all possible.'[20]

Not unexpectedly, the growing tide of agrarianism frightened the men of property: in November 1918, the RIC inspector general could sense 'the steady growth of Sinn Féin from a small body to . . . vast dimension' but noted that 'persons of stake' viewed 'this popular movement with apprehension'.[21] Calls for redistribution were made in the chambers of the newly established Dáil Éireann; on 4 April 1919, Alistair MacCabe moved and Countess Markievicz seconded that 'This assembly pledges itself to a fair and full redistribution of the vacant lands and ranches of Ireland among the uneconomic holders and landless men.'[22] However, there were also revolutionaries in the Dáil who were from propertied backgrounds, and when agrarianism spiralled out of control, the Sinn Féin 'respectables' realised they had created a Frankenstein monster – a metaphor sometimes used in the Victorian press to describe the Irish land question – that might rampage out of their control, and so they adopted a dual control mechanism: they sent the IRA into the most disaffected areas to put down the agrarianism and set up Dáil land courts to adjudicate on disputes.[23] These tactics met with considerable success in the War of Independence, but when the scale of agrarianism reached new heights in the Civil War period, the Free State government found another way through the legislative process to exert control, to wean people away from social revolution, and to accept the authority of the new state and give it international credibility: the 1923 Land Bill promised the compulsory acquisition and redistribution of lands.[24]

Most of these lands belonged to traditional aristocratic or gentry landlords: among the largest of the dozens of untenanted estates to be acquired and redistributed by the Land Commission between 1923 and 1936 were the 12,250-acre estate of Sir John Leslie in Donegal; the 5,714-acre Persse estate in Galway; the 3,888-acre estate of Lord Ashtown in the same county; and the 2,370-acre estate of Lord Cloncurry in Kildare.[25] Demesnes had come under tremendous pressure in the 1919–23 period, and demands for their acquisition and redistribution explained the motivation behind the burning of a great many of the three hundred Big Houses mapped to date.[26] This social dimension to the revolution has only gained traction in more recent times, since the publication of this author's *Decline of the Big House in Ireland* (2001).[27] Before that, it was a phenomenon almost completely ignored. Peter Hart, for example, following the Lynch argument of 1966, contended that 'not only did the Irish Revolution not bring social transformation, there was no socially revolutionary situation in Ireland even in prospect' because 'most farmers owned their farms by 1922'.[28] In his influential study of revolutionary Cork, Hart disregarded the fact that dozens of country houses were burned there, which is most surprising because he could not have missed Tom Barry's references to the same in *Guerilla Days in Ireland*. Barry described, with much triumphalism, the IRA's burning of Big Houses in reprisal for crimes perpetrated on Sinn Féin supporters by the Crown forces in Cork:

> Castles, mansions and residences were sent up in flames by the IRA immediately after the British fire gangs had razed the homes of Irish republicans. Our people were suffering in this competition of terror, but the British Loyalists were paying dearly, the demesne walls were tumbling and the British ascendancy was being destroyed.[29]

Furthermore, Barry also hinted that it was not all about politics or deeply ingrained ancestral grievances, for when the Britishers fled, the

IRA officers 'encouraged local landless men to settle on the lands and to use them'.[30]

When the Cumann na nGaedheal minister for agriculture, Patrick Hogan, introduced the Land Bill in May 1923, his party colleague, James Burke, did not have to explicate when he argued that 'implicit in this event alone is the undoing of the conquest of Ireland'.[31] Burke's monochromatic version simply morphed all conquests, colonisation schemes, plantations, centuries of complex political manoeuvrings and social engineering with land redistribution at their core, into one simple overarching narrative, concluding that it was time to take the land from the alien oppressors and return it to the deserving Gael. Hogan, and his friend and minister for justice Kevin O'Higgins, knew full well that the reality of 'undoing the conquest' could never match the rhetoric. Above all, they had to adopt a diplomatic approach in the interest of future international credit ratings.[32] In private, Hogan emphasised to Cosgrave that 'a considerable amount of the estates remaining unpurchased are small estates . . . These are all poor estates and anything like the terms demanded by the tenants would leave the owners with absolutely nothing, in fact would leave the estate insolvent and unable to pay their charges.'[33] And in the more public arena of the Dáil: 'No matter how obnoxious a landlord may be personally his legal position as vendor confers on him certain rights which cannot be ignored without running the risk of such diminution of the credit of the nation.'[34]

Not to understand why the first independent Irish government found it incumbent to prioritise the passing of a land act in 1923 is not to understand the Irish revolutionary period in its totality.[35] Adopting a local case-study approach, this chapter sets out to validate this argument. In doing so, it interrogates the relationship between the IRA and agrarianism at local level, where patriots and agrarianists, often one and the same, came together to stage their own micro revolution in the hope that it would lead to the final overthrow of the old order and the redistribution of lands. It can be argued that the government put a stop to this by using a coercion and conciliation approach; the Public Safety (Emergency Powers) Act worked in tandem with the Land Act, both passed almost simultaneously. By extension, the Irish revolution took a conservative course, not, as some may argue, because there was no prior potential for a social dimension, but rather because middle-class revolutionaries such as Hogan and Higgins stopped it in its tracks. But even that interpretation may be compared to observing a Breughel painting, admiring the broad canvas, but not seeing the detail of what the people were getting up to. Local studies are probably the best way to understand the Irish revolution and to reveal the anomalies.

LOCAL PERSPECTIVES

Under the 1903 Land Act, Edward John Beaumont-Nesbitt of Tubberdaly, Rhode, King's County had sold around 6,500 acres of his 8,000-acre estate. He retained his demesne because, other than life as a rentier, farming was all he knew, and he had no intention of leaving Ireland. He felt no need to do so; as a landlord, even during the long and often bitter Land War of the 1880s and 1890s, his relationship with his tenantry had remained stable.[36] However, in time, his retention of so much land, and his unionist politics, would become problematic. He got some hint of this on the eve of the first county council elections in Ireland, when on the last day of 1898 a letter appeared in the nationalist *Leinster Leader* from the anonymous 'Ratepayer':

> Mr Nesbitt is an Englishman who came to this country a few years ago, and during his short stay took such a lively interest in public affairs, and had the welfare of the country so much at heart, that when the last Home Rule Bill was before Parliament, he exerted himself so much as to organise a meeting in Edenderry to oppose a measure that would prove disastrous to the country. Mr Nesbitt's entire retinue of Scotch and English servants attended the meeting, and, like their master, signed a petition against Home Rule for a country of whose requirements they knew nothing.[37]

There were a number of grievances at play in this letter: firstly, Beaumont-Nesbitt was presented as an Englishman, an outsider, a new 'planter', who did not understand or care about Ireland. He was, in fact, born in Ulster and inherited the estate from his spinster aunt in the 1880s. 'Ratepayer' presented him as a staunch unionist. That was true. But his representation as sectarian and discriminatory towards Catholics in terms of his employment policy was more complex. As was the case with most landlords of the era, his house and estate management staff shared his religion and were often taken in from outside the area,[38] but those employed on the estate farm and mill were local Catholics, mainly from Rhode and the surrounding areas. The creation of myths that engendered hostility, especially those that had roots in the 1880s and were ready to ignite, had consequences.

The First World War brought great change to the family. Two of Beaumont-Nesbitt's sons fought and on 27 November 1917 the youngest son, Wilfrid (born 1894), a captain in the Grenadier Guards, was killed at Fontaine. It was a blow from which his parents struggled to recover.[39] For a time during the war, with Home Rule on the statute books, and southern unionist opposition and organisation on the decline, it looked as if there might be some local rapprochement between opposing parties. In March 1915, Beaumont-Nesbitt and the nationalist chairman of the county council convened a meeting in Tullamore, 'for the purpose of impressing upon the young people of the County the urgent duty which is cast upon them of joining the army in defence of their King and Country, in the present terrible crisis of the fortunes of the Empire'.[40] Any optimism was misplaced. In the family memory, the fallout from the Easter Rising of 1916 had a damaging effect on their local standing: Beaumont-Nesbitt's eldest son, Frederick, later recorded in his memoirs: 'I do not recall a single incident during my boyhood when hostility was shown either to myself or a member of my family, at least not until the outbreak of Easter week 1916.' It is more likely that 1916 became the site of memory for something that happened a few years later.

In 1919 the labourers on Tubberdaly's 240-acre demesne went on strike for four months for higher wages and better working conditions.[41] It was a growing trend in midland counties such as Offaly and neighbouring Kildare.[42] Three of the ringleaders were dismissed: Christopher Jones, a carpenter, John Connor, a labourer, and Matthew Geraghty, the sawyer. The rise of Sinn Féin, its success at the 1918 General Election, the establishment of Dáil Éireann, the speeches of the likes of Laurence Ginnell in the area, and the rise of Labour had changed the deferential landscape.

For years, Jones, who Beaumont-Nesbitt described as 'a jolly bad carpenter', had lived in one of the estate cottages rented from a tenant farmer who held around 35 acres. When the farmer emigrated, Beaumont-Nesbitt bought the tenant interest, grazed it, but allowed Jones to stay on in the cottage.[43] After initiating the strike, Beaumont-Nesbitt ordered Jones to vacate the cottage, but Jones stayed put. Beaumont-Nesbitt later told his sister that '... when the bad times came he [Jones] put stock on my land, turned mine off, and later on when I was letting the grazing, he threatened to shoot anyone who disturbed him'.[44] It was not until May 1921 that Beaumont-Nesbitt got a decree for possession of the cottage but, as he put it, 'owing to the state of the country' he was unable to enforce it. Beaumont-Nesbitt would later write of Jones: 'He has given me all the trouble he can ever since he was unemployed, and I look upon him as the ringleader of most of the attempts to damage my property.'[45]

Those attempts were numerous. On 11 July 1921, the morning on which the Anglo-Irish truce was called, Beaumont-Nesbitt's Scottish estate steward, Lewis Fraser, was attacked by a gang of men who came to his home. He made good his escape, but his house was burned down. The following month he was replaced by Henry McMullan. Full of bravado, McMullan called all the employees together and told them that 'if Jones was allowed to so graze the lands, it would lead to others doing the same, and eventually Mr Nesbitt might be forced to give up the lands with the result that they would be out of employment'. He asked the men to help him drive Jones' cattle off the demesne. Most complied, but there was a cohort of around seven who did not. That night a group of around that size called to McMullan's house, dragged him out, and threatened to shoot him.[46] Jones was not in the gang, but McMullan would later claim that he instigated it, that the men who threatened to shoot him said 'Jones had no place else to put his cattle'.[47]

The culmination of the hostilities was the burning of Tubberdaly on 15 April 1923, during the Civil War. A number of points need to be made here in relation to the wider national picture. As studies by Gemma Clark and Gavin Foster have shown, the Civil War changed the landscape of everyday violence, including a rise in agrarian crime, a rise that greatly disturbed Patrick Hogan and Kevin O'Higgins.[48] Related to this was the escalation in country house burnings, twice as many as during the War of Independence and more geographically dispersed.[49] In many areas, motivations were increasingly driven by land issues, including in Offaly, where Ciarán Reilly has found 'land related issues played a predominant role'.[50] Reilly references a meeting of Tullamore rural district council in April 1923, held about a week after Tubberdaly was burned, where Councillor Dunne boasted (mistakenly) that Offaly led the way in Big House burnings and put it down to the fact that 'it had been the most planted part of the country', thereby associating such actions with the undoing of the Tudor colonisation scheme of the sixteenth century. However, the editor of the *Midland Tribune* rebuked Dunne: 'the burnings in Offaly is not a matter to boast of', he wrote, 'land hunger and not the Gaelic state or republic was the motive of a good many of them'.[51]

It is challenging to ascribe any single motivation to the burning of a country house. Tubberdaly is no exception. Beaumont-Nesbitt himself claimed there was a political dimension. When filling in a compensation appeal form for the Irish Grants Committee, an organisation established in London in 1922 to assist refugees from Ireland, and later to grant interim loans while they awaited compensation payments, he wrote:

'I was Lord Lieutenant of the county and well-known as a Unionist, and the policy of the republican party in the Free State at the time was to select Unionists for reprisals when they destroyed property. I am satisfied that it was the primary cause . . .' However, that was in answer to the question, was the burning 'occasioned in respect or on account of your allegiance to the Government of the UK?'[52] That was a prerequisite for compensation in the first place.

There are those who believe that the burning should be linked to the execution of two local anti-treatyites, Joseph Byrne and Patrick Geraghty, on 27 January 1923, under the Public Safety Act of November 1922. While it is true that the Offaly IRA reputedly burned a number of big houses as a reprisal for these executions, including Greenhills, where 'the leader announced they were republicans who had come to burn the house as a reprisal for the execution of Patrick Geraghty', the burning of Tubberdaly was almost two months after the executions, so the reprisal motive can almost certainly be ruled out.[53]

It does not mean that anti-treatyites were not involved. Jones' son, also Christopher, was certainly a member of the IRA. His IRA pension application form shows he was a member of the 1st Offaly Brigade, 3rd Battalion, D Company between 1 April 1920 and 30 September 1923, for which he successfully received a pension under the Military Service Pensions Act, 1949, and a Service (1917–21) Medal without Bar. Jones' witnesses included Patrick Cox, formerly OC of D Company, and Col. Liam Egan, OC of the Eastern Command. Jones claimed active service as a dispatch courier, took part in raids for arms, blocked roads and participated in attacks on several RIC Barracks. The file also claims that he was on the run from April 1921, arrested and beaten by British forces in May 1921, and interned in Hare and Rath camps until his release in November 1921.[54]

After the Truce, he took the anti-treaty side. His record claims he was on the run with an Active Service Unit (Flying Column) before he was imprisoned successively in Templemore, County Tipperary, Newbridge and the Curragh in Kildare from October 1922 until February 1924. The summary makes no mention of his role in the burning of Tubberdaly. However, the pension file of his sister, Mary Swords, is open. She was a captain in the 3rd Battalion of the Offaly Cumann na mBan.[55] According to Col. Liam Egan: 'She was a member of the Jones family of Tubberdaly, all of whom rendered constant and unselfish service to the National Cause.'[56] On her active service record are listed the 'Destruction of Ballyburly and Greenhill Houses' and the 'Destruction of Tubberdaly House'.[57] Significantly, Patrick Cox witnessed that she had acted as lookout for the IRA when they burned Frazer's house at Tubberdaly.[58]

Mary Swords' role in the burning of country houses and the attack on Frazer were obviously acknowledged as acts of patriotic endeavour. However, some of the local IRA were not just fighting patriots, they may also have been agrarianists with a specific agenda. On 2 July 1923, Eamonn Coogan, the Garda Deputy Commissioner, wrote a revealing report to O'Higgins' department of home affairs: 'The trouble is not strictly labour ... The campaign was originated with a view to terrorizing Mr Nesbitt and his employees and ultimately to succeed by such methods to have the ranch divided up and distributed.'[59]

Local land issues, entwined with labour disputes, therefore provided the main motivation for the burning of Tubberdaly. The burning took place after three years of local agrarian unrest in the midst of civil unrest, which provided the opportunity to burn the house in order to ensure that Beaumont-Nesbitt would not return. Jones and his followers, including the Geraghtys, had been occupying demesne buildings and lands. Two successive stewards had been intimidated, threatened with murder, and eventually driven away from Tubberdaly. Nesbitt himself had been forced to exile in London, though he remained relatively unperturbed. He told the Irish Grants Committee in 1926: 'I am in quite comfortable circumstances and have a sufficient income not to have been more than inconvenienced by what has occurred.'[60] It is legitimate to argue, therefore, that Christopher Jones Sr, his followers and his own children decided to take advantage of the times to improve their status in life, which, in truth, was probably what most young IRA men had hoped the War of Independence and, if necessary, the Civil War, would do for them. Tubberdaly illustrates a mercenary aspect adopted by some; there is no reason to see that as casting aspersions on those members of the IRA who were motivated by patriotic fervour. But one has to accept there were plenty of people as interested in their own social and economic gain as in the attainment of a republic. Students of IRA pension files will have to be able to read between many lines.

After the burning, sometime in May 1923, Beaumont-Nesbitt had written to the Irish government telling them of his situation. The government was in the process of preparing the new land bill. Two weeks before the burning of Tubberdaly, Patrick Hogan had informed W. T. Cosgrave that land grabbing by 'landless men who would not be entitled to land under any scheme' had become endemic.[61] (Eunan O'Halpin thinks Hogan 'wildly exaggerated' his claims but that very much remains to be seen.[62]) Hogan made it clear to Cosgrave that the landless men have 'neither a first nor a second claim to land'.⁶³ In other words, the lowest rural class was not to be catered for, a result replicated in land reform legislation in Scotland from the 1880s also.

The middle-class conservatives within Sinn Féin had come to prominence, and Hogan and Kevin O'Higgins, minister for home affairs, were among the more influential. They both came from respectable middle-class landed and professional backgrounds. Educated at elite private schools and then UCD, they had no respect for the aims or methods of agrarian agitators.⁶⁴ Before the Civil War broke out in earnest, and in reaction to reports of increased agrarian crime, O'Higgins asked: 'What lies ahead? Civil War? A social revolution?'⁶⁵ The Civil War followed but O'Higgins was determined that there would be no social revolution. Later he wrote a piece called 'Mexican politics', in which he clearly indicated that he wanted no peasant revolt, as had happened in Mexico under Emiliano Zapata (1879–1919).⁶⁶ At the very time that Christopher Jones Sr's activities in Tubberdaly were being reported to his office, O'Higgins made public his contempt for the men who had 'gone out in an entirely selfish, wilful and criminal spirit to seize land by the strong hand'.⁶⁷ He promised to 'bring to bear on the Minister for Agriculture, and whatever influence I can bring to bear upon the Executive Council . . . to seeing that such people do not benefit by this Act'.⁶⁸ On 14 June 1923, he told the Dáil:

> They cannot have law and violence. They cannot have an act and their own plunder and, in so far as I can secure it, I will see that they do not have it . . ., and by the time this bill reaches its closing stages, I hope to be able to assure the Dáil that there is not in any county, over which we have for the time being responsibility and jurisdiction, one acre of land in the possession of any person but the legal owner.⁶⁹

The politics of land redistribution were now being used to threaten any potential enemies of the state. This was resented by socialist republicans such as Peadar O'Donnell, who would later write that: 'All the leadership wanted was a change from British to Irish government; they wanted no change in the basis of society.'⁷⁰ And IRA volunteers came to see this clearly themselves. Thomas Carragher, who fought in the War of Independence in Monaghan, later reminisced eloquently:

> During the period of the Truce, the politicians and respectables took over. It was they who interpreted our dream, the dream we fought for. It was they would decide the terms to which we must agree. In the mind of every soldier was a little republic of his own in which he was the hero. But his dream was shattered. The process-server that he once made easy to talk to was back in

business, the same gripper, the same sheriff with the same old laws while the little hero was back at his plough.[71]

Of course, Hogan also had to consider the future of the agricultural economy. In early July, he met with Beaumont-Nesbitt in Dublin.[72] Prior to the meeting, an inspector of the Land Settlement Department had reported to Hogan on the importance of Beaumont-Nesbitt's thoroughbred Aberdeen Angus herd and advised that he 'should get ample protection for this herd and his splendid yards etc.'.[73] He further pointed out that Beaumont-Nesbitt's yearly wage bill was at least £1,400.[74] He suggested the arrest of Jones and four others.[75] Almost concurrently, on 10 July, Beaumont-Nesbitt received a letter from Jones:

> Sir, This is the fourth letter I wrote you. Got no reply about the farm. I have my case entered this two years. I expect you have a letter from IRA Headquarters. I am going to cut the meadows. I have no other means. I'll pay you for grass and clear you of all debts. I am willing to buy the farm honestly as no one else will be allowed to do so.[76]

It deserves a little unpacking: Jones presumably had made application to Beaumont-Nesbitt to buy the farm he was occupying (that went with the cottage). Beaumont-Nesbitt could have sold it to him, as he had purchased the tenant right from the farmer who had emigrated to America. But he was not prepared to facilitate Jones, a fact he made clear in his letter to Mrs Savage-Armstrong:

> There are several of my old labourers whom I want to help as much as I can, and if I do sell I think that I can arrange that these get helped first, and thereby I can put a spoke in the wheels of some that I do not want to help. I am quite philosophic about it all, I've had my innings and am out now, and if I can help any decent men to get a living out of the wreck, that is all I care about.[77]

Jones was willing to act in a reasonable manner, as he saw it, by paying for the cut meadow. As in the Land League days, he anticipated that no outsider would bid on the farm, and he could claim, with some authority, that he had the local anti-treatyite IRA behind him.

On 13 July 1923, Hogan wrote to O'Higgins: 'Mr Nesbitt is a very useful man, a first class farmer and employs a very large number of labourers, and he has done a lot for livestock in this country. It is a case that should be dealt with very firmly and I think it would be well to get a report from the Committee of Order as to the present condition.'[78] The letter suggested Cumann na nGaedheal's empathy for the large farming class, which was to be much derided by their political opponents in the years ahead. Hogan followed the communication up on 14 July with a note to O'Higgins: 'Jones is the principal cause of the trouble down there and he should be arrested at once. Could you have that arranged?'[79] It was just over two weeks before the 1923 Land Act was passed on 3 August. O'Higgins had to stand by his Dáil speech of 28 May: '[any persons] who go out in defiance of the law or in defiance of the Parliament to press their claims by their own violence and their own illegalities [would] be placed definitely outside the benefits of this Bill'.[80]

On 24 July 1923, Jones was charged at Tullamore with being 'in illegal possession of a farm of land, the property of Mr Nesbitt' and remanded in custody to Tullamore District Court Sessions on 3 August.[81] According to Garda William Hickey of Rhode, Jones said to him: 'Ye are no Irishmen to come and arrest me. I wrote to Mr Nesbitt on three or four occasions offering him a price for the land, but he never replied to any of my letters. I had to find some means of living.'[82] The date of the remand hearing was significant. It was two days after the government enacted the Public Safety (Emergency Powers) Act on 1 August 1923. The Act was directed against all enemies of the Free State government who 'have created a spirit of rebellion'. Among the crimes punishable by arrest, imprisonment and whipping were 'wrongful entry on and retention of possession of land without color [sic] or pretence of title or authority'.[83] When Jones came back before the Tullamore court, he was charged with 'unlawfully and by force entering the lands of Tubberdaly ... and retaining the land by force and excluding Mr Nesbitt by force and threats from the use of the lands from Sept[ember] 1922, to the present time'.[84] However, Jones, who had no legal representation, was released on bail to be returned for trial at a later date. A frustrated Deputy Commissioner Coogan pointed out that because Jones' offence took place before 3 August, 'he could not be made amenable under the Public Safety Act'.[85] To Coogan, Jones was 'a thoroughly lawless scoundrel, and his family being connected with the Irregulars, he would get a certain amount of assistance from that section of the people in the locality'.[86] The guards were trying 'to detect him in an offence punishable under the Public Safety Act' but 'no overt act could be traced to him'.[87]

Beaumont-Nesbitt was now in residence in Penton Lodge in Hampshire. Under the Damage to Property (Compensation) Act he claimed £24,574 (with separate claims for other properties bringing it up to around £35,000) for the destruction of Tubberdaly. He was awarded only £8,100.[88] Like many of other burned-out country house owners, he was not prepared to accept a 'reinstatement clause' that would have forced him to rebuild on the original site, even though he would have received considerably more. He was resigned to all of this, accepting that 'there is no use trying to fight out my corner' and that 'if I started to rebuild or build anything new, I should just be robbed'.[89] He may have been misinformed that the Irish people were asking 'when [will] the English come back?' but more accurate in his assessment that 'the so-called Free State is broke, and that for generations there will be poverty and want far greater than ever occurred in the remembrance of anyone now living'.[90]

He never returned to Ireland. In 1925 the Land Commission purchased the demesne and paid Beaumont-Nesbitt £8,138, of which £2,038 was in cash and £6,100 in 5 per cent compensation stock (which he sold for £5,777).[91] Many years later, when his grandson, Brian, visited the ruins of Tubberdaly in 1991, he felt 'a mixture of anger against the blackguards who burned it, nostalgia for something I never knew – and regret that the site had been invaded by so many buildings ...'.[92] When around the same time, this author spoke with a descendant of one of 'the blackguards', resident on the demesne, he had a very different remembrance: 'We burned the bastards out!'

After Jones' trial in August 1923, the sources are very confusing, a confusion that could be avoided if the Land Commission records were made readily available to researchers. It is not clear who was in charge at this stage: the state or local power brokers? In June 1924, Jones was before the Tullamore quarter sessions again. He was now described as 'a small farmer' but the charge remained the same.[93] This time he pleaded guilty to trespass and his solicitor argued 'there were certain mitigating circumstances in the case. Accused like a good many other people at the time, foolishly thought he could get a bit of land, he put his cows on Mr Nesbitt's farm.'[94] The judge discharged him with a fine of £50.[95] On 24 July 1924, Coogan wrote to the secretary of the department of justice that the farm Jones had grabbed was now 'quite derelict ... neither used by the owner nor is it let to tenants and is in that position for the past eighteen months'. No one had interfered with it since Jones was first arrested in July 1923.[96] Presumably Jones did not work it, fearing consequences under the Special Powers Act, but neither would anyone else touch it. In 1925 Beaumont-Nesbitt claimed that Jones, 'with a good many' of Beaumont-Nesbitt's former labourers, 'decided that if any dividing up takes place no one is to come in until they are satisfied'.[97]

AFTERLIVES

And, it seems, no one did. For almost ten years, the Cumann na nGaedheal government failed to deal with the redistribution of the Tubberdaly demesne. In many other areas it had used the 1923 Land Act as an opportunity to distribute patronage through the redistribution of lands, but equally a lethargic approach protected the large holders, allowing the traditional rural elites to emerge again to social and political prominence and thereby prevent the feared social revolution on the horizon.[98] The Act was also used to punish the supporters of the anti-treaty side by excluding them from redistribution schemes, as they were excluded from many other spheres of employment.[99]

By late 1931, the writing was on the wall for the government; the country was fed up with austerity, and rural Ireland was frustrated with the delays in land redistribution so much promised in 1917–23. Fianna Fáil was on the rise, and expediting land redistribution was at the core of its rural policies. In 1926 De Valera had told the Fianna Fáil *ard fheis* that it was the party's aim 'to complete land purchase, break up the large grazing ranches, and distribute them as economic farms amongst young men and agricultural labourers, such as those compelled at present to emigrate'.[100]

Revealingly, it was not until October 1931 that a meeting was held in Rhode to form a branch of Cumann na nGaedheal, a case perhaps of locking the stable door after the horse had bolted. John O'Connor lamented the 'very strange' and 'long promised distribution of the lands of Tubberdaly', and that 'since the place was put in the hands of the Land Commission there was a decided change for the worse'.[101] It was more stagnation than change; and O'Connor only felt comfortable in hinting at it: 'Some strange things had happened which were not for the good of the people of the district.'[102] These may never be revealed but undoubtedly there had been local issues that no Land Commission inspector could solve, at least not before he sanctioned the title of those who had grabbed the land ten years before.

At that Cumann na nGaedheal meeting there was no mention of Joneses or Geraghtys who had continued to reside on the demesne, staunch Fianna Fáil supporters. Jones' sister, Mary, told the IRA pensions board that her brother 'has been an ardent worker for F[ianna] F[áil] all down the years'.[103] In February 1932, Fianna Fáil came to power, and a month or so later, De Valera released all political prisoners, allowed the order declaring the IRA illegal to lapse, and suspended the tribunal set up by the Cosgrave administration to deal with political crime. Three months later, the new minister for lands and fisheries, former republican P. J. Ruttledge, replied to an answer in the Dáil that a scheme for the redistribution of the Tubberdaly demesne would be 'put into operation at an early date'.[104] A month later, the newly elected Fianna Fáil representatives, Patrick Boland and P. J. Gorry, met with a 'large deputation', including the 'uneconomic holders of Rhode', to hear an 'important development in connection with the proposed distribution of the lands of Tubberdaly'.[105] The meeting was chaired by Patrick Cox, Christopher Jones Jr's former IRA officer, who had supplied references for him and his sister. John O'Connor turned up at this meeting as well; there was nothing like a land division scheme to overcome party loyalty. O'Connor said those present 'did not deplore the going of such as he [Beaumont-Nesbitt] from Ireland, but they did deplore the fact that nothing had been done to substitute the livelihood got from him'.[106] The irony of the comment was lost on himself.

The following year, Fianna Fáil introduced its own Land Act, and changed the hierarchy of allottees, giving preference to discharged labourers, uneconomic holders in the immediate vicinity of the estate being divided and landless men 'of a deserving class'. Preference in all categories was to be given to IRA veterans.[107] In the Dáil, Hogan was scathing: 'You are accepting landless men quite apart from herds and other suitable persons. That is good politics, I admit, but it is rotten economics and rotten national administration.'[108] 'Land for Old IRA Men' campaigns made newspaper headlines in Offaly and elsewhere. Frank Aiken, who was temporary minister for lands in 1933,[109] had his department draw up a 'List of members in Battalion areas deserving of land allotment with suggestions as to estates for acquisition in those areas'.[110] Appendix 5 was a 'List of old IRA members who suffered victimisation in the matters of business, land allotment, careers, public positions and employment'.[111] In 1936, when Christopher Jones Jr was making an application for an IRA pension, the review board received an enquiry from the Irish Land Commission to say that he had applied for land and to confirm whether he had given 'first class meritorious IRA service during the Pre-Truce period', to which the board replied in the affirmative. At that stage he was turned down for a pension (which was only eventually granted in 1953), but Jones (and the Geraghty family, descendants of Matthew) were officially installed in their demesne farms and houses (which they seem to have held on to since the burning). In the end, local power brokers might be said to have outmanoeuvred Hogan and O'Higgins.

When the Irish government began construction of the Electricity Supply Board power stations at Rhode and Ferbane in the late 1950s, symbols of a modernising Ireland, recycled materials from houses burned in Offaly, including Tubberdaly, were used in the construction.[112] When Christopher Jr ('Kit') Jones died in June 1964, his obituary in the *Irish Press* stated that his funeral took place with full military honours. He was a War of Independence hero. His story and that of his father and the Tubberdaly labourers emphasises that the political shenanigans around local land redistribution schemes in the 1920s and 1930s will make for a number of delicious PhDs some day! That will only be possible with the making available of the Irish Land Commission records to the research public, and then, and only then, will the course of the Irish revolution be revealed in all its complexities.

NOTES

* Here southern Ireland is intended as the twenty-six-county area that came to form the Irish Free State after 1922.
1. R. M. Kain and R. Wyse Jackson, both quoted on the cover of Ernie O'Malley, *On Another Man's Wound* (Dublin, 1979 edn).
2. Ibid., p. 182.
3. Ibid., p. 96.
4. C. Townshend, *Political Violence in Ireland* (Oxford, 1983), p. 339; P. Bew, 'Sinn Féin, agrarian radicalism and the War of Independence', in D. G. Boyce (ed.), *The Revolution in Ireland* (London, 1988), pp. 217–34; T. Dooley, *'The Land for the People': The Land Question in Independent Ireland* (Dublin, 2004), pp. 16–20, 26–56.
5. P. Lynch, 'The social revolution that never was', in T. D. Williams (ed.), *The Irish Struggle, 1916–1926* (London, 1966), p. 41; J. J. Lee, *Ireland, 1912–1985: Politics and Society* (Cambridge, 1989), p. 71; J. M. Regan, *The Irish Counter-Revolution, 1921–36* (Dublin, 1999), p. 377; P. Hart, 'Defining the Irish Revolution', in J. Augusteijn (ed.), *The Irish Revolution, 1913–1923* (Basingstoke, 2004), p. 27.
6. *Report of the Proceedings of the Irish Convention* [cd 9019], HC 1918, x, 697.
7. *Report of the Proceedings of the Irish Convention* [cd 9019], HC 1918, x, 697, p. 87; H. J. Monaghan, 'Administration of Land Acts', in F. C. King (ed.), *Public Administration in Ireland* (Dublin, 1944), p. 130.
8. *Agricultural Statistics for Ireland with Detailed Report for the year 1917* [cmd 1316], HC 1921, lxi.135, p. 14.
9. To take but three examples from tillage, beef and dairying sectors: wheat rose from 8.8 shillings a ton in 1914 to 21.6 shillings in 1920; beef from just over £3 per ton to almost £8; and butter from 108.6 shillings to 320.6; *Return Showing to the Latest Year Available, for Ireland as a*

Whole, the Annual Average Prices for Each Year from 1881 . . . HC 1921, xli. 93.
10. R. Gerwarth, *The Vanquished: Why the First World War failed to end, 1917–1923* (London, 2016), p. 35; D. Smith, *Former People: The Last Days of the Russian Aristocracy* (New York, 2012); J. Schloten, *Comrade Baron: A Journey Through the Vanishing World of the Transylvanian Aristocracy* (Nevada, 2016).
11. *Agricultural Statistics for Ireland with Detailed Report for the year 1917* [cmd 1316], HC 1921, lxi.135, p. 14. While some way in the future, but, nonetheless, also illuminating is the fact that in 1940 Eamonn Mansfield, on behalf of the Irish Land Commission, carried out a statistical survey to determine how many farms fell below the Commission's definition of viability, and found that every county in the Free State had a majority of holdings below £20 valuation, ranging from 55 per cent in Dublin to 90 per cent in Leitrim and Donegal, with a twenty-six-county average of 70.5 per cent; Eamonn Mansfield, 'Congestion in the various counties', [1940] (NAI, Dept of Taoiseach files, S14399).
12. James Fintan Lalor, *The Writings of James Fintan Lalor* (Dublin, 1895); H. Patterson, *The Politics of Illusion: A Political History of the IRA* (London, 1997 edn), p. 13.
13. R. V. Comerford, *Fenians in Context: Irish Politics and Society, 1848–82* (Dublin, 1998 edn [1st edn 1985]), p. 115.
14. Isaac Butt, *Land Tenure in Ireland: A Plea for the Celtic Race* (Dublin, 1866), p. 92.
15. R. V. Comerford, *Ireland* (London, 2003), pp. 9, 266.
16. Telegram sent by John Devoy to James O'Connor, October 1878; quoted in T. W. Moody, *Davitt and the Irish Revolution 1846–82*, p. 250; F. Campbell, *Land and Revolution: Nationalist Politics in the West of Ireland* (Oxford, 2005); D. S. Jones, *Graziers, Land Reform and Political Conflict in Ireland* (Washington, 1995).
17. John Devoy, *The Land of Eire* (1882), p. 20.
18. Labhras MacFhionnghail, *The Land Question* (Dublin, 1917), pp. 15, 19.
19. E. O'Connor, 'Agrarian unrest and the Labour movement in County Waterford 1917–1923', *Saothar*, vi, (1980), pp. 40, 54–5.
20. Kevin O'Shiel, Bureau of Military History witness statement (NAI, WS1770), p. 941. In 2003 Fergus Campbell published Shiel's memoir that had been serialised in the *Irish Times* in 1966 in *Archivium Hibernicum* and concluded: 'This memoir demonstrates the necessity for reconsidering the social component of the Irish revolution.' F. Campbell, 'The last land war? Kevin O'Shiel's memoir of the Irish Revolution (1916–21)', *Archivium Hibernicum*, 57 (2003), pp. 155–200, quotation on p. 170; see also Eda Sagarra, *Kevin O'Shiel: Tyrone nationalist and Irish statebuilder* (Sallins, 2013).

21. Inspector General Confidential Monthly Report, November 1918 (TNA, police reports, CO904).
22. *Minutes of Proceedings of the First Parliament of the Republic of Ireland 1919–21*, p. 121.
23. A. Mitchell, *Revolutionary Government in Ireland: Dáil Éireann 1919–22* (Dublin, 1995); M. Kotsonouris, *Retreat From Revolution: The Dáil Courts 1920–24* (Dublin, 1994).
24. See below; T. Dooley and T. McCarthy, 'The 1923 Land Act: Some new perspectives', in M. Farrell, J. Knirck and C. Meehan (eds), *A Formative Decade: Ireland in the 1920s* (Sallins, 2015), pp. 132–56.
25. P. J. Sammon, *In the Land Commission: A Memoir 1933–1978* (Dublin, 1997), pp. 264–78.
26. T. Dooley, *The Decline of the Big House in Ireland* (Dublin, 2001), pp. 171–207.
27. A. O'Riordan, *East Galway Agrarian Agitation and the Burning of Ballydugan House, 1922* (Dublin, 2015), p. 55; also on big house burnings, see D. Fitzpatrick, *Politics and Irish life, 1913–21* (Dublin, 1977), pp 53–71; C. J. Reilly, 'The burning of country houses in Co. Offaly during the revolutionary period, 1920–3', in T. Dooley and C. Ridgway (eds), *The Irish Country House: Its Past, Present and Future* (Dublin, 2011), pp. 110–33; J. S. Donnelly Jr, 'Big house burnings in Cork during the Irish Revolution, 1920–21', *Éire-Ireland*, 47:3 & 4 (2012), pp. 141–97.
28. Hart, 'Defining the Irish Revolution', p. 27
29. Tom Barry, *Guerilla Days in Ireland* (Cork, 1955 edn), p. 116.
30. Ibid., p. 117.
31. *Dáil Debates*, Vol. 3, 28 May 1923, 1147.
32. Dooley and McCarthy, 'The 1923 Land Act'.
33. NAI, Dept. of Taoiseach files, S3192, Patrick Hogan to W. T. Cosgrave, 18 April 1923.
34. *Dáil Éireann Parliamentary Debates*, Vol. iii, 28 May 1923, p. 1165.
35. The most important work on the 1923 Land Act to date unfortunately remains unpublished: J. T. Sheehan, 'Land purchase policy in Ireland: From the Irish Convention to the 1923 Land Act' (unpublished MA thesis, St Patrick's College Maynooth, 1993).
36. See, for example, the report of annual sports day on the Tubberdaly demesne in the *Leinster Leader*, 5 July 1902.
37. 'Ratepayer' to editor in *Leinster Leader*, 31 December 1898.
38. Dooley, *Decline of the Big House*, pp. 160–5.
39. http://ourheroes.southdublinlibraries.ie/node/7551 [accessed 11 April 2018].
40. C. J. Kingston to under-secretary, Dublin Castle, 16 March 1915: http://www.rte.ie/centuryireland/images/uploads/further-reading/Ed48-KingsCountyRecruitingCombo2.pdf [accessed 11 April 2018].

41. NAI, Dept. of Justice files, 5/822, Memo by E. J. Beaumont-Nesbitt [hereafter EJB], 'Tubberdaly, near Rhode, King's County', 28 May 1923.
42. On Kildare, see T. Nelson, *Through Peace and War: Kildare County Council in the Years of Revolution 1899–1926* (Kildare, 2015).
43. EJB to Mrs M. Savage-Armstrong, 19 January 1925; quoted in P. Buckland, *Irish Unionism, 1885–1923: A Documentary History* (Belfast, 1973), p. 382.
44. Ibid.
45. NAI, Dept. of Justice files, 5/822, Memo by EJB, 'Tubberdaly, near Rhode, King's County', 28 May 1923.
46. *Freeman's Journal*, 17 April 1923; NAI, Dept. of Justice files, 5/822, Eamonn Ó Cúgáin [Eamonn Coogan] to secretary of Home Affairs, 2 July 1923.
47. *Freeman's Journal*, 4 August 1923.
48. G. Clarke, *Everyday Violence in the Irish Civil War* (Cambridge, 2014); G. Foster, *The Irish Civil War: Politics, Class, and Conflict* (London, 2015).
49. Dooley, *Decline of the Big House*, pp. 187–92.
50. Reilly, 'The burning of country houses in Co. Offaly', p. 111.
51. *Midland Tribune*, 5 May 1923.
52. TNA, Compensation files, CO 762/64/12, Application to Irish Grants Committee, 13 December 1926.
53. *Leinster Leader*, 3 February 1923; P. McConway, 'The Civil War in Offaly', *Tullamore Tribune*, 2 January 2008.
54. Christopher Jones, IRA pension application, No. 2907, MSP34REF18628, http://mspcsearch.militaryarchives.ie/detail.aspx [accessed 17 May 2021).
55. IRA pension claim form, Mary Swords, 9 February 1952, MSP34REF62664. I would like to thank Ciarán Reilly for bringing Mary Swords to my attention.
56. Reference of Col. Liam Egan included in ibid.
57. Swords pension claim form.
58. Reference of Patrick Cox included in ibid.
59. NAI, Dept. of Justice files, 5/822, Eamonn Ó Cúgáin to secretary of Home Affairs, 2 July 1923.
60. EBN Irish Grants Committee form.
61. NAI, Dept. of Taoiseach files, S3192, Patrick Hogan to W. T. Cosgrave, 7 April 1923.
62. O'Halpin, *Defending Ireland: The Irish State and its Enemies since 1922* (Oxford, 1999), p. 33.
63. Hogan to Cosgrave, 7 April 1923.
64. On their role in the formulation of the 1923 Land Act, see Dooley and McCarthy, 'The 1923 Land Act'; also E. M. Hogan, 'James Hogan, a biographical sketch', in D. O Corrain (ed.), *James Hogan: Revolutionary, Historian and Political Scientist* (Dublin, 2001); J. P. McCarthy, *Kevin*

O'Higgins: Builder of the Irish State (Dublin, 2006); J. M. Regan, *The Irish Counter-Revolution 1921–1936: Treatyite Politics and Settlement in Independent Ireland* (Dublin, 1999).
65. UCD, O'Higgins papers, P197/135, Kevin O'Higgins, Memo, 30 December 1922.
66. UCD, O'Higgins papers, P197/137, Kevin O'Higgins, 'Mexican politics'; *Free State*, 18 March 1922; UCD, O'Higgins papers, P197/141, Address by Kevin O'Higgins to the Irish Society at Oxford University, 31 October 1924; Regan, *The Irish Counter-Revolution 1921–1936*, pp. 244–5.
67. *Dáil Éireann Parliamentary Debates*, Vol. 3, 28 May 1923, p. 1161.
68. Ibid., 14 June 1923, p. 1971.
69. Ibid., p. 1972.
70. R. English, *Radicals and the Republic: Socialist Republicanism in the Irish Free State 1925–1937* (Oxford, 1994), p. 31.
71. MCM, Marron papers Tom Carragher.
72. NAI, Dept. of Justice files, 5/888, John Kelly to minister of agriculture, 4 July 1923.
73. Ibid.
74. Ibid.
75. Ibid.
76. NAI, Dept. of Justice files, 5/888, Copy letter, Christopher Jones to Sir [EJB], 10 July 1923.
77. EJB to Mrs Savage-Armstrong, 19 January 1925; Buckland, *Irish Unionism*, p. 382.
78. Patrick Hogan to minister of home affairs [Kevin O'Higgins], 13 July 1923, ibid.
79. Ibid.
80. *Dáil Éireann Parliamentary Debates*, Vol. 3, 28 May 1923, pp. 1162–3.
81. NAI, Dept. of Justice files, 5/888, Superintendent Sean Liddy to Commissioner of Civic Guard, 28 July 1923.
82. *Offaly Independent*, 11 August 1923.
83. *Public Safety (Emergency Powers) Act*, No. 28, 1 August 1923.
84. *Freeman's Journal*, 4 August 1923; *Offaly Independent*, 11 August 1923.
85. NAI, Dept. of Justice files, 5/888, Eamonn Ó Cúgain to secretary, minister for home affairs, 30 January 1924.
86. Eamonn Ó Cúgain to secretary, minister for home affairs, 30 January 1924, ibid.
87. Ibid.
88. TNA, Compensation files, CO 762/64/12, EJB to secretary of Irish Grants Committee, 3 May 1927.
89. EJB to Mrs Savage-Armstrong, 19 January 1925; Buckland, *Irish Unionism*, p. 382.
90. Ibid.

91. TNA, Compensation files, CO 762/64/12, Application to Irish Grants Committee, 1927.
92. Brian Beaumont-Nesbitt to Bobbie Tyrell, 29 September 1991 (private possession).
93. *Drogheda Independent*, 14 June 1924.
94. Ibid.
95. Ibid.
96. NAI, Dept. of Justice files, 5/888, Eamonn Ó Cúgain to secretary, department of justice, 24 July 1924.
97. EJB to Mrs Savage-Armstrong, 19 January 1925; Buckland, *Irish Unionism*, p. 382.
98. Dooley, 'Land for the People', esp. pp. 57–98.
99. Foster, *The Irish Civil War*; J. M. Regan, *The Irish Counter-Revolution, 1921–1936* (Dublin, 1999).
100. Fianna Fáil, *A Brief Outline of the Aims and Programme of Fianna Fáil* (Dublin, n.d.), p. 4.
101. *Offaly Independent*, 10 October 1931.
102. Ibid.
103. Mary Swords to IRA pension Board, 6 September 1962; MSP34REF62664.
104. *Dáil Éireann Parliamentary Debates*, Vol. 41 No. 15, 19 May 1932: http://oireachtasdebates.oireachtas.ie/debates%20authoring/debateswebpack.nsf/zoomin?readform&chamber=dail&memberid=343&pid=PeadarSeanDoyle&year=1932&month=05&day=19 [accessed 11 April 2018].
105. *Offaly Independent*, 11 June 1932.
106. Ibid.
107. Land Act 1933, No. 38 of 1933; Dooley, 'Land for the People', pp. 99–131.
108. *Dáil Éireann Parliamentary Debates*, Vol. 48, 13 July 1933, p. 2400.
109. R. Fanning, 'Aiken, Francis Thomas (Frank)', in James McGuire and James Quinn (eds), *Dictionary of Irish Biography* (Cambridge, 2016): (http://dib.cambridge.org/viewReadPage.do?articleId=a0070) [accessed 5 April 2020].
110. UCD, Aiken papers, P104/2886 (29), 'List of members in Battalion areas deserving of land allotment with suggestions as to estates for acquisition in those areas'.
111. UCDA, P104/2886 (38), Appendix 5, 'List of old IRA members who suffered victimisation in the matters of business, land allotment, careers, public positions and employment'.
112. Reilly, 'Burning of country houses in Offaly', p. 131.

6

The Liberties of the Land: Preserving the Commons in England in the Later Nineteenth and Early Twentieth Centuries

Ben Cowell

INTRODUCTION

ON A SUNNY MORNING in June 2015, a cross section of the British establishment gathered on a patch of common land near the banks of the River Thames to mark the 800th anniversary of an act of monarchical circumscription. The document now known as Magna Carta was, after all, agreed somewhere on 'the meadow which is called Runnymede, between Windsor and Staines', though the precise location of the events of June 1215 remains uncertain.[1] Perhaps there was some irony in the fact that the eighth centenary of King John's bitter clash with his barons was being commemorated through harmonious public ceremonials led jointly by the Queen, her Prime Minister (newly returned to his role at a general election held the previous month) and her Archbishop of Canterbury.[2] A succession of speakers addressed the audience from a stage erected especially for the occasion, each attempting to outdo the last in heaping admiration onto a piece of parchment now regarded as the bedrock of the British political system and a guarantor of human rights and liberties.

Not everyone that day, however, shared in the apparent consensus of the occasion. Up on Cooper's Hill, the wooded bluff overlooking Runnymede, a rather different set of political attitudes prevailed. A group calling themselves Diggers had first made camp here three years earlier, in June 2012. The Diggers objected to a proposal for the site to be redeveloped as housing, and to register their opposition had established an eco-village in the woods. On their blogsite, in what they called their 'Declaration from the Dispossessed', the group declared their intention 'to go and cultivate the disused land of this island; to build dwellings and live together in common by the sweat of our brows.' The blog read as a modern-day Magna Carta, in which the limits of exploitation were laid down in writing by this group of 'peaceful people': 'We call on

Figure 6.1 View of Runnymede from Cooper's Hill, with a distant view of Windsor Castle. (Edmund John Niemann – National Trust)

the government and all landowners to let those who are willing, make good use of the disused land. Land that is currently held from us by force.'[3] Their efforts were directly inspired by history: both the evocative resonance of Runnymede itself and the memory of the original Digger community of 1649 established by Gerrard Winstanley on common land at St George's Hill, Weybridge, 12 miles away.[4] The eco-village survived over the summer of 2015, until the inhabitants were evicted by court order in September of that year.

The occupation of Cooper's Hill reminds us that land continues to be a contested resource. Common land, which combines elements of both absolute private property and customary, communal resource, has on occasion borne witness to some of the most intense disagreements over land and land ownership.[5] Common land has a complex history, occurring in different forms at different times and in different geographical locations. Commons were often the marginal and least productive lands of a parish, excluded from direct cultivation and instead reserved for grazing or as an occasional source of food, fuel and timber. Cultivated fields might at times also be commonable: thrown open to grazing after the harvest had been taken. Common rights were those rights that attached to specific properties: the right to graze a certain number of animals on the parish's common lands, for example. Such rights were carefully managed by local courts. Beyond these rights, the poorest elements in rural communities often depended on the resources found on the commons and exercised more informal and customary forms of access to them. The ability to travel across commons (even where there might be no formal rights of way), to take wood or fuel, or to catch the occasional rabbit for the supper pot, might make all the difference for those eking out life on the margins of rural society.

The act of enclosure most often disregarded these customary uses of the commons. Whether achieved by mutual agreement or through Parliamentary statute, enclosure was the process by which communal practices of land management in a parish gave way to a system of entirely individualised landholdings. Open fields were divided into fenced plots and assigned to those recognised as having a stake in the parish's landholdings. Surviving areas of common land were those that either escaped enclosure entirely or were formally recognised as areas of common in enclosure acts and subsequent legislation. The legal process of enclosure therefore implied the formal recognition of the existence of common rights over a parcel of land, and compensation for the loss of those rights when the commons and open fields were partitioned and subdivided. Whether this compensation was sufficient, and whether enclosure had detrimental social consequences, are matters on which historians continue to disagree, albeit that the loss of the commons would undoubtedly have been felt most keenly by the poorest.[6] Commons gained further statutory identity in the twentieth century: Runnymede was officially registered as common land under the Commons Registration Act (1965).[7]

Historians have pointed to examples of resistance to enclosure, as evidence of the importance of common land resources to the poorest in society. Attention has been drawn to fence breaks, wood stealing, tree maiming, riots and other public disturbances, to demonstrate how enclosure could be a contested process, with the aggressive actions of landowners prompting reactions from the poorer sort.[8] Localised forms of enclosure protest have been witnessed throughout British history and in other contexts around the world.[9] Numerous examples have been recorded where those involved in these acts of resistance had blackened their faces, principally to avoid identification and arrest under the cover of darkness.[10] Otmoor in Oxfordshire was enclosed by Act of Parliament in 1815; night-time anti-enclosure protests here in 1830 involved crowds of people with blackened faces, some of them also armed, and with some of the men further disguised as women.[11] An earlier and even more notorious example of face blacking was associated with poaching gangs in southern England in the 1720s. The gangs' activities led to the extreme provisions of the Black Act of 1723, which made it a capital offence even to be found in a forest or royal park with a blackened face.[12]

This essay explores the history of the movement to resist the enclosure of commons by more legalistic means in the second half of the nineteenth century and into the early decades of the twentieth century. It argues that the commons preservation movement, which was an aspect of the debates about land reform in the later decades of the nineteenth century, contributed to the reinvention of commons as 'public' places rather than the localised resources of specific communities of commoners. The essay goes on to explore the tensions that could arise as a result of this redefinition by considering the history of the meadows at Runnymede themselves and their protection by the National Trust in the early decades of the twentieth century. By declaring Runnymede open to all, and by assuming a regulatory role over the management and operation of the site, the National Trust incurred the displeasure of locals from the very outset, demonstrating the difficulties involved in trying to adapt historic and localised commoning traditions to modern circumstances. As will be seen, these tensions came to the fore at another royal celebration held at Runnymede in July 1932.

COMMONS PRESERVATION AS A POLITICAL ISSUE, c. 1860–1880

The protection of remaining areas of common land became a noted political issue in the middle decades of the nineteenth century. By this time, most of England had already undergone enclosure. In 1760, perhaps three-quarters of England was already enclosed. Parliamentary enclosures from 1760 were responsible for the enclosure of 6.5 million acres. Howkins estimates that by 1845 there were just 2.5 million acres of common land left.[13] The pace of enclosure was such that by 1873 just 1.7 million acres of common land remained.[14]

As Roberts has noted, the political priorities of the commons preservation movement varied over time.[15] In the first half of the nineteenth century, the prevailing instinct to enclose (and thereby to improve farming practices) gave way among some to a growing concern over the loss of freely accessible countryside, and the deleterious effect that this had on the well-being of local populations. Antecedents for the commons preservation movement could be seen in the debates over the protection of public open spaces during the 1833 Select Committee on Public Walks. The General Enclosure Acts of 1836, 1840 and 1845 quickened the concerns of those worried about the loss of the relatively limited areas of remaining commons and open spaces. These concerns were highlighted too by radicals such as Thomas Spence, and later the Chartists.[16]

The commons preservation movement entered its next phase in the mid-1860s, by which time the high peak of Parliamentary enclosure had already passed. The specific occasion that spurred many into political action was the threatened enclosure of Wimbledon Common by its owner, Earl Spencer. Spencer's scheme to turn the principal part of Wimbledon Common into a parkland, fenced and regulated, stirred significant dissent from politicians with little or no connection to Wimbledon itself. The case prompted select committee investigations, which recommended that commons in the metropolitan area should remain unenclosed and available for public access. The Metropolitan Commons Act gained assent the following year and empowered the enclosure commissioners in the metropolitan area to receive proposals from lords of the manor for how commons could be managed as public spaces.[17]

A further development was the foundation in July 1865 of the Commons Preservation Society, one of the country's first environmental campaigning groups.[18] The Society's stated aims were 'to watch the interests of the public in the Commons round London', and it fought a series of high-profile battles against enclosure in the 1860s and 1870s.[19] Emboldened by the Wimbledon Common case, the Society launched campaigns against the enclosure of, among others, Hampstead Heath, Epping Forest, and Berkhamsted Common in the Hertfordshire Chilterns. In each of these cases a similar pattern of action ensued. The Society would bring the threat of enclosure to public attention. It would then encourage a local resident with sufficient influence and resources to launch a legal challenge against the threatened enclosure – in Hampstead, Gurney Hoare, at Berkhamsted, Augustus Smith.[20] At the advice of the Society's lawyers, this legal challenge would invariably be taken to the Court of Chancery rather than the common law courts.

The commons protection debate prompted an outpouring of legal and historical opinion, such as the *Six Essays on Commons Preservation* that were published in 1867 following the Wimbledon case.[21] Publications such as these placed the origins of commons within the context of the rise of feudal property rights, drawing on the work of historians such as Maitland, Seebohm, Maine and Vinogradoff. But the commons preservation movement also effected a reinterpretation of commons as public places, over which rights of access for all prevailed. George Shaw Lefevre, the Commons Preservation Society's chairman, stated that his ambition was to 'restore to the commons something of the attributes of the ancient Saxon folk land'.[22]

Each of the cases fought by the Commons Preservation Society involved scrutiny of the historical record. Epping Forest became a particular rallying cry for commons preservationists after a legal case was brought against a local resident in the early 1870s.[23] The City of London corporation was persuaded to exercise its position as one of the commoners of the Epping Forest area to mount a defence of common rights in the forest area. The success of the corporation's case in 1874 meant that all enclosures that had been carried out there since 1851 were declared invalid.[24] An Act of 1878 transferred the entire 6,000 acres of Epping Forest to the City of London, which remains the legal owner and manager of the land today.

THE DEVELOPMENT OF COMMONS PRESERVATION, 1880–1907

The decision of the City of London corporation to champion the cause of commons preservation may in retrospect seem unexpected. Roberts points out that it may have been part of the corporation's attempts to demonstrate its modernity in the face of criticism of its medieval rights and privileges.[25] Equally, the City of London filled a gap: there was no property-owning organisation capable of taking on the ownership and management of commons at this time, as the social housing reformer Octavia Hill had discovered when she consulted Robert Hunter on the options for saving Sayes Court in Deptford, the ancestral garden of John Evelyn.[26] The Commons Preservation Society continued to use legal argument to object to enclosures, as well as to defend footpaths and rights to roam (in 1899 it merged with the National Footpaths Society to become the Commons and Footpaths Preservation Society). But its influence was ultimately surpassed by a new force for commons protection: The National Trust.

The National Trust was registered as a company in January 1895, although the idea of a company holding land on behalf of the general public was first sketched out by Hunter in a speech to the Association for the Promotion of Social Science in 1884.[27] Hunter had been a major figure in the Commons Preservation Society, serving as its lawyer and subsequently the chair of its branch in Haslemere, Surrey.[28] But Hunter recognised the limits of the Society's methods, which depended on the success of legal action in forcing landowners to step back from proposed commons enclosures. Hunter developed his ideas about the potential for a national landholding trust in correspondence with Hill, who held a strong moral regard for the benefits of commons and open spaces. For Hill, the issue of commons preservation aligned closely to her work in alleviating the conditions experienced by the urban poor.[29]

From its inception, the National Trust was conceived as a charitable landholding entity that would acquire areas of land and hold them in perpetuity in the public interest. The Trust's first property, gifted in 1895, was an open coastal site in Wales, Dinas Oleu, donated by Fanny Talbot, a friend and correspondent of Ruskin. (In addition to his influence on Hill, Ruskin had been an inspiration to Hardwicke Rawnsley, another of the Trust's founders.[30]) Hunter's devotion to the cause of commons preservation had a major influence on the development of the National Trust. Many of the Trust's early acquisitions were open, green spaces – places like Ide Hill in Kent (1899), Wicken Fen in Cambridgeshire (1899), Box Hill (1914) and Bookham commons (1924) in Surrey, Maidenhead and Cookham commons in Berkshire (1934), and Berkhamsted, bought for the Trust along with the Ashridge estate in 1925 following a fundraising campaign by the historian G. M. Trevelyan.[31]

Hunter served as the Trust's first chairman and prepared the Trust's founding constitutional documents. He had the foresight to recognise that, as the Trust's estate grew, the charity needed firmer foundations. The return of a Liberal government in 1905, along with the acquisition by the Trust of Hindhead Common (including the Devil's Punch Bowl) in Surrey in 1906, may have been the spur for Hunter to engineer a private member's bill that would finally give the Trust a statutory footing. The National Trust Act (1907) enshrined the charity's powers in law, giving it the special responsibility for holding land inalienably, meaning that the Trust's property could not be disposed of without Parliamentary consent. The 1907 Act did more than this, however. It specifically empowered the Trust to acquire common land, reflecting the origins of the organisation from within the commons preservation movement. Statutorily, the Trust was required to keep its own commons undeveloped: common land was instead to be kept 'unenclosed and unbuilt on as open spaces for the recreation and enjoyment of the public'. The only buildings that were permitted on such spaces were 'sheds for tools and materials', and any attempt to enclose or encroach upon these lands was to be resisted by the Trust using 'all lawful means'. A further clause permitted the use of Trust common land for games or for holding 'meetings or gatherings for athletic sports'.[32] As will be seen, these clauses were relevant when it came to the management of one of the most famous of the Trust's commons: Runnymede.

THE 'SAVING' OF RUNNYMEDE MEADOWS

The meadows at Runnymede are recognised internationally because of their association with Magna Carta. Originally known as 'The Provisions of Runnymede', the document was dispatched in multiple copies soon after King John had agreed to its terms somewhere on or near the meadows in June 1215. By so doing he agreed to new limits on the powers of the monarch, whether to raise taxes without consent or otherwise act beyond the limits of the law. Just months later, the agreement was declared null and void by the King and the Pope. Nonetheless, the significance of the document grew in the years that followed. The Charter was reissued on the crowning of John's successor, Henry III, in 1216. It acquired the name 'Magna Carta' to differentiate it from a second document, issued in 1217, the 'Charter of the Forest'. The forest charter took the chapters of the original document that dealt with forest law (chapters 44, 47, 48 and 53) and expanded them into a longer document setting out the boundaries of monarchical control over environmental resources. Some commentators have seen in the Charter of the Forest a document of equal if not greater significance than the Great Charter from which it came, since it spelled out, perhaps for the first time, a statement of environmental rights and responsibilities. Both the Magna Carta and the Charter of the Forest have been influential texts for struggles involving rights and freedoms across the globe.[33]

Runnymede was described as a meadow on the face of the 1215 charter, but beyond that there is little evidence for how the thirteenth-century landscape of the site might have looked. Its identification as the location of the June 1215 agreement might be purely arbitrary, or equally might have some significance. There is some evidence for an Anglo-Saxon tradition of signing peace treaties at sites next to rivers, or the spot may have been selected because of its location midway between the outer boundaries of the orbit of London and the King's base at Windsor Castle. The land now known as Runnymede formed part of the manor of Egham held by Chertsey Abbey until dissolution in 1537, at which point possession reverted to the Crown. A Parliamentary Survey of 1650 records the meadow of Runnymede among the lands appurtenant to the manor house at Egham.[34]

Because of their riverside location, the meadows at Runnymede were prone to flooding. The meadows had an important agricultural function, being used for hay growing from February through to Old Lammas Day (12 August), after which parts were fenced off as grazing for cattle, horses and sheep. In 1811 ten tenants were recorded as having the use of the land for its hay, and thereafter all tenants of the manor of Egham were permitted to graze livestock. A central part of the meadows was traditionally left unenclosed. The meadows in the eighteenth century were perhaps more famous for their regular horse races than for their role in constitutional history. The Runnymede races were recorded taking place during the reign of Queen Anne and were revived a century later under William IV. On the event's revival, the King was reported to have made a speech recalling 'that it was here that our liberties were obtained and ever secured' and pledging to ensure that those liberties would be protected in future.[35] Ironically, Parliamentary enclosure was one of the means by which this had happened. An Act of 1813–14 ordered the enclosure of Egham's common fields and pastures, but specifically reserved the rights of pasturage over Runnymede and its neighbouring meadows 'for certain people' subject to the caveat that from time to time the 'inclosures should be thrown down to enable the horse-races held there to be continued as usual'.[36]

Although the last of the horse races was held in 1886, Runnymede continued to be known as a site of public recreation, for riverside picnics and for weekend walks. After the First World War, Lloyd George's government attempted to put Runnymede up for sale: the meadows were included as Lot 8 on a list of Crown lands available for purchase in 1921. Lloyd George himself reportedly anticipated that a private contractor would buy the land and convert it to a permanent fairground. But if that was the intention, he did not account for the vigorous objections of local people. Helena Normanton (1882–1957), a pioneering lawyer who lived nearby, instigated a campaign of action to protect Runnymede from being developed in this way.[37] The government backed down and withdrew the Runnymede meadows from sale. Together with the vicar of Egham, Reverend Albert Cecil Tranter, and Robert Wynn Carrington, Marquess of Lincolnshire (1843–1928), Normanton established a Magna Carta Commemoration Committee to oversee the use of the meadows for annual Magna Carta celebrations. Nicholas Vincent and Steven Franklin have explored the running tensions within and beyond this committee, not least in its attempts to regulate the use of the Runnymede meadows and its vying with the International Magna Carta Day Association for hegemonic influence over the direction of the annual festivities.[38]

The Magna Carta Commemoration Committee continued to take an interest in the long-term protection of the Runnymede site, and in 1926 opened discussions on how best to secure the ownership of the meadows.[39] The permanent solution came from Lady Fairhaven, the widow of Urban Broughton (1857–1929). Broughton, an English-born engineer, made a fortune in America through business as well as through his marriage to Cara Rogers, daughter of the wealthy industrialist Henry Huttleston Rogers. Broughton was Conservative MP for Preston between 1915 and 1918, and owned a substantial property near to Runnymede at Englefield Green. His gift of Ashridge House to the Conservative Party in 1928 may have been one of the factors behind the peerage that he was due to be granted in the 1929 honours list, but his death in January of that year meant he was never able to assume the title. Instead his eldest son became the first Lord Fairhaven, while his widow was granted the courtesy title of Lady Fairhaven. Lady Fairhaven subsequently came forward to offer to purchase the site of Runnymede meadows and to transfer them to the National Trust in memory of her late husband. The purchase was completed by December 1929, and with satisfaction Helena Normanton wrote that this latest act of commons preservation had protected Runnymede from development:

> It seems almost incredible now, as we draw our breaths in ease, that only by a fluke has it escaped the fate of so much Thames riparian soil, that disease which Dean Inge has styled 'bungalitis'. It is a repulsive thought that our children's children might have had to seek the site whereon our country's liberties were obtained beneath a clustering covey of bungalows something like Peacehaven![40]

The proposed acquisition of the site by the National Trust was not without its tensions, however. The transfer of the property from the Fairhaven family to the Trust took several years to implement, during which time the charity established a management committee chaired by Lord FitzAlan to oversee the meadows. Without the full legal authority of ownership, the Trust resorted to persuasion, urging the visiting public 'particularly during the holiday season, to co-operate ... in seeing that order is maintained and that nothing is done to impair or injure the amenities of this historic spot, which is now held for their benefit'.[41] Examples of disorderly behaviour included the use of the meadows as a runway for light aircraft, and the holding of mass sporting events. The Magna Carta Commemoration Committee had wrestled with the problem posed by a local flying club in 1928 and 1929. The Trust went one step further and banned the flying club from using Runnymede at all, and at the same time also banned cars from parking on its land at the site.[42] Nevertheless, early the following year a correspondent for the *Nottingham Journal* recorded his astonishment at seeing a thousand spectators watching a rugby match on the meadows. Many had 'halted in their afternoon run, and were parked alongside the road' (as no doubt the correspondent himself had done). He went on to observe, somewhat balefully, that the nearby banks of the River Thames 'were lined with anglers of both sexes who had also used their cars to assist them to reach their sport'.[43]

Disagreements over different local users' interests in the sites it managed would have been nothing new to the National Trust at this time. But a more fundamental objection to the Trust's management of Runnymede was soon to emerge, based on Runnymede's status as a common. Working with Runnymede's management committee, the architect Sir Edwin Lutyens (1869–1944) was commissioned to prepare plans for buildings at the two main entrances to the meadows, on the road from Windsor to Staines running parallel with the River Thames. Lutyens devised a scheme for two kiosk structures at the Egham end of the road, while the Windsor end would be graced by two more substantial lodges.[44] Stone pillars, two at each end, would bear inscriptions to explain the significance of the Runnymede site and Urban Broughton's gift to the nation. These pillars would function like scaled-down versions of the famous Cenotaph that Lutyens was commissioned to build in Whitehall to commemorate the fallen of the Great War.

Lutyens' plans were eventually realised, but not without causing the National Trust a deal of effort and anxiety. Initially, the Trust was accused of commissioning the building of the larger cottages at the Windsor end merely in order to frustrate the plans of the County Council to build a more substantial bypass across the meadows.[45] Opponents of the Trust locally then appealed to the 1814 Egham Enclosure Act to argue that the Trust in fact had no authority to build on Runnymede. This was a more serious objection, which necessitated the hiring of the Council Chamber at Egham Urban Council for a special hearing by the Ministry of Agriculture and Fisheries in January 1932. The Trust put forward a retrospective application for approval of the building work that had been undertaken. This approval was apparently sought with reference to the Enclosure Act, rather than to the National Trust Act of 1907 (which expressly forbade the Trust from building on any common land that it owned). Leading the charge, General George Grogan (1875–1962), veteran of the Somme, maintained that the Trust had infringed the 1814 Act. Moreover, he objected to the ugliness of the cottages (one of which was to serve as a public lavatory, for which he saw no need) and took issue with the fact that the Trust had not sought sufficient approval for the building work from the local council before starting work. General Grogan was supported by Mr Harrison, who claimed the Trust was indeed seeking 'to override everybody local' and urged the Council to deny permission.[46] Further concerns were raised about the propensity of the site to flood, the fact that the Trust had failed to appoint any Egham residents onto its management committee, and about the visual intrusion represented by the buildings. One objector stated that Runnymede 'should not be used as a memorial for private people', and that the Trust was overreaching itself, for example by denying people the right to camp on the meadows, saying that the Trust had acted against 'Christian Charity' in depriving 'the poor lads from the London slums of the rights to enjoy the country during the week-end'.

The Trust responded by arguing that the area due to be built on was just 500 square yards (4,500 square foot) of the 182 acres of Runnymede. The Trust added that the proposals would benefit local inhabitants. A caretaker would live in one of the cottages, which would help to limit vandalism on the site. The building work was being undertaken at the National Trust's expense, and the failure to lodge a planning application had been a consequence of the earlier disagreement over the bypass (wherein the Trust had assumed that Surrey County Council, and not Egham Urban Council, was the appropriate planning authority). The local authorities, along with Reverend A. C. Tranter from the Magna Carta Commemoration Committee, pledged their support to the National Trust.[47] At the conclusion of the hearing in April, the Trust was granted retrospective power to overrule the 1814 Act and build on Runnymede, in the face of local hostility. The Trust expressed regret at the situation and agreed to meet residents to discuss the membership of its management committee.[48]

Alas for the Trust, this was not the end of the matter. A few months later, in July 1932, a royal event was planned for the official opening of Runnymede as a National Trust property. The Prince of Wales, the future Edward VIII, agreed to visit Runnymede on Friday 8 July to pull the cord and release the drapes that covered the memorial pillars. During the night, however, and under the cover of darkness, someone visited Lutyens' buildings and liberally sprayed the pristine new stonework with creosote. Upon discovering the act, the Trust's representatives did all they could to remove evidence of the damage, but the creosote had sunk into the surface of the Portland stone and could not be scrubbed away before the royal visitor's arrival. As one newspaper reported, the buildings 'looked much as a lorry looks when it has ended a long winter journey over bad roads. All their clean freshness had been spoiled.'[49] The Prince, when he eventually appeared (wearing a 'straw "boater" and a very "summerish" lounge suit … without

Figure 6.2 Magna Carta memorial vandalism, July 1932 (*The Scotsman*, 9 July 1932).

waistcoat'), was game enough to pull the cord anyway and give a speech in honour of the National Trust and Lord Fairhaven and his mother Lady Fairhaven, without whose 'generous and patriotic action', the Prince maintained, 'these famous meadows, the most famous, perhaps, in the history of our country, might have become exploited by the jerry builder'.[50] Diplomatically the Prince avoided referring directly to the vandalism, though he later commented to the press that he considered it a 'blackguardly thing'.

Newspapers took a detailed interest in the story, and variously reported that the action must have been undertaken using either industrial syringes or 'a spraying machine' taken to the site by motor car.[51] Commentators were quick to ascribe motives to the vandals, generally linking the action to the local upset at the actions of the Trust in allowing a portion of the meadows to be built over. The *Gloucester Citizen* may have implied as much when it reported that the local police did not 'suspect any local "Reds" or other agitators as the culprits'.[52] The *Sheffield Daily Telegraph* was unusual in showing some degree of empathy towards the vandals, commenting that 'local opinion should certainly have larger share in deciding these matters' and that the creosoting incident had 'undoubtedly resulted from local resentment having been despotically ignored by bureaucracy'.⁵³ Most newspapers, however, decided that the protagonists were beyond the pale. Later that summer, when Lord Ashby closed Ashby Park to public access because of the problem of littering, the *Coventry Evening Telegraph* could not resist taking a collective swipe at the 'vandals who attacked the Runnymede Memorial, the middle-class motorist too lazy to take picnic packages home, and the working-class beanfeast party who leave their broken beer bottles in the hedgerows', all of them part of the problem that beset open-air recreation sites across the country.⁵⁴

CONCLUSION

The National Trust's *Trusted Source* webpages, produced in conjunction with the University of Oxford, contain a whole series of brief essays listed under various topic headings, one of which is 'Landscapes and Nature'. Here, browsers will find a section entitled 'What are commons?' sitting immediately adjacent to an essay explaining 'Why was Magna Carta sealed at Runnymede?'.⁵⁵ Common rights and civil liberties continue therefore to be conceived as interconnected issues, with the open meadows at Runnymede serving a dual function: as both the crucible within which such concepts were forged and as a totem for the continued observance of those rights.

The specificity of local commoning traditions, however, gives warning to the dangers of over-generalisation. Common land continues to be ill served by those who profess otherwise to be knowledgeable about its history. In 2019 George Monbiot was part of a team of authors that produced a report for the Labour party entitled *Land for the Many*. Commons were referenced throughout the document, as both the historic subject of aggressive aristocratic and gentry enclosure and as a potential model for the future governance of land. In a section entitled 'Learning from the Past', the report's authors described common land as 'where the majority of the population once lived and worked, exercising collective rights to farm and forage for food and fuel'.⁵⁶ Given that commons were frequently formed from the least productive, marginal lands of a parish, the idea that the 'majority of the population once lived and worked' on them is something of a non sequitur. The notion too that there were once 'collective rights' for all over such lands simplistically conflates common rights (which were forms of property rights held by individual, named commoners) with customary rights (not legally held rights at all, but rather claims to the produce of the land that might be tolerated at the discretion of a local community). Few historians would agree with Guy Standing when he asserts that before the Parliamentary enclosures all land was 'common, public land'. Standing goes on to suggest that the Charter of the Forest was 'perhaps the greatest single victory for the common man in British history'.[57] The elision here of the 'common' with the 'public', as we have seen, is an idea mainly of late nineteenth-century invention. Writers like Standing echo the refrain of radicals down the ages, that the land was 'stolen' (usually from 'the people') at some unspecified point in history (usually just after the Norman Conquest).[58]

This essay has shown that the management and subsequent protection of common land has a long and complex history. Most common land had already disappeared by the time the commons preservation movement mobilised into action in the mid-1860s. The battles fought by the Commons Preservation Society ensured that large and familiar landscapes (Hampstead Heath, Wimbledon Common, Epping Forest) remain open to public access today. Had it been formed thirty years earlier, the National Trust itself would no doubt have been a logical custodian for these landscapes. But the Trust's own formation came at the very end of the nineteenth century, when new modes of governance were being explored in order to guarantee the survival of commons (and other properties) for public access rather than for local subsistence. The National Trust today owns 35,000 hectares of common land, or nearly 10 per cent of the total registered common land in England; common land accounts for almost a fifth of the Trust's entire landholdings. Nonetheless, the protections promoted by the Commons Preservation Society and the National Trust did not necessarily extend to the continuation of local, customary uses of the commons. Organisations like the National Trust could in this way assume roles that might appear every bit as patrician and aloof as the landowners they had supplanted. New regulatory regimes imposed in the name of conservation might serve to eradicate commoning cultures that had prevailed for centuries, obliterating them beneath new strictures about the right, and wrong, uses of the commons.[59]

It might stretch credulity to suggest that the spraying with creosote of Lutyens' buildings and monumental pillars at Runnymede was in the tradition of those eighteenth- and nineteenth-century forms of resistance to enclosure that involved attacks on property under the cover of darkness. Nevertheless, an element of the local population, unhappy with the enclosure of a small part of Runnymede, resorted to a night-time 'blacking' of the new stonework that had been commissioned for the common during the National Trust's custodianship. The vandalism of a monument to a wealthy, titled family was interpreted at the time as a localised expression of discontent with enclosure, mimicking, whether consciously or not, displays of anti-enclosure sentiment witnessed in manifold other contexts.

NOTES

1. D. Carpenter (ed.), *Magna Carta* (London, 2015), p. 69.
2. The celebrations of June 2015 are explored further in G. Smith and A. Green, 'The Magna Carta: 800 years of public history', in J. B. Gardner and P. Hamilton (eds), *The Oxford Handbook of Public History* (New York, 2017), pp. 387–401.
3. Available at http://diggers2012.wordpress.com/about/ [last accessed 18 January 2020].
4. See A. Howkins, 'Diggers to Dongas: The land in English radicalism, 1649–2000', *History Workshop Journal*, 54 (Autumn, 2002), pp. 1–23.
5. C. P. Rodgers, E. A. Straughton, A. J. L. Winchester and A. Pieraccini, *Contested Common Land: Environmental Governance Past and Present* (London, 2011), p. 10. See also D. Wall, *The Commons in History: Culture, Conflict, and Ecology* (Cambridge and London, 2014).
6. For which, see the discussion in J. M. Neeson, *Commoners: Common Right, Enclosure and Social Change in England, 1700–1820* (Cambridge, 1993) and the discussion in L. Shaw-Taylor, 'Parliamentary enclosure and the emergence of an English agricultural proletariat', *Journal of Economic History*, 61:3 (2001), pp. 640–62.
7. D. R. Denman, R. A. Roberts and H. J. F. Smith, *Commons and Village Greens* (London, 1967), p. 478.
8. See Neeson, *Commoners*, chapter 9; B. Bushaway, *By Rite: Custom, Ceremony and Community in England 1700–1880* (London, 1982); A. Charlesworth, *An Atlas of Rural Protest in Britain 1548–1900* (Philadelphia, 1983); C. Griffin, 'Protest, practice and (tree) cultures of conflict: Understanding the spaces of "tree maiming" in eighteenth- and early nineteenth-century England', *Transactions of the Institute of British Geographers*, New Series, 33:1 (2008), pp. 91–108.
9. P. Linebaugh, *Stop Thief! The Commons, Enclosures and Resistance* (Oakland, CA, 2014).
10. A. Howkins and L. Merricks, '"Wee be black as Hell": Ritual, disguise and rebellion', *Rural History* (1993), 4:1, pp. 41–53.
11. D. Eastwood, 'Communities, protest and police in early nineteenth-century Oxfordshire: The enclosure of Otmoor reconsidered', *Agricultural History Review* (1996), 44:1, pp. 35–46, p. 39.
12. E. P. Thompson, *Whigs and Hunters: The Origin of the Black Act* (Harmondsworth, 1975).

13. A. Howkins, 'The use and abuse of the English commons, 1845–1914', *History Workshop Journal*, 78 (2014), pp. 107–32, p. 110.
14. J. R. Wordie, 'The chronology of English enclosure, 1500–1914', *The Economic History Review*, 36:4 (1983), pp. 483–505.
15. M. J. D. Roberts, 'Gladstonian Liberalism and environmental protection, 1865–76', *English Historical Review*, cxxviii, 531 (2013), pp. 292–322; J. Winter, *Secure from Rash Assault: Sustaining the Victorian Environment* (California, 2002).
16. M. Chase, 'Chartism and the land: "The Mighty People's Question"', in M. Cragoe and P. Readman (eds), *The Land Question in Britain, 1750–1950* (Basingstoke, 2010), pp. 57–73.
17. Roberts, 'Gladstonian Liberalism', pp. 297–8.
18. Also one of the longest-running: it continues today as the Open Spaces Society. See K. Ashbrook, *Saving Open Spaces: The Campaign for Public Rights to Enjoy Commons, Green Spaces and Paths* (Stroud, 2015). See also the discussion in P. Readman, *Land and Nation in England: Patriotism, National Identity, and the Politics of Land, 1880–1914* (Woodbridge, 2008), pp. 113–16.
19. The classic account is given in George Shaw Lefevre, *English Commons and Forests. The Story of the Battle During the Last 30 Years for Public Rights over the Commons and Forests of England and Wales* (London, 1894).
20. For Berkhamsted, see B. Cowell, 'The Commons Preservation Society and the campaign for Berkhamsted Common, 1866–70', *Rural History*, 13:2 (2002), pp. 145–61.
21. H. Peek (ed.), *Six Essays on Commons Preservation* (London, 1867).
22. Shaw-Lefevre, *English Commons and Forests*, p. 360.
23. E. Baigent, 'A "Splendid Pleasure Ground [For] the Elevation and Refinement of the People of London": An historical geography of Epping Forest 1860–95', in E. Baigent and R. Mayhew, *English Geographies 1600–1950: Historical Essays on English Customs, Cultures and Communities in Honour of Jack Langton* (Oxford, 2009), pp. 104–26.
24. Roberts, 'Gladstonian Liberalism', p. 298.
25. Ibid., p. 311.
26. G. Darley, *Octavia Hill: Social Reformer and Founder of the National Trust* (London, 2010), pp. 277–8.
27. R. Hunter, *A Suggestion for the Better Preservation of Open Spaces: A Paper Read at the Annual Congress of the National Association for the Promotion of Social Science, Held at Birmingham, in September 1884*. Copy held in the archives of the National Trust.
28. For evidence of Hunter's voluminous knowledge of the subject of commons preservation, see Sir R. Hunter, *The Preservation of Open Spaces and of Footpaths and Other Rights of Way* (London, 1896).

29. See the chapters in E. Baigent and B. Cowell (eds), *'Nobler Imaginings and Mightier Struggles': Octavia Hill, Social Activism and the Remaking of British Society* (London, 2016).
30. P. Clayton, B. Cowell and V. Griffiths, *The Three Founders of the National Trust: Octavia Hill, Robert Hunter and Hardwicke Rawnsley* (London, 2020); A. Swenson, 'Founders of the National Trust (act. 1894–1895)', in L. Goldman (ed.), *Oxford Dictionary of National Biography* (Oxford, 2008).
31. D. Cannadine, 'Conservation: The National Trust and the National Heritage', in D. Cannadine, *In Churchill's Shadow: Confronting the Past in Modern Britain* (London, 2002), pp. 224–43, p. 232.
32. 7. Edw.VII, Act to incorporate and confer powers upon the National Trust for Places of Historic Interest or Natural Beauty, section 29. Available at https://nt.global.ssl.fastly.net/documents/download-national-trust-acts-1907-1971-post-order-2005.pdf [last accessed 1 March 2020].
33. P. Linebaugh, *The Magna Carta Manifesto: Liberties and Commons for All* (Berkeley and Los Angeles, 2008).
34. 'Parishes: Egham', in H. E. Malden (ed.), *A History of the County of Surrey: Volume 3* (London, 1911), pp. 419–27. Available at http://www.britsh-history.ac.uk/vch/surrey/vol3/pp419-427 [last accessed 23 February 2020]. More information has been taken from P. Williams, *Runnymede: A Pictorial History* (Egham, 1995).
35. Information drawn from notes assembled by Helena Normanton and held at Egham Museum.
36. 54 Geo. III, cap. 153, quoted in Malden, *History of the County of Surrey* (1911).
37. J. Workman, 'Normanton, Helena Florence (1882–1957)' in L. Goldman (ed.), *Oxford Dictionary of National Biography* (Oxford, 2004).
38. B. Cowell, *Runnymede and Magna Carta* (London, 2015); N. Vincent and S. Franklin, 'Runnymede and the commemoration of Magna Carta (1923–2015)'. Available at https://magnacarta.cmp.uea.ac.uk/read/feature_of_the_month/ Jul_2015 [last accessed 29 February 2020].
39. Woking, Surrey Archives Ac1498/10, as quoted in Vincent and Franklin 'Runnymede' (2015).
40. Helena Normanton notes, Egham Museum.
41. As reported in *The Scotsman*, 18 April 1930.
42. As reported in the press, for example *Portsmouth Evening News*, 16 May 1930.
43. *Nottingham Journal*, 16 February 1931.
44. The lodges went on to play a significant role in the history of the National Trust, albeit briefly. At the outbreak of war in September 1939 the Trust's central headquarters were evacuated to these lodges. They turned out to be completely unsuitable and the office was moved again to West Wycombe in Buckinghamshire. M. Bloch, *James Lees Milne: The Life* (London, 2009), p. 119.

45. *Daily Herald*, 27 May 1931.
46. As reported in *Surrey Advertiser*, 23 January 1932.
47. Ibid., 27 February 1932.
48. Ibid., 16 April 1932.
49. *Yorkshire Post and Leeds Intelligencer*, 9 July 1932. The vandalism was widely reported, for example in the *Coventry Evening Telegraph* (8 July 1932), *The Scotsman* (9 July 1932), *Portsmouth Evening News* (8 July 1932), *Taunton Courier, and Western Advertiser* (13 July 1932), *Western Gazette* (15 July 1932) and *Illustrated London News* (16 July 1932).
50. *Yorkshire Post and Leeds Intelligencer*, 9 July 1932.
51. The theory of the *Western Gazette*, 15 July 1932.
52. *Gloucester Citizen*, 19 July 1932.
53. *Sheffield Daily Telegraph*, 27 July 1932.
54. *Coventry Evening Telegraph*, 15 August 1932.
55. Available at https://www.nationaltrust.org.uk/lists/landscapes-and-nature [last accessed 9 March 2020].
56. G. Monbiot (ed.), R. Grey, T. Kenny, L. Macfarlane, A. Powell-Smith, G. Shrubsole and B. Stratford, *Land for the Many: Changing the Way our Fundamental Asset is Used, Owned and Governed* (London, 2019), p. 61.
57. G. Standing, *Plunder of the Commons: A Manifesto for Sharing Public Wealth* (London, 2019), pp. 8, 13.
58. See also, for example, G. Shrubsole, *Who Owns England? How We Lost our Green and Pleasant Land & How to Take it Back* (London, 2019); Howkins, 'Diggers to Dongas'.
59. See also the discussion in C. J. Griffin and I. Robertson, 'Moral ecologies: Conservation in conflict in rural England', *History Workshop Journal*, 82 (2016), pp. 24–49; Howkins, 'Uses and abuses'.

PART III

Legislation and its Impacts

7

The Introduction of the 'Gregory Clause' and Ireland's Great Famine

Ciarán Reilly

And be it enacted. That from and after the first day of November next, after the passing of this Act, no person who shall be in the occupation of any land of greater extent than the quarter of a statute acre shall be deemed and taken to be a destitute poor person under the provisions of the first-recited Act, or of the Acts amending the same, or of this Act; and if any person so occupying more than the quarter of a statute acre shall apply for relief, or if any person on his behalf shall apply for relief, it shall not be lawful for any board of guardians to grant such relief within or out of the workhouse ... [1]

There never yet was invented a more dangerous or destructive instrument for debasing, degrading, and ruining the poor, and crippling the resources of the rich, than this same clause.[2]

INTRODUCTION

IN THE COURSE OF the proceedings of the British House of Commons on 29 March 1847, William Gregory (1816–92), a county Galway landowner and MP for Dublin, proposed a clause to the Irish Poor Law Bill then under discussion as a means of alleviating the distress caused by the onset of Famine. Known officially as the 'Quarter Acre Clause', but thereafter more commonly referred to as the 'Gregory Clause', after much discussion the proposal eventually passed into law. This contentious clause had a detrimental impact on how the Great Irish Famine played out at a local level and would become a byword for landlord neglect and clearance. Almost as soon as it became law it had the effect of filling the already overcrowded Irish workhouse system and dominated debate both during and after the Famine. Moreover, the clause haunted Gregory and his legacy.[3]

First elected to Parliament for Dublin in 1842, when he defeated the former Lord Lieutenant of Ireland, Lord Morpeth, even then it was argued that Gregory lacked experience, and some predicted that he would find it difficult to prosper as a parliamentarian: 'It will be the cause that will triumph for the man is too young ... quite untried in politicks [sic]', wrote the county Wicklow-based Elizabeth Smith.[4] According to *Hansard*, Gregory, who represented Dublin (1842–7) and Galway (1857–72) in Parliament, spoke on 384 occasions in the house during his career. It is doubtful whether any of his contributions were as important, or indeed controversial, as that he gave in the Commons in March 1847, shortly before his first stint as an MP came to an end. In recent years, Gregory, who has long been depicted as one of the villains in the Famine narrative, has undergone somewhat of a reassessment by historians. Brian Walker, for example, argues that Gregory was harshly treated by his contemporaries and historians alike. Indeed, Walker argues that Gregory may even have been misquoted during the 'Quarter Acre' debate in the House of Commons, questioning the reliability of *Hansard* transcriptions at this time.[5] This essay does not seek to further that debate but instead examines the context in which the Gregory clause was framed and implemented, and places it within the wider changing public opinion towards the poor and the ongoing relief efforts in Ireland.

By the end of 1846, after two consecutive crop failures, it was evident that the two major government-sponsored relief schemes in operation in Ireland – the public works (which provided employment for the poor) and outdoor relief (through soup depots and kitchens) – were being grossly abused by those who sought assistance from them. Impersonation and deception were rife, and with resources stretched, relief committees across the country began to scrutinise their lists for fraud. Although many were successful in routing the scheme of defrauders and those who were not entitled to assistance, the government decided that both schemes were to be wound up. In their place, the government introduced a new Irish Poor Law Bill, where poor law unions took charge of local poverty and where the cost of this scheme was met entirely by poor law rates. Naturally, the suggestion was widely criticised by poor law unions already on the verge of bankruptcy, and ratepayers who themselves were now feeling the effects of continued famine. It was argued that such a proposal was unfeasible, as there was a significant portion of the population who did not own land and thus who were not ratepayers. When on 12 March Gregory queried in the House of Commons whether the government intended limiting the new relief bill to non-occupiers of land, the British Prime Minister, Lord John Russell, advised that he should bring a clause forward himself to that effect.[6] Returning on 27 March, Gregory duly did. He stated that the clause he was putting forward would 'guard the provisions of the bill from abuse' and so urged that those holders of land of quarter of an acre or more would not be entitled to the relief. Crucially, he argued, this would still allow the person to hold a small plot of potato ground and his cabin.

There followed a lively debate in which Gregory looked for support for the clause. In an oft-quoted passage, the accuracy of which Walker recently contested, Gregory was recorded as saying that if the Act had the effect of reducing the number of small farmers, 'he did not see of what use such small farmers could possibly be'. Defending his position, Gregory claimed that:

> Since he gave notice of his intention to move this clause, he had been in Ireland. He consulted persons the most intelligent and the most conversant with the condition of the people, and was by them assured that the limits of holding which he had formerly designed, 'half an acre,' was by far too extensive; and that there was no chance of the law working satisfactorily if persons holding more than 'a quarter of an acre,' were allowed to apply for relief. He accordingly inserted 'quarter of an acre' in the clause.[7]

Remarkably, and in light of what would follow, there was little opposition to the clause from Irish members in the House of Commons. On the contrary, some saw it as being both beneficial to the working of the Poor Law Bill and also to the improvement of Ireland going forward. Richard Bellew (1803–70), MP for Louth, believed that the clause would:

> most essentially aid the well working of the Bill in Ireland, and would tend to the gradual absorption of the small holdings now so extensively held, as well as the conversion of masses of starving peasantry into useful and well-paid labourers. Without such a clause, the poor law would tend rather to retard than to expedite this happy result.[8]

However, there were some opponents. George Poulett Scrope, MP for Stroud, objected to the implementation of the clause so suddenly, the consequence of which would be 'the complete clearance of the small farmers in Ireland – a change which would amount to a perfect social revolution in the state of things in that country'.[9] Perhaps the most pertinent question in the whole debate was posed by Colonel Rawdon, MP for Armagh (1840–52), who asked to what extent the clause would affect the rights of descendants. This was an important consideration, given the nature of leasing in Ireland in the 1840s and the fact that holdings were often divided among family members and thus many would suffer when a family entered the workhouse. It was a difficult choice which faced thousands of smallholders across the country, as outlined by Herbert Curteis, MP for Rye, who believed that the 'provision would be most unpopular in this country'. According to Curteis:

> the clause was meant to benefit the Irish landlords – a class which deserved little sympathy from the House or the country. What was a quarter of an acre of land? The peasant grew potatoes on it. Suppose his crop failed him; he must, in such case, give it up and go into the workhouse, or starve. It might be that the poor man, having a lease, would not surrender it. What then – must he hold it and starve?[10]

REACTIONS AND RESPONSES

In Ireland, the reaction to the clause was one of widespread condemnation, led in the main by newspaper editors. The editor of the *Cork Examiner*, in particular, was a vocal critic of the Act, writing that while the 'founder of the Society of St Vincent De Paul has a place among the blessed . . . the originator of the damnable Gregory Clause deserves a berth in Limbo'.[11] The editor, who also compared him to Oliver Cromwell, hoped that any future legislation Gregory was involved in would be drafted conscious of the fact that his 1847 Act was 'the most infamous measure that ever blackened the statue book of England by its inhuman cruelty'. He was not alone in his condemnation. Even before the new law was implemented and tested, many newspaper editors spoke out against the Act and the detrimental effect it would have. The *Dublin Weekly Register*, for example, claimed that it was an 'extermination clause with a vengeance' and that significantly, 'the means of testing whether one qualified for relief was in the hands of those who stood to gain most from it'. Predicting a bleak future, the editor predicted the clause 'would make way for cattle and sheep instead of people' and that 'the clearance code is now controlled by law!'.[12]

One of the most vocal critics of the clause was Fr John Sheehan of Ennistymon, county Clare, who witnessed at first hand the horrors which were inflicted by this new 'workhouse test', or what he called 'a life destroying clause'.[13] For Sheehan, the clause had done more damage than all other legislation relating to eviction over the course of the previous half century. County Clare was one of the parts of the country most affected by the clause, owing both to the nature of landholding and the callousness of landlords and workhouse officials. There were a number of harrowing stories of those who were refused entrance to the workhouse or relief because of this 'bungling legislation'. For example, in 1848 a man named Corbett in Glounagruss, near Meelick in county Clare, who had a wife and six 'helpless' children, died after being denied access to the outdoor relief because he owned a small plot of ground from Lord George Quinn.[14] In Limerick, there were numerous cases of people denied entry to the workhouse, including one of a man named Purcell, because of the clause and who subsequently died of hunger on the road.[15] It was a similar situation with another man named Purcell and his wife in Capanahanagh, county Limerick, who were refused entry to the workhouse because of the clause and so were left to starve.[16] It was little wonder that local parishes came together to object to the clause. In 1848 the inhabitants of the Tuam Poor Law Union drafted a petition to Parliament for 'a more humane test' for admittance to the workhouse or for outdoor relief.[17] Their plea fell on deaf ears and by July 1849 it was claimed that the Act would soon make the area around Tuam 'a vast waste of pauperism'.[18] There was widespread criticism that the clause had filled the workhouses, which had now become overburdened and heavily in debt. In solving one problem, the Gregory clause had created another.

However, privately and in some quarters, there was support for the clause. In the case of the aforementioned Elizabeth Smith, the wife of a county Wicklow landowner, the Gregory clause would finally solve their problem of dealing with 'the hordes of beggars' on their estate. In her personal diary, Smith appeared content that the Poor Relief bill 'precludes the holder of more than a rood of land from being in any way assisted', which would solve many of their personal problems. In particular, she was referring to the 'hordes' of smallholders who 'struggle on in their own miserable way as well as their low state of habits and feelings admit of, there are hardly more of them than are required even now, under this idle system of husbandry'. Whether her feelings were publicly aired is not known, but certainly her diary shows little empathy for their plight, continuing:

> The beggars are the small holders, entitled to no relief, and so we shall gradually get rid of them; they must give up their patches and take to labour. I am anxious to see the Bill for I feel pretty sure its provisions are in the main good.[19]

While Smith's sentiments displayed little sympathy for the plight of the poor, they did reflect the changing attitude towards the provision of relief. Local committees faced continued financial pressures from the distribution of relief as subscriptions began to dwindle. While these committees had been successful in the past during times of scarcity (such as in 1822 and 1831), their efforts then were usually temporary and made redundant by a subsequent bountiful harvest. By the summer of 1847, almost three million people were in receipt of this temporary relief, although by August that number, for a range of reasons, had been reduced to just over 2.5 million. While the Gregory clause continued to dominate discussion in political circles in early 1847, across the country relief committees began to scrutinise their lists as it became apparent the system was being abused, thereby denying those in genuine need of accessing relief. In May 1847, relief committees were informed that they must conduct a strict audit of the relief system within their own area and to

> use every means in their power to ascertain facts, and to fix the culpability on individuals, in order that they may be punished or exposed, and thus prevent an impression gaining grounds that such practice acquire as impunity from being common in the country.[20]

Many committees appointed teams of inspectors to visit the holdings of the relief recipient to ascertain claims.[21]

Abuses in the system were rife even where resident landowners sat on relief committees. Newspapers such as the *Anglo Celt* frequently called out those guilty of fraud and impersonation, publishing details of the abuse. Outraged at the continued misuse of relief committee provisions, others such as the *Cork Examiner* lambasted this behaviour, asking 'can it be true that coachmen, in the employment of gentlemen, gate-keepers, wood-rangers, and for all we know, ladies' maids, are receiving relief?' At Ardrahan, county Galway, the relief committee struck off a number of people from their lists who it was claimed were capable of looking after themselves and thus should not be in receipt of relief.[22] Likewise, at Strokestown in county Roscommon an inquiry into the recipients of relief found dozens of defrauders, including those receiving money from America; landholders of more than 10 acres; people using aliases; and the McKeon girls, four in all, who claimed to be orphans but their father was discovered to be in England and sending them money.[23] In Kilnaleck, county Cavan, it was a similar scenario. A series of abuses were halted following an inquiry carried out by Captain Hotham, when sixty-five people were struck from the list as they were deemed ineligible to receive relief. They included James Plunket of Leharry, an able-bodied weaver; Thomas McKiernan, who with his brother owned over 4 acres of land; and Edward Skelly, who had a crop of grain. There were others like Catherine McEntee, who was found to have misrepresented herself as 'silly' and was in receipt of relief although not entitled to do so. The defrauders also included shoemakers, blacksmiths and other tradesmen who did not pass the relief 'test'.[24]

Relief committees also scrutinised those employed on the public work schemes. Although a large number of the cottier class petitioned for help, representing themselves to be in 'great distress', there were others who sought to make the most of the public work schemes. In the barony of Tullygarvey in county Cavan, for example, there were a number of instances of impersonation in relation to the public works principally among farmers who sent their sons, although they did not qualify to do so. This particular abuse of the system had been highlighted by Sir George Grey during the debate in the House of Commons in March 1847. Grey's position was unambiguous, arguing that these smallholdings 'were the bane of Ireland' and

> that among persons seeking for relief on the public works were the holders of small farms, many of whom gave up the cultivation of their own little holdings in order to earn 6s a week under the Government system. It would be unwise to allow persons who held a considerable quantity of land to receive relief.[25]

Despite the scrutiny and vigilance, it was almost impossible to prevent abuse. In county Cork it was claimed that the greatest abuses were committed at the very time they were trying to eradicate them.[26] Likewise, the *Kerry Evening Post* lamented the fact that it was impossible to avoid abuse because so great was the impersonation and false claims.[27] However, despite the growing pressure to do so, some committees were reluctant to believe that abuses were committed in their area or at the very least report them. Under the chairmanship of Thomas Moriarty, the Ventry Relief Committee, for example, claimed in late 1847 that no abuses had occurred within their area.[28]

IRISH LANDLORDS AND EVICTION

Equally important to consider in the debate on the introduction of the Gregory clause was the changing attitude towards eviction by landlords and others. After initially granting abatements of rent and forgiving arrears in the early months of the Famine (and some were rather generous in that respect), by late 1846 landlords now turned their attention to eviction and clearance. This had begun in advance of the introduction of the Gregory clause and some landlords had made special provision for doing so.[29] Those like the Earl of Rosse in King's County (now Offaly) introduced estate rules with strict terms for the behaviour of tenants going forward. Many of these were impossible for tenants to adhere to, while more were unwilling to do so.[30] For Irish landlords this was necessary, given the sensation that the infamous Gerrard evictions, for example, had caused. It was now realised by all and sundry that eviction was 'a sure passport to celebrity'.[31] In Aghadda, county Cork, in March 1846, Reverend Townsend deplored the 'horrid clearance system', which had commenced in the county and which involved hundreds of people removed from their holdings.[32] In the same month, tenants were evicted near Ballylinan, Queen's County (now Laois), which prompted an assassination attempt on the estate under-agent who had served the writs.[33] The same was true of county Roscommon, where Lord Kilmaine evicted fifty-three families in April, most of whom owed in excess of three years' rent.[34] And throughout county Limerick the 'sacrifice of the mass and prayers' were offered for evicted tenants in Ballingarry and Killmallock.[35] Curiously, there was little opposition displayed at these eviction scenes. In March, when forty people were evicted from the Coote estate at Ballingarry, the presence of the military it was argued was 'most needless'.[36] These early examples of clearance, save the notorious eviction on the Gerrard estate in county Galway, garnered little attention from the public as a whole.[37]

This is important in terms of the association of the Gregory clause and eviction, which dominates much of the discourse about the Famine. There were a host of reasons why tenants were evicted, including criminal or secret society activity; voting at election against the landlord's wishes; and unsurprisingly, matters of religion were often cited for the removal of tenants, although such claims were always strenuously denied by landlord and agent alike.[38] Indeed, this clearance tide had begun in earnest after 1838 following the introduction of the Irish Poor Law Act and the creation of the workhouse system.[39] Landlords began to clear land safe in the knowledge that the newly established workhouse system would cater for the ejected. Eviction again escalated following a downturn in agricultural output from 1841 to 1843, when rental arrears accumulated on most estates. At Mountmellick, Queen's County, for example, more than a hundred people were evicted from lands owned by a Mr Tilly of Dublin.[40] In May 1844, the Earl of Orkney evicted 290 people in Tipperary, while the Earl of Norbury cleared a number of his tenants in the same county.[41] On the eve of the Famine it was claimed that evictions in county Carlow were being carried out to create 'a Protestant colony', while two months before the potato blight struck, the people of Castleconnell, county Limerick, were said to have 'felt the full weight of the eviction notice'.[42] No part of the country was spared eviction. In counties such as Wexford and Kilkenny, where landlords and their agents were widely praised in the early stages of the

Famine for their benevolence, by 1847 it was lamented that many now turned their attention to eviction.[43]

In time, many of these evictions were lost to popular social memory or muddled in the discussion regarding the Gregory clause, of which they were not associated. There were appalling instances of malevolence associated with these evictions. During the course of an eviction in January 1845 a Catholic priest in King's County (now Offaly) recalled that he had seen 'a wretched mother, with her three children, actually lying in the snow while the house was being levelled'.[44] Likewise, at the Beamish estate at Clonakilty, county Cork, in September 1847, where ninety-five people were removed, it was claimed that one poor woman was 'being buried to death amongst the ruins from which she had not the strength to drag her weakened limbs'. Another poor man, labouring under the effects of fever, was described as being demented, as the eviction was carried out.[45] At Drimnagh, county Roscommon, an entire townland was levelled in 1847 when 210 people were removed from the Barton estate.[46] Likewise, the *Cork Examiner* correspondent lambasted the Waterford landlord Arthur Kiely-Ussher for the removal of over seven hundred people at Ballysaggartmore in May 1847, reporting that

> an awful sight was before my eyes, I found twelve to fourteen houses levelled to the ground. The walls of a few were still standing but the roofs were taken off, the windows broken in, and the doors removed. Groups of famished women and crying children still hovered round the place of their birth, endeavouring to find shelter from the piercing cold of the mountain blast, cowering near the ruins or seeking refuge beneath the chimneys.[47]

These examples are offered merely to highlight the context in which the Gregory clause was introduced. Eviction was ubiquitous and the Gregory clause was just one wave which afflicted Ireland in the 1840s. The 'Gregory phase' was a more silent phase involving single families, but nonetheless saw little sympathy for the plight of the poor, as 'crowbar brigades' and 'hut tumblers' moved in to erase from the landscape the poor who made their way to the workhouse. This lasting legacy of bitterness towards eviction had more to do with the manner in which the levelling took place than to the criteria attached to the Poor Law Bill. Fuelling much of the animosity towards eviction was the part the local community played in the eviction process. In Ballycumber, King's County, for example, tenants were paid to pull down their neighbours' houses and many took advantage of doing so.[48] There was little remorse or charity on their part as they tormented those who were gripped with fever and hunger. Such was the zealousness of the 'levellers' that whole townlands could be erased in an afternoon. In Clondoogan, county Meath, in 1848, for example, it took only a few hours to level seventeen houses and in the process clear a whole townland.[49] Unsurprisingly, the bailiffs and hut levellers were the targets of much of the violence that followed. These brigades were hated figures in their local communities, described as 'monsters' and 'ogres' content with 'carrying out the devil's work'.[50] In many ways, then, the role of the local community was more important than the role of Gregory. These were the evictions which lingered in popular social memory. Of course, those who abandoned houses to enter the workhouse were unlikely to feature in the following week's provincial newspaper and we have no way of knowing the exact numbers concerned here.

Who made the most of the 'Gregory Clause' or partook in eviction separate to the provisions of the bill? Significantly, a sizeable proportion of the evictors were merchants, shopkeepers, doctors and other professional people, all of whom had acquired landholdings across the country in the decades prior to the Famine. Indeed, according to the *Dublin Evening Mail*, the 'agents of extermination' were not confined to the owners or cultivators of land, querying 'how many shopkeepers and tradesmen of Dublin have been driven into the same work?'.[51] Schools, colleges and institutions, including the College of Physicians, Trinity College Dublin, the Erasmus Smith Schools, the Commissioners of Education and Mercers Hospital, undertook eviction as a means of creating a more solvent tenant for their business model.[52] As one of the largest landholders in Ireland, with more than 195,000 acres, evictions on the Trinity College estates were particularly numerous during the Famine, owing to the long-standing management practice of leasing the lands to middlemen who subsequently relet them to undertenants. When pressure was applied by the college during the Famine, these middlemen evicted *en masse*; in county Kerry alone, more than six hundred people were from evicted from college property in early 1849.[53]

As the Poor Law Bill was debated in Parliament in 1847, those like the aforementioned Smiths of Baltiboys, who were friendly with the Gregorys and entertained them at their home in Wicklow, argued that the provision of relief could not be sustained by landlords. In April 1847, Smith noted in her diary that her husband

> has been writing to Lord John Russell about the injustice of rating the proprietors by Electoral Divisions six or eight or ten of them together, and to pay in equal proportions towards the support of all the paupers in the Division, instead of by townlands, each landlord burdened separately with his own, by which arrangement the good would reap the benefit of their care and the

bad would be deservedly charged with the maintenance of the beggary their neglect had fostered.[54]

Once again, Smith noted that the lower orders were using the relief schemes to their own advantage. Indeed, even on their estate there were those, she wrote, like Jem Doyle 'whom we employ out of charity, disinclining to work one rainy day went to the relief stores, much astonished to find that being in service he could get nothing when he preferred idling'.[55] Whether or not the Prime Minister replied to Smith's correspondence is unclear but a few days later there was a change in attitude about the poor in general. On 15 April she wrote in her diary:

> I am almost sick of the dishonesty of these poor miserable creatures. In every way, in all classes, lying, cheating, defrauding, concealing – every sort of underhand meanness is practised among them. Here has come to light such a tissue of evil as really disgusts one – how can it be otherwise – brought up in sin and sloth for the purpose of struggling through misery we are absurd to expect correct principles from so low a state of morals; patience – one had need indeed to be made of it, to endure life with such surroundings.[56]

Smith again returned to the abuse in the relief system and that little was being done to check it. In May she wrote:

> There are crowds of them who have been receiving relief as destitute all winter now coming into the market with cartloads of sound potatoes for which they are receiving extravagant prices and the 'greatest of praise' from their equals; 'think of that now! There's cuteness.' The want of probity strikes none of them. It requires unremitting watchfulness to keep farmers and tradesmen in decent circumstances from appropriating a share of the relief stores; they apply unblushingly for everything going, anything.[57]

These outbursts displayed a significant change in her attitude since January of that year when she wrote that to 'rouse' the poor from 'their natural apathy may be the work of future years. To feed them must be our business this.'[58]

Months of debate followed the introduction of Gregory's clause, during which time it was pointed out that there were a number of problems inherent with it. Firstly, the haphazard system of leasing and subdivision of land in the half century prior to the Famine meant that landholdings were saturated with many different families, while others held common ground.[59] This was a problem, which Sharman Crawford called attention to in the House of Commons as he proposed a motion to defeat or block the clause. According to Crawford, the poverty of one individual could spell ruin for many who would be forced to quit their holding.⁶⁰ In March 1848, Crawford moved for leave to bring in a bill to amend the Irish Poor Relief Extension Act and in particular to repeal the by now notorious '10th Section'. Debating the impact of the clause on Ireland, John Reynolds, who had replaced Gregory in the General Election of 1847 as MP for Dublin, claimed that he was only returned to Parliament for his opposition to the Act. For Reynolds, 'the quarter of an acre clause appeared to have been prepared for the particular benefit of the landlords, and furnished them with a powerful weapon for dispossessing the poorer sort of tenantry'.⁶¹ The debate was divisive. Colonel Edward Conolly of Castletown House in county Kildare opposed Crawford's motion, stating that 'landlords of Ireland had not profited by the quarter-acre clause. To say they had was a grossly unfounded aspersion upon them.'⁶² Edmond Roche, 1st Baron Fermoy (1815–74), reiterated these claims and argued that Irish landlords had not profited from the Gregory clause and 'it was nonsense to suggest it'. Roche also dispelled the suggestion that the poor would use the workhouse system if allowed to remain on the land, noting that 'there was nothing of which the Irish poor had a greater abhorrence than the workhouse; and he knew that the majority of them would rather die by the ditch side than enter it.'⁶³ Even Morgan J. O'Connell, son of the Liberator and MP for Kerry, would not support the motion, asking members to consider 'what would be the state of the country if relief were to be extended to all persons'?⁶⁴ There were others who objected to what Crawford proposed but perhaps one is worthy of mention. Sir William Somerville, Chief Secretary of Ireland from 1847 to 1852, opposed the motion weakly, arguing that

> the poor-law has nothing to do with that state of things. If the poor man goes to the workhouse to seek relief, and that during his absence from his home his landlord comes and levels his house, I believe that he might have done just the same thing if the man had only gone to market or elsewhere.⁶⁵

Of course, as a landlord in county Meath, Somerville in 1848 evicted a large number of tenants from his estate at Brownstown, near Navan. The removal of thirteen families prompted the *Limerick and Clare Examiner* newspaper to query whether the chief secretary could be cognisant of such proceedings. The tenants, the newspaper noted, were 'scarcely out of their homes when the houses were levelled'.⁶⁶ There were other similar cold conclusions. Reflecting the changing attitudes towards the poor, Colonel Francis Dunne, MP for Queen's County, argued that if 'the right to relief were to be extended to all classes, it was impossible that the country could support the burden'.⁶⁷

This chapter has examined the context within which the Gregory clause was introduced and implemented. Crucially, it allows for a greater understanding of the mindset of those who shaped and supported the clause through Parliament and in private. The changing nature of public and private opinion towards the poor is central to understanding the impact of the Gregory clause and indeed to how the Famine played out at a local level. Historians and others have long argued over the exact number of people who were evicted during the Famine years.[68] Owing to the imprecise nature of the record keeping by police and others, it is difficult to arrive at a definitive figure. Equally so, it remains unclear just how many of those were removed from the land because of the Gregory clause. While Gregory has been described as a victim of the Famine in that his reputation never recovered from the introduction of the clause,[69] it is difficult to argue with the assertion that it was a 'god send to the exterminator'.[70] These evictions occurred outside of the spotlight of the local newspaper or periodical of record. A family here, a family there. The levelling of houses continued throughout the Famine, as those on the verge of starvation gave up possession and entered the workhouse, swelling the numbers of what Paschal Mahoney has described as the 'grim bastilles of despair'.[71]

NOTES

1. An Act to make further Provision for the Relief of the destitute Poor in Ireland, 8 June 1847, 10 Vic., c. 31.
2. *Cork Examiner*, 16 February 1848.
3. See B. Walker, 'Villain, victim or prophet?: William Gregory and the Great Famine', in *Irish Historical Studies*, 38:152 (2013), pp. 579–99.
4. Diary of Elizabeth Smith, 30 January 1842 (in private possession).
5. See Walker, 'Villain, victim or prophet?', pp. 579–99.
6. House of Commons Debates, 12 March 1847, Vol. 90 cc. 1242–3, pp. 1242–3.
7. House of Commons Debates, 29 March 1847, Vol. 91 cc. 575–613.
8. Ibid.
9. Ibid.
10. Ibid.
11. *Cork Examiner*, 28 May 1849.
12. *Dublin Weekly Register*, 3 April 1847.
13. *Freeman's Journal*, 26 June 1849.
14. *Limerick and Clare Examiner*, 14 June 1848.
15. *Dublin Weekly Register*, 11 March 1848.
16. Ibid.

17. *Freeman's Journal*, 2 January 1849.
18. *Kerry Examiner*, 6 July 1849.
19. Diary of Elizabeth Smith, 8 April 1847 (in private possession).
20. *Cork Examiner*, 9 June 1847.
21. See, for example, for the operation of the Rathkenny Relief Committee, county Cavan (Clements Papers, Maynooth University, uncatalogued collection).
22. *Cork Examiner*, 16 July 1847.
23. See Ciarán Reilly, *Strokestown and the Great Famine* (Dublin, 2014), p. 22.
24. *Anglo Celt*, 6 October 1848.
25. House of Commons Debates, 29 March 1847, Vol. 91 cc. 575–613.
26. *Cork Examiner*, 17 December 1847.
27. *Kerry Evening Press*, 9 February 1848.
28. Ibid., 9 October 1847.
29. National Library of Ireland, EPH, D34, 'To the tenantry on the estate of John Mac Donnell, Esq.' [issued by] Charles W. Hamilton, 27 December 1846; L. P. Curtis, *The Depiction of Eviction in Ireland, 1845–1910* (Dublin, 2011).
30. Birr Castle Archives, J/3, 'Rules for the management of the Rosse estate'. See also *King's County Chronicle*, 3 February 1847.
31. *Freeman's Journal*, 10 April 1846.
32. Ibid., 4 March 1846.
33. Ibid.
34. *Connaught Telegraph*, 29 April 1846.
35. Ibid., 18 March 1846.
36. Ibid.
37. For more on the Gerrard eviction, see T. Crehan, *Marcella Gerrard's Galway estate, 1820–70* (Dublin, 2013).
38. See case of tenants evicted at Drumlish in county Longford in 1847 in *Dublin Weekly Register*, 23 October 1847.
39. See C. Reilly, 'Clearing the estate to fill the workhouse: King's County land agents and the Irish Poor Law Act of 1838', in V. Crossman and P. Gray (eds), *Poverty and Welfare in Ireland 1838–1948* (Dublin, 2011), pp. 145–63.
40. *Nation*, 20 May 1843. See also *Nenagh Guardian*, 1 July 1843.
41. *Limerick Reporter*, 10 May 1844.
42. *Cork Examiner*, 11 June 1845. See also *Dublin Evening* Post, 7 June 1845.
43. *Nation*, 23 October 1847.
44. *Wexford Independent*, 25 January 1845.
45. *Limerick & Clare Examiner*, 2 October 1847.
46. See *Freeman's Journal*, 27 August 1850. I am grateful to Jody Moylan for bringing this to my attention.
47. *Cork Examiner*, 24 May 1847.

48. *Nation*, 20 November 1849.
49. *Dublin Evening Post*, 22 August 1848.
50. *Connaught Telegraph*, 19 May 1852.
51. *Dublin Evening Post*, 29 November 1848.
52. See, for example, R. McCarthy, *The Trinity College Estates, 1800–1923: Corporate Management in an Age of Reform* (Dundalk, 1992); *Report from Commission of Board of Education in Ireland on Schools founded by Erasmus Smith*, H.C. 1810 (194), x, appendix 2, pp. 22–7; and *Evidence before Endowed Schools Commission*, H.C. 1857–8 (2336).
53. *Cork Examiner*, 4 May 1849.
54. Diary of Elizabeth Smith, 9 April 1847 (in private possession).
55. Ibid., 13 May 1847.
56. Ibid., 15 April 1847.
57. Ibid., 9 May 1847.
58. Ibid., 12 January 1847.
59. See, for example, the case of Strokestown, county Roscommon, in Reilly, *Strokestown*.
60. House of Commons Debates, 9 March 1848, Vol. 97 cc. 338–61.
61. Ibid.
62. Ibid.
63. Ibid.
64. Ibid.
65. Ibid.
66. *Limerick & Clare Examiner*, 22 November 1848.
67. House of Commons Debates, 9 March 1848, Vol. 97 cc. 338–61.
68. See J. S. Donnelly Jnr, *The Great Irish Potato Famine* (Stroud, 2001), pp. 138–40. See also T. P. O'Neill, 'Famine evictions', in C. King (ed.), *Famine, Land and Culture in Ireland* (Dublin, 2000), p. 29. In the 1880s a British government inquiry was told that almost 900,000 families had been evicted in Ireland during the previous fifty years, although how many of these occurred during the Famine was unclear. Michael Davitt, founder of the Irish Land League and himself a victim of eviction from his home in county Mayo during the Famine, estimated that almost 190,000 families or 950,000 people were dispossessed. More recently, historians including W. E. Vaughan have estimated that 250,000 people were evicted in the period from 1846 to 1854, while Tim O'Neill argues that the number was closer to 580,000. However, as the constabulary were only required to record eviction statistics from 1849 and many people were readmitted to holdings as caretakers, a definitive figure of how many were evicted during the Great Famine remains elusive.
69. See Walker, 'Villain, victim or prophet?', pp. 579–99.
70. *Freeman's Journal*, 26 June 1849.
71. See P. Mahoney, *Grim Bastilles of Despair: The Poor Law Union Workhouses in Ireland 2016* (Cork, 2016).

8

Small Landholdings and Society: The Legacy of Small Landholder Legislation in the South-west of Scotland, 1911–Present Day

Micky Gibbard

IN CONTEMPORARY BRITAIN, SCOTLAND is very much regarded as the pioneering force in progressive attitudes towards land use, management and reform. Historically, this is best demonstrated through successive attempts at policies and legislation which have championed land settlement and reform. In the Highlands and Islands, addressing the 'land question' has been shown in the increasing rights and protections of the crofting community, beginning with the Crofters Holdings (Scotland) Act 1886 and developing throughout the twentieth century and via the internationally celebrated Land Reform (Scotland) Act 2003 and its amendments of 2016.[1] Such initiatives have their roots in a long lineage, with the 'land question' enduring in Scotland throughout a large part of the nineteenth century, partially addressed in the Highlands and Islands by the aforementioned 1886 Act, and Scotland in its entirety via the Small Landholders (Scotland) Act 1911.[2] There is a tendency in the literature to focus on the Highland and Island experience of land settlement, with little attention paid to the Lowlands; it is the legacy and impact of the 1911 Act and successive legislation of the Land Settlement (Scotland) Act 1919 in the South-west Lowlands that are the focus of this chapter.[3]

Crofting (essentially small farming) in the Highlands and Islands has a vital cultural and emotional aspect around which the 1886 Act was formed. The foundation of the Napier Commission in 1883 highlighted the hardships – historic and contemporary – of the crofting community and it is not surprising that the Liberal government was keen to right the wrongs of land clearance still within living memory. The rights and securities granted under the 1886 Act are held as a significant moment in the fight for land within the crofting counties and have been widely celebrated by a number of historians.[4] While the 1886 Act was a response to deep-set grievances, the impetus for the 1911 Act was more radically proactive, even within the wider context of the land question in Scotland. What this Act allowed was for the newly formed Board of Agriculture for Scotland (hereafter BoAS) to establish landholding schemes on private land across Scotland and extend the rights and securities achieved under the 1886 Act to the whole of the country.[5] The final piece of significant legislation in this period came in the form of the Land Settlement (Scotland) Act 1919, which extended the powers of the 1911 Act, allowing for BoAS to purchase land, and granted access to more Treasury funds which, in turn, made land settlement in Scotland more readily achievable. This Act was passed under different circumstances, in part as a response to the post-war cry for land among rural communities.[6] Minor changes were made to the legislation in 1931 in the form of the Small Landholders and Agricultural Holdings (Scotland) Act, and collectively these Acts remain in the statute books as the Small Landholders Acts 1886–1931.[7] The above account of land settlement legislation in Scotland, while simplifying the multifaceted impetus for the passage of these Acts, nonetheless demonstrates a drive for land reform and settlement in Scotland within a short period of legislative history from 1886 to 1931. Most importantly, it meant the establishment of 'small landholdings', a form of land tenure now in terminal decline.

The term 'small landholding' is a legal definition for a type of tenancy coined at the time of the 1911 Act. It consists of a tenanted agricultural holding of less than 50 acres with an annual rent not exceeding £50.[8] This form of tenure was not dissimilar to a croft defined under the 1886 Act, in that the 1911 Act secured three core rights: security of tenure, fair rent and tenant compensation for improvements to the land. Following the establishment of 1,551 new holdings and 1,517 holding enlargements on private land, 1,721 new holdings and 392 enlargements on land purchased by BoAS up to 1931, and limited new establishments up to 1943, the Crofters (Scotland) Act 1955 designated (in some cases, redesignated) small landholdings within crofting counties as 'crofts'. The extant small landholdings outside these areas, however, maintained their own legal distinction.[9] It is at this point we see a split in the continued development and legacy of these two types of holding. Within the crofting counties, continued policy focus and legislative amendments have led to the extension of the rights and securities of crofters in the Highlands and Islands, including the significant 'right to buy' developed through the Crofters (Scotland) Act 1993 and, more recently, via the Land Reform (Scotland) Act 2003.[10] Small landholdings, on the other hand, have been left in something of a legislative cul-de-sac. While their number is dwindling – an estimated sixty-eight in 2018 – there has been renewed political focus on these 'Cinderella sister' holding schemes, and as such, contributions to the historiography must reflect such changes.[11]

The historiography of land settlement has developed around the view that the Highlands and Islands are more significant in the historical context of the land question in Scotland than the rest of the country. Such a contention is not without its merits and, indeed, the case of the Highlands and Islands has been historically more compelling than the remainder of Scotland, not just in the sheer number of holdings established, but the social and cultural aspects of the 'fight for land'. This does not mean that the schemes established outwith the crofting counties do not have valuable source material that can be used to unpick the realities and legacy of small landholdings in the Lowlands. In light of renewed political attention and the increasingly dwindling numbers of extant small landholdings, it is timely to address this historiographical oversight. In doing so, we can not only highlight the distinctiveness of the Lowland experience but serve to reinforce the importance of the historiographical focus based around collective memory and attachment to the land in the Highlands and Islands.

This chapter will critically analyse this underexplored aspect of Scottish land reform and settlement throughout the twentieth century. Small landholdings remain a quirk in Scottish land law, with limited legislative provision for over one hundred years; it is this uniqueness that makes them significant. The study will be approached by casting a critical look on empirical aspects of an individual land settlement scheme in the South-west Lowlands: Grassmillees, Ayrshire, proposed in 1920 and fully established by 1922.[12] Grassmillees represents a significant case study for several reasons, most notably its extensive documentation, but also the large size of the scheme and high retention rate of small landholders. This will allow us to more fully interrogate the legacy of these holdings up to the present day. This legacy is a growing identity of 'small landholders' that, while a minority, has been created by the lack of legislative developments brought into sharp relief by advancements in the Highlands and Islands. It will be argued that the uniqueness of small landholdings in the Lowlands has not been self-defining, but rather forms a stark point of contrast with the continued developments in Highland and Island land law. It will do so in three ways: by outlining land settlement developments to provide context; providing the empirical background of the Grassmillees holding scheme; and exploring how the legacy of little legislative or policy focus on the Lowlands has created a small landholding identity and how this can be used to strengthen rural identities across all of Scotland.

BACKGROUND TO LAND SETTLEMENT

The land question in nineteenth- and twentieth-century Scotland had been a vital component of political discussions, electioneering and, most importantly, rural identity. Such is the strength of the issue that it endures in contemporary political debates, and while this chapter deals with a marginal group, it stands to show how pervasive the issue is in Scottish rural society.[13] It is important, nonetheless, to be reminded that Scotland is by no means distinct; Ewen Cameron rightly points out that noting the distinctiveness of the Scottish land question carries difficulties which might undermine regional diversity.[14] This regional diversity has a long history, with deep-set cultural differences between Highland, Island and Lowland. As regards the land in modern history, this is best demonstrated in the differing approaches and outlooks of agricultural improvers in the eighteenth century and in the infamous Highland Clearances, which wrought devastating social change on the Highlands and Islands up to the 1860s.[15] Such processes have reshaped the importance of access to agricultural land across Scotland. The most significant aspect of this is seen in the way that land is historically viewed by those who worked it: in the Highlands and Islands forming a more vital cultural component related to regional identity, shared history and memory, and in the Lowlands carrying greater agricultural and economic connotations.[16]

The use of the land question in electioneering gained the Liberal party continuous success in Scotland from 1832 onwards, and the strength of feeling for land settlement in the Highlands and Islands began truly to gather momentum in the 1870s and early 1880s.[17] The eventual culmination of the 1886 Act marks the first legislative divide between the Highlands and Islands (the 'crofting counties') and the remainder of Scotland, primarily achieved on the strength of feeling about famine and poverty in the wake of the Clearances. This is not to say that the land question was not used as a political device outwith the crofting counties, and this chapter is framed around legislation that extended the powers of the 1886 Act to the whole of Scotland.

Following a protracted period of debate between 1906 and 1911, the Small Landholders (Scotland) Act 1911 came into force in April 1912. The Act gave BoAS the power to establish small landholdings (both new holdings and enlargements) on privately owned land and establish a form of dual ownership (meaning that the proprietor had ultimate ownership of the land, but the tenant owned buildings and improvement); significantly, this, via a process of arbitration through the newly formed

Scottish Land Court (SLC), could theoretically be achieved without the landowner's consent. This was the cause of significant misgivings, particularly among Lowland landowners who sought to obstruct the passage of the Act, which Cameron states reveals 'more about the attitudes of the Lowlands than the Highlands'.[18] The reaction of Lowland landowners to the passage of the Act was lobbied through the newly founded Scottish Land and Property Federation (SLPF) and much of the basis of their argument was that land settlement was an infringement on the rights of landowners.[19] Their input to the debates around the various iterations of the Small Landholders Bills delayed the Act's passage significantly, but most important were the clauses introduced to appease landowning interest. To pacify the vociferous opposition of the SLPF, a clause was introduced for the creation of Statutory Small Tenancies (SSTs), which gave a different legal distinction to holdings upon which the landowner had paid for improvements.[20]

Despite the continued opposition to various iterations of the Small Landholders Bill, following the concession of establishing SSTs under a distinctly less radical policy, the 1911 Act came into force the following year. The initial impact of the Act was staggering, with the preliminary applications for new holdings and enlargements totalling 5,532 by the end of 1912.[21] Of these initial applications for small landholdings, around 80 per cent came from within crofting counties. Given the cultural attachment and pre-existing landholding schemes established by the Congested Districts Board in the Highlands and Islands, this was unsurprising, although there was a hope that the application bias towards the crofting counties would balance out over time as small landholders in the south became increasingly aware of the benefits.[22] This would not be the case and in the period between 1911 and 1919, of the 14,651 total applications received by BoAS, 76 per cent were from within the crofting counties.[23] In terms of successful applications, the total number of holdings established and enlarged in this period under the provisions of the 1911 Act was 1,287, with 80 per cent within the crofting counties.[24] Nonetheless, as Cameron and Leah Leneman have noted, land settlement in this period was far below demand and landowners employed delaying tactics via loopholes in the amount of compensation they could receive.[25]

While the 1911 Act set a precedent to establish and enlarge holding schemes across all of Scotland, the outbreak of the First World War in July 1914 effectively put an end to land settlement, with scheme establishment figures falling between 1915 and 1918. In the South-west Lowlands, some schemes that had been suggested in 1912 and 1913 simply hit an administrative wall as the already skeleton staff established on the 1911 Act was yet further reduced by wartime conscription.[26] Legislative developments gathered steam again in 1918 when the new Land Settlement Bill was drafted, which featured significant revisions to the 1911 Act to make land settlement more achievable. The passage of the Land Settlement (Scotland) Act 1919 was uncontroversial and forms a stark point of contrast with the 1911 Act, making its passage in a mere six months, with prominent Scottish landowners including the Duke of Buccleuch, whose father vehemently opposed the 1911 Act, stating in a Lord's debate that 'as regards the Bill there is in the main no hostility towards it'.[27] The 1919 Act maintained the 'small landholding' distinction to the whole of Scotland but eliminated some of the clauses landowners could exploit to slow the land settlement process. It also allowed BoAS a more substantial budget and the ability to purchase land on which to establish schemes, in part to make up for the failures of settlement on private land under the 1911 Act. Up to 1931, BoAS established slightly more new holdings (1,721 to 1,551) on land purchase under the 1919 Act.[28] In the wake of the First World War, there was, too, a policy of prioritising the applications of ex-servicemen, which is seen in the details of tenants awarded small landholding tenancies following the passage of the 1919 Act. Additionally, while there was officially no legislative distinction between crofting and non-crofting counties, following a period of prioritisation of ex-servicemen, there was an unofficial policy that the Highlands and Islands be given precedence for settling small landholders.[29]

As noted, the historiography has tended to focus on the Highlands and Islands in its own right, and thus studies on small landholdings in Scotland are reflective of this trend. This history of land settlement in Scotland is dominated by a small group of scholars, all of whom focus on Highland exceptionalism. James Hunter and Ewen Cameron are among the most cited of this group of historians. Cameron focuses largely on the high numbers of applications and new holdings on the isles of Lewis and Skye under the 1911 and 1919 Acts, and argues that the case of the Highlands as an 'area of special policy' was borne of historicised politics as opposed to a simple need to furnish rural populations with small landholdings.[30] There are detailed accounts of land impacted by the Acts discussed above, and Iain Robertson and Robert Chambers both employ an empirical approach in exploring in-depth land settlement, particularly of the inter-war period.[31] Robertson provides us with the cultural underpinning of land raids which, prior to 1924, had a meaningful impact on driving land legislation and steering policy focus towards the Highlands and Islands, noting the power of collective memory in driving the Highland and Island impetus for land settlement. Similar to Hunter and Cameron, Robertson and Chambers adopt a Hebridean focus, which does not skew the historical reality that the vast majority of holdings were in the Highland and Island region, with a particular concentration on Lewis and Skye. Such works serve to justify the focus of this chapter on the minority experience of land settlement in Scotland through considering extant small landholdings and interesting 'exceptions' to wider experience. The only scholars to make use of extended discussion of land settlement in the Lowlands is Leah Leneman, who carried out extensive research into the pattern and experience of land settlement *on the ground*.[32] Leneman tends to employ a much less analytical approach, focusing on empirical accounts, and makes no links between sweeping generalisations made and detailed case study work.

What this brief historiographical overview demonstrates is the prevailing view that the Highlands and Islands not only have greater archival depth but a greater attachment to memory and heritage that is perhaps absent in Lowland land settlement. This is reflected in the literature and in approaches to legislation and policy, particularly from the late nineteenth century, and it is certainly true that the Highlands and Islands benefited more from the developments of 1911 and 1919 than anywhere else in Scotland. Important throughout debates around land settlement, particularly regarding the inclusion of the whole of Scotland, is Cameron's assertion that 'while the Highland debate was conducted in the realms of history and memory, the Lowland discussion was dominated by the more prosaic themes of agriculture and commerce'.[33] The implication of this was that more land settlement schemes were established in the Highlands and Islands – between 1911 and 1931 around 60 per cent of new holdings and over 99 per cent of enlargements.[34] In the first instance, this is a region with experience of land settlement prior to the passage of the 1911 Act. That crofts were already in existence is self-evident in the definitions laid out under the 1886 Act, but further, the actions of the Congested Districts Board pursued land settlement in the Highlands and Islands from 1897 until the passage of the 1911 Act. Second, the sheer numbers of applicants for small landholdings from the Highland and Island region far outweighs those elsewhere. It has been argued by some that the particularly problematic history of the Highlands and Islands, as well as an atavistic connection to the land in part, explains the reasons behind this.[35]

In land settlement, the active process of drawing on Highland and Island history and memory developed in tandem with policy and legislature.[36] There is something of a mutually beneficial bond between the practice of history and policymaking that lends itself to the development of land settlement and land reform legislation. In historicising the debates on land settlement to give justification to its aims, it is not difficult to see that the case for the Highlands and Islands is rather more meaningful and developed than in the remainder of Scotland: notably, the Highland Clearances give a collective impetus for renewed land legislation that rural society in the Lowlands lacks. This has ensured that Highland and Island historiography of the land serves to justify new reforms and legislation, while those same reforms give meaning to and contextualise historiographies. This is the reason for both a lack of literature on the Lowland experience of land settlement and, similarly, the lack of any legislative change since the final iteration of the Small Landholders Acts 1886–1931. With that in mind, it is not surprising that contemporary developments in legislature in the Highlands and Islands are marked by contributions by historians which both draw on history and memory while providing an impetus for further change.

GRASSMILLEES, AYRSHIRE

Within Scottish land settlement, the area outwith the crofting counties accounted for 2,448 new holdings (a little over 50 per cent of the total new holdings) and around 1 per cent of the enlargements across Scotland.[37] Of the new holdings established outwith the crofting counties, the South-west comprised around 45 per cent, with Ayrshire maintaining the highest concentration.[38] Up to 1931, Ayrshire had seventeen schemes established on private land, eleven of which before the 1919 Act, with a further six schemes established on land purchased by BoAS under the powers of the 1919 Act.[39] These are important distinctions to make and it should be further noted that the selection of Grassmillees is in part reflective of it being established on private land. This approach is justified by the fact that the majority, if not all, of the extant small landholdings remain on private estates, as the contractual obligations of small landholders on land purchased by BoAS have been settled and no longer exist. Grassmillees as a case study is also reflective of the exceptionally high number of extant holdings on the scheme – eight of the original fifteen holdings – and the availability of archival material. These advantages will be used to indicate possible histories and legacies of the wider South-west and Lowlands more generally.

In Ayrshire, several small schemes were established on private land between 1912 and 1918, with two much more substantial schemes established in 1914 (prior to the First World War) and 1918 (which settled a number of ex-servicemen).[40] Following the passage of the 1919 Act, a greater allocation of Treasury budget meant that a number of large schemes were established throughout the Lowlands. Of the six schemes established on land purchased by BoAS, only Collenan and Maxwood farms were acquired in the immediate wake of the 1919 Act, with two schemes with a large number of small landholders proposed on private land in 1920 and 1921 respectively.[41] The former of these, Grassmillees Farm, in the parish of Mauchline around 12 miles northeast of Ayr, is the best documented and among the largest surviving of the schemes.[42]

The case in Grassmillees is not unique in small landholding creation, even after the vital changes made under the 1919 Act. Originally proposed in 1920, it took two years to finalise through a seemingly drawn-out process.[43] Grassmillees, as we shall see, was representative of the labyrinthine processes under BoAS, landowner obstruction and complex interactions with local authorities, all of which slowed the scheme. The proposal for establishing holdings on Grassmillees Farm first appears in the records in March 1920, when Gillespie and Paterson, the agents of the landowner, the Trustees of Sir Claud Alexander of Ballochmyle, were notified of BoAS's interest in establishing fifteen small landholders of between 'three or four and 40 acres'.[44] The farm originally comprised around 189 acres of mixed farming land, tenanted to John Brown between 1905 and 1920, with a new tenant, Robert Paton, set to take entry from Martinmas 1920.[45] Compensation claims, as with many holding schemes, comprised the bulk of negotiations following BoAS's indication that Grassmillees was a preferential site, and it was clear that they would have to settle a substantial compensation payout to the landowner, as well as to Brown for his equipment and Paton for 'loss of profits and disturbance'.[46] Despite the potential for expensive compensation, the need for land settlement in the parish of Mauchline was regarded as a priority in the South-west and Grassmillees represented what was seen as the cheapest opportunity to settle ex-servicemen in the area.[47] Nonetheless, a substantial compensation figure was settled at £2,161 for Paton, regarded as 'hush money' to facilitate quicker completion of the scheme, and £540 to Brown, both of which were negotiated within a reasonably short time frame.[48] There were, however, difficulties in settling the claim of the landowner, with some significant differences in opinion on what might be settled. Up to February 1921, BoAS papers indicate that the landowner compensation approved by the Secretary for Scotland was £1,030, which increased to around £1,627 at the approval of the Director of Land Settlement on 14 February 1921.[49] At this time, too, the landowner had suggested their compensation claim would be £7,930 – dramatically unrealistic, and likely used as a delaying tactic.[50] A meeting on 30 March indicated that 'the agents for the Estate stated that they might be prepared to consider a settlement of the proprietors' claims for compensation at £2,500'.[51] BoAS, nonetheless, was not willing to pay above £1,800 and this impasse persisted into 1922, when the landowner lodged a claim of £6,605 with the Scottish Land Court.[52] The ruling from this hearing settled the compensation claim of the landowner at £2,200 plus 'reasonable legal expenses', throwing out a number of the claims of the landowner, including loss of rent and mineral rights.[53] During this process, BoAS were selecting applicants, all of whom were ex-servicemen, and comments on their character, experience and service records, as was always the case in settling small landholders, reveal a varied rural but not necessarily agricultural background.[54]

At Grassmillees, Leneman notes that the circumstances of its foundation illustrate wider problems of the 'long drawn out squabbles' regarding land settlement and landlord delaying tactics, even after the passage of the 1919 Act.[55] What is perhaps overlooked in her outline of the scheme is quite how wide-reaching these 'squabbles' were. Aside from the disputes over compensation there were several competing interests exacerbated by the more developed Lowland areas with more complex patterns of land ownership. BoAS was unprepared for the bureaucracy of land settlement in the Lowlands. At Grassmillees, delays were the result of protracted negotiations between BoAS and the Water Subcommittee of Mauchline Parish Council, regarding supply across and access to pipes where holdings might be constituted, Ballochmyle Quarries, regarding the placement of buildings on one of the holdings, and the Glasgow and South Western Railway Company, regarding an access road.[56] While the delays involved in this were by no means uncommon, they certainly appear to manifest themselves more obviously in Lowland holding schemes.[57]

As noted, the success and exceptionality of Grassmillees hinged on the basis that it had a high retention rate, with all the holdings remaining until 1938, when a disabled ex-serviceman, David Naismith Livingstone, a blind poultry farmer, resumed the remainder of his holding, keeping the house and garden; houses were developed on the land.[58] The rest of the holdings remained until 1954 when another holder, Alexander Auld, transferred his loans and holding to his brother, William, a tenant on an adjacent holding.[59] Following this, an intimation from William Auld to leave his holdings in 1957 and a lack of documentation post-1958 suggests that both holdings were resumed at some point in the late 1950s.[60] These three resumptions apparently all took place largely for a lack of suitable inheritors or an inability to work the holding, indicating that resumption was for arbitrary reasons, as opposed to either a lessening need of the holdings to remain, or the landowner's inducement to consolidate farmland once the call for land settlement had begun to abate.

That there were only three resumptions until at least 2013, excepting one holding with an undocumented history, reflects a desire to inherit these holdings and to remain a small landholder despite the increasingly out-of-date legislation in the wake of continued developments for crofters post-1955. This desire is further supported by the fact that Grassmillees experienced standard rent increases by the landowner in 1965, 1972, 1978, 2013 and 2017.[61] Those that were resumed following 2013 received settlements to retain house and gardens and give up access to the land, presumably for the construction of houses, as in the case of the Livingstone holding in 1938.[62] While this is certainly the case on all holdings schemes, we might surmise that the dwindling numbers across the remainder of the Lowlands are likely a combination of difficulties in finding suitable inheritors, old age, or at the inducement of a landowner offering compensation to resume the holding and sell the land. Numbers at Grassmillees and across various schemes on Arran (which boasts the highest combined concentration) still suggest a desire to inherit small landholdings. At Grassmillees, from 1938, it appears that adjacent holders James Gilliland and his son, Thomas D. Gilliland, had their holdings referred to collectively in any correspondence in the Department of Agriculture's (DoA) papers, and the holdings are now collectively tenanted to a farm 15 miles north-east of Mauchline, T. D. Gilliland and Sons.[63] Additionally, at least five of the extant holdings are third or fourth generation direct descendants of the original holders.[64] Despite the Lowland regions having limited experience of land settlement before 1911, the willingness to bequeath holdings despite successive rent increases might be indicative of a growing attachment to the land and that there is a growing identity as a 'small landholder'. This is not to denigrate the difficult past and shared cultural and physical hardship of crofters in the Highlands and Islands, but is a demonstration of an 'other' identity that has emerged in the Lowlands as a result of static legislative procedures.

SUCCESS AND LEGACY

When considering land settlement in the Lowlands today, framing discussion around success and legacy is important. Officially, the legacy of land settlement is considered a success. This was reported in the annual reviews of BoAS and DoA, and it seems that an obsession with *the number* of those settled on small landholdings was certainly the ultimate aim. In the Highlands and Islands, both Cameron and Leneman have questioned to what extent land settlement can be considered a 'success', tending towards the view that the legislation was enacted on a piecemeal basis and thus did not meet the needs of the applicants.[65] The Lowlands represent a more complex and nuanced account of success and legacy, and defining these in short- and long-term contexts is essential. That Grassmillees only experienced one resumption by 1955 implies that the short-term success of the scheme was high; similarly, the long-term success is seen in at least twelve of the holdings remaining up to 2013. Nonetheless, it is vital to consider success within the context of purpose, which, at the time of Grassmillees' foundation, was to provide ex-servicemen with land and the means to provide for themselves. At Grassmillees, all of those settled on the scheme were ex-servicemen, reflective of the policy of their settlement on land prior to demobilisation, and so arguably Grassmillees was a success.[66] This can also be said of the vast majority of Lowland settlement schemes established post-1918, which had a much higher proportion of ex-servicemen being settled than in the Highlands and Islands.[67] Success, however, can also be measured by the absence of what pre-existed the scheme, and Grassmillees Farm was considered among the most fertile in the parish. If, then, we were to use agricultural productivity as a criterion, small landholdings, particularly in the fertile South-west Lowlands, were a failure. This was evident even as early as the 1940s, when an economic report noted:

> It is clear, whatever criterion may be used, that small holdings cannot be equally successful in all forms of agricultural production. All the evidence in this Report points to the fact that small holdings are not so well adapted to mixed farming practice as to the more 'intensive' forms of production.[68]

While highly fertile land is not uniform across the Lowlands in its entirety, small landholdings cannot be considered as contributing to wider agricultural needs. In the long term, Grassmillees might be considered a failure, as since 1998 only one holding has continued to work the land.[69]

The divergence of small landholding history occurred with the passage of the Crofters Act 1955, whereafter the Highlands and Islands (the crofting counties) continued to maintain an evolutionary approach to the legislature and policymaking. In the Lowlands, the abandonment of any future policy and the approach of BoAS and DoA following the establishment of strict enforcement of non-involvement in the schemes aside from loan repayments, presented the burden of responsibility to the landowner.[70] From the late 1950s, the decline of these holdings began as estates started to buy them out on the basis of being a historical anachronism. For the small landholder, their terms began to look increasingly unfavourable, particularly in contrast with the ever-increasing rights and securities enjoyed by crofters. As a result, by 2018 only an estimated sixty-eight small landholdings remained in existence in Scotland. To dismiss this number as insignificant would be to favour the more utilitarian view of agricultural policy in Scotland; these holdings represent a portion of rural society in the Lowlands with their historical roots growing ever deeper. It is a nascent culture and identity but a strong one, most notably demonstrated by Arran small landholdings refusing to take the opportunity to convert small landholdings to crofts under the 2010 extension of the crofting counties. Malcolm Combe has noted that this indicates 'there is no appetite for conversion or that the existing conversion process is not appealing'.[71] This might suggest a willingness to maintain the distinction of 'small landholding', although the terminal nature of their decline, Combe further notes, makes them prime candidates for 'modernisation and reform'.

Under land settlement in the Lowlands, there was no consideration of the potential for a cultural shift in rural society, as there was in the Highlands. The narrow imperative on the part of the government to furnish those who required it with land and limited engagement thereafter has allowed for a nascent culture and identity of small landholders to flourish. No collective memory exists to draw upon and thus the absence of a rallying point has limited the lobbying for development of land legislation in the region. A by-product of this laissez-faire approach has been just that: a rallying point around which to forge an identity as a small landholder seeking the extension of rights and securities afforded to crofters to secure inheritance and enable the right to buy.

CONCLUSION

This chapter has argued that an emergent culture and identity of small landholding has been forged not through contemporary radical policies, collective land agitation or political lobbying, but by an absence of precisely these. The success of land settlement across Scotland as a whole is a point of contention, with many historians suggesting that while the intentions are to be celebrated, policies were piecemeal and did not necessarily pursue land settlement to the extent needed. From the inception of the 1911 Act to 1943, BoAS and DoA only settled around 25 per cent of the demand for small landholdings, and even considering withdrawn applications, managed a little under 40 per cent.[72] The success of land settlement as a whole is not, however, the point of contention here. While the discussion of a history of land settlement has provided important context in this chapter, the most pertinent point is that the collective memory and history of the Highlands and Islands was a vital inducement for forcing through land legislation between 1886 and 1931 and again from 1955 to the present day. The crofting identity, culture and community has been forged on past historical injustices and the radical policies that sought to rectify these. This, combined with substantial numbers with a marginal crofting life on infertile soil, has maintained a voice among legislative influences and policymakers. That voice is, of course, something to be celebrated, but it is important to consider the position of small landholders.

In the case of Grassmillees, a group of small landholders with a nearly one-hundred-year history and ties to the land has been created. The original group of small landholders who took entry of the scheme around 1922 no longer have shallow historical roots on the land that has been worked by successive generations of their descendants, who through this inheritance have formed familial attachments to both the land and the role of the small landholder. This is especially the case on the Isle of Arran, a district with the highest concentration of extant schemes, all of which have a similarly long history. What is interesting about Grassmillees in the present day is that of the remaining holdings only one is worked by the tenants, while at least two others are leased to the owner of a larger farm and the remainder let their fields for grazing.[73] The reality is that many of the buildings on these small landholdings were constructed by the current tenant's grandparents or great-grandparents and the land, until recently, had been worked by successive generations of the same family. It might be the case that the agricultural legacy in these small landholdings is disappearing, but the emotional attachment to the land survives, perhaps suggesting that the 'small landholder' as an emergent identity in rural Scotland is in terminal decline. Work by the Scottish Government between 2016 and 2020 has sought to shed light on the history and possible legislative future of this form of tenure, but there are significant archival and oral histories still to be unlocked in the history of extant small landholdings in Scotland. This chapter has attempted to point towards bridging the gap between legislative developments and the small landholders themselves; there is still, however, important work to be done before this form of tenure disappears completely.

NOTES

1. Crofters Holdings (Scotland) Act 1886, 49 & 50 Vict., c. 29; Land Reform (Scotland) Act 2003, asp 2; Land Reform (Scotland) Act 2016, asp 18.
2. Small Landholders (Scotland) Act 1911, 1 & 2 Geo. V, c. 49.
3. Land Settlement (Scotland) Act 1919, 9 & 10 Geo. V, c. 97; this chapter considers the 'South West' as the historic counties of Ayrshire, Bute (which includes the Isle of Arran), Dumfriesshire, Kirkcudbrightshire, Lanarkshire, Renfrewshire and Wigtownshire.
4. The crofting counties were originally in the historic counties of Argyll, Caithness, Inverness, Ross and Cromarty, Sutherland, Orkney and Shetland. The Crofting Reform (Designation of Areas) (Scotland) Act 2010 extended this definition to encompass Moray, parts of Argyll and Bute, Arran, Great Cumbrae and Little Cumbrae, where some small landholdings remain extant. The most notable works on this include James Hunter, *The Making of the Crofting Community* (Edinburgh, 2018); Ewen Cameron, *Land for the People? The British Government and the Scottish Highlands, c. 1880–1925* (East Linton, 1996); T. M. Devine, *Clanship to Crofters' War: The Social Transformation of the Scottish Highlands* (Manchester, 1994).
5. For the Highlands and Islands, this meant that the term 'croft' was legally defunct between 1911 and 1955, and this form of tenure was designated as a 'small landholding'.
6. For more on the post-war rural Lowlands, see Richard Anthony, *Herds and Hinds: Farm Labour in Lowland Scotland, 1900–1939* (East Linton, 1997).
7. Small Landholders and Agricultural Holdings (Scotland) Act 1931, 21 & 22 Geo. V, c. 44.
8. Small Landholders (Scotland) Act 1911, section 26. The Isle of Lewis had special provision for small landholders not exceeding 30 acres or £30 in annual rent (section 27).
9. National Records of Scotland [hereafter NRS], AF66/95, Summary of Settlements Reported to 31 December 1931. It should be noted here that these figures are the sum for *total* land settlement in Scotland and therefore include establishment under the Congested Districts (Scotland) Act 1897 and the Small Colonies Holdings (Scotland) Acts of 1916 and 1918,

although it should be stressed that the vast majority of land settlement in Scotland was achieved under the 1911 and 1919 Acts.
10. Crofters (Scotland) Act 1993, c. 44.
11. Annie Tindley, 'Small landholdings: Landownership and registration', *Scottish Government Project Report* (Edinburgh, 2018), p. 6; Idem, 'Small landholdings in Scotland: Piloting a new land register', *Scottish Government Project Report* (Edinburgh, 2020). See also 'Review of legislation governing small landholdings in Scotland', *Scottish Government* (Edinburgh, 2017).
12. NRS, AF83/1174-1188.
13. See, for instance, Hunter, *The Other Side of Sorrow: Nature and People in the Scottish Highlands* (Edinburgh, 2014).
14. Cameron, 'Setting the heather on fire: The Land Question in Scotland', in Matthew Cragoe and Paul Redman (eds), *The Land Question in Britain, 1750–1950* (London, 2010), p. 109.
15. These are best summarised in Frederic Albritton Jonsson, *Enlightenment's Frontier: The Scottish Highlands and the Origins of Environmentalism* (Yale, CT, 2013); Eric Richards, *Leviathan of Wealth: Sutherland Fortune in the Industrial Revolution* (Edinburgh, 1973); idem, *A History of the Highland Clearances* (London, 1982).
16. On memory, see Charles W. J. Withers, 'Landscape, memory, history: Gloomy memories and the 19th-century Scottish Highlands', *Scottish Geographical Journal*, 121:1 (2005), pp. 29–44; Iain J. M. Robertson, *Landscapes of Protest in the Scottish Highlands after 1914: The Later Highland Land Wars* (London, 2013). On Lowland agriculture, see Anthony, *Herds and Hinds*; David Turnock, *The Making of the Scottish Rural Landscape* (Edinburgh, 1995).
17. Cameron, 'Setting the heather on fire', p. 109.
18. Ibid., p. 116.
19. NRS, GD325.
20. Small Landholders (Scotland) Act 1911, section 32.
21. BoAS Annual Report, 1912, p. viii.
22. Cameron, *Land for the People?*, p. 145. The schemes established in the Highlands and Islands before 1911 were largely under the Congested Districts (Scotland) Act 1897, 60 & 61 Vict., c. 53.
23. BoAS Annual Report, 1919, Appendix II.
24. Ibid., Appendix II.
25. Cameron, *Land for the People?*, p. 146; Leneman, *Fit for Heroes? Land Settlement in Scotland after World War One* (Aberdeen, 1989), p. 54.
26. This is especially true of the schemes on the Isle of Arran.
27. HL Deb 11 December 1919, Vol. 37, c. 896.
28. NRS, AF66/95.
29. Cameron, *Land for the People?*, p. 169.

30. Ibid., pp. 163–4; Idem, 'The Scottish Highlands as a Special Policy Area, 1886 to 1965', *Rural History*, 8:2 (1997), pp. 195–215.
31. Robertson, *Landscapes of Protest*; Robert Chambers, 'For want of land: A study of land settlement in the Outer Hebrides, Skye and Raasay between the two World Wars' (unpublished PhD Thesis, University of Aberdeen, 2013).
32. Leneman, *Fit for Heroes?*
33. Ibid., p. 116.
34. NRS, AF66/95.
35. Robertson, *Landscapes of Protest*.
36. This has manifested most recently in James Hunter, 'Peopling emptied places' (Scottish Land Commission, 2019).
37. NRS, AF66/95. These figures relate to the *total* land settlement between 1897 and 1931. In the Lowlands this is largely under the provisions of the 1911 and 1919 Acts.
38. Ibid.
39. Ibid.
40. Schemes established in Ayrshire under the powers of the 1911 Act include Downieston (1912), Bargany (1913), Busbie (1914 and 1931), Alton Albany (1914), Pinmerry (1914), Dupin (1918), Wyllieland (1914), Dinmurchie (1914), Auchengate (1915), West Altercannoch (1916) and Burnton (1918); there was also one scheme established post-1931 on land purchased by BoAS, Mainholm Small Holdings Scheme (1934).
41. Schemes established in Ayrshire on land acquired by BoAS include Collenan (1919), Maxwood (1919), South Craig (1925), Auchincruive (1929), Auchenwynd (1930) and Mosshead (1930).
42. Other schemes established in Ayrshire on private land post-1919 include Nether Barr (1921), Old Mill (1921), Ploughland (1927), Downan (1930) and an extension to Busbie (1931).
43. NRS, AF83/881-884; AF83/1265-1267.
44. NRS, AF83/1174.
45. Ibid.
46. NRS, AF83/1179, 'Tenant's compensation'.
47. Leneman, *Fit for Heroes?*, pp. 178–80.
48. NRS, AF83/1179. See also Leneman, *Fit for Heroes?*, p. 179.
49. NRS, AF83/1176.
50. Ibid.
51. Ibid.
52. *The Scotsman*, 24 March 1922.
53. AF83/1178, SLC Order, 14 November 1922.
54. NRS, AF83/1182.
55. Leneman, *Fit for Heroes?*, p. 178.
56. Details of these 'squabbles' are found throughout NRS, AF83/1174-1188.
57. This was especially true of schemes on the Isle of Arran, for instance, Springbank and Bennicarrigan.

58. NRS, AF83/1185; 'resumption' refers to where an estate regains the ability to let or alter the holding as they see fit, no long subject to the powers of the Small Landholders Acts, 1886–1931.
59. NRS, AF83/1187.
60. Ibid.
61. Grassmillees Land Register (2020), https://data.ncl.ac.uk/articles/Grassmillees_Land_Register/12066114 [accessed 30 April 2020].
62. Grassmillees Land Register (2020).
63. Ibid.
64. Ibid.
65. Cameron, Land for the People?, pp. 202–4; Leneman, Fit for Heroes?, pp. 203–8.
66. NRS, AF83/1182.
67. NRS, AF66/95.
68. NRS, AF43/290, Archibald Murchie, 'An Economic Survey of Small Holdings in Scotland, 1934'.
69. Grassmillees Land Register (2020).
70. At Grassmillees, this is found continually throughout AF83/1174-1188.
71. Malcolm Combe, 'Small holdings, big complexities', Journal of the Law Society of Scotland, 62:4.
72. Land Settlement in Scotland: Report of the Scottish Land Settlement Committee (1944–5), pp. 18–19.
73. Grassmillees Land Register (2020).

9

The Case for Separate Agricultural Legislation for Wales

John Gwilym Owen and Nerys Llewelyn Jones

INTRODUCTION

IT IS WELL KNOWN that the majority of the Welsh Land Commissioners recommended in 1896 that there should be a separate Land Court for Wales established in law.[1] However, such a Court was never implemented and unlike Scotland and Ireland, Wales was to remain legislatively indistinguishable from England in these matters by reference to The Agricultural Holdings (England) Act 1875, The Agricultural Holdings (England) Acts 1883–1900 and The Agricultural Holdings Act 1906. The rhetoric and patriotic fervour of some radical Liberal Welsh MPs in the years leading up to the establishment of the Welsh Land Commission in 1893, and its reporting in 1896, has been subject to comprehensive analysis by historians such as David W. Howell, J. Graham Jones and Matthew Cragoe.[2] In comparison, the years immediately following the publication of the *Report* have received very little scholarly attention. This paper will demonstrate how calls for separate treatment for Wales in respect of agricultural matters, including demands to implement the Land Court, continued after 1896. This is significant for two reasons: firstly, it sheds light on a hitherto under-researched aspect of legal history, namely the calls for separate legislation for Wales in respect of agricultural matters, both *before* the setting up of the Commission and in the years *immediately after* the time when the Commission reported; and secondly, it contextualises suggestions made later in this article that, by reference to the current law on arbitration to settle disputes between landlord and tenant in England and Wales, arbitration is not fit for purpose. Welsh Government is considering reform of agricultural tenancy law in Wales.[3] As agriculture has been devolved in Wales since The Government of Wales Act 1998, Wales could choose to pursue a distinctive agenda from England in agricultural matters under discussion in this article. It will be argued that by placing this narrative in its full historical context, proposals for reform in Wales may be understood more clearly.

The article will examine the background to the Commission together with the calls for reform which continued in the period following the reporting of the Commission in 1896.[4] This reveals a longer-term perspective on the 'Welsh Land Question' than that which is usually outlined in the historiography and will reveal what appears to be a homogenous Welsh agenda. The authors will analyse the legislation set out in the preceding paragraph together with contemporary and current law relating to disputes in respect of rent, tenant right and succession. The paper will conclude by suggesting that specifically Welsh proposals for reform of the law in Wales in respect of these matters could be made. These issues will be analysed by reference to the following six discrete sections and end with an overarching conclusion.

BACKGROUND TO THE WELSH LAND COMMISSION AND THE BASIS OF ARBITRATION

Across nineteenth-century Wales there was a radical nonconformist agenda to uproot the power and influence of the gentry, partly fuelled by agricultural depression.[5] The problems were rooted in wider debates about religion, politics, education and the future of Wales. This movement included a drive for separate or distinctive legislation for Wales, for example the Sunday Closing (Wales) Act 1881 and the Welsh Intermediate Education Act 1889.[6] These Acts were important as they promoted Welsh identity and were applicable only in Wales and not England. Indeed, prior to the Sunday Closing (Wales) Act 1881, there had been no Act dealing just with Wales since the Tudor Acts of Union 1536–43. One of the features of the disestablishment movement was to try to undermine the role and influence of both landed estates and the Anglican Church. This was aligned to the political movement to overpower the influence of the Tories in Wales, as highlighted by Graham Jones:

> Rural inter-relationships were undermined by a basic cleavage between landlords and tenants in religion, language and political outlook (a divide which did not feature in England) potently reinforced by memories of the elections of 1868 . . .[7]

Thomas Ellis (1859–99) MP was a leading proponent for reform. He was brought up on the Rhiwlas estate near Bala, whose family had been evicted from their farms in 1859 and 1868. He was much influenced by these events, as indeed by events in Ireland; and by the Irish Land Act 1881 and the Crofters Holdings (Scotland) Act 1886, which had attempted to improve the position of the Irish and Scottish agricultural tenant. There had been continuous attempts to introduce a Welsh Land Bill to Parliament across the late 1880s and 1890s, and Ellis had played a prominent part in these debates. In a House of Commons speech in 1892 concerning the Tenure of Land (Wales) Bill (No. 27), he said that 'after the election of 1859 in the Counties of Carnarvon, Cardigan, Carmarthen, notices to quit came like snow-flakes'.[8] In the same speech he talked of 'the evil of insecurity of tenure' and 'the terror of the notice to quit' in seeking to negotiate higher rents. He also pointed to the fact that custom had played a prominent part in tenancy agreements in Wales but no longer as they were expressly excluded in the agreement. He gave examples of old customs whereby on the death of a tenant a farm would pass to a son or other family member, and how an incoming tenant paid market value for stock and an amount for goodwill. As stated, he argued that landlords charged too much rent and did not provide sufficient security of tenure. Other prominent complaints included lack of compensation for improvements and disturbance by game, such complaints being largely confined to the political platform and the columns of radical newspapers.

Often referred to in Dublin as the 'Parnell of Wales', Ellis was also present at the Mitchelstown massacre when police attacked and killed tenant farmers. However, land agitation in Wales was intermittent and transient.[9] Further, unlike in Ireland, the Welsh land reform movement was generally peaceful.[10] This is important as the alleged good relationship[11] between landlords and tenants in Wales was very much a driving force in the ultimate rejection of a Land Court, even after it had been recommended by the Commission. It is true that whereas there was antagonism in Wales, especially at the time of the 1868 elections, relations seemingly did improve from that point. J. Graham Jones has stated:

> ... Wales of the 1880s, where at least piecemeal evidence of relatively harmonious rural inter-relationships and mutual respect between landlords and tenantry stands in striking contrast to the acrimony and unrelieved antagonism of the contemporary social scene in Ireland.[12]

By 1893 the problems in Wales were not the same as those in Ireland; for example, there was not a problem with landlord absenteeism in Wales as there was in Ireland.[13] However, there was a concern that the methods and tactics of Irish agrarian radicals could be replicated in

Wales and it was this 'Irish card' which was seized upon by radicals such as Tom Ellis. As in Ireland and Scotland, the government's response was to delay legislative action by appointing the Land Commission in 1893 to investigate these issues, and it was while he was an MP (1886–99) that Ellis[14] put pressure on Gladstone to appoint a Royal Commission on Land for Wales whose terms of reference were 'to inquire into the conditions upon which land is held, occupied, and cultivated in Wales and Monmouthshire'.[15]

What was persuasive was that in Wales, in the traditional landlord and tenant relationship, mutual obligations were recognised to one another outside of the strictly contractual legal and economic relationship outlined largely in annual tenancy agreements.[16] This meant that landlords, often through their agents, could sit down with tenants and negotiate by means of a flexible private negotiation. However, one must be careful in analysing what this meant. This statement is probably not true in the context of negotiating the terms of the tenancy, which were set out in standard tenancy agreements on each estate, and the annual nature of these agreements vested significant power in favour of landowners. This meant that tenants were expected to accept the terms or lose their tenancy. The statement relating to a flexible private negotiation is probably true in terms of disputes over revaluations of land leading to increases in rent; and disputes over compensation due for tenant-funded improvements, and that arbitration was only applicable in limited circumstances. In this respect, Vincent refers to evidence given by a valuer in giving evidence to the Commission that '. . . [t]he rent is fixed by valuation on this estate by a practical valuer and a tenant farmer'. The same surveyor goes on to say that this was 'practically the universal system' in circumstances giving rise to adjustments of rent.[17]

Vincent then goes on to consider the position where a landowner tried to contract out of the Agricultural Holdings Act 1883 and concludes that it really made no difference:

> . . . and when the tenancy comes to an end, the tenant goes to his lawyer, who laughs at the whole business, and recovers for him precisely the amount of compensation under the Act which he would have obtained if the clause purporting to avoid the Act had not been inserted.[18]

This relationship of mutual obligation and responsibility referred to above was critically important in the life of rural Wales and included a flexibility on the part of landowners of smaller estates who had the potential to develop more intimate relations with their tenants. The owners of larger estates could afford to be more generous in terms of investing in improvements, paying compensation for improvements, in negotiating rents and in respect of providing more security of tenure. It was argued that a Land Court would be too rigid in that it would have interfered with the freedom of contract between landlord and tenant and would not have provided the same degree of flexibility as the traditional status quo.[19] There were arguments in favour of a Land Court on the basis that it would have created a safety net for those tenants whose landlords were financially unable to negotiate privately over these matters, but ultimately such arguments did not find favour. However, as will be seen later in the article, a significant feature in the rejection of a Land Court was political, as it was perceived as being linked to Home Rule for Wales.

As such, private negotiation with arbitration available where this fails, has been the basis for the settling of disputes between landlords and tenants in Wales and in England. Indeed, this fact is recognised in the current consultation on Agricultural Tenancy Reform in Wales.[20]

This paper now turns to consider relevant agricultural legislation both before and immediately after the Commission of 1893–6.

THE AGRICULTURAL HOLDINGS (ENGLAND) ACT 1875 AND THE AGRICULTURAL HOLDINGS (ENGLAND) ACTS 1883–1900

Notwithstanding reference to England in the above legislation, this legislation applied to both England and Wales.

The Agricultural Holdings (England) Act 1875 (the 1875 Act)

The 1875 Act came into force on 14 February 1876, predating the 1893 Commission.[21] It was passed predominantly for economic reasons as agriculture needed to be supported, but there were political difficulties in view of 'the constraints of the prevailing political beliefs (freedom of contract, free trade and *laissez faire*)'.[22] There were no provisions in the 1875 Act dealing with security of tenure, and half a year's notice expiring on a tenancy termination date was sufficient to bring an agricultural tenancy to an end in cases not involving a tenant's bankruptcy.[23] The main provisions of the 1875 Act dealt with an agricultural tenant's right to compensation for unexhausted improvements, which comprised three classes and different amounts of compensation payable according to the class of improvement.[24] Examples from each class included: drainage of land; erection or enlargement of buildings; laying down of permanent pasture; the making or improving of roads or bridges; chalking of land

and clay burning; and application to the land of purchased manure.²⁵ It is also important to note that the compensation provisions were not mandatory, and by agreement between the parties, or more likely by the landowner's preference, these provisions could be avoided in the tenancy agreement.²⁶ If the compensation provisions were not avoided, the 1875 Act laid down a procedure for the settlement of disputes by reference to a referee/umpire.²⁷

The Agricultural Holdings (England) Act 1883 (the 1883 Act) *and The Agricultural Holdings (England) Act 1900* (the 1900 Act)

The 1883 Act came into force on 1 January 1884 and although it repealed the 1875 Act it in fact extended the number of improvements for which compensation was payable and had provision for dispute resolution like the 1875 Act.²⁸ ²⁹ The biggest changes were the provisions prohibiting contracting out of the payment of compensation by agreement. It 'marked for the first time the compulsory intervention of the law in the supposedly voluntary bargains between tenants and landlord'³⁰ and increased the notice period in giving notice to quit from a half year to a full year.³¹

The preamble to the 1900 Act states that it received the Royal Assent on 8 August 1900 and came into force on 1 January 1901.³² It preserved much of the 1883 Act³³ but it provided for the first time a procedure whereby disputes were to be referred to arbitration by name before a single arbitrator in default of any dispute procedure set out in the tenancy agreement.³⁴ There are two points to be made here; firstly, the authors have noted reference in an 1882 newspaper article to proposals for arbitration predating the 1900 Act. An article in the *Bristol Mercury* dated 4 March 1882 makes reference to a County Government Bill omitting provisions for a Land Court for England and Wales, making reference instead to a Court of Arbitration; and secondly, there does not appear to be any practical difference in the dispute resolution procedures under the 1875 and 1883 Acts and the 1900 Act other than in name only, i.e., there appears to be no real difference between a referral to a referee/umpire and an arbitrator, as both were entitled to make awards. Therefore, it might fairly be said that statutory arbitration goes back to 1875 in agricultural disputes.

We now turn to consider the Welsh agenda for separate Welsh agricultural legislation in the years leading up to the Commission which sat between 1893 and 1896 and the apparently forgotten Welsh agenda in the years immediately following the Commission's report in 1896. The divergence between the pre- and post-Commission context is conveniently encapsulated by J. Graham Jones:[35]

> By the time of its [the Commission's report] appearance, the Liberal Government had fallen from office, to be succeeded by a notoriously unsympathetic Tory administration which survived for ten years. Moreover, a striking improvement in the social and economic prosperity of rural Wales meant that the issue largely lacked substance by the time the report appeared.

There was a particularly Welsh dimension to the 1900 Act, and there is evidence of repeated attempts by Francis Channing (1841–1926), Liberal MP for Northamptonshire East, to introduce his own bill on a regular basis since at least 1887.[36] It has already been noted that Thomas Ellis had been attempting to introduce to Parliament a 'Welsh Land Bill' from around the same period and that it was Ellis' Tenure of Land (Wales) Bill in 1892 which encouraged Gladstone to appoint a Royal Commission. Ultimately, it was a government bill in 1900 which led to the 1900 Act, which was a watered-down version of Channing's bills and recommendations for a Welsh Land Court by the Commission. The evidence will show anger among some Welsh MPs generated by the fact that the government had not passed separate Welsh legislation as it was worried about demands for Home Rule.

THE HANSARD DEBATES LEADING UP TO THE 1900 ACT

The Agricultural Holdings Bill was first presented on the motion of Channing et al. on 28 January 1887.[37] It followed a debate beginning on 25 January 1886 with a speech made by the Chancellor of the Duchy of Lancaster (Chaplin) about the agricultural depression. Chaplin quotes Barclay, MP for Forfarshire, who entered the debate. Barclay had criticised existing legislation, particularly in the Scottish and Irish context, but did not discuss Wales. Channing alleged in August 1887 that the government had 'persistently blocked this Bill'.[38] An amended bill was brought in by the same MPs in October 1888, another on 22 October 1889 and another on 18 February 1890.[39] The subject of valuation and compensation for improvements was first brought up in the Commons by Channing on 9 June 1890.[40] A new bill to consolidate and amend was brought in by Channing (now making reference to England and Wales) on 26 November 1890,[41] and another on 10 February 1892.[42] Channing presented his proposals on an almost annual basis, with evidence of Welsh MPs entering the debate in 1897, notably after the conclusion of the Welsh Land Commission. Samuel Smith, the Liberal MP for

Flintshire, stated that '[he] regretted that the Speech from the Throne took no notice of the important Report of the Welsh Land Commission'. He talked about 'great dissatisfaction in Wales if no action was taken upon the Report' and went on to say that 'a crisis had arrived which could not be surmounted except by a system of judicial rents and fixity of tenure, as was the case in Ireland'.[43] Support for the Welsh agenda was not confined to Welsh MPs. The Liberal MP Sir Henry Campbell Bannerman raised concern about the lack of priority given to the bill and mentioned 'unanimous recommendations of the Welsh Commission' which he stated had been 'disregarded'.[44] However, the *Liverpool Mercury* reported on 24 June 1899 that in the debate in the House of Lords the day before, the then Conservative Prime Minister, Lord Salisbury, had been against a Land Court in Wales. Opinion on this was mixed, with the *Boston Guardian* reporting on 1 July 1899 that Earl Carrington strongly supported the establishment of a Land Court for Wales.[45]

A full debate on the government bill took place on 9 April 1900, in which Welsh MPs took part.[46] The Liberal Swansea MP, Mr Brynmor Jones, had been a member of the Commission and he referred to the lack of provision of specifically Welsh legislation. In the context of the recommendation for a Land Court, he said he thought they 'had hit upon a measure which would secure the proper and equitable adjustment of the rights of landlord and tenant'. He went on to say that '[t]he Commission unanimously said that the circumstances in Wales were such as to demand separate treatment by a separate Bill'. As for the issue as to whether the Commission sympathised with Home Rule in Wales, he said that 'was not in the mind certainly of Lord Kenyon and was certainly not in my own mind'.[47] Another Liberal Welsh MP, Herbert Roberts (Denbighshire, West), spoke about the specific objectives of Welsh farmers. He supported the bill with a heavy heart and went on to say:

> It is perfectly useless, therefore, to try and explain to the House the reasons for which we make an urgent claim for special land legislation on political, historical, and racial grounds. I am prepared to support the Bill so far as it goes. I grant that from the point of view of machinery it will be an improvement on the Act of 1883. I wish to say that we in Wales cannot look upon it as in any sense or degree a satisfactory solution of the Welsh land problem; and we must leave it to the future and to other conditions – Parliamentary conditions, perhaps – under which we may look forward to receiving satisfactory legislation on this important question.[48]

There is also evidence of a Welsh agenda following the 1900 Act in the debates leading up to the passing of the Agricultural Holdings Act 1906 (the 1906 Act), to which the discussion now turns.

THE AGRICULTURAL HOLDINGS ACT 1906

The 1900 Act was amended by the 1906 Act, which received the Royal Assent on 21 December 1906 and came into force on 1 January 1909. Damage by game had been a major source of discontent in Wales, as it had in Ireland and Scotland. Consequently, the 1906 Act introduced certain new measures, such as the right to compensation for damage to crops by game (defined as deer, pheasants, partridges, grouse and black game), with the amount of such compensation to be determined by way of arbitration.[49] Further provisions included freedom of cropping and disposal of produce, 'notwithstanding any custom of the country and or the provisions of any contract of tenancy';[50] compensation for unreasonable disturbance with differences to be referred to arbitration;[51] the consent of the landlord not being required for repairs to buildings 'being necessary for the proper cultivation or working of the holding, other than repairs which the tenant is himself under an obligation to execute';[52] and the right of either the landlord or the tenant to have a record of the condition of the holding (buildings, fences, gates, roads, drains, ditches and cultivation) made within three months of the commencement of the tenancy.[53]

THE HANSARD DEBATES POST-1900

In a debate about local government in Wales on 18 March 1903, MPs repeatedly brought up the subject of devolution, and it is clear that feelings were running high at the time.[54] Brynmor Jones, Liberal MP (Swansea District), while criticising the President of the Local Government Board,[55] stated that Lord Kenyon and Sir John Llewelyn had recommended 'certain clauses for Wales' in the Agricultural Holdings Bill, but that the President of the Local Government Board had refused, referring to him as '[l]ike Mephistopheles . . . as far as Wales was concerned, the spirit of the everlasting "no"'. It was a patriotic speech, which referred to when the Welsh legal system became unified with that of England in 1830. He said that the Member for Plymouth 'had hardly grasped the true position of Wales in regard to the United Kingdom' and went on to say that '[i]t was perfectly true that in 1830 the Welsh Judicature was suppressed, but not in accordance with the feelings of the Welsh people'. Further, he said, '[t]he right hon. gentleman thought that what was good for Wiltshire was good enough for Wales, but this Resolution was a protest against that attitude'. In summing up he went on to say:

> ... Wales was a separate entity by virtue of its history and its social and economic conditions, and by virtue of the fact that its own language was spoken by over 50 per cent of its inhabitants; and that in all the essential elements which went to form a nationality Wales was distinct from any other county in England, Scotland or Ireland. That point had never been fairly and squarely met by the right hon. Gentleman. They wanted from the Government a definite recognition of this for many purposes, for Wales was a separate entity. They were not wild and sentimental persons imbued with any notion of separation from the United Kingdom. Why was Wales always treated like this?

We have already noted reference to specifically Welsh legislation at the end of the nineteenth century, namely the Sunday Closing (Wales) Act 1881 and the Welsh Intermediate Education Act 1889. The Cymru Fydd movement was established in 1886 to promote Home Rule for Wales and lasted until 1896. This debate can perhaps be seen as part of a drive in Wales at this time for Welsh independence, and within a few years of the debate the Welsh Board of Education was formed in 1907.

CONTEMPORARY AND CURRENT LAW

Bearing these historical points in mind, the discussion will now turn to the modern law in respect of agricultural tenancies in England and Wales, and suggest that Wales could introduce further legislation which diverges from that which exists in England.[56] However, and in order to provide a more comprehensive account, before turning immediately to the contemporary and modern legislation applicable in Wales, there will be a brief discussion outlining the key features of agricultural legislation between the 1906 Act and the current legislation. This section will therefore contain three sub-sections: a brief explanation of the key features of the legislation between 1906 and the law applicable today; relevant contemporary and modern agricultural law; and problems with arbitration. There then follows an overarching conclusion suggesting that proposals for reform in Wales should consider the historical narrative.

Key features of the legislation between the 1906 Act and contemporary and modern agricultural legislation

The provisions of the 1900 Act and the 1906 Act were consolidated in the Agricultural Holdings Act 1908 (the 1908 Act), which was followed by amending Acts in 1913, 1914, 1920 and 1921. There then followed a consolidation in the Agricultural Holdings Act 1923 (the 1923 Act). However, there was still no security of tenure over and above what had been provided in the notice provisions contained in the 1883 Act, which had been carried forward through successive Acts. As for rent increases, section 12(5)(a) of the 1923 Act provided that any demand for an increase in rent which was not agreed had to be referred to arbitration and in determining that rent an arbitrator was not to take into account any of the tenant's improvements.[57] The detailed provisions in the 1923 Act relating to the right of the tenant to compensation for improvements[58] were very similar to those contained in current agricultural legislation detailed below, and disputed matters were to be referred to arbitration.[59] The provisions introduced in the 1906 Act were in relation to compensation for damage by game; freedom cropping and disposal of produce and the right to a record of the condition of the holding were carried over into the 1923 Act.[60]

The authors have not noticed any Welsh agenda between the 1906 Act and the 1923 Act, although two points should be noted. In 1919 a Welsh department of the Ministry of Agriculture and Fisheries was formed.[61] Further, a question put by Sir Herbert Roberts to Mr Runciman, the President of the Board of Agriculture, is of interest to the discussion. Roberts asked the President whether there was dissatisfaction in north Wales concerning arbitrators nominated under the 1908 Act who could not speak Welsh and were not au fait with Welsh farming. The President responded by saying that he was only aware of one such case but that the arbitrator would have the services of an interpreter and that he was conversant with Welsh farming methods.[62] Although this refers to a particular case, as has previously been noted, pressure was being put on successive governments at this time for Welsh autonomy. This might suggest that there may have been a public outcry over a certain case around language and politics, and how they were bound up with wider issues concerning identity and agrarian politics. The discussion now turns to consider the more modern law in respect of the matters under discussion.

Contemporary and current agricultural law

Following on from the 1923 Act, the next major piece of legislation was the Agriculture Act 1947 (the 1947 Act). The main provisions for the purposes of this article are contained in sections 31, 68 and 73 of the 1947 Act.[63] By virtue of section 31, for the very first time tenants were provided with security of tenure, as that section introduced restrictions on termination by notice of tenancies of holdings. The tenant had the right to serve notice on the landlord within one month after the giving of the notice to quit requiring the Minister of Agriculture to consent to the operation of the notice to quit. The Minister was empowered to delegate such functions[64] to newly formed County Agricultural Executives, which were established by the 1947 Act.[65] However, the notice would be incontestable if certain grounds were made out in the notice, for example, if the tenant had not been farming in accordance with the rules of good husbandry set out in Part II of the 1947 Act; or if the tenant had failed to pay rent due within two months of serving of a notice requiring payment of unpaid rent.[66] However, it should be borne in mind that the death of a tenant would automatically bring a tenancy to an end notwithstanding any assignment or sub-letting thereof.

Section 68 of the 1947 Act established the Agricultural Land Commission. Section 68(5) provided that functions of the Commission pertaining to Wales and Monmouthshire were to be delegated to a sub-commission entitled the Welsh Agricultural Sub-Commission, and Section 68(6) provided that 'one of the persons appointed to be a member of the Commission shall be a person appearing to the Minister to be qualified as having special knowledge and experience of agriculture in Wales'. However, it was by virtue of section 73 of the 1947 Act that an Agricultural Land Tribunal in Wales came into existence, as the Minister was mandated to 'constitute such number of areas, as he may consider expedient, and for each area so constituted there shall be established an Agricultural Land Tribunal'. This was not a Welsh Land Court with special powers in respect of Wales. Rather, the Agricultural Land Tribunal in Wales was treated the same as other Agricultural Land Tribunals established in England. It was the Minister of Agriculture who ordered the provision and procedure for the various Agricultural Land Tribunals.[67] It should be noted that these measures replaced the local county agricultural committees[68] which had been in existence in Wales prior to the 1947 Act. The 1947 Act was repealed and re-enacted (with what had not been repealed of the 1923 Act by the 1947 Act) in the Agricultural Holdings Act 1948. The 1948 Act maintained the provisions in the 1947 Act for 'good estate management' on the part of the landlord and 'good husbandry' on the part of the tenant. As has been conveniently summarised by Seabrooke, the law had now reached a point at which the legislation had improved the position of the tenant:[69]

> ... it greatly strengthened his security of tenure; it introduced a 'fair rent' basis for rental assessment; it ensured a right to financial compensation for improvements by the tenant which result in residual benefit to the farm on the termination of a tenancy; it granted a right, in certain circumstances, for the tenant to claim compensation for the disturbance if forced to quit the farm as a result of notice to quit served by the landlord.

Various amending legislation followed the 1948 Act, the most important of which for the purposes of this article are summarised below.

From a historical perspective, perhaps the most interesting change was the one brought about by The Agriculture Act 1958 (the 1958 Act). As has been seen, matters pertaining to notices to quit had been determined by the Minister of Agriculture under the 1947 Act. Therefore, at that time, the Minister of Agriculture dealt with the operation of notices to quit, but other matters as detailed in this article (i.e. disputes as to rent and compensation claims) were referred to arbitration. However, following the 1958 Act the Minister's functions relating to hearing claims concerning the operation of notices to quit were transferred to the Agricultural Lands Tribunal. The debate on 18 March 1958[70] details the heated exchanges between the then Minister of Agriculture, Fisheries and Food (Mr John Hare) with certain MPs who opposed the change. The Minister stated that '[t]he Franks Report recommended the setting up of subordinate land tribunals to take over the judicial functions at present carried out by the agricultural executive committees' (i.e. the County Executive Committees set up under s.71 of the 1947 Act, detailed above). The Minister stated that 'judicial functions ought not to be carried out by Ministers or their agents' and summarised the government's position as follows:

> We propose that applications for consent notices to quit, applications for certificates of bad husbandry, applications for tenants to carry out improvements without the landlord's consent, all should be heard by the agricultural land tribunals, and we propose that the Lord Chancellor should make rules of procedure for those tribunals.

The Minister got his way and the 1958 Act enacted that the functions of the Minister and the County Executive Committees in determining consent for the operation of notices to quit passed to the Agricultural Land Tribunals. The 1958 Act did not alter any of the provisions relating to arbitration. For example, disputes concerning rent and compensation for improvements were still to be referred to arbitration. The Minister said during the debate on 18 March 1958:

> The overwhelming majority of farm rents, as the House well knows, are fixed by agreement between landlord and tenant. Nothing in the Bill alters that. If they cannot reach agreement, there is provision for arbitration under the 1948 Act; and nothing in the Bill alters that.

Although supporting the Bill, Sir C. Mott-Radclyffe highlighted good relations between landlord and tenant in the agricultural community:

> [t]he landowner and tenant in the agricultural industry well understand each other's problems. That is why the system works. I have often thought that if in certain other industries, notably nationalised industries, relations were as good as they are in the agricultural industry, we should not have any balance of payment problems.

Although enacted, the change faced heavy opposition in the Commons, especially from Mr Thomas Williams (Don Valley). This was because there was concern that the professional lawyers sitting in the Agricultural Land Tribunals would not have the relevant experience of dealing with agricultural matters as would members of the County Executive Committees. Mr Thomas Williams summarised this as follows during the debate:

> The valuable experience of county agricultural executive committees is completely lost; the intimate relations within the industry are ignored and for all practical purposes the final arbiters on questions of farming efficiency, sound estate management and greater hardship will be lawyers mostly without farming experience at all.

One Welsh MP, Mr Tudor Watkins (Brecon and Radnor), was concerned that 'security of tenure will be undermined by the Bill'. He pointed out that '[w]e have a great cause in our fight for security of tenure in Wales which goes back to the beginning of the century and before then'. Thus, the Agricultural Land Tribunal's powers were enhanced. However, as McNall has pointed out, there was discontent with the Tribunal, resulting in many types of dispute being referred to arbitration.[71] This will be discussed below but some understanding of the present law is required. However, as this article is primarily concerned with historical developments, only a summary of the current law is offered here to place calls for reform in Wales in a historical context.

By virtue of the Government of Wales Act 1998, the National Assembly for Wales was able to legislate for the first time on matters pertaining to agriculture.⁷² As already noted, whereas there are some differences in legislation between England and Wales in respect of agricultural matters, for the purposes of the explanations provided below, those differences are not material. Following legislation passed in 1976, 1977, 1984, 1986 and 1995, the current law in relation to agricultural holdings in England and Wales, insofar as it is relevant for this article, may be conveniently summarised as follows.

In general, with agricultural tenancies in existence before 1 September 1995 (Agricultural Holdings Act Tenancies) there is lifetime security of tenure, with tenancies entered into before 12 July 1984 having succession rights for two generations on death or retirement subject to satisfying certain eligibility requirements. For tenancies after 1 September 1995 (Farm Business Tenancies) there is no security of tenure, with Farm Business Tenancies being commonly let for a set period of years and determinable on the death of the tenant. Further, the current legislation on Agricultural Holdings Act Tenancies allows for either landlord or tenant to call for a rent review every three years and to demand compensation for improvements on the determination of the tenancy subject to consent being given in the case of long-term improvements. The current legislation provides that in the event of a dispute concerning any of these matters, certain matters are to be referred to arbitration and certain matters to the Agricultural Land Tribunal.⁷³

More recently the Agriculture Act 2020 has introduced amendments to Agricultural Holdings Act Tenancies and Farm Business Tenancies under Schedule 3. First, it is now possible to refer to the Chair of the Agricultural Law Association and the President of the Central Association of Agricultural Valuers in addition to the President of the Royal Institution of Chartered Surveyors for an arbitrator to be appointed under both the Agricultural Holdings Act 1986 and Agricultural Tenancies Act 1995. Both organisations have set up new panels for the purposes of these appointments which not only include qualified chartered surveyors but also other qualified professionals.⁷⁴ Second, it provides that in relation to a rent review under the Agricultural Holdings Act 1986, a matter can not only be referred to an arbitrator but also to a third party determinator to make a decision in that regard, with the procedural issues that previously existed now being remedied.⁷⁵ It will be interesting to see what effect this has in practice and whether more will seek to use the Third Party Determination (TPD) procedure now that the issues outlined below have been rectified and whether the options in relation to appointments are fully utilised.

Problems with arbitration

The problem with arbitration is that it can be expensive.[76] Schedule 4 of the Deregulation Act 2015 amends the Agricultural Holdings Act 1986 Act by providing for TPD in place of arbitration, although this has had little application in practice due to procedural issues with its use. However, this does not apply to notices to quit, which continue to be dealt with by either the Tribunal or by way of arbitration, as appropriate.[77]

CONCLUSIONS

This article takes the position that as agriculture is devolved in Wales, separate Welsh legislation concerning TPD could be introduced to extend to cover notices to quit as well as those areas in respect of which it is offered as an alternative to arbitration.[78] Whether this is desirable is a matter to be worked out by practitioners. The purpose of this article is to set out the development of relevant agricultural law in a historical context specific to Wales. This article has drawn attention to the specific Welsh agenda both before and in the years immediately following the Commission of 1893–6. The rejection of a Welsh Land Court favoured by the majority of the Commissioners was greeted with derision by certain MPs, as we have seen. However, more broadly, views were mixed on the point and some argued against a Court, based on perceived good relations between landlords and tenants, with some exceptions. That said, there is clear evidence of a Welsh agenda. This article has shown that this waned as the years rolled by and although Wales never did get a Welsh Land Court, it did get devolution in respect of agricultural matters and a Welsh Agricultural Land Tribunal. Where appropriate to do so, Wales should go its own way in respect of agricultural matters[79] and history teaches us that there is a strong imperative to do so, as this article has attempted to demonstrate. There are already differences in terms of agricultural law between England and Wales in relation to agricultural tenancies, in addition to other legal mechanisms which govern the implementation of financial and other support for farmers. Welsh Government has taken a different approach to Westminster in the implementation of the Common Agricultural Policy, and this article serves to remind us of the reason why a different approach may be warranted and encouraged in Wales.

We await the outcome of the consultation held in 2019 by Welsh Government on the future of agricultural tenancies in Wales, and it will be interesting to see what amendments are tabled to the existing legislation in Wales in comparison to that in England, which may lead to further comments by the authors once the full details are available.

NOTES

The authors are grateful to Dr Marie Parker, Bangor Law School, for assisting in providing helpful references to newspaper articles and to Dr Christopher McNall, Barrister-at-law, 18 St John Street Chambers Manchester, for providing certain helpful material. The authors are also very grateful to Peter Foden for assisting in researching the Hansard debates; Dr Shaun Evans, Director of the Institute for the Study of Welsh Estates, Bangor University, for his assistance, encouragement and support; Professor Annie Tindley FRHistS, Professor in Modern British History, Newcastle University, for reading a previous draft of this paper and for making constructive comments; and to Mr Einion Thomas, former Archivist, Bangor University Archives, for making certain material available to us. The references to the Hansard debates are cited pursuant to the Open Parliament Licence v3.0.

1. See generally, D. Lleufer Thomas, *The Welsh Land Commission: A Digest of Its Report* (London, 1896).
2. J. Graham Jones, 'Select Committee or Royal Commission?: Wales and "The Land Question", 1892', *Welsh History Review*, 17:2 (December, 1994), pp. 205–29; see articles in Cragoe and P. Readman (eds), *The Land Question in Britain, 1750–1950* (Basingstoke, 2010) and Matthew Cragoe, *An Anglican Aristocracy, The Moral Economy of the Landed Estate in Carmarthenshire 1832–1995* (Oxford, 1996).
3. Welsh Government Consultation Document Number: WG37107 Agricultural Tenancy Reform. A consultation on tenancy reform and call for evidence on farm business repossessions and mortgage restrictions over let land, 9 April 2019.
4. Several tenant farmers reported that they were afraid to give evidence before the Commission: 'They are afraid of the notice to quit.' See Royal Commission on Land in Wales and Monmouthshire, Minutes of Evidence Cmd. 7439 1894 p. 644. As discussed later in the article, tenants did not get security of tenure until the passing of the Agriculture Act 1947. Reports of landlords evicting tenants were not uncommon in cases where tenants refused to comply with landlords' demands for increased rental payments: see *The Holyhead Chronicle*, 15 December 1916.
5. See C. S. Orwin and E. H. Whetham, *History of British Agriculture, 1846–1914* (London, 1964), chapters 3, 9 and 10.
6. See K. O. Morgan, *Rebirth of a Nation 1880–1980* (Oxford, 1981); K. O. Morgan, *Wales in British Politics* (University of Wales, 1970); W. Griffith, 'Devolutionist tendencies in Wales 1885–1914', in D. Tanner,

C. Williams, W. Griffith and A. Edwards (eds), *Debating Nationhood and Governance in Britain, 1885–1945: Perspectives from the 'Four Nations'* (Manchester, 2006), pp. 89–117.
7. Jones, 'Select Committee or Royal Commission?', pp. 205–29, p. 205.
8. HC Deb 16 March 1892, Vol. 2 cc961–1026.
9. Jones, 'Select Committee or Royal Commission?', pp. 205–29, p. 208.
10. D. W. Howell, 'The Land Question in nineteenth-century Wales, Ireland and Scotland: A comparative study', *Agricultural History Review*, 61:1 (2013), p. 96.
11. See R. A. Jones, *The Land Question and a Land Bill* (Wrexham, 1887), p. 7, where Jones states in the context of The Agricultural Holdings Act 1883: 'Landlords from Wales have written anonymously to the press to point out that they are on excellent terms with their tenants. Doubtless there are such cases ... But such statements, when made in perfect good faith, are not necessarily true.'
12. See J. Graham Jones, 'Michael Davitt, David Lloyd George and T. E. Ellis: The Welsh experience, 1886', *Welsh History Review*, 18:3 (June, 1997), pp. 450–82, p. 454.
13. See Cragoe, *An Anglican Aristocracy*.
14. See generally, *Speeches and Addresses by the late Thomas E. Ellis, M.P.* (Wrexham, 1912).
15. James Edmund Vincent, *The Land Question in North Wales* (London, 1896), p. 58.
16. Vincent, op. cit., p. 45; pp. 95–7 and p. 113; p. 124; pp. 126–39 and p. 152; p. 154; p. 187; p. 230 and p. 235. See also E. H. Whetham, 'The Agriculture Act, 1920 and its repeal – The "Great Betrayal"', *Agricultural History Review*, 22 (1974), pp. 36–49. See also C. S. L. Orwin and E. H. Whetham, *History of British Agriculture, 1846–1914* (London 1964), chapters 2 and 6.
17. Vincent, *The Land Question in North Wales*, p. 152.
18. Op. cit., p. 187.
19. The matter was, however, controversial. For instance, there is an article in the *Aberystwyth Observer* dated 20 December 1884 referring to support for a Land Court and setting out the arguments against on the basis that it 'upset all cordiality between landlord and tenant'.
20. Welsh Government Consultation Document Number: WG37107, para 3.7.
21. Agricultural Holdings (England) Act 1875, s. 2.
22. A. Densham, 'Agricultural tenancies: Past and present', in Susan Bright (ed.), *Landlord and Tenant Law: Past Present and Future* (Hart, 2006), p. 114.
23. Agricultural Holdings (England) Act 1875, s. 51. Therefore, if a tenancy were for twelve months from 29 September 1877 until 28 September 1878, notice would have to have been given before 28 March 1878, expiring on 28 September 1878, to bring that tenancy to an end during that year of the

tenancy. However, this rule did not apply in cases involving the tenant's bankruptcy.
24. Ibid., sections 7–9.
25. Ibid., s. 5.
26. Ibid., s. 54.
27. Ibid., s. 21. For the detailed provisions, see sections 22, 31 and 33.
28. Agricultural Holdings (England) Act 1883, sections 53 and 62.
29. Ibid., sections 8 and 9 and Schedule 1.
30. F. M. L. Thompson, *English Landed Society in the Nineteenth Century* (London, 1971), p. 196.
31. Agricultural Holdings (England) Act 1883, sections 55 and 33. Therefore, if a tenancy were for twelve months from 29 September 1885 until 28 September 1886, notice would have to have been given at any time before 28 September 1886, expiring on 28 September 1887, to bring the tenancy to an end. The provision gave the tenant security of tenure of twelve months in addition to his existing term.
32. Agricultural Holdings (England) Act 1906, s. 13.
33. Ibid., see para 1 Schedule 6 for the repeals.
34. Ibid., s. 2 and Part 1 Schedule 4.
35. Jones, 'Select Committee or Royal Commission?', p. 229.
36. For context on land reform in England, see Michael Tichelar, *The Failure of Land Reform in Twentieth-Century England: The Triumph of Private Property*, Part I – available on Google Books. Articles in Cragoe and Readman (eds), *The Land Question in Britain, 1750–1950*.
37. HC Deb 28 January 1887, Vol. 310 c. 239.
38. HC Deb 25 January 1886, Vol. 302 cc. 348–403.
39. HC Deb 21 May 1890, Vol. 344 c. 1545.
40. HC Deb 9 June 1890 vol 354 cc. 327–9327.
41. HC Deb 26 November 1890, Vol. 349 c. 113.
42. HC Deb 20 February 1892, Vol. 1 c. 163.
43. HC Deb 19 January 1897, Vol. 45 cc. 42–112. However, calls for a separate Land Court for Wales were being made long before the Commission sat, as has been set out previously. Other examples include evidence in newspaper reports: in the *Gloucester Citizen* dated 16 June 1886, following a conference of tenant farmers in Rhyl which was attended by several MPs; some seven years later, on 28 October 1893, the *South Wales Daily News* contains a report stating that farmers in south Wales had been against arbitration, preferring instead a Land Court. This should be contrasted with a report in the *St James's Gazette* dated 18 September 1896, which took a contrary view.
44. HC Deb 7 February 1899, Vol. 66 cc. 78–176.
45. The Earl of Carrington was the Chair of the Welsh Land Commission which had recommended the setting up of a Land Court.
46. HC Deb 09 April 1900, Vol. 81 cc. 1534–624.

47. Both were members of the Commission.
48. This is of interest in that we can have legislation which applies to both England and Wales that works perfectly well in technical terms, but which does not meet the needs of the people of Wales in terms of the administration of justice.
49. The Agricultural Holdings Act 1906, s. 2.
50. Ibid., s. 3.
51. Ibid., s. 4. This section provided that compensation for unreasonable disturbance included (1) where the landlord without good and sufficient cause terminated a tenancy by notice to quit; (2) where the landlord refused to renew a tenancy having been requested in writing to do so at least one year before the termination of the tenancy; and (3) where it could be proved that a rent increase had been demanded by reason of an increase in value of the holding due to improvements executed by or at the cost of the tenant.
52. Ibid., s. 6.
53. Ibid., s. 7.
54. HC Deb 18 March 1903, Vol. 119 cc. 1171–205.
55. Walter Hume Long (1854–1924).
56. The only current difference is that created by The Agriculture (Model Clauses for Fixed Equipment) (Wales) Regulations 2019 No. 1279 (W.223).
57. Agricultural Holdings Act 1923, s. 12(5)(b).
58. Ibid., sections 1, 2–6 and 11–12.
59. For the detailed provisions relating to arbitration, see sections 16–17 and Schedule 2 Rules as to Arbitration Agricultural Holdings Act 1923.
60. Ibid., sections 11, 12, 30 and 32.
61. See T. G. Watkin, *The Legal History of Wales*, 2nd edn (Cardiff, 2012), p. 191.
62. HC Deb 24 July 1913, Vol. 55 cc. 2219–20.
63. See W. Grant, 'Agricultural policy', in P. Dovey (ed.), *Developments in British Public Policy* (London, 2005), p. 8: 'Post-war agricultural policy generally – not just in Britain – was dominated by the objective of food security, which led to an emphasis on the maximisation of production as the principal goal of agricultural policy.'
64. Agriculture Act 1947, s. 71.
65. Ibid., s.72.
66. See sections 30 (1) and 31 (1); (2); and (3) of the Agriculture 1947 Act. The Minister was required to withhold consent unless satisfied that one or more of the grounds specified in s. 31 (3) (a)–(e) had been made out.
67. Ibid., s. 73 (3) (a)–(c). For land lying partly in Wales and partly in England, see s. 75.
68. Set up under the provisions of Part II of the Ministry of Agriculture and Fisheries Act 1919. The Councils of Agriculture, the Agricultural Advisory Committee and county agricultural committees were dissolved by virtue of s.76 of the Agriculture Act 1947.

69. W. Seabrooke, 'The place of the agricultural tenancy in modern farming in England and Wales', *Agricultural Administration*, 18 (1925), pp. 25–37, pp. 29–30.
70. HC Deb 18 March 1958, Vol. 584 cc. 1109–225.
71. 'Dispute Resolution Third Party Determination: who, what, why?', *Agricultural Law Association Bulletin*, 81 (Summer, 2015), pp. 3–4. For statutory arbitration, see also David Sutton, Judith Gill and Matthew Gearing (eds), *Russell on Arbitration* (Sweet and Maxwell), p. 720, para. A3-008.
72. See Watkin, *The Legal History of Wales*, p. 197.
73. For example, any disputes under the Agricultural Tenancies Act 1995 have to be referred to arbitration (although Third Party Determination can apply if there is provision for this in the tenancy agreement: see sections 28–29 of the 1995 Act and also in relation to Agricultural Holdings Act Tenancies the provisions of Schedule 4 Deregulation Act 2015 now apply); as must disputes concerning the validity of a notice to remedy or a notice to quit under Cases A, B, D or E of Schedule 3 of the Agricultural Holdings Act 1986. However, any application for succession under the Agricultural Holdings Act 1986 must be made within the prescribed time limit to the relevant Agricultural Land Tribunal for determination by that Tribunal.
74. Agriculture Act 2020 Schedule 3 Part 1 and Part 2.
75. Agriculture Act 2020 Schedule 3 Part 1 Section 2.
76. McNall, *Agricultural Law Association Bulletin*, 81 (Summer, 2015).
77. Ibid.
78. For a helpful summary, see McNall, op. cit.
79. The Welsh Government consultation document on Agricultural Tenancy Reform is referred to in the introduction to this article.

10

'The price of our loyalty?' Ulster Landlords, Tenants and the Northern Ireland Land Act of 1925

Olwen Purdue

INTRODUCTION

ON 28 MAY 1925 the Act to amend the law relating to the Occupation and Ownership of Land in Northern Ireland was passed by the Westminster government, thus completing the compulsory transfer of land from the hands of Northern Ireland's landed class into the hands of its tenants, just two years after similar legislation had been passed by the Free State government.[1] This piece of legislation has passed largely unnoticed. At the time it went through Parliament quietly and without much interest either at Westminster or in the national press; and subsequently, in terms of historical scholarship on the land question, it rarely rates a mention. The social history of the early years of Northern Ireland has only recently begun to attract scholarly attention, most works on the period having focused on issues relating to the political history of the period.[2] Meanwhile, the principal scholarly work on the land question in twentieth-century Ireland, Terence Dooley's *The land for the people*, deals only with the twenty-six counties that became the Republic of Ireland.[3] Yet for northern landlords and tenants alike, the Northern Ireland Land Act was significant both in practical economic terms and in terms of the light it shed on issues of identity, legitimacy and the age-old tensions surrounding land, its ownership and its occupation.

As scholars such as Phillip Bull have demonstrated, by the end of the nineteenth century the land question had become synonymous with the national question throughout much of Ireland. A binary had developed between, on the one hand, the landlords who owned the land and who identified with and desired to maintain Ireland's place within Britain and the Empire and, on the other, the tenants who had become increasingly desirous of ending both landlordism and British rule in Ireland and who associated the landlord class with the economic and political system they wished to overthrow.[4] Bringing an end to the economic framework of landlordism and to the political framework of British rule in Ireland had become one unified aim. Yet to see the dynamics of land and politics at this point in Ireland's history solely in these terms would be to miss the complexity of the relationship that existed between landlords and tenants, particularly in the north of the country. Work on the land question in Ulster has recognised the fact that the dynamics were often different there due to the existence of a third dimension – the large number of Protestant tenants, both Anglican and Presbyterian, for whom the relationship between land reform and national identity was not so symbiotic.[5]

The constitutional question, when it came to the fore, tended to suppress divisions over land tenure that might have existed among Protestant tenants and their landlords; but that is not to say that these divisions did not exist. The momentum for land reform and the feelings of frustration at the system of land ownership that existed were very strong in Ulster, as even a quick glance at the Bessborough Commission report of 1881 reveals.[6] Ulster Protestant tenants may have shared, to some degree, a sense of history, religious affiliation and identity with their landlords; however, many of them did not share their understanding of the basis of land ownership in Ulster and of the way that ownership and right to occupation should be interpreted.[7] Furthermore, the Presbyterian farmers of counties Antrim and Down were also separated from their Anglican landlords along confessional grounds, thus widening the cultural gulf between them. Pressure for land reform emerged at an early stage and in a highly motivated and organised fashion in these Presbyterian parts of Ulster; only the threat of Home Rule was able to unite northern unionist Protestants in a common cause, temporarily pasting over these fissures. Against this background, this chapter aims to explore the final step in ending landlordism in the six north-eastern counties of Ulster through compulsory purchase in the form of the Northern Ireland Land Act, its economic implications for tenants and landlords in the north and the way in which it was received by northern Protestant farmers.

LAND REFORM IN THE NORTH OF IRELAND

In 1876 the government published a set of papers referred to by contemporaries as the 'New Domesday Book', properly the *Return of owners of land of one acre and upwards, in the several counties, counties of cities and counties of towns in Ireland*.[8] This remarkable volume, which captured a snapshot of land ownership in late-Victorian Ireland, revealed

Table 10.1 Number of landlords owning estates of 2,500 acres and above in the six counties of the north of Ireland, 1876

Number of acres	Number of families
40,000 +	5
30,000–40,000	6
20,000–30,000	10
10,000–20,000	24
2,500–10,000	65

Source: J. Bateman, *The Great Landowners of Great Britain and Ireland* (London, 1881).

the extent to which rural Ireland was dominated by large estates owned by an elite group of gentry or nobility families. The wealthiest and most influential families owned vast estates in both Ireland and Britain, some of which ran to upwards of 100,000 acres, while many others owned tens of thousands of acres of land across the island of Ireland. The pattern of land ownership in the six counties of the north-east followed this pattern of a concentration of land in the hands of a few; indeed, there seems to have been a preponderance of very large estates in the region. As Table 10.1 shows, there were 110 landowners with estates of 2,500 acres or above whose principal country house and core estate was situated in these six counties; out of this group, 20 per cent were in possession of estates of 20,000 acres or more.[9] Hughes, referring to the number of 'truly great estates' in the north, writes that 'two thirds of [Irish] estates valued at over £20,000 had their core areas located in either Leinster or Ulster and one-third of the most influential of owners had the cores of their estates located in what is now Northern Ireland'.[10]

Whether granted as a reward for loyal service during the seventeenth century or bought with the proceeds of hard graft or good fortune in the eighteenth and nineteenth centuries, whether owned by the same family for generations or purchased more recently by those who had accumulated wealth through trade, these estates conferred on the families that owned them not only wealth but social prestige and significant political influence. Throughout the nineteenth century these families dominated the local administration of law and order, justice and public services; they were closely tied by social and political ties to Britain's ruling landed elite; they sat in Parliament, held key positions in government and represented British authority in the far reaches of empire. This apparently unassailable position of political and social ascendancy was built on the foundation of the ownership of large landed estates; yet, as the Famine had all too clearly demonstrated, this foundation was far from secure. Now, as the nineteenth century drew to a close, it was about to be dismantled in order to make way for a new type of landowner, the 'peasant proprietor'.

For landowning families in the six north-eastern counties that were to become Northern Ireland, this process, begun in earnest by the Ashbourne Act of 1885 and accelerated by the Wyndham Act of 1903, was brought to a conclusion by the Northern Ireland Land Act of 1925, a compulsory purchase Act which finally transferred any remaining tenanted holdings into the hands of those who occupied them.[11] Within half a century of the publication of the 'New Domesday Book', the remaining great estates of the north-east were being dismantled by an Act passed by the Westminster government for that part of Ireland which remained within the United Kingdom. Important as it was, however, little attention has been given to this Act – to its conception, its terms or its impact on Northern Ireland's remaining landed families or their tenants.

As early as 1881, before any serious attempt had been made to establish a peasant proprietary, the Earl of Antrim had predicted that the days of Ireland's large landed estates were numbered. In the wake of Gladstone's second land act of 1881, he wrote to his agent that,

> One of the reasons I want to sell Glenarm . . . is that this Land Act [1881] is by no means the end any more than the 1870 Act, and anything the Irish clamour for will be given them by the Radicals. I feel quite sure that within a few years, ten or thereabouts, some Act will be passed which will force the landlords to sell to the tenants and in that case the Castle, gardens, etc. will never sell as their value would be lost as no-one would care to buy a large house, stables, garden, park etc. with no property round it.[12]

Although the earl had overestimated the rate at which the dismantling of landlordism would proceed, his basic predictions proved to be accurate. For some landlords, badly affected by the agricultural depression and rent strikes of the early 1880s, unable to continue borrowing on the strength of their Irish land and disillusioned by government interference in the management of their estates represented by Gladstone's land act of 1881, Lord Ashbourne's land purchase act of 1885 was seen as an opportunity to cut their losses. By 1888 over five thousand individual holdings had been sold to tenant farmers in the province of Ulster, twice as many as in the other three provinces put together. This figure did not, however, represent significant movement of land ownership on the great estates of the north; rather it was the small landowners, those in possession of estates of less than 1,000 acres and who bore the brunt of rent strikes and agricultural depression, who were selling at this point.[13] Of the few great northern landowners that did sell land, most only parted with small estates, generally outlying property at some distance from their principal country estate.

Greater incentive was necessary before these landowners could be persuaded to part with their ancestral acres, and this was to materialise two decades later in the shape of the Wyndham Act of 1903. Offering a 12 per cent bonus on all sales and more attractive terms for landlords and tenants alike, this Act proved much more successful in moving the land out of the hands of great proprietors and into the hands of those who occupied and worked their smallholdings.[14] Some families, such as the earls of Gosford, the Staples family of Lissan and the McClintocks of Seskinore in county Tyrone, sold practically all of their tenanted land at this point. Others – the dukes of Abercorn, the earls of Kilmorey and the earls of Caledon among them – sold off significant sections of their property, thus benefiting from the Act's generous terms in order to clear some of their encumbrances and invest the remaining capital, while still retaining an income from their remaining tenanted property and their status as large landowners.

An important point that emerges from a study of the sales on these estates, however, and one which is often lost in the examination of the impact of the land purchase acts, is that although the Wyndham Act and a subsequent piece of legislation passed in 1909 led to the sales of large numbers of holdings, they did not represent the end of landlordism in the north. On the contrary, by the time that Northern Ireland was created in 1921, a significant number of farmers remained as tenants, renting their land from landlords. In the six counties, 550,800 acres of tenanted land had been sold under the pre-Wyndham land acts, 1,219,800 acres under the Wyndham Act and a further 139,600 under the Act of 1909. This still left over 900,000 acres in the hands of landlords.[15] In county Down, Baron Dunleath held tenaciously onto all but 770 acres of the land which he had so recently acquired.[16] The Annesley family, while selling off their Cavan estate, kept all their estates in county Down apart from 342 acres which had been sold under Wyndham. The Nugents of Portaferry had sold no land at all.[17] In county Armagh the Armstrongs of Dean's Hill sold 280 acres under an early land act. However, by 1921 they still retained 2,000 of the 2,280 acres the family had owned in 1878.[18] In county Fermanagh, the earls of Belmore and Enniskillen each retained around 10,000 acres of tenanted land, while Sir Victor Brooke, who had sold over 13,000 acres in the 1880s, still retained over 14,000 acres of his estate.[19]

In county Antrim, in particular, a significant number of landlords either sold no land at all or retained the larger part of their estate. Although Sir Francis Macnaghten of Dunderave sold the 950 acres which the family had acquired in county Armagh, he did not part with any of his principal 7,100-acre county Antrim estate. Likewise, G. C. Macartney of Lissanoure did not sell any of his 12,800 acres, Francis Turnly held onto his entire 6,500-acre estate at Drumnasole and the Dobbs family to their 5,000-acre estate near Larne.[20] While Lord O'Neill did sell over 25,000 acres under the Wyndham Act, generating a sum of £200,000, he retained over 34,000 acres of tenanted land in the county.[21] By 1921, seven out of the twenty-five sample landowners, or 28 per cent, were still in possession of at least 95 per cent of their land, while over half of them still owned over 50 per cent of their original land.

Of those landlords who had sold no land at all, most had their core estates in either counties Down or Antrim, and their estates were what might be considered as 'middling', i.e. between 5,000 and 20,000 acres. There are a number of possible explanations as to why these particular landowning families were not interested in selling their estates. Firstly, many of their estates were in a relatively sound economic position, therefore it might be assumed that their owners had not the pressing financial need to sell land that some of the older and larger landed families experienced. While a number of the north's great landowners had actually been unable to sell for the very opposite reason, i.e. their estates were so heavily encumbered that to sell them would involve such a massive debt repayment that little would remain to invest, most of these particular estates had been run along sound business lines and debts were not allowed to accumulate. The Perceval-Maxwells, for example, had worked hard over the previous half-century to greatly reduce the debts on their estates and were now managing the running of the estates very closely; the Nugents of Portaferry had likewise managed their finances carefully, selling stocks and bonds rather than borrowing should a large sum of money be required for some purpose or another.[22] Secondly, for many of these 'middling-sized' landowners, their Ulster estates represented their entire property, unlike the 'great' landowners who may have owned large estates in England or Scotland as well as in other parts of Ireland. Their reluctance to sell off parts of their estates can, therefore, be understood. A third factor is that many of the estates which remained largely intact had been purchased within the previous century or so by families with backgrounds in trade rather than granted in earlier centuries through patronage. The Macartney and Turnley families, for example, had both become established as landed proprietors in north Antrim during the eighteenth century and owed their landed status to the business enterprise of earlier generations. William Young of Galgorm and John Mulholland of Ballywalter Park, both of whom had made their fortunes in the linen trade, had only recently purchased their estates and were beginning to acquire the social and political advantages that came with being a substantial landowner. These and others like them retained a strong business sense and a desire to make their estates work as a going business concern; thus they were inclined to view any attempt by the government at promoting land purchase as nothing short of confiscation.

COMPULSORY PURCHASE NORTH AND SOUTH

Whatever the attitudes of northern landlords towards land purchase, their days as landed proprietors were numbered. In 1918 the land purchase sub-committee of the Irish Convention – a body set up to try to achieve consensus on the land question – had devised a scheme for the compulsory purchase of remaining tenanted land, something which would replace once and for all the old system of land tenure with a situation where all the occupiers of the land enjoyed ownership of it. The Convention's recommendations were that all untenanted land in the congested districts should be transferred to the Congested Districts Board for a set fee. It also recommended that ownership of all tenanted land should automatically pass either to the occupier or to the state and that bonds at 5 per cent should be issued for the payment of the landlords. In order to ensure a continued income for the landlords, the bonus would still be paid, although not at the flat 12 per cent that had benefited so many under Wyndham.[23] Although these proposals were accepted by the government and placed before Parliament as a new land bill in 1920, more pressing constitutional developments caused the suspension of such issues and the bill was shelved. With the passing of the Government of Ireland Act of 1920, any further legislation concerning land purchase necessarily became the responsibility of the two separate jurisdictions.

In the years immediately following Partition, northern landowners anxiously watched developments in the Free State, where further land legislation was being quickly pushed through by the new government. The result was the Hogan Act of 1923, an Act which legislated for the compulsory purchase of all tenanted lands and, in some cases, lands which were held in hand by the landlord. The Act declared that

> All tenanted land wherever situated and all untenanted land situated in any congested districts county and all such untenanted land situated elsewhere as the Land Commission shall ... declare to be required for the purpose of relieving congestion or of facilitating the resale of tenanted land, shall, by virtue of this act, vest in the Land Commission on the appointed day.[24]

Although the Act contained some safeguards protecting lands used by landlords for their own purpose – home farms, etc. – these safeguards were not sacrosanct and any land could be forcibly purchased should the Land Commission deem it necessary. In other ways, too, as Lord Oranmore and Browne pointed out in the House of Lords, the terms of the Hogan Act fell far short of the terms agreed at the 1918 Land Convention:

> Southern Irish landlords received less good terms and they received no bonus. As a result of this, there is no doubt that ... many Irishmen with estates which are burdened with debts will find themselves ruined.[25]

Lord Lansdowne echoed these sentiments in a letter written to *The Times* in 1926 in which he stated that:

> under the act the landlord's income may be reduced by from 25 to 35 percent, or even more, notably in cases where the land taken from him has been untenanted. To many vendors, expropriation on these terms implies the complete disappearance of the all-too-slender margin of income which remained to them.[26]

A subsequent Act aimed at speeding up the process of land transfer was passed in 1931. Fianna Fáil Minister for Lands, Frank Aiken, stated at the time that the safeguards which had been given to home farms and demesne lands had 'operated to impede the work of the Land Commission in the relief of congestion', indicating that such untenanted lands would be fair game in the near future.[27] Subsequent years would see the untenanted land remaining to southern country houses being purchased by the Land Commission in the interest of relieving congestion, leaving many of these houses shorn of the land that was so necessary for their maintenance. As Dooley has concluded, for many remaining landed families this 'was tantamount to ruin'.[28]

In Northern Ireland the whole question of compulsory purchase also loomed large. The failure of the British government to pass a compulsory land purchase bill concurrently with the Government of Ireland Act had been seen by many as a dereliction of duty; not only would the new jurisdictions lack the mechanisms and borrowing power to enable them to oversee this effectively, but it was considered by some to be too contentious a matter to be dealt with by the devolved governments. Lord Oranmore and Browne, for example, in criticising the government for having failed to pass land purchase legislation in tandem with the Government of Ireland Act, argued in 1921 that

> the Prime Ministers of Northern and Southern Ireland would at once be pressed to deal with this question and that great pressure would be put on them by the more extreme members to do so in a manner which would not be thought equitable by any party in this country.[29]

As land purchase, therefore, remained to be completed in both of the new jurisdictions, it was listed, along with matters pertaining to national security, taxation and the postal service, as one of the 'Reserved Matters' which would remain under the jurisdiction of the Imperial Parliament.[30] While the establishment of the Free State left the southern government free to pursue its own land purchase legislation, in Northern Ireland, by contrast, land purchase remained a reserved matter to be legislated for at Westminster. This would prove significant in that it prevented the devolved government from being able to exert influence on the matter in the way that Oranmore and Browne had anticipated. It also protected the new government from itself coming under local pressure over what would be an extremely divisive matter. In contrast to the fairly straightforward political and ideological framework within which the southern government responded to the question of land reform, in Northern Ireland, where the new government's support base consisted of members of the landed class as well as a significant number of discontent 'unbought' tenant farmers, the issue was potentially explosive. The fact that the whole matter of land purchase remained a reserved matter would act as a useful buffer between the Unionist government and those sections of their electorate who clamoured for land reform and was used throughout the early years to deflect the issue every time it was raised.

Among the northern landed class there was a range of attitudes towards compulsory purchase. While there were some for whom any attempt by the government to force them to sell their estates was seen as gross interference in their rights of property, others felt that the existing situation where purchased and unpurchased holdings existed side by side – a partial 'peasant proprietorship' – was detrimental to farmers in general and impeded agricultural progress in the north. Hugh de Fellenburg Montgomery, a prominent Tyrone landlord and an early advocate of land purchase, felt that for the good of all classes of landowners and farmers it was necessary that land purchase should be completed as soon as possible. His concern was that the government might not honour its earlier commitment to facilitate this process. 'It looks now,' he wrote,

> as if the Government were going to repudiate their promise of passing a Land Purchase Bill to deal with unsold tenanted agricultural estates. I look upon the future of that sort of property as very doubtful indeed, and I think it might be well to make a beginning by selling a few of the unsold farms where the tenants have plenty of cash, for cash to the tenants at a price that would not be ruinous.[31]

For the tenant farming class, this was a pressing and deeply contentious issue. Tenants and their representatives were anxious to see further legislation enacted sooner rather than later, and a great deal of discontent existed among many remaining tenant farmers at the fact that they were still paying rents while farmers on neighbouring estates were now in possession of their own farms. On 12 December 1922, the matter was raised in the Northern Ireland Parliament by William Coote, MP for Fermanagh and Tyrone, who demanded to know whether the British government was going to take any steps to fulfil its pledge 'to transfer the remaining property of the owners of lands in Northern Ireland subject to the Land Acts to the occupiers on terms fair to both parties, and on the basis agreed to by the Land committee of the Irish Convention of 1917–1918'.[32] In reply, Minister of Finance, Hugh Pollock, reminded the House, as he would do many times over the next few years, that as, under the Government of Ireland Act, the question of land purchase in Northern Ireland was a reserved matter to be legislated for by the Imperial Parliament, there could be no debate on the matter in the Northern Ireland Parliament. Despite this fact, however, the issue was repeatedly raised by elected representatives, who demanded to know whether the Northern Ireland government was putting sufficient pressure on the Imperial Parliament and if it was aware of the importance to the farming community of getting compulsory purchase passed as soon as possible.

Frustrated by the lack of progress on the completion of land transfer, a number of tenant farmers formed an organisation called the Unbought Tenants' Association. This was particularly active in county Antrim, where there was a strong representation of Presbyterian tenant farmers and a long tradition of tenant right activism; but also where landlords seemed less willing to part with their property. As Graham Walker has pointed out, this group of Protestant farmers represented a 'strain of agrarian Presbyterian radicalism' that was particularly antagonistic to landlordism.[33] It could be traced back to north Antrim's Route Tenants'

Association of the 1850s and perhaps even further to the United Irishmen of 1798; and, it might be argued, traced forward to a different manifestation of resistance to the 'establishment' in the evangelical Protestantism that would eventually be represented politically by the Reverend Ian Paisley. It is also possible that county Antrim farmers were less preoccupied with the issue that dominated the political consciousness of both Protestants and Catholics in the counties close to the newly established border in anticipation of the decision soon to be made by the Boundary Commission. Only in the east, where the population was to a degree removed from this political uncertainty and the communal tensions that accompanied it, could tenant farmers focus instead on social and economic issues such as land transfer. Alongside the Unbought Tenants' Association was the Ulster Farmers' Union, a more representative, mainstream and 'respectable' organisation, and one which had some support among political representatives for northern constituencies in the Imperial Parliament. These representatives arranged for a deputation representing both the Ulster Farmers' Union and the Unbought Tenants' Association to travel to London where, on 2 February 1925, they met with the Home Secretary, Sir William Joynson Hicks.[34]

In 1925 the Unbought Tenants' Association fielded candidates in the elections to the northern Parliament. W. R. Todd and Patrick Conlon were selected to stand for county Armagh, R. N. Boyd and James Skeffington for county Tyrone, James Wood for county Down and George Henderson for county Antrim. The *Irish Times*, in an article on the election in Tyrone, commented that the selection of Boyd and Skeffington was 'unlikely to deflect many votes from the other parties'.[35] Likewise in county Armagh, another border county, there was limited interest in the land question. In county Antrim, as has already been mentioned, there was a considerably greater amount of interest in the plight of the unbought tenants, and meetings were held in locations across the county, many of which had a long tradition of tenant activism. In Ballymoney, for example, a meeting described by the *Northern Whig* as 'lively' passed a unanimous vote of confidence in Henderson, one speaker declaring that 'it was only fair that there should be one representative to look after the agricultural interests of North Antrim'.[36] That the movement had some degree of support in the county was demonstrated in the results of the election, with Henderson securing 8,720 votes and taking his seat in the Northern Ireland Parliament.[37]

The fact that land purchase needed to be completed in Northern Ireland was not lost on Westminster and, with a view to formulating a bill without any delay, a committee under the chairmanship of Lord

Eustace Percy (himself a landowner) was established to 'consider what should be the terms of future land purchase in Northern Ireland and to make recommendations for legislation accordingly'.[38] In the introduction to the committee's report, published on 20 May 1923, it was explained that they took for their basis the recommendations contained in the Irish Convention report of 1918, the value of which lay in the fact that they were reached by the common consent of landlord and tenant alike. The main points of this were that tenants' annuities would be fixed at a rate similar to those already established in their particular area, that landlords would 'receive payment at face value in stock bearing interest at a rate unlikely to render any serious depreciation unlikely', and that the state should pay a bonus which, added to the purchase price, would ensure for landlords an income on a par with the rental they had been receiving. The committee accepted almost all the recommendations of the Convention, only finding difficulty in the recommendation that the landlord should receive payment in 5 per cent British Guaranteed Stock. Rates of interest for government borrowing having fallen considerably in the five years since the Convention made its report, it was felt that stock at 4.5 per cent would be more appropriate.

REACTIONS TO THE NORTHERN IRELAND LAND BILL

The bill was passed quickly and with very little debate. Some English MPs expressed their disapproval of the very generous terms on offer to the Northern Ireland government. Several hard-pressed local authorities throughout Britain had tried and failed to secure Treasury loans in order to facilitate the creation of new housing or health provisions, yet here was the Northern Irish government being freely offered exactly such a facility in order to pay off its landed class. Furthermore, the proposed Act would allow landlords to retain any minerals which were deemed to be of value, something which was generally seen as overly favourable to the landed class. While these issues were explored at some length by a number of English members, it was noted, however, that those members present from Northern Ireland had been unusually quiet throughout the debate![39] That this was a 'landlords' bill' was also the cry when it was debated in the Northern Ireland Parliament. Tenants' representatives expressed strong opposition to the bill, complaining that it was weighted very much in the landlords' favour and that its terms compared very unfavourably to the terms offered to southern tenants by the Hogan Act. George Henderson, now MP for Antrim, claimed that the government had done nothing to secure a better deal for Northern Ireland's tenant farmers. Contrasting the high annuities that northern tenants would have to pay with those now being paid under the 'Free State Land Act', he argued that this was already creating great discontent among the 'better class of tenant farmer'. 'These men', he went on to say, 'really ask themselves this question: is this the price that we are going to have to pay for our loyalty? Are men across the Border going to receive on the completion of land purchase a reduction of 7s in the pound whereas we are put off with 3s 7½ d?'[40]

Others raised the objection, already made at Westminster, that Clause 16 allowed the landlord to retain his rights to any mineral supplies, something which would be important for landowners such as the Earl of Antrim, who had been exporting limestone and iron ore for years. From the tenants' point of view, according to Samuel Kyle, leader of the Northern Ireland Labour Party, this would prevent occupiers of holdings from obtaining cheap supplies of lime to improve their soil and constituted 'sheer, unmitigated robbery'. Warming to his theme, he stated that nothing else could be expected from an administration that had consistently put the interests of the landed class before those of the tenants:

> It seems to me that the Government of Northern Ireland have sold the unbought tenants to the landlord class. In that they are not departing from their historic role. Invariably the Members on the opposite side of this House have defended the landlord class in all circumstances, and it is because I believe that, that I, too, want to enter my protest against the agreement which they have arrived at with the British Government so far as these unbought tenants are concerned.[41]

In concluding, Kyle drew an interesting parallel between Henderson, the member for Antrim, and those county Antrim tenants who had been at the forefront of the early tenant-right movement during the 1870s:

> I am indeed glad to see that the tenant farmers of Northern Ireland are going to go back to the traditions of their forefathers, because it was in County Antrim that tenant-right was fought for and where the farming class, the agricultural labourers, were compelled to fight their landlords a hundred years ago, and less than a hundred years ago. I am indeed glad to see that there is some spirit of the men of a hundred years ago in the men of County Antrim to-day.[42]

This point was reiterated by Thomas McAllister, nationalist member for Antrim, who suggested that Henderson had been returned at the general election earlier that year simply and solely on the issue of tenant dissatisfaction with the proposed bill, 'and', he added, 'it would have been the same in every other county had not the Border question intervened'.[43]

The British government continued to assert that it was a case of 'take it or leave it' and, despite opposition from certain quarters, most parties involved accepted that the completion of land purchase was necessary and should be effected straight away. Agreement was reached between representatives of the Northern Ireland government, the landed interest and the Ulster Farmers' Union in February 1925,[44] and on 28 May 1925 the bill passed into law.[45] The rate of the purchase annuity was set at four pounds and fifteen shillings, whereas under the Wyndham Act it had stood at three pounds and five shillings. The rate of interest was also changed from 3.5 per cent to 4.5 per cent. Landlords would be paid in 4.5 per cent bonds with interest at the rate of 4.5 per cent payable per annum. They would also receive a bonus which would be calculated as a percentage of the rent, varying according to county and to whether the rents were first, second or third term judicial rents. In practice, the bonus generally worked out at roughly 10 per cent of the purchase price. While this was not quite as generous as that received under Wyndham, it was substantially more than southern landlords were receiving under their recent compulsory purchase act. Not without good cause did Lord Oranmore and Browne 'most heartily congratulate our [landed] brethren in the North on the very good terms they have obtained'.[46]

All tenanted land from the appointed day would vest in the Land Commission. There were, however, some exceptions which stood to benefit a number of landlords: any holding which was not primarily agricultural or pastoral, any holding occupied by someone who worked on the grounds or home farm of a big house, and any holding which 'possesses a substantial value or utility whether potential or actual as building ground or is a town park' was exempt from compulsory purchase. In most cases, however, if the land was tenanted then the landlord had no choice but to sell and the next few years saw the final break-up of northern landed estates. In some cases entire estates were compulsorily purchased; in other cases those estates owned by landlords who had chosen to sell only part of their property under Wyndham had to go. The remaining tenanted land which was now bought from the landlords and sold to tenants under the terms of the 1925 land act came to a total of 805,500 acres. In total, 38,500 tenants purchased their estates from 1925 onwards.[47] The process of creating a peasant proprietorship which had made its first tentative beginnings in 1881 was now complete.

IMPLICATIONS OF THE LAND ACT FOR THE NORTHERN LANDED CLASS

Despite the complaints of 'confiscation' that arose from some landed quarters, the north's landlords had every reason to congratulate themselves. The compulsory purchase of their remaining tenanted acres had been inevitable; all that had ever been in question was the terms that they were likely to get, and on that score they had little ground for complaint. Although the 12 per cent flat rate bonus they were offered under Wyndham was no longer available, the fact that they got a bonus at all placed them in a much better situation than that of their southern counterparts.

The real significance of the Act for the long-term future of the country house in Northern Ireland, however, and that which left northern landed families in a much better position than those in the rest of the island, lay in the fact that landlords were able to retain any land that was not let to tenants. This was in stark contrast to the situation in the Free State, where much harsher land purchase terms from the landlords' perspective led to many being left with very little land, something that, in turn, hastened the departure of many landed families and the decline of the class as a whole. The land which was traditionally attached to a country house was essential in order to generate the income necessary for its maintenance. Without it, a house had little chance of survival. Dooley refers to one western landowner who depended on his remaining 150 acres to generate enough income to maintain his big house, commenting that

> much more than 150 acres was required to maintain a great mansion. Unfortunately for those landowners who wanted to remain in Ireland, and who were not driven out by events of the revolutionary period from 1919 to 1923, the Free State government had little sympathy for anyone holding on to thousands of acres when there were so many smallholders and landless men clamouring for land.[48]

In Northern Ireland, by contrast, many landed families remained in possession of thousands of acres simply due to the fact that, not being let to tenants at the time when the Northern Ireland Land Act was passed, this land was held to be exempt from compulsory purchase, something that was to prove vital for the continued survival of many northern landed families. Out of twenty-five sample landed families examined as part of an earlier study, eight remained in possession of 5,000 acres or more, while all but three retained at least a thousand acres (see Table 10.2).[49]

Table 10.2 Land remaining on twenty-five sample estates after 1925

Name	Size of original estate, 1878	Acres sold after 1925	Acres remaining after 1925
Abercorn	69,930	1,600	13,430
O'Neill	65,920	34,130	6,600
Kilmorey	43,960	4,900	15,900
Antrim	34,400	680	6,700
Caledon	32,110	8,000	8,780
Erne	31,389	40	12,500
Brooke	27,990	1,910	12,230
Annesley	23,350	18,610	4,390
Bruce	20,800	17,200	2,360
Belmore	19,400	9,810	1,950
Stronge	12,950	50	2,810
Macartney	12,800	6,360	6,440
Montgomery (Blessingbourne)	12,550	4,800	3,780
Gosford	12,180	–	80
Templetown	11,900	–	2,900
Perceval-Maxwell	8,470	4,131	1,738
Montgomery (Benvarden)	7,800	1,120	1,750
Macnaghten	7,360	5,500	1,630
Turnly	6,500	3,300	3,200
Dobbs	5,060	4,590	470
Nugent	4,638	3,602	1,040
McClintock	4,553	118	465
Staples	4,070	170	370
Armstrong	3,181	1,865	1,036
Lenox-Conyngham	2,526	23	2,530

Source: *Belfast Gazette* and Land Commission Papers.[50]

Lord O'Neill, for example, was left with over 6,000 acres of land in county Antrim. Although a large part of this consisted of a large area of raised lowland bog, including the ecologically important Sluggan Bog to the north of Randalstown, he also owned several thousand acres of prime farmland surrounding his house and demesne. Ironically, this good fortune owed itself to the excesses of previous generations of the family who had laid out much of this land as a vast deer park during the nineteenth century. As such, it was now deemed as being held by the landlord for his own purposes and, therefore, safe from compulsory purchase. This proved to be a vital factor in ensuring the success of the O'Neills' move from landlords to large-scale farmers, the amount of workable land available to them being essential if their property was to remain viable. Similarly, the Brookes retained over 12,000 acres in Fermanagh, much of which they continue to farm to this day. The

Caledons, with 8,780 acres in county Tyrone and the Antrims with over 6,500 acres in county Antrim, both successfully made the transition from owners of landed estates to managers of estates companies.

The Abercorns, having sold around 56,500 acres under various land acts, retained somewhere in the region of 15,000 acres in Tyrone and Donegal following the Act of 1925.[51] Although the duke, in his capacity as Governor of Northern Ireland, resided at Hillsborough Castle, his son, the Marquis of Hamilton, lived at Baron's Court and managed the estate. On 6 February 1928, the remaining lands at Baron's Court were settled on the marquis, thus giving him full ownership of the property.[52] This period saw the movement of this once great estate towards direct farming of the land, closely managed by the Marquis of Hamilton himself. This is evident in the vast number and range of farm accounts available from the early twentieth century onwards, which demonstrate the growing importance of the farm in generating an income both from the sale of eggs, milk, timber and livestock and through the letting of land to local farmers. Not only was farming an obvious way of making money from their land but there were also significant tax advantages to farming your own land in the post-war years as new income tax and surtax rebates on repairs, maintenance and capital expenditure suddenly made the upkeep of estates more financially viable.[53]

The Perceval-Maxwells of Finnebrogue in south county Down also survived the compulsory purchase act remarkably well. The sale of around one-quarter of their 8,400-acre estate under the Wyndham Act in 1919 had raised a total of £35,360 and, after all encumbrances were paid off, a residue of £33,102 had remained to be paid into the estate. When the rest of the tenanted estate was sold in 1928, the family retained a further residue of £32,365 out of a total purchase price of £46,115.[54] When these sums were added to those raised by the sale of the southern property, the Perceval-Maxwells were placed on a very firm financial footing indeed. The property, which now consisted of 1,000 acres of prime farming land, passed to Lt-Colonel the Rt Hon. Robert David Perceval-Maxwell and, on his death in 1932, to his son, John. John Perceval-Maxwell took a keen interest in the development of new improved farming methods and injected much time and money into the breeding of Shorthorn and Hereford cattle at Finnebrogue. Most importantly for the survival of Finnebrogue, he had the enthusiasm and, with the wealth which he had inherited, the opportunity to develop his farm into a highly profitable concern.[55]

The fact that many of Northern Ireland's gentry and aristocracy turned increasingly to farming for a living was evidenced by the number of heirs to country houses who chose to attend agricultural college during the early decades of the twentieth century. In the past, where the vast majority of sons of landed families would have attended institutions such as Sandhurst, these years witnessed a dramatic swing in favour of Cirencester Royal Agricultural College or even Greenmount Agricultural College near Antrim. This was a situation that increased rather than diminished as the twentieth century progressed. Today, the present Duke of Abercorn, Lord O'Neill, Hugh Montgomery of Benvarden and Richard Blackiston Houston have all attended the Royal Agricultural College at Cirencester, while Patrick Forde of Seaforde and Capt. Robert Lowry of Blessingbourne have both attended Greenmount.[56] Thus, those who were taking on estates during the 1950s and 1960s had developed a sound personal understanding of farming and were aware of the latest ideas in estate management, something which would help to turn around the declining fortunes of a number of estates.

The reality for most landed families is that farming, in itself, is rarely profitable enough to generate an income sufficient for the maintenance of a large country house and its grounds; what has made a difference to many, however, is the fact that they still owned enough land to allow them to supplement their income from farming with other economic activities. For many northern landed families this opportunity to diversify, made possible by the generous terms of the Northern Ireland Land Act, was crucial in ensuring their continued economic survival. Those still in possession of upland areas, for example, were encouraged by the Northern Ireland government to plant coniferous forests. A grant scheme was introduced in 1927 to encourage owners of estates to plant more trees on their property as a cash crop.[57] In 1943 this campaign of afforestation was stepped up by the formation of a new 'strategic policy', the main thrust of which was that annual state planting should be increased to 800 hectares. Large grants were offered to landlords as an incentive to plant on their estates and an increasing number of them took advantage of this opportunity. Others leased their land to the forestry service. In 1922 the 3rd Duke of Abercorn leased 3,000 acres of his land to the forestry service for a period of ninety years. This provided a steady income over those years and now means that this land is back in the hands of the Abercorns.[58] The Earl of Antrim also leased large areas of his estate to the forestry service, something which was an important source of income on the Antrim estate,[59] while at Lissan, near Moneymore, 100 acres is still on long-term rental to the Forestry Commission.[60] Other options included the development of natural resources such as mineral deposits or access to the coast.

One of the more contentious terms of the Northern Ireland Land Act was that under which a landlord retained his rights to any mineral reserves which had been on his estate. For remaining owners of country estates this was of great importance as it ensured that they could continue to receive an income from this source, thus leaving them less dependent on the vagaries of agriculture. The Mourne estate of the earls of Kilmorey, for example, contained a ready supply of granite, not only the principal building material in the immediate area but exported to the rest of Ireland and, indeed, the British Isles. The Antrim estate in north Antrim contained important deposits of iron ore and bauxite as well as limestone, all of which had been mined extensively from the nineteenth century. In order to fully exploit this natural resource, the earls of Antrim had built harbours, improved roads and created railway links from the quarries to the harbours. The iron ore, as well as the limestone which was an important element in the steel-making process, were then shipped to the great iron foundries of the Clyde valley in Scotland.[61] At Lissan, near Cookstown, the river which ran through the estate produced large quantities of sand and gravel, important materials in the building trade. This has continued to generate an important income for the Staples family up until the present time.[62]

Finally, the continued ownership of thousands of acres has allowed landed families to effectively develop their properties for tourism purposes, something which has only begun to show its true potential as a generator of revenue in the past few years. On country estates across Northern Ireland, not only has the 'big house' been made available for exclusive guest accommodation, but the grounds have been developed to provide a wide variety of sporting and leisure activities. Colebrooke Park in Fermanagh, former home of Northern Ireland Prime Minister, Viscount Brookeborough, is now open for functions such as weddings and conferences. What makes it attractive is not only the historical significance and grandeur of the house, but the vast parkland surrounding it. Promotional literature offers:

> fishing, clay pigeon shooting, archery and other outdoor activities are available on this sweeping Fermanagh Estate. For those who may wish to enjoy a less energetic stay there are long riverside and shrub garden walks and there are purpose built 'hides' for watching the abundant wildlife in this remarkable haven. These include deer, otters, mink, buzzards, kingfishers and many others.[63]

The grounds of Glenarm Castle, home of the earls of Antrim, have recently been developed to provide luxury corporate events such as weekend shoots, fishing weekends, etc. Other activities include flower festivals, opera evenings and highland games, all held in the extensive grounds. Randal McDonnell, heir to the estate, has also developed a successful rose garden which is open to the public for most of the year. At Shane's Castle, home of the O'Neills, recent events have included light opera and rock concerts, steam rallies and medieval fairs, all of which help to generate an income for the estate and which are only possible where a large area of land is freely available.

CONCLUSION

The compulsory purchase of remaining landed estates represented by the Northern Ireland Land Act of 1925 may have ended landlordism in Northern Ireland; however, it certainly did not destroy the landed class. Instead, by its favourable terms and, most importantly, by the fact that it preserved for landed families the land which they held in hand, it allowed them to develop their remaining resources in a way that would enable them to continue to maintain their country houses and demesnes and remain living and playing an active part in the life of the region. Through the opportunity to farm remaining land on a viable basis, to develop other natural resources on their estates and, in latter days, to capitalise in the tourist and leisure market which has finally taken off in Northern Ireland, owners of many country houses continue the struggle to maintain their cash-greedy, labour-intensive mansions. In contrast to the situation in the Free State, where compulsory land purchase legislation left an open door for the stripping of land from country houses by a land-hungry population, the compulsory purchase legislation passed by Westminster protected the interests of the landed class, not only in the short term but, by ensuring that they remained in possession of their untenanted land, for many years to come.

NOTES

1. Northern Ireland Land Act, 1925 [15 & 16 Geo. 5. On. 34].
2. See, for example, P. Bew, P. Gibbon and H. Patterson, *The State in Northern Ireland 1921–72: Political Forces and Social Classes* (Manchester, 1979); Patrick Buckland, *The Factory of Grievances: Devolved Government in Northern Ireland 1921–39* (London, 1979).
3. T. A. M. Dooley, *'The Land for the People:' The Land Question in Independent Ireland* (Dublin, 2004).

4. P. Bull, *Land, Politics and Nationalism: A Study of the Irish Land Question* (Dublin, 1996).
5. W. E. Vaughan, *Landlords and Tenants in Mid-Victorian Ireland* (Oxford, 1994); R. W. Kirkpatrick, 'Origins and development of the land war in mid-Ulster 1879–85', in T. W. Moody (ed.), *Ireland Under the Union: Varieties of Tension* (Oxford, 1980); J. R. B. McMinn, 'The Land League in north Antrim 1880–82', *The Glynns*, 11 (1983), pp. 35–40; F. Thompson, *The End of Liberal Ulster: Land Agitation and Land Reform 1868–1886* (Belfast, 2001).
6. *Report of Her Majesty's Commission of Enquiry into the Working of the Landlord and Tenant (Ireland) Act, 1870, and the Acts amending the Same* [C 2779], HC 1881, xviii, p. 1. *Minutes of Evidence*, pt i [C 2779], HC 1881, xviii, p. 73. *Minutes of Evidence and Appendices*, pt ii [C 2779], HC 1881, xix, p. 1. (Bessborough Commission.)
7. See O. Purdue, *The Big House in the North of Ireland: Land, Power and Social Elites 1878–1960* (Dublin, 2009), p. 33.
8. *Return of owners of land of one acre and upwards,* in the several counties, cities and towns in Ireland [C 1492], HC 1876, lxxx, p. 61.
9. J. Bateman, *The Great Landowners of Great Britain and Ireland* (London, 1881).
10. T. Jones Hughes, 'The estate system of landholding in nineteenth century Ireland', in William Nolan (ed.), *The Shaping of Ireland* (Dublin, 1986), p. 140.
11. For a fuller discussion of land purchase in the north of Ireland, see Purdue, *The Big House*, pp. 64–91.
12. Public Record Office of Northern Ireland [PRONI], Antrim papers, D/2977/5/1/11/16/59&60 Antrim to McDonald, 14 and 19 August 1881.
13. *Return giving the names of the landowners the purchase of whose properties under the Land Purchase (Ireland) Act 1885 has been sanctioned by the Irish Land Commission,* return of completed sales to December 1888, HC, 1889 lxi, p. 685.
14. B. L. Solow, *The Land Question and the Irish Economy 1870–1903* (Cambridge, MA, 1971).
15. *Ulster Year Book* (Belfast, 1938), p. 44.
16. ILC papers, Dunleath estate, PRONI, LR1/1248, 1270, 1194.
17. Ibid., Annesley estate, PRONI, LR1/755; Nugent estate, PRONI, LR1/1105, 1332–4, 2139.
18. Ibid., Armstrong estate, PRONI, LR1/757, 1207.
19. Ibid., Belmore estate, PRONI, LR1/104L, 192, 465; Enniskillen estate, PRONI, LR1/2274, 2336; Brooke estate, PRONI, LR1/106AL.
20. Ibid., Macnaghten estate, PRONI, LR1/914; Macartney estate, PRONI, LR1/1684–86; Dobbs estate, PRONI, LR1/1828, 2306.
21. Ibid., O'Neill estate, PRONI, LR1/39L, 46L, 1052.
22. C. A. Wilson, *A New Lease on Life: Landlords, Tenants and Immigrants*

in Ireland and Canada (Montreal, 1994); Nugent estate accounts, 1880–1930, PRONI, D/552/B/3/1/110–112.
23. *Report of the Irish Convention's Sub Committee on Land Purchase*, 22 March 1918, PRONI, D/3727/E/45/1/40–92.
24. Quoted in T. Dooley, *The Decline of the Big House in Ireland: A Study of Irish Landed Families 1860–1960* (Dublin, 2000), p. 131.
25. *Hansard 5 (Lords)*, lxi (London, 1925), p. 243.
26. *The Times*, 2 February 1926.
27. Dooley, *Decline*, p. 133.
28. Ibid., p. 134.
29. *Hansard (Lords)*, Vol. 45, 13 July 1921, p. 1079.
30. A. G. Donaldson, 'The constitution of Northern Ireland: Its origins and development', *The University of Toronto Law Journal*, 11:1 (1955), p. 12.
31. PRONI, Montgomery papers, D/627/F/2/5, Montgomery to Christie, n.d. 1921.
32. *The parliamentary debates (official report)*, first series (Vol. 1): *First session of the first parliament of Northern Ireland, 12 Geo V, House of Commons, session 1922*, p. 1889.
33. G. Walker, *A History of the Ulster Unionist Party: Protest, Pragmatism and Pessimism* (Manchester, 2004), p. 69.
34. *Irish Times*, 2 February 1925.
35. *Irish Times*, 24 March 1925.
36. *Northern Whig and Belfast Post*, 3 April 1925.
37. Ibid., 7 April 1925.
38. *Report of the committee on land purchase in Northern Ireland 1923* [Cmd 1967], HC 1923, xii, pt i, p. 531 (Percy Report).
39. *Hansard 5 (Commons)*, clxxx (London, 1924–5), pp. 1358–60.
40. *Hansard NI (Commons)*, i, Vol. 6 (1926), p. 246.
41. Ibid., p. 251.
42. Ibid., p. 252.
43. Ibid., p. 259.
44. *The Times*, 13 February 1925.
45. *An Act to amend the Law relating to the Occupation and Ownership of Land in Northern Ireland; and for other purposes relating thereto* (15 and 16 George V, ii (28 May 1925)).
46. *Hansard 5 (Lords)*, lxi (London, 1925), p. 244.
47. *Ulster Year Book*, p. 44.
48. Dooley, *Decline*; for a more detailed account of land legislation in the Free State, see idem, *'The Land for the People': The Land Question in Independent Ireland* (Dublin, 2004).
49. Purdue, *The Big House*.
50. See Purdue, *The Big House*, bibliography. The *London, Edinburgh* and *Belfast Gazettes* are the official newspapers of record in the United Kingdom. The *Belfast Gazette* was first published in 1921 and legal notices,

such as the transfer of land under the land purchase act, were required to be published in it.
51. Duke of Abercorn, personal interview, 25 June 2005.
52. PRONI, Abercorn estate papers, D/623/A/367/333, Ross to Inspector of Taxes, 7 November 1932.
53. P. Mandler, *The Fall and Rise of the Stately Home* (New Haven, CT, 1999), p. 356.
54. PRONI, LR1/722 and LR1/1290–91, ILC sale papers, Perceval-Maxwell estate.
55. A. P. W. Malcomson, introduction to Perceval-Maxwell papers, PRONI, D/1556.
56. *Who's Who in Northern Ireland 2004* (Ayrshire, 2004).
57. History of forest service, www.forestservice.gov.uk.htm [accessed 10 September 2005].
58. Abercorn, 25 June 2005.
59. Earl of Antrim, personal interview, 10 June 2005.
60. Hazel Dolling, personal interview, 20 October 2003.
61. Antrim, 10 June 2005.
62. Dolling, 20 October 2003.
63. Colebrooke Park, https://colebrooke.info [accessed 5 February 2020].

PART IV

Landowner Responses

11

Landed Responses to Land Reform in Scotland and Ireland, c. 1860–1903

Annie Tindley

I feel that any Government ought to see the propriety of keeping in this country a class independent enough to withstand any revolutionary projects or combinations that might be started in country districts by secret societies or other means; and the very fact that the attack on us has been avowedly based on the intention of driving us from the country shows that the Government have an interest in retaining us in the country.[1]

INTRODUCTION

THIS CHAPTER WILL CONSIDER how the landed and aristocratic classes responded to the challenge of legislative land reform in Scotland and Ireland in the late nineteenth century. As an elite social group, they were in this period still broadly coherent, linked by blood, marriage and a shared culture of expectations as to both their privileges and responsibilities.[2] But by the later nineteenth century some of their most dearly held assumptions were under sustained political attack, particularly in Scotland and Ireland. Even for those landowners in England and Wales who were not facing directly troubling changes in land tenure law, the sight of their peers doing so elsewhere was enough to generate concern and a degree of joint action.[3] Perhaps most concerning for landed elites was the way in which those who had once been natural political allies in government and Parliament began to see some degree of the 'abducting away of the landlord's rights' as inescapable, even politically desirable.[4] The loosening aristocratic and landed grip on the levers of power at Westminster, local government and their landed estates, defined the content and tactics of landed responses to these challenges. As they found themselves increasingly on the losing side of votes on land reform legislation in Parliament, landowners began to draw on the tactics of their radical opponents, establishing property defence associations to coordinate their responses and marshal their evidence, speaking collectively to concentrate the power of their objections, and utilising the tools of extra-parliamentary lobbying, the press and public relations. This was something of a radical departure for the landed interest: almost by definition they were used to holding the reins of political, territorial and cultural power in Britain and Ireland. By the late nineteenth century this was unravelling under pressure from a wide range of seemingly disparate sources: the move to an industrial and urban-centred economy and society, political reform, the (gradual) rise of mass education and working-class political movements and leadership. Landowners began to realise that their face no longer fitted as the expected and 'natural' governing classes in Britain or Ireland, destabilising both their long-held pragmatic expectations but, more importantly, their implicit identity and sense of purpose.[5]

Much of this outlook can be reconstituted from the private correspondence between landowners at this time. In 1880 Lord Dufferin, an Ulster landowner, diplomat and colonial governor, wrote to his Liberal colleague and fellow Irish landowner, Lord Lansdowne, on the impending doom of William Gladstone's proposals for Irish land reform, enacted the following year:

> Having for generations misgoverned Ireland through the instrumentality of a dominant Protestant minority, the time had come for that minority, now powerless at the polls, to be sacrificed to the voting masses. I foresaw that no English government would have the courage, the virtue or the good sense to withstand and control the gathering agrarian agitation, and I have consequently sold almost all my property. The little that I retain I keep in my own hands for fear lest if I let it to a tenant, Parliament might some fine morning declare him the proprietor. Having spent all the energies of my life, and a great part of my fortune in improving my estate, it has caused me a bitter pang to part with it, but I would sooner live at the North Pole than submit to the tyranny and injustice which is in store for the Irish landlords.[6]

This analysis, although somewhat histrionic, was prescient and nuance was present: the belief that as a collective, landlord interests were to be sacrificed by once supportive political interests in the face of a new kind of society was not too far from the truth. The next logical step was that landlord interests must collectivise to prevent that outcome. This dramatic picture of landed decline should not be overstated, however, particularly for the period before 1911. While it was very much the case that the landed interest regarded themselves as under sustained and existential attack, particularly from the mid-1870s, the historian should not take this entirely at face value. Much of the evidence points to their continuing grip on national and local politics – for example, in the proportion of cabinet members from landed families, or MPs – as well as the enduring power of paternalistic social structures on their landed estates.[7] Many families owned land across national boundaries or were related to those who did. They congregated politically at Westminster and socially in London's clubland and their country estates. As such, the ways in which they framed land issues and reform were necessarily shared, whether in England, Scotland, Wales or Ireland, despite the legislative and chronological differences in land tenure reforms between the different jurisdictions in the late-Victorian and Edwardian period.[8]

This chapter will examine their conceptions of land and property, their responses to the legislative challenges made to those assumptions, and how – and with what success – they organised themselves collectively in an attempt to neutralise or slow the pace of reform. This analysis will be mapped against the wider context of political, social, economic and territorial changes faced by the landed classes in this period, commonly identified as one of decline, if not outright fall.[9] How far did legislative land reform play a part in this decline, or was it just one of a number of more important symptoms of the wider malaise affecting the landed in Britain and Ireland and elsewhere in Europe?[10] Lastly, this chapter assesses how effective the collective response of the landed interest was in meeting these challenges, and what, if any, enduring legacies it has generated in the twenty-first century.

'RULE BY THE BEST': LANDED CONCEPTIONS OF PROPERTY AND THEIR CHALLENGERS

> The fact is, that there is such a spirit of dissatisfaction and such a sense of insecurity gone abroad, that it may become dangerous on the part of the Government, if they don't do something to ameliorate the condition of the people. The people feel that they have no country.[11]

The British and Irish landed classes were a group which in the mid-nineteenth century still maintained a coherent vision of their property, position and status.[12] It was this vision that came under increasing attack and which they were forced to defend and – under duress – adapt. A number of interrelated factors concentrated and reinforced landed identities and responses in this period. These included the ownership of landed estates and the cultures engendered on them; land law, especially the principles of inalienability, entail and primogeniture; the public schools and Oxbridge; politics, London clubland and service to Crown and state.[13] Traditionally this would have taken the form of military leadership as well as the organisation of recruitment into the armed forces from their estates, and this was to some extent still the case even in an increasingly professionalised military context in the nineteenth century.[14] Increasingly, however, it was in the form of local and national political leadership, including dominance in the Houses of Parliament and the cabinet, that overtook military duties as the most common mode of service for the landed and aristocratic. The more self-aware landowners recognised that their position was increasingly conditional on their fulfilling the duties of property rather than enjoying its privileges: residence, charity, social and moral leadership, paternal estate management.[15] As a group, they believed they had both the right to rule and the requisite character and education to do so, and to this extent they demonstrated a form of class consciousness which was exemplified in the tense and existential debates over land reform flaring up by the 1860s.[16]

The extent to which any changes in land tenure or the principles underpinning their power in land would critically undercut the landed classes is best exemplified by considering their continued territorial dominance into the 1870s, when across Britain and Ireland approximately seven thousand families owned four-fifths of the land. In Ireland and Scotland in particular, their territorial dominance was striking, as was the level of land concentration, with 78.4 per cent of land in Ireland held privately and 92.8 per cent in Scotland.[17] These figures were moving into the public realm by the 1870s, with the publication of John Bateman's *The Great Landowners of Great Britain and Ireland*, a seminal text and the starting point for a new generation of land reformers.[18] These figures also highlight the practical implications of land reform measures on the operation of private land ownership: landowners came under political attack because of their territorial monopoly, which went from a source of strength to one of weakness.[19] After Bateman, a series of official government enquiries and commissions into rural conditions merely confirmed their monopoly, their enjoyment of 'unearned' incomes and evidenced calls for radical change.[20] Their understanding of their past – honour, service, status – was demolished by campaigners who painted a very different picture – domineering, selfish, unintellectual, unmerited status and privilege.[21] These were not just the views of a radical peasant fringe; increasingly, these views were shared by the growing urban middle and professional classes, who were demanding power as well as wealth and whose cultural spokesmen in the form of novelists such as Charles Dickens, and even to some extent Anthony Trollope, were busy lampooning the aristocracy and their poor record in providing 'rule by the best'.[22]

Although they were a coherent elite, there were of course variations which had an impact on their response to the challenges of land reform. One of these was the well-documented leavening of old status with new wealth in the nineteenth century, introducing by marriage or purchase the new cultural norms and expectations of wealth separated from land and different financial strategies.[23] Whether new or old, one of the most enduring aspects of landed culture was paternalism and 'rule by the best'. The continued expectation of paternalistic behaviour on rural estates sat increasingly awkwardly in the capitalist and industrial society of the later nineteenth century, and much *sturm und drang* between landowners and their tenants across Britain and Ireland stemmed from this conflict of expectations. A fine example of this in action can be found in the words of the land agent acting for Lord Macdonald on Skye when, in a testy opening exchange with the commissioners investigating conditions for small tenants in the Scottish Highlands and Islands, he was asked to guarantee that no tenant giving evidence need fear eviction if they were critical of his employer:

> I expect that he will tell the truth, the whole truth, and nothing but the truth, and so far as I am concerned as factor, I will visit in no way anything upon him, and I believe Lord Macdonald will do nothing ... but this I would say, if we hear any man making a grossly false statement against us, which we can prove to be false, I do not think that in human nature it would be found we should like to continue that man as our tenant.[24]

Tenants and reformers might ask why should not their behaviour and attitudes change in line with those of their landlords? A poem in Scottish Gaelic produced in the same period, 'A song between a tenant and a landlord' by Calum Campbell Macphail, nicely skewers these contradictions and presents the fictional landowner as inflexible and power-crazed in the face of justified tenant outrage:

> [Landlord] If you were obedient to my will
> I would control you in a noble fashion
> But since you have staged a rebellion
> You will be given a fight which you will not win.[25]

Landowners who were seen to have abandoned their paternalistic inheritance in order to prioritise their financial position at the expense of their tenantry were heavily criticised, particularly during times of acute crisis such as the Great Irish Famine, enclosures in England or the Clearances in Scotland.

Any discussion of a coherent transnational response to tenant agitation and revolt across Britain and Ireland should reflect the firmly and genuinely held contemporary belief that agitation was transnational too. In the Scottish Highlands in the early 1880s, landowners and their agents as well as some sections of the press blamed the Irish for the upsurge in lawlessness and disorder on their estates. Historians have debated the point since, and although a consensus is difficult to identify, there is agreement that through the press and key individuals such as Michael Davitt, Edward McHugh and Angus Sutherland, there was a cross-fertilisation of tactics and organisational and financial support across radical networks in Dublin and Glasgow in particular.[26] This was grist to the landowner mill of blaming agrarian disorder on 'outside agitators', who had corrupted their otherwise loyal tenants with false promises.[27] Scottish and Welsh reformers were careful about what they did and said in relation to Irish agitation, however, due to its violent reputation and from 1879 its alignment to the national question, which was not a strong force in Scotland or Wales at the time.[28] Landowners would learn from their opponents in organising their own responses, by seeking to combine more than they had previously.[29]

Land reform was not the only threat facing the landed classes in Britain and Ireland: there was a wider ecosystem of problems that they were not well equipped to deal with, including a number of crises in the agricultural economy, which sliced into their economic and financial resources.[30] Overall the long-term picture was brutal: agriculture's share of GNP went from 20 per cent in 1860 to 7 per cent in 1914, although landowners struggling in the early 1870s were not to know the long-term extent of the crisis.[31] The situation was worst for those families who were gripped by debt with little room for manoeuvre and who were proportionally more reliant on rental income than those fortunate enough to have paying investments elsewhere.[32] Agricultural prices and rental income declined and in some places collapsed; often, landowners sought to pass the pressure on to their tenants, which generated resistance and agitation especially from 1879, when a severe economic downturn hit rural Britain and particularly Ireland. The response of Irish landowners was important for their peers in Britain because it convinced the British government that Irish landlords were authors of their own destruction and – critically – were not worth saving.[33] As the Liberals under William Gladstone began to move towards a historicist position on land, landowners found themselves fighting on two fronts: that of the present and immediate land reform proposals, and that of the 'past', obliged to defend their families' historical records on estate management, questions of destitution, famine, clearance and emigration.[34] The other key threat, and the one which arguably contributed more to the weakening of aristocratic power than any land reform, was reforms to taxation, principally death duties, but famously also the measures in David Lloyd George's 1909 People's Budget, including the 'super tax' and taxes on luxury goods such as motor cars, alcohol and petrol.[35] After a monumental struggle, Lloyd George was able to get his budget passed, but only after a constitutional crisis and the permanent clipping of the wings of the Lords. One of the reasons for his eventual success was the way in which he and fellow anti-landlord radicals were able to draw on examples from a century of rural destitution, famine, clearance and emigration, as well as the at times unhelpful, even embarrassing, contemporary responses and public pronouncements made by landowners. The first meant that anti-landlordism, especially in Scotland and Ireland, could be rapidly activated and the second meant that contemporary fuel could be added to the fire of historical controversies.[36]

Long term it also led to declining land values in some places, most critically in Ireland, making it difficult for landowners to sell their way out of trouble.[37] Having said that, and despite the gloomy voices among the landed classes and the press, land values remained stable in many parts of England and Scotland, supported by the desire of farming tenants to become owner occupiers in the former and the high international value placed on commercial sport in the latter.[38] The passage of the 1881 Irish Land Act and the 1886 Crofters Holdings (Scotland) Act – both pieces of legislation which the Conservatives had been unable to prevent – land purchase measures seemed to many landowners the only viable option for the future. The attraction of this policy was that it allowed the state to buy them out where possible, and the Conservatives supported this desire with a series of land purchase measures in Ireland and Scotland.[39] Land and its ownership in Britain and Ireland had gone from being the bedrock of elite wealth and status to being both economically and politically vulnerable; for some a millstone around their family's necks. Landlordism was not a monolithic force: there was much variation in wealth, status and the extent to which the foregoing crises affected individuals and families, which led to a multiplicity of responses and a significant minority who did not respond in any way at all.[40]

COUNTER-AGITATIONS: THE RESPONSE OF LANDOWNERS

Landowners as a group were facing many challenges, but in relation to that posed by legislative land reform – which was after all a narrowly defined if existential threat – they were able to generate a collective defence.[41] This took two main forms. First, there was the intellectual defence posed by a minority of landowners who thought and published about land reform, opposing it on intellectual and often historical grounds. These leading voices often drew on a wellspring of data gathering and support from other landowners or their land agents, who busied themselves in digging up facts and figures to support their arguments.[42] Second, there were measures of practical defence that could be taken, including lobbying government and local law enforcement to stamp out illegal agitation, including trespass and rent strikes, as well as attempts to direct the fate of land reform legislation by influencing Parliament and by attempting to suggest more palatable alternatives.

There were some precedents for landowners working together to protect their interests, such as their internecine battles with the Crown Estate over rights to the foreshore in Scotland, which, due to the importance of the revenues deriving from the manufacture of iodine from kelp in wartime, raged in the early to mid-nineteenth century and beyond.[43] In 1861 these proprietors banded together to form the Association of Seaboard Proprietors in Scotland, which had its roots in local Commissioners of Supply and whose principal objective was to have legally settled in their favour once and for all their absolute property rights in the foreshore of their estates.[44] Many of the tactics developed by this Association were replicated in relation to land agitation and tenure reform: publicising their grievances, lobbying the highest levels of government, combining in order to spread the cost and risk of legal action, and bringing on board some of the most active and talented land agents and legal experts to fight their corner.[45] The Association remained active for decades and involved itself in the controversies of the 1880s, highlighting again the grievances of the kelp proprietors, this time fighting off efforts from the Crown and the public in terms of access to and revenues from the foreshore and attempting to direct government attention to industrial development. The leading personnel of this group was closely interlinked with later anti-land reform groups: for instance, George Loch, the commissioner for the dukes of Sutherland, who set up the first meeting of the Association. The 3rd Duke of Sutherland was a leading light in the Defence of Property in Ireland Mansion House group, one of a hundred aristocrats, including five other dukes.[46] Another link was in the legal counsel used by the Association, Skene and Peacock, a long-standing Edinburgh firm with a strong reputation for defending landed interests across Scotland.[47]

Although perhaps not famed as a class for their intellectual prowess, there was a significant minority of landowners who took it upon themselves to develop an intellectual defence of the status quo. They undertook research – often into the management history of their own estates – to develop case studies, including international and imperial comparisons, and attempted to use these to push against the growing tide of anti-landlord public and political opinion.[48] In this, they sought to defend firstly their historical record, and once that had been established, to use that as the basis for their argument that they should continue as the guardians of the land, justifying their power and social status. They also based their arguments on more abstract principles, sacrosanct pillars of progress, liberty and property. First, they vindicated Britain's parliamentary democracy and attacked radical calls for its reform and particularly what they labelled socialism; second, they sought to vindicate the constitutional role of the House of Lords, still their political bastion; third, they justified social and economic inequality as 'essential to Nature'; and lastly, they re-emphasised the governing capacity of the aristocracy for the benefit of all.[49]

Landowners were faced with radically opposed visions of their own history as a class to those they had nurtured over centuries themselves. This was especially the case in Ireland, where the impact of a historicist turn in thinking about land ownership and the duties of those owners was particularly detrimental to landed reputations. 'Instead of a native landowning class rooted in the soil,' explained the Bessborough Commission report, 'the landlords of Ireland were as a class alienated from the mass of the people by differences of religion, manners, and sympathy, and were many of them, strangers and "absentees".'[50] This was just one illustration of what became by the early 1870s an orthodox view on Irish society and land reform, one which was also prevalent in Scotland and India.[51] Landowners saw this shift to a historicist framework – correctly – as highly detrimental to their interests, as political reformers from the radical fringes to the heart of the Liberal party argued that past wrongs should be righted in the present. The 8th Duke of Argyll, a member of William Gladstone's cabinet and leading spokesperson against Liberal land reform measures from 1870 onwards, strenuously argued against the historicist position.[52] He pointed out that history was purely interpretive and an unstable foundation upon which to rest legislation.[53] He also argued that any government interference in the rights and management of property in land would operate as a slippery slope towards all kinds of abuses and make landowners like himself – and by extension the traditional ruling classes – vulnerable to mob rule and 'communistic' tendencies.[54]

One counterargument made by landowners and their agents was to deny that conditions were as drastically bad as claimed historically:

in other words, they sought to 'correct' the versions of history being put forward vocally by reformers.[55] Typical of such a view was that expressed by Evander McIver, one of the Duke of Sutherland's agents on his northern estates, before the Napier Commission: 'Under every proprietor and factor, let them be as kind and good and liberal as they may, there will be some dissatisfied spirits.'[56] In other words, critical testimony coming out of the woodwork from the late 1860s about past estate management practices should be discounted as the usual gripes and grumbles the poor always expressed towards their betters.[57] Another common argument was that the dissatisfaction and agitation which dogged the 1870s and 1880s were evidence of improving conditions disappointed by short-term economic depressions and therefore of the long-term success of landlord policy.[58] The Bessborough Report made this argument: 'Ireland is now richer and has fewer grievances of a social or political sort than at any previous period of her history. For this very reason the great grievance that remains has now come to the front, and demands an instant remedy.'[59] The realists among the landed classes recognised, however, that any attempt to rationalise – as they saw it – was now doomed to failure. One of these was Lord Dufferin, who felt strongly enough on the matter to build up a portfolio of speeches, pamphlets and reviews between 1866 and 1870.[60] These constitute some of the best-constructed liberal defences of Irish landlordism of the time, although his actual practical impact was tellingly limited, making little or no impression upon the economists, agitators and politicians who identified the origins of Ireland's problems as being rooted in its landlords.[61] Dufferin fumed to the only person who would understand: Argyll, then secretary of state for India:

> Do any of your 15 deities, sitting in your ministerial Olympus, cast an eye towards these forlorn regions? If you do, you may perhaps learn that a good many people have been shot lately, and it may occur to you, in a languid sort of manner that not an unimportant function of government is the preservation of life and property ... People may talk as they choose, but these crimes are but the simple translation with fact of the benevolent theories which have been so complacently professed of late by our transcendental moralists and philosophers.[62]

Dufferin's efforts expose the tactics utilised by landowners in defence of their interests: public and private lobbying. There were two further elements to this lobbying: first, as already discussed, an attempt to push back against and prevent legislative reform; and second, an attempt to come up with and deliver more palatable alternatives to offer government a way of actively meeting demands but in ways which were perceived as less damaging to landed interests.[63] In Ireland alone, eight national associations were set up for this purpose, dedicated to countering the demands of land reform, between 1879 and 1887.[64]

A further example can be seen in an unusual 'conference of landlords' at Inverness, hosted in January 1885 and reported widely in the Scottish press. This meeting had been set up under pressure from the Liberal government on Highland landowners to compromise with their tenants and thereby avoid the necessity of the government stepping in with a legislative alternative.[65] It was attended by a sprinkling of landowners and their land agent and legal representatives, including George Malcolm, agent for Ellice of Invergarry and an individual who would become a leading light in the landed defence against land reform in Scotland. The meeting was not a striking success, no doubt due to the broad political spectrum, wide range of financial circumstances and local and regional differences represented. They were able to agree on three resolutions, however, including leases for those tenants not in arrears, revised rents and limited compensation for improvements, none of which were as far-reaching as the Three Fs (Free Sale, Freedom from Eviction and Fair Rent) already enshrined in the 1881 Irish Land Act.[66] Instead, the conference attempted to refocus the debate away from land tenure reform onto the economic development of the region through improved roads, railways and harbours in order to promote the fishing industry, seen as a key alternative to agriculture, as well as state assistance for emigration programmes.[67]

If there was limited landed coordination in Scotland, the exception was the tireless George Malcolm, who saw early on the benefits of presenting a unified message, rather than one fractured by local histories and controversies.[68] His evidence before the Napier Commission was regarded as so useful as a landed defence that it was subsequently published as a pamphlet that his employer assiduously doled out to the major Liberal figures of the day.[69] He took a leading role in preparations for the Deer Forest Commission (1892–5) too, this time under the banner of secretary to the Highland Property Association, established in 1892. In exchange for statistical information from estates as to their deer forests and other sporting operations, Malcolm read and corrected drafts of the statements they were planning to make to the Commission. This was principally to encourage consistency across the landowning lobby in the face of this government 'attack', but also promoted confidence among other agents facing the Commission.[70] As with the Napier Commission, Malcolm's evidence to the Deer Forest Commission consisted of a long, statistics-heavy statement, although this time explicitly with the backing of the Highland Property Association, the president and vice-president of which were the Duke of Atholl and Cameron of Lochiel (who had served as a commissioner on the earlier Napier Commission) respectively, and included a membership of practically every significant landowner in the region.[71] The Association emphasised the scale of investment which had gone into Highland, and wider Scottish, estate management from the 1790s, much of it carefully tabulated for the commissioners.[72] Landowners in Scotland were keen to emphasise the level of their personal and familial investment into their estates as evidence of their critical role and commitment to a paternalistic model.[73] They were also able to positively compare their record to that of Irish landowners, demonstrating that at times self-interest came before transnational peer solidarity, especially in the context of different legislation in the different jurisdictions. Indeed, the failures of Irish landlordism were often made a useful foil for the successes of landlordism elsewhere, something that was increasingly strenuously rejected by energetic Irish landlords.[74] 'But what we are concerned to say is that,' as Mr Montgomery of Fermanagh proclaimed in a landlord's meeting in Dublin in 1887, 'as a class, the landowners of Ireland will bear comparison with any class in Europe ... Many of us who have had experience in county government know that all public works are done by the landowning class, and that if that class is removed, and has left the country, there is in many parts of the country really nobody to step into their place.'[75] Altogether, the creation and financial support of these landlord combinations – albeit mainly focused in or on Ireland, where the threat to landed interests came first and was greatest – belies the traditional collective image of landowners as impotent and inactive in the face of their own decline.

Landowners looked to other tactics.[76] One of these was an attempt to refocus government attention on economic diversification and communications infrastructure across regions most severely affected by both economic stagnation and tenant agitations, such as the Scottish Highlands and the west of Ireland.[77] This tactic was a political feint away from land tenure reform and focused on planning and funding railways, harbours, reclamations, home industries and small-scale agricultural and housing improvements through large-scale government capital investment.[78] After the passage of the 1886 Crofters Act for the Scottish Highlands, for instance, the incoming Conservative government offered two conciliatory gestures; first, a one-off and immediate grant of £30,000 to relieve pressures on local rates, and second, the establishment of a new commission (West Highlands and Islands) to investigate and make recommendations for investment in infrastructure projects such as harbours, roads and railways.[79] This was an old tactic, of course, used to great effect when packaged into drainage and other improvement acts during the Great Irish and Highland Famines of the 1840s and 1850s, and re-established through Conservative legislation in the 1890s in both Ireland and Scotland through the Congested Districts Boards (CDBs).[80] The CDBs had two main functions: first, to ameliorate conditions in congested parishes through grants for equipment, fencing, agricultural improvement and infrastructure, and second, to facilitate the state acquisition of land for sale on the open market, to be purchased and then divided and offered to struggling small tenants and cottars.[81] The CDBs in both Scotland and Ireland had more success with their economic development policies, investing large sums into new piers, harbours and roads, as well as agricultural assistance in the form of improving breeding stock and plants, and training schemes for both men and women, to prepare them for practical trades, seamanship and domestic service and the home industries. Land purchase was a much knottier proposition, but that it was legislated for and would see both budgets and powers increase in Ireland in 1903 and Scotland from 1911 is evidence of the at least partial success of landlord lobbying and organisation.[82]

CONCLUSIONS

> The defence of property is as sacred a duty as the defence of liberty, and men are as much bound to sacrifice their lives for the one as for the other.[83]

So went the argument of many a landed and aristocratic defender of property in the late nineteenth century, in terms which echoed across the newspapers, journals, pamphlets, speeches and Houses of Parliament in the face of the most sustained attack on their power in the modern period. This chapter has considered first, what the collective response was, and second, how successful it was in defending long-standing privileges. Although in many ways a highly individualistic or dynastic social group, the threat of land reform, alongside other worrying trends, did incentivise landowners to collectivise at least to some extent. In many ways this is unsurprising: their social coherence had long been underpinned by collective action – in private clubs, the country house circuit, the London season and of course the Houses of Parliament. Around this generalised sense of collective action there were of course outliers: some landowners who simply refused – on principle – to engage with the debates, the agitators and as far as they could the legislation. For these bitter-enders, any compromise was a betrayal of the fundamental principles which underpinned civilised society and the rule of law. At the other end of the spectrum were those pragmatists who were willing to accept some curbs to their traditional powers in exchange for survival. It was often this group who recognised most clearly the importance of how their conduct and reputation – and perceptions of both – were increasingly turning public and political opinion against them. As a result, they placed most emphasis on defending the historical and contemporary reputation of land ownership. In 1887, for instance, a number of Irish landlords met in Dublin to strategise their best chance of survival, articulating the severest threat: their very conduct – past and present – and reputation:

> But now, we, the landowners of Ireland, are enabled to speak for the first time with a united voice, and the question which we have to ask ourselves is, 'What is the first use that it is our duty to make of our newly acquired powers?' Should it not be to clear ourselves from the charges which have been brought against us and to vindicate our character and our good name? We have been placed upon our defence. Calumnies and accusations have been heaped upon us for years past, but no reply has come from us . . . And why? For the simple reason that we were not united. We have had to bear in silence the pain and obloquy of all the reproaches which have been heaped upon us. (Applause.) But if, now that we have met, we should fail to reply to these charges, if we do not speak out now, it would be taken for granted by the world that the reason was because we had no reply to make and no refutation to offer.[84]

Expressed here was the realisation, arguably come far too late, that reputation was all: the dawning concern that decades, perhaps centuries, of individualistic and dynastic behaviour was coming home to roost.[85] So much of the long history of the ideal paternalism underpinning aristocratic and landed dominance was implicit and symbolic, crystallised in the dusty genealogies and addresses hanging in forgotten corridors of country houses. Extraordinarily threatening circumstances from the mid-nineteenth century forced them to slowly collaborate and dust off their arguments, but it was almost too late. The socio-economic fabric of British and Irish life had changed so much that a collective life rope was no longer in the power of the British government to throw; politically it was no longer possible, and even if it was, the perception of the landed record on rapacious estate management and abject response to rural crises such as destitution and famine could no longer be ignored with generations of their own tenantry, rural reformers and political agitators working hard to expose them to the public eye. It was this, more than any specific land reform act, which played the chief part in their long decline: just one of a number of more important symptoms of the wider malaise affecting the landed in Britain and Ireland and elsewhere in Europe.

The efforts made towards collective action from the 1880s across Britain and Ireland generated some interesting organisational legacies, particularly in Scotland where the concentration of private land ownership remains very high into the twenty-first century. The Highland Property Association continued to fight the landed corner, eventually becoming a nationwide organisation in the Scottish Landowners Federation.[86] This organisation gradually professionalised throughout the twentieth century, lobbying on all matters relating to landed interests, from forestry to subsidy regimes. This is reflected in its various names: the Scottish Rural Property and Business Association and latterly Scottish Land and Estates, with its tagline, 'Helping rural Scotland thrive'.[87] The lessons learned the hard way in the late nineteenth century, including the spectre of the almost complete dismantling of Irish landlordism by the 1920s, have been applied with a fair degree of effectiveness in Scotland, where since 1999 a new programme of land reform legislation has been rolling out under the auspices of the Scottish Parliament. In England and Wales, the collective profile of landowners is much less visible and often subsumed into heritage and farming organisations but the principles remain the same: safety in numbers and reputational protection remain as vital in the 2020s as they were in the 1880s.

NOTES

1. National Library of Ireland, Irish Landowners' Convention, BB7734: *The Irish Land Question: Proceedings and Speeches at the Landowners' Convention held on September 14th and 15th 1887 at the Leinster Hall*, Mr H. de F. Montgomery (Fermanagh), p. 9.
2. F. Campbell, *The Irish Establishment 1879–1914* (Oxford, 2009), pp. 7–30; J. A. Mangan, *Making Imperial Mentalities: Socialisation and British Imperialism* (Manchester, 1990), pp. 1–3.
3. For more on the merits of a transnational approach more broadly, see E. Delaney, 'Our island story? Towards a transnational history of late modern Ireland', *Irish Historical Studies*, 37 (2011), pp. 604–11; J. M. Mackenzie, 'Irish, Scottish, Welsh and English Worlds? A four-nation approach to the history of the British empire', *History Compass*, 6:5 (2008), pp. 1250, 1255–6; M. Cragoe, '"A contemptible mimic of the Irish": The Land Question in Victorian Wales', in M. Cragoe and

P. Readman (eds), *The Land Question in Britain, 1750–1950* (Basingstoke, 2010), pp. 97–102; D. Howell, 'The Land Question in nineteenth century Wales, Ireland and Scotland: A comparative study', *Agricultural History Review*, 61:1 (2013), pp. 84, 93, 99.

4. Public Record Office of Northern Ireland [hereafter PRONI] Dufferin & Ava Papers, D1071, H/B/C/95/93, Lord Dufferin to the 8th Duke of Argyll, 24 December 1880.
5. For example, W. Bence-Jones, *The Life's Work in Ireland of a Landlord who tried to do his Duty* (London, 1880); G. F. Trench, *Are the Landlords Worth Preserving, or, Forty Years' Management of an Irish Estate* (London and Dublin, 1881).
6. PRONI, D1071, H/B/F/175, ff. 7, Dufferin to Lansdowne, 4 July 1880; B. Solow, *The Land Question and the Irish Economy 1870–1903* (Massachusetts, 1971), pp. 15–23, 43. See Bolton's discussion of definitions of Irish Ascendancy elites in G. Bolton, 'The idea of a colonial gentry', *Historical Studies*, 13 (1968), pp. 308–10, 315.
7. This information is brilliantly tabulated in D. Cannadine, *The Decline and Fall of the British Aristocracy* (London, 1990), pp. 711–26.
8. P. Readman, *Land and Nation in England: Patriotism, National Identity and the Politics of Land, 1880–1914* (Woodbridge, 2008), pp. 137–42; E. Delaney and C. O'Niall (eds), 'Beyond the nation: Transnational Ireland', *Eire-Ireland*, 51:1–2 (2016); N. Whelehan (ed.), *Transnational Perspectives on Modern Irish History* (London, 2015).
9. For instance, K. T. Hoppen, 'Landownership and power in nineteenth century Ireland: The decline of an elite', in R. Gibson and M. Blinkhorn (eds), *Landownership and Power in Modern Europe* (London, 1991), pp. 168, 175–7.
10. D. Lieven, *The Aristocracy in Europe, 1815–1914* (London, 1992); E. Frie and J. Neuheiser, 'Introduction: Noble ways and democratic means', *Journal of Modern European History*, 11:4 (2013), pp. 434–48.
11. PP 1884 XXXIII-XXXVI *Evidence and Report of the Commissioners of Inquiry into the condition of the Crofters and Cottars in the Highlands and Islands of Scotland* [hereafter Napier Commission Evidence], Reverend James Cumming, Sutherland, p. 1596.
12. J. Ridden, 'Making good citizens: National identity, religion and liberalism among the Irish elite, c. 1800–1850', unpublished PhD thesis (King's College London, 1998), pp. 7–9, 12–21.
13. D. Castronovo, *The English Gentleman: Images and Ideals in Literature and Society* (1987), pp. 75–88; J. Gathorne-Hardy, *The Public School Phenomenon* (London, 1977), pp. 137–9.
14. Cannadine, *Decline and Fall*, pp. 264–70.
15. A. Adonis, 'The survival of the great estates: Henry, 4th Earl of Carnarvon and his dispositions in the 1880s', *Historical Research*, 64 (1991), pp. 56–7; L. Proudfoot, 'The management of a great estate: Patronage, income

and expenditure on the Duke of Devonshire's Irish property, c. 1816–1891', *Irish Economic and Social History*, 13 (1986), pp. 32–5, 40, 54; D. M. McHugh, 'Family, leisure and the arts: Aspects of the culture of the aristocracy of Ulster, 1870–1925', unpublished PhD thesis (University of Edinburgh, 2011), pp. 36–8, 53–4.
16. Cannadine, *Decline and Fall*, pp. 13–16, 367.
17. Cannadine, *Decline and Fall*, p. 9.
18. J. Bateman, *The Great Landowners of Great Britain and Ireland* (London, 1883); J. V. Beckett, 'Agricultural landownership and estate management', in E. J. T. Collins (ed.), *The Agrarian History of England and Wales: Vol. VII 1850–1914* (Cambridge, 2000), pp. 701–6.
19. Cannadine, *Decline and Fall*, pp. 3–21 for an overview. See also F. M. L. Thompson, 'English landed society in the twentieth century I: property – collapse and survival', *Transactions of the Royal Historical Society*, 5th series, 40 (1990), pp. 1–6; J. Habakkuk, *Marriage, Debt and the Estates System: English landownership, 1650–1950* (Oxford, 1994), pp. 623–34; A. Adonis, *Making Aristocracy Work: The Peerage and the Political System in Britain, 1884–1914* (Oxford, 1993), pp. 165–71.
20. Beckett, 'Agricultural landownership', pp. 694–6.
21. A. Taylor, *Lords of Misrule: Hostility to Aristocracy in Late Nineteenth and Early Twentieth Century Britain* (Basingstoke, 2004), pp. 2–15; J. W. Burrow, *A Liberal Descent: Victorian Historians and the English Past* (Cambridge, 1981), pp. 1–3, 12–22.
22. For example, C. Dickens, *Little Dorrit* (London, 1857) and A. Trollope, *The Way We Live Now* (London, 1875); Taylor, *Lords of Misrule*, pp. 2–15; Cannadine, *Decline and Fall*, pp. 239–42; Castronovo, *English Gentleman*, pp. 77–9; E. F. Biagini, *Liberty, Retrenchment and Reform: Popular Liberalism in the Age of Gladstone, 1860–1880* (Cambridge, 1992), pp. 50–8; L. P. Curtis, *The Depiction of Eviction in Ireland, 1845–1910* (Dublin, 2011), pp. 1–8.
23. Numbers of estates purchased by new men of wealth peaked in Britain in the 1850s and 1860s; D. Brown, 'New men of wealth and the purchase of land in Great Britain and Ireland, 1780 to 1879', *Agricultural History Review*, 63:2 (2015), pp. 286–8, 298; R. Pahl, 'New rich, old rich, stinking rich?', *Social History*, 15 (1990), pp. 229–39; T. Nicholas, 'Businessmen and landownership in the late nineteenth century', *Economic History Review*, 5:2 (1999), pp. 27–44; F. M. L. Thompson (ed.), *Landowners, Capitalists and Entrepreneurs* (London, 1994), pp. 139–70.
24. *Napier Commission Evidence*, Alexander Macdonald, Skye, p. 2.
25. D. E. Meek (ed.), *Tuath is Tighearna: Tenants and Landlords* (Edinburgh, 1995), p. 229; C. Dewey, 'The rehabilitation of the peasant proprietor in nineteenth century economic thought', *History of Political Economy*, 6:1 (1974), pp. 17–19, 38–41.
26. A. Mackenzie, 'Ireland and the Irish Land Act from the Highland point of

view', *Celtic Magazine*, 10 (1884–5); A. Newby, 'Scotia Major and Scotia Minor: Ireland and the birth of the Scottish land agitation, 1878–82', *Irish Economic and Social History*, 31 (2004), pp. 23–6; J. Hunter, 'The politics of Highland land reform, 1873–1895', *Scottish Historical Review*, 53 (1974), pp. 48–9, 57–8; M. Davitt, *The Fall of Feudalism in Ireland* (London, 1904).
27. See, for example, E. McIver, *Memoirs of a Highland Gentleman: Being the Reminiscences of Evander McIver of Scourie*, (ed.) Reverend G. Henderson (Edinburgh, 1905), p. 75.
28. Newby, 'Scotia Major', p. 28; C. Townshend, *Political Violence in Ireland: Government and Resistance since 1848* (Oxford, 1984), pp. 105–6, 115–18.
29. E. McLaughlin, 'Competing forms of cooperation? Land League, Land War and cooperation in Ireland, 1879–1914', *Agricultural History Review*, 63:1 (2015), pp. 89–90, 108, 111; T. W. Guinnane and R. I. Miller, '"Bonds without bondsmen": Tenant-right in nineteenth century Ireland', *Journal of Economic History*, 56:1 (1996), pp. 113–21.
30. Cannadine, *Decline and Fall*, p. 26.
31. C. O'Grada, 'Agricultural decline, 1860–1914', in Floud and McClosky (eds), *The Economic History of Britain since 1700, Vol. 2 1860 to the 1970s* (Cambridge, 1981), p. 175; Beckett, 'Agricultural landownership', pp. 693, 694; P. Readman, *Land and Nation in England: Patriotism, National Identity and the Politics of land, 1880–1914* (Woodbridge, 2008), pp. 137–42; R. Perren, 'The landlord and agricultural transformation, 1870–1900', *Agricultural History Review*, 18 (1970), pp. 37–42.
32. L. P. Curtis, 'Incumbered wealth: Landed indebtedness in post-famine Ireland', *American Historical Review*, 85 (1980), pp. 334–6, 363–7; F. M. L. Thompson, 'II: new poor and new rich', *Transactions of the Royal Historical Society*, 6th series, 1 (1991), pp. 2–3.
33. R. V. Comerford, 'The Land War and the politics of distress', in W. E. Vaughan (ed.), *A New History of Ireland, Vol. 6: Ireland under Union, 1801–1921, II, 1870–1921* (Oxford, 2010), pp. 28, 42–7; O. MacDonagh, *States of Mind: A Study of Anglo-Irish Conflict 1780–1980* (London, 1983), pp. 34, 37–9, 42.
34. C. Dewey, 'Celtic agrarian legislation and the Celtic Revival: Historicist implications of Gladstone's Irish and Scottish Land Acts', *Past and Present*, 64 (1974), pp. 34–40, 43–9, 50–6; K. T. Hoppen, *Governing Hibernia: British Politicians and Ireland 1800–1921* (Oxford, 2016), pp. 179–88, 191–5; H. C. G. Matthew, *Gladstone, 1809–1898* (Oxford, 1999), pp. 435–9, 444–51; T. M. Devine, *The Great Highland Famine: Hunger, Emigration and the Scottish Highlands in the Nineteenth Century* (Edinburgh, 1988), pp. 83–105. See much of the evidence of the Napier Commission, for example, Angus Sutherland, pp. 2431–3: 'Our grievances had their origin in the years 1814–19', referring to the Clearances. For a wider imperial context, see P. Marshall, 'The imperial factor in the Liberal Decline, 1880–1885', in

J. Flint and G. Williams (eds), *Perspectives of Empire: Presented to Gerald S. Graham* (Harlow, 1973), pp. 133, 144; T. Koditschek, *Liberalism, Imperialism, and the Historical Imagination: Nineteenth-century Visions of a Greater Britain* (Cambridge, 2011), pp. 330–2.
35. Cannadine, *Decline and Fall*, p. 48.
36. Cannadine, *Decline and Fall*, pp. 49–50, 56–61, 69–71.
37. J. Beckett and M. Turner, 'End of the old order? F. M. L. Thompson, the land question and the burden of ownership in England, c. 1880–c. 1925', *Agricultural History Review*, 55 (2007), p. 273.
38. Ibid., pp. 287–8.
39. As reflected in the fact that all land acts passed in Ireland after the 1881 Act were land purchase acts (1885, 1887, 1891, 1896, 1903, 1909) rather than landlord and tenant regulation acts (1870, 1881): Cannadine, *Decline and Fall*, pp. 63–7.
40. E. A. Cameron, *Land for the People? The British Government and the Scottish Highlands, c. 1880–1925* (East Linton, 1996), p. 32; C. A. Bayly, *The Birth of the Modern World, 1780–1914: Global Connections and Comparisons* (Oxford, 2004), pp. 295–8.
41. Elites in other European nations tried similar tactics: see, for example, M. Rendle, 'Conservatism and revolution: The all-Russian union of landowners, 1916–18', *Slavonic and East European Review*, 84:3 (2006), pp. 481–3.
42. See, for example, D. S. A. Cosby, *The Irish Land Problem and How to Solve It – A Defence of the Irish Landlords* (London, 1901); W. Bence-Jones, *The Life's Work in Ireland of a Landlord who tried to do his Duty* (London, 1880); Trench, *Are the Landlords Worth Preserving?*
43. J. MacAskill, *Scotland's Foreshore: Public Rights, Private Rights and the Crown, 1840–2017* (Edinburgh, 2018), pp. 1–5.
44. Ibid., p. 15.
45. Ibid., pp. 16–17, 23–38.
46. Curtis, 'Landlord responses to the Irish Land War, 1879–1987', *Eire/Ireland* (Fall–Winter, 2003), p. 176.
47. MacAskill, *Scotland's Foreshore*, pp. 23–8, 30; C. Dewey, 'Celtic agrarian legislation and the Celtic Revival: Historicist implications of Gladstone's Irish and Scottish Land Acts', *Past and Present*, 64 (1974), pp. 50–6.
48. Curtis, 'Landlord responses', pp. 144, 166–8.
49. Adonis, *Making Aristocracy Work*, pp. 257–8.
50. PP 1881 [Cd. 2779, I, II, III] *Report and Evidence of Her Majesty's Commissioners of Inquiry into the working of the Landlord and Tenant (Ireland) Act, 1870, and the acts amending the same* [hereafter *Bessborough Evidence*], p. 4; J. C. Beckett, *The Anglo-Irish Tradition* (Belfast, 1976), pp. 85–91.
51. T. Foley and M. O'Connor (eds), *Ireland and India: Colonies, Culture and Empire* (Dublin, 2006), pp. xiii–xviii; T. Ballantyne, 'The sinews of

empire: Ireland, India and the construction of British colonial knowledge', in T. MacDonagh (ed.), *Was Ireland a Colony? Economics, Politics and Culture in Nineteenth Century Ireland* (Dublin, 2005), pp. 148, 157–8; R. C. D. Black, 'Economic policy in Ireland and India in the time of J. S. Mill', *Economic History Review*, 21:2 (1968), pp. 321–5, 328, 330; B. Crosbie, *Irish Imperial Networks: Migration, Social Communication and Exchange in Nineteenth-century India* (Cambridge, 2012), pp. 1–23; S. B. Cook, *Imperial Affinities: Nineteenth Century Analogies and Exchanges between India and Ireland* (New Delhi, 1993), pp. 9–15, 21–6, 32–7.

52. As well as giving numerous speeches on these issues in Parliament, the 8th Duke of Argyll published extensively on them. The most relevant here are: Argyll, 'New Irish Land Bill', *Nineteenth Century*, 9 (1881); Argyll, 'Land reformers', *Contemporary Review*, 48 (1885); Argyll, *Irish Nationalism: An Appeal to History* (London, 1893).

53. 8th Duke of Argyll, 'A Model Land Law: A reply to Arthur Williams MP', *Fortnightly Review*, 41 (1887), pp. 764, 784.

54. J. W. Mason, 'The Duke of Argyll and the Land Question in late nineteenth century Britain', *Victorian Studies*, 21 (1978), pp. 149–70. See also contemporary arguments made by Richard Bourke: Z. Laidlaw, 'Richard Bourke: Irish liberalism tempered by empire', in D. Lambert and A. Lester (eds), *Colonial Lives Across the British Empire* (Cambridge, 2006), pp. 118–44; J. W. Mason, 'Political economy and the response to socialism in Britain, 1870–1914', *Historical Journal*, 23:3 (1980), pp. 565–87; D. Omissi, '"A most arduous but noble duty": Gladstone and the British Raj in India, 1868–98', in M. E. Daly and K. T. Hoppen, *Gladstone, Ireland and Beyond* (Dublin, 2011), p. 181.

55. E. D. Steele, *Irish Land and British Politics: Tenant-right and Nationality, 1865–1870* (Cambridge, 1974), pp. 3–10, 32.

56. *Napier Commission Evidence*, Evander McIver, p. 1707.

57. A. Jackson, *Colonel Edward Saunderson: Land and Loyalty in Victorian Ireland* (Oxford, 1995), pp. 167–9, 181–3.

58. T. Dooley, *The Decline and Fall of the Dukes of Leinster, 1872–1948* (Dublin, 2014), pp. 39–40, 45–6.

59. Bessborough Report, p. 5.

60. Dufferin, *Contributions to an Inquiry into the State of Ireland* (London, 1866); Dufferin, *Irish Emigration and the Tenure of Land in Ireland* (Dublin, 1870); Dufferin, *Mr Mill's Plan for the Pacification of Ireland Examined* (London, 1868); F. Thompson, *The End of Liberal Ulster: Land Agitation and Land Reform 1868–1886* (Belfast, 2001), p. 63.

61. Steele, *Irish Land and British Politics*, pp. 201, 230, 234–5, 308.

62. PRONI, D1071, H/B/C/95, ff. 30, Dufferin to Argyll, 11 January 1869; Howell, 'The Land Question in nineteenth century Wales, Ireland and Scotland', pp. 84, 93, 99.

63. For example, NLI, C723: Irish Landowners' Convention: Statement to be

submitted to HM's ministers by the deputation on behalf of the Landowners' Convention, February 3rd 1888, p. 3. Similar tactics were used in India: G. R. G. Hambly, 'Richard Temple and the Punjab Tenancy Act of 1868', *English Historical Review*, 79:310 (1964), pp. 47–50, 55–6, 61.
64. Curtis, 'Landlord responses', pp. 169–70.
65. 'Conference of landlords at Inverness, 14 January 1885', *Transactions of the Gaelic Society of Inverness*, Vol. II (1884–5), p. 134; see also Lord Napier, 'The Highland crofters: A vindication of the report of the Crofters Commission', *Nineteenth Century*, 17 (1885).
66. 'Conference of landlords', p. 136; G. Campbell, 'Land legislation for Ireland', *Fortnightly Review*, 19 (1881), pp. 18–29.
67. 'Conference of landlords', pp. 136–7; Cameron, *Land for the People*, pp. 28–31.
68. The whole of his evidence is at *Napier Commission Evidence*, pp. 2822–67.
69. This included the dukes of Argyll, Atholl and Buccleuch; Gladstone, Lord Grey and James Lowther MP, speaker of the House of Commons: National Library of Scotland, Ellice of Invergarry papers, Acc. 12560, 2, letters to Edward Ellice, 1883.
70. Malcolm's evidence to the Deer Forest Commission can be found at *1895 XXXVIII-XXXIX Royal Commission (Highlands and Islands, 1892), Report and Evidence, 1895* [hereafter *Deer Forest Commission Evidence*], pp. 1290–362; National Library of Scotland, Sutherland Estates Papers, Acc. 10225, Crofters ZN/e, tabular information on Assynt for the Deer Forest Commission; Acc. 10225, Factor's correspondence, 1497, Box to Wright, 13 May 1893; E. A. Cameron, 'The Political influence of Highland landowners: A reassessment', *Northern Scotland*, 14 (1994), p. 33.
71. The full list is on *Deer Forest Commission Evidence*, p. 1362.
72. See, for example, *Deer Forest Commission Evidence*, pp. 1304–5.
73. For more on the crossover between landed and imperial paternalism, see B. Porter, *The Absent-minded Imperialists: Empire, Society and Culture in Britain* (Oxford, 2004), pp. 228–31; C. Boylan, 'Victorian ideologies of improvement: Sir Charles Trevelyan in India and Ireland', in T. Foley and M. O'Connor (eds), *Ireland and India: Colonies, Culture and Empire* (Dublin, 2006), pp. 1–4.
74. Curtis, 'Landlord responses', p. 186.
75. National Library of Ireland: Irish Landowners' Convention, *BB7734: The Irish Land Question: Proceedings and speeches at the Landowners' Convention held on September 14th and 15th 1887 at the Leinster Hall, Mr H. de F. Montgomery (Fermanagh)*, p. 8; Curtis, 'Landlord responses', pp. 184–6.
76. L. P. Curtis, 'The Anglo-Irish predicament', *Twentieth Century Studies*, 4 (1970), pp. 57–61.
77. A. Warren, 'Gladstone, land and social reconstruction in Ireland, 1881–1887', *Parliamentary History*, 2 (1983), pp. 154–9.

78. T. W. Guinnane and R. I. Miller, 'The limits to land reform: The Land Acts in Ireland, 1870–1909', *Economic Development and Cultural Change*, 45 (1997), pp. 591–4, 607–8.
79. PP 1890 XXVII, 1890–91 XLIV *Reports of the Committee appointed to inquire into certain matters affecting the interests of the population of the Western Highlands and Islands of Scotland*; I. M. M. MacPhail, *The Crofters War* (Stornoway, 1989), pp. 216–18.
80. Cameron, 'Political influence', pp. 27–8, 33–5.
81. A. S. Mather, 'The Congested Districts Board for Scotland', in W. Ritchie, J. C. Stone and A. S. Mather (eds), *Essays for Professor R. E. H. Mellor* (Aberdeen, 1986), pp. 196–8.
82. Cameron, 'Political influence', pp. 35–6; Mather, 'The Congested Districts Board', pp. 199–202; A. Gailey, *Ireland and the Death of Kindness: The Experience of Constructive Unionism 1890–1905* (Cork, 1987), pp. 1–3, 6.
83. *Bessborough Evidence*, Lord Dufferin, p. 1022, Q.33162.
84. National Library of Ireland: Irish Landowners' Convention, *BB7734: The Irish Land Question: Proceedings and speeches at the Landowners' Convention held on September 14th and 15th 1887 at the Leinster Hall, Mr Henry Villiers Stuart (Waterford)*, p. 7.
85. T. Dooley, 'Landlords and the land question, 1879–1909', in C. King (ed.), *Famine, Land and Culture in Ireland* (Dublin, 2001), pp. 116–28.
86. National Records of Scotland, GD325, Papers of the Scottish Landowners Federation.
87. https://www.scottishlandandestates.co.uk [last accessed 14 May 2020].

12

'The battle of the Welsh nation against landlordism': The Response of the North Wales Property Defence Association to the Welsh Land Question, c. 1886–1896[1]

Shaun Evans

INTRODUCTION: THE WELSH LAND QUESTION

ON 11 DECEMBER 1886, 'a large and representative meeting of landowners' convened at the Queen's Hotel, Chester, to consider the 'present land agitation in Wales and [...] the apparent disposition to attack generally the rights of property of all kinds'.[2] The establishment of a North Wales Property Defence Association (NWPDA) was envisioned as an organised landowner response to the Welsh Land Question (*Pwnc y Tir*), which by 1886 had emerged as a 'burning issue', commanding enormous attention in the columns of the Welsh press.[3] Although the relationship between landowner and tenant always had the potential to generate social and economic grievance, from the 1860s it emerged as a key political and cultural battleground for the future of Wales and its status as a nation.[4] David W. Howell has concluded that 'during the 1860s and 1870s longstanding criticism of the gentry as political leaders ripened into a total attack on their very existence as a class'.[5] This was spearheaded by a radical, nationalist and nonconformist movement which identified Gladstone's Liberal party as the political vehicle for achieving its objectives.[6] Men like Henry Richard (1812–88), Michael D. Jones (1822–98) and Tom Ellis (1859–99) came to believe that their visions of national revival could only be achieved by dismantling the dominance traditionally exerted by the squirearchy, gentry and aristocracy over all aspects of Welsh society and politics, including in the sphere of parliamentary representation.[7] Attempts to emancipate Wales from the influence of its landowners were supported by 'the myth of the *gwerin*', a powerful ideological undertaking to redefine Wales as uniformly nonconformist in religion, radical in politics and Welsh in language.[8] This idealised impression of Welsh identity deliberately excluded landowners, who in contrast with their tenants were portrayed as homogenously Anglican, Tory and English-speaking: 'the mere fact that a man or a woman is a Welsh landowner is quite sufficient in itself for a certain type of Welsh nationalist to mark down him or her as an outsider, a pariah, in Wales [...] the Welsh gentry are ruled out as having any part in Wales as a nation'.[9] This narrative of cultural division, which positioned a *gwerin* majority in opposition to a minority of 'anglicised' and 'alien' gentry, was a conscious attempt to undermine the traditional operation of society based on the landed estate, and divide every village and valley into two communities, embodied in the popular Welsh proverb *'Trech Gwlad Nag Arglwydd'* ('the land is mightier than its lord').[10]

Since the autumn of 1879, agricultural depression had caused significant hardship in the life of rural Wales.[11] It was these economic conditions, coupled with the cultural and political drivers outlined above, which provided the foundation for a Welsh Land Question in the 1880s.[12] From the beginning of 1886, radical Welsh-language newspapers, especially Thomas Gee's (1815–98) influential *Baner ac Amserau Cymru* (*Y Faner*), 'launched incessant attacks against the manifold evils inherent in Welsh landlordism'.[13] An article of November 1886 asserted that 'the battle of the Welsh nation against landlordism is beginning in earnest' and included the vicious claim that the gentry were 'the devourers of the marrow of their [tenants'] bones'.[14] To add to this mix, from August 1886 a series of occasionally violent protests erupted across parts of north Wales, fuelled by the perceived injustice of a largely nonconformist tenantry having to make tithe payments to the Anglican Church.[15] In the so-called 'Welsh Tithe War' (*'Rhyfel y Degwm'*), which continued into the 1890s, the economic hardship faced by tenant farmers conjoined with the principal objective of radical nonconformists: disestablishment of the Church of England in Wales. An array of local farmers' clubs and associations sprang up across Wales to petition landowners for rent abatements or permanent reductions, which were approved in a significant number of cases.[16] However, the tithe question provided another route for radicals to attack landowners and their agents, including through the formation of an Anti-Tithe League under the leadership of John Parry (1835–97) of Llanarmon, which quickly morphed into attempts, spearheaded by Gee, to create a Welsh Land League towards the end of 1886, with the aim of combining the numerous farmers' clubs established across the country.[17]

During the 1886 general election, held under the provisions of the Third Reform Act, radical candidates such as Tom Ellis used their platforms to politicise land, decrying the oppressiveness of *'landlordiaeth'* ('landlordism') and arguing for special legislation to deal with what they viewed as the particular causes and effects of poverty and misery in the Welsh countryside.[18] This aligned closely with the broader 'Home Rule' objectives of the emergent *Cymru Fydd* movement.[19] Taking inspiration from Trevelyan's recently enacted Scottish Crofters Act (1886) and Gladstone's Irish Land Act (1881), Welsh radicals promoted a programme of Welsh land reform comprising the 'three Fs': fair rents, fixity of tenure, and freedom of sale with compensation for improvements and disturbance by game.[20] There was 'frequent invocation of the Irish experience', noticeably when Michael Davitt (1846–1906), founder of the Irish Land League, and other leading land reformers, including G. B. Clark (1846–1930), were invited to tour Wales from February 1886 to mobilise public support for E. Pan Jones' (1834–1922) 'land for the people' campaign.[21] Although Davitt's visit is widely held to have been a failure and the various incarnations of Gee's Welsh Land League turned out to be completely ineffective, it was this context which spurred landowners into action:

> The Association was formed at a period when the Land and Tithe Agitation was at its height. The radical press from week to week was full of violent attacks against property-owners, with exaggerated stories of landlord tyranny and oppression [...] some of the radical papers went so far as to say that landlords ought to be swept away from the face of the earth.[22]

At the start of 1886 it was claimed that 'landowners are slow to believe that farming is undergoing a revolution'; by the end of the year they had been convinced of the need to respond to a movement which threatened to undermine the foundation of their position in society.[23] Although Welsh landowners believed the comparison with the tumultuous Irish context was incredulous, the progress of the Irish Land War and the vigour of the Irish Land League were cause for concern: 'the fate of the Irish landowners', faced with the provisions of the Irish Land Commission and Ashbourne Act (1885), 'has given them a timely warning', wrote one commentator.[24] The draft scheme for the establishment of NWPDA was sent out to landowners with a newspaper report of a large public meeting of farmers in Denbigh, and the inaugural meeting in Chester included a lengthy consideration of J. Bryn Roberts' (1843–1931) proposed Land Bill for Wales, the first of many he attempted to introduce to Parliament over the next decade.[25] The threat of separate legislation for Wales, coupled with the prospect of an organised Welsh Land League and fears of Irish methods taking root, were the key factors informing the establishment of NWPDA, based on the model of the Irish Property Defence Association. As one radical columnist put it: 'the fact that they recognise the present situation sufficiently grave to justify the establishment of a NWPDA is significant'.[26]

WELSH LANDOWNERS AND THE ESTABLISHMENT OF THE PROPERTY DEFENCE ASSOCIATION

The formation of NWPDA was fronted by lords Penrhyn (1836–1907) and Harlech (1819–1904). George Sholto Douglas-Pennant had recently succeeded to the Penrhyn influence on the death of his father in March 1886, inheriting the second-largest estate in north Wales, including one of the most productive slate quarries in the world. His painful defeats in the general elections of 1868 and 1880 had firmly demonstrated that the Penrhyn estate was 'a primary theatre for the playing out of a fierce confrontation about the nature and future of Welsh society'.[27] The other main instigator, William Ormsby-Gore, possessed a sizeable estate around his main seat at Brogyntyn, near Oswestry, and further west in Caernarfonshire and Merioneth.[28] It is probably significant that he also possessed a landed interest in Ireland (21,019 acres in county Sligo and 7,480 acres in county Leitrim in the 1870s) and was Conservative MP for those counties for much of the 1840s to the 1870s.[29] These backgrounds and perspectives vested the two main instigators of NWPDA with an acute awareness of land politics across Ireland and Wales.

Membership was made available to all north Wales landowners through payment of an annual subscription based on their gross income from land; their land agents were admitted without additional cost.[30] Full membership lists were kept secret until 1898, at which point the Association had just under a hundred members, including nine female landowners.[31] However, the Association submitted evidence from 192 landowners to the Welsh Land Commission, with an estimated combined landmass of around 840,000 acres, viewed by Lord Penrhyn as constituting 'about one-half of the acreage of north Wales'.[32] The extent to which the owners of some major estates, such as Wynnstay, Nannau, Chirk and Glynllifon, formally engaged with the scheme is unclear. In autumn 1892 it was noted that 'leading landowners in Anglesey', namely Sir Richard Williams-Bulkeley (1862–1942) of Baron Hill, Lord Boston (1860–1941) and Sir George Meyrick (1827–96) of Bodorgan, had 'declined previously to join', and in the same year Lord Sudeley (1840–1922) of Gregynog complained that he and other major Montgomeryshire landowners had never heard of the Association.[33] Although membership was never ubiquitous among north Wales landowners, the lists of provisional and executive committee members drawn up from 1887 across the early 1890s imply that the description of NWPDA as 'representative' of the region's landowners was fully justified. The executive incorporated the owners of extensive estates such as Penrhyn (71,000 acres in 1892), with smaller landowners such as the successful banker T. D. Thomas (1812–1902) of Parc Postyn (3,500 acres in 1892) in Denbighshire, and everything in between.[34] The executive also included numerous land agents; those of the Penrhyn, Gwynfryn and Faenol (or Vaynol) estates – W. E. Sackville-West (d. 1905), Walter Jones (d. 1904) and N. P. Stewart – played major roles in the activities of the Association. The resident agent William Bell (d. 1894) represented the interests of Bodrhyddan, whereas Isaac Taylor (d. 1896), Richard Birch (d. 1915) and Evan Powell (1834–1903) spoke on behalf of the numerous estates they administered from their practices.[35] The executive included landowners with estates situated across the region, from Penrhos in north-west Anglesey, down to Peniarth in Merioneth, Rhiwlas in the heart of northern Wales, Kelsterton on the Welsh outskirts of Chester and Brogyntyn on the Denbighshire–Shropshire border. These estates operated within very different cultural milieus. Membership also extended to leading English aristocrats with estates in Wales, notably the Duke of Westminster (1825–99), who held lands in Halkyn, Flintshire; Lord Stanley of Alderley (1827–1903), who owned Penrhos, and the Earl of Denbigh (1823–92), proprietor of the Downing estate in Flintshire. However, most of the members were resident Welsh gentry, including individuals such as Lord Mostyn (1856–1929), W. D. W. Griffith (1840–1927) of Garn and W. R. M. Wynne (1840–1909) of Peniarth, whose ancestors had been part of the fabric of Welsh society for centuries and who took great pride in their Welsh heritage. The executive also included Welsh-speaking landowners such as Griffith, H. J. Ellis Nanney (1845–1920), owner of the large Gwynfryn estate in Caernarfonshire and Merioneth, and O. Lloyd Evans (d. 1901) of Broom Hall. Many other members, even if not Welsh-speaking, had intense interests in promoting and preserving Welsh heritage and culture – collecting Welsh manuscripts and antiquities, researching Welsh genealogy and supporting *eisteddfodau*.[36] These were joined by a host of landowners who had recently acquired estates in Wales, through purchase, marriage or inheritance: NWPDA's vice-chairman, H. D. Pochin (1824–95), originally from Leicestershire, made his fortune as an enterprising industrial chemist in Manchester, allowing him to purchase the Bodnant and Golden Grove estates; the Scotsman Henry Robertson (1816–88), a mining engineer, prolific railway builder and owner of numerous iron, steel and coal works in north Wales, who resided at Palé Hall, Llandderfel; and Samuel Sandbach (1856–1928), whose grandfather, a leading Liverpool merchant, had purchased Hafodunos with profits linked to transatlantic slavery. Most executive members were actively involved in the governance and administration of their localities, and many had previously served as MPs. Though most were pronounced Conservatives, the involvement of Liberals such as Pochin, Robertson, Sir Robert Cunliffe (1839–1905) of Acton and especially W. Cornwallis-West (1835–1917) of Ruthin Castle allowed the Association to present itself as 'in no sense a political or party organisation'.[37]

The diversity of landed identities represented on the executive goes some way towards complicating the simplistic Welsh gentry caricature presented in the contemporary radical press. These landowners joined together through NWPDA to protect a shared mainstay of their existence: their relationship with land. Though many members could draw on significant industrial wealth or political influence, it was ownership and management of land which provided much of the foundation for the position they occupied in society. The Welsh Land Question was, fundamentally, a challenge to the traditional social structure presided over by the aristocracy, gentry and squirearchy, based on local hierarchal relations and mutually dependent roles and responsibilities which conditioned life on the patchwork of landed estates which enveloped Wales.[38] It is remarkable that these landowners, who had been the dominant force in Welsh society since at least the sixteenth century, felt the need to follow their counterparts in Ireland and establish an organisation to 'defend the rights of property and to protect it against the efforts of agitators to interfere between landlord and tenant'.[39] NWPDA's response to the Land Question provides valuable insights into landowner attitudes towards land, tenant relations, agriculture and estates, as well as their perceptions of societal roles and responsibilities.

CONFRONTING THE LAND AGITATION: THE OUTLOOK AND ACTIONS OF THE PROPERTY DEFENCE ASSOCIATION

From the outset, the Association was at pains to stress affinity with tenants; 'promoting the feeling that the interests of landlord and tenant were identical'.[40] The notice of the scheme circulated to prospective members asserted that the Association was 'formed in no hostile spirit, or as a combination against the tenant farmers in any shape or form';

instead, the initial meeting 'expressed the utmost sympathy and good feeling toward the tenant farmer' in the context of the agricultural depression, and it was agreed that 'landowners should meet their tenants fairly and liberally'.[41] Members recognised the difficult economic circumstances of the time, but on the basis of their experience and relations with their tenantry, sincerely believed that there was no need, nor widespread tenant-led desire, for major legislative reform. They argued that 'in truth and in fact landlordism does not to any substantial extent exist in north Wales'; that the 'agitation upon the Welsh Land Question was unreal in origin and had not its source in any genuine sense of grievance on the part of the agricultural community'.[42] The Association quickly concluded that 'the so-called land agitation has been purely a matter of journalistic enterprise' driven by 'incessant interference by outside agitators, often totally unconnected with any interest in land'.[43] This interpretation aligns with Howell's contention that 'the Welsh Land Question – the agrarian indictment against the landowners – was largely the invention of Welsh nonconformist radicalism' and that 'they often pressed anti-landlord allegations which had no basis in fact'.[44] It was the Welsh radical press that NWPDA identified as the instigator of the agitation and its primary antagonist.[45] In opposition to the narrative of oppression and division, the Association presented a picture of mutually beneficial partnership, insisting that the estates system 'involves certain substantial advantages to the tenant' and highlighting the strength of traditional bonds within rural society:

> Men who know the country can understand, although the radicals of the towns cannot, the feeling which inspires a landowner with regard to his hereditary estates, the affection with which he regards tenants whose faces and voices have been familiar to him from childhood.[46]

It was the significance placed on landowner–tenant relations which made the Association strongly resistant to any land reform legislation which would interfere with both the freedom of contract characterising tenancy agreements and the broader mass of uncontracted social roles and responsibilities wrapped up with the relationship. Many members were active participants in the House of Lords, and a London sub-committee was formed to 'watch' parliamentary legislation – an activity which was also supported through subscription to the Liberty and Property Defence League.[47] NWPDA resolved to 'oppose in all possible ways any attempt to get special land legislation for Wales as distinct from England'.[48] This was primarily informed by a desire to counteract comparisons with England, Ireland and Scotland, arguing that the circumstances in Wales were 'entirely distinct from that of Ireland [and] the crofting areas of Scotland', but that landowners in Wales were 'neither worse nor better than their English brethren'.[49] The Association was, however, concerned that the barrage of negative reports was gradually 'creating ill-feeling amongst the farmers and working classes' and that virtually all allegations were being allowed to propagate without refutation.[50] Countering the narrative expounded by the radical press within Wales and radical politicians at Westminster emerged as the biggest challenge for the Association, viewing its mission as a collective fight for the future of estates as a mainstay in the life of Wales.

On 23 December 1886, W. D. W. Griffith wrote to Lord Penrhyn to express his 'fear that not much further progress can be made with the work of the Association until a good paid secretary is appointed'.[51] After a thorough search, and numerous letters of recommendation, in 1887 NWPDA appointed George H. M. Owen (d. 1895) as secretary. It was an inspired choice. Still in his twenties, Owen – a solicitor based in Caernarfon, who was already secretary to various local Conservative clubs and associations – was quickly earning a reputation as 'one of the best-known party organisers in the UK'.[52] One of his referees commented that he was 'thoroughly qualified to discharge the duties; he understands the country and the people of Wales well; can read and write the language and has tact and judgement.'[53] Owen injected a real sense of drive, organisation and professionalism to the activities of the Association and quickly became its most important asset. Two of the central aspects of his demanding and multifaceted role were recruitment and marketing. Sixty-four landowners had enrolled by July 1887, but membership had to be as high as possible, firstly to cover the costs of the Association's activities and secondly to justify its claim to represent the views and interests of the region's landed interest.[54] On appointment, Owen was supplied with a list of landowners and he determinedly set about writing to the region's gentry about the aims and purpose of the Association, with invitations to join.[55] His correspondence with C. A. Wynne-Finch (1841–1903), preserved in the Foelas estate archive, also shows that he played an important role in maintaining contact with members, providing updates on activities and sustaining a sense of collective action.[56] Early in 1888, advertisements were included in local newspapers which presented Owen as the point of contact for all landowners 'interfered with by the Welsh Land League'.[57]

In setting out the criteria for the secretary of the Association, Griffith noted that:

> It is desirable that the secretary should have a thorough knowledge of the Welsh language and be able to read and write fluently in it, to enable him to watch the Welsh papers, to draw attention of the Association to anything requiring notice and to be able to reply to, and expose any misstatements that may be put forth.[58]

Owen came to refer to this as his 'press-watching process', and 'defending Welsh landowners against the attacks made upon them by the Welsh vernacular press' became his most significant contribution to the Association's work.[59] Newspapers in Wales had never been a 'neutral medium for the transmission of factual information'.[60] Conversely, Welsh-language papers such as *Y Faner*, *Y Genedl Gymreig* and *Y Werin*, and English-language equivalents such as the *North Wales Express and Observer*, were 'unashamedly propagandist', deeply involved in efforts to shape an 'imagined community' and redefine the boundaries of Welsh identity.[61] By 1886 these papers were full of inflammatory articles, which in the view of the Association promoted 'narratives designedly or recklessly written so that they represent anything rather than the truth'.[62] Owen identified 'the *Baner* published by Gee & son of Denbigh [as] the chief organ in this movement'.[63] The main problem for the Association was that landowners tended not to read these papers, or could not understand the Welsh text; they were 'not coming under the notice of those gentlemen who were being attacked [and] for the most part were allowed to go uncontradicted', the danger being that 'masses of the working class population accepted and largely adopted the principles of the leaders of the agitation as the truth'.[64] The fightback against this propaganda started with an objective 'systematically to collect the violent and incorrect statements that have been made'.[65] These articles were then translated into English, with printed copies sent to those landowners who were attacked, in addition to members of the cabinet, MPs and major English newspapers.[66] The translations were also used to boost recruitment.[67] A translation from *Y Werin* narrated that 'we consider that Welsh farmers on a host of estates are little better than West Indian slaves, except that their bodies are not the personal property of the landowners'.[68] Such translations were circulated to inform, alarm and energise landowners into collective action. This campaign also included the employment of a 'short-hand writer well acquainted with the Welsh-language' who secretly attended and recorded the proceedings of Welsh Land League meetings; an English translation of the official manifesto of the League was also circulated to encourage membership.[69]

Efforts to counter the prevailing narrative of the Welsh Land Question began soon after the formation of the Association. In 1887 the agents of the Penrhyn and Faenol estates agreed to be interviewed by the radical *North Wales Express* for a special feature on 'The Land Question from the Landowners' Standpoint', in which they challenged a host of allegations and assumptions about the operation of estates.[70] Owen was attentive in submitting written responses, in Welsh and English, to derogatory articles, 'exposing and refuting all misstatements and insidious assertions put forth by local agitators and the Welsh Press'.[71] Towards the end of 1889, he wrote to Lord Penrhyn with news of a 'mysterious circular directed to the clergy & landed gentry of Wales, proposing the formation of a scheme for boycotting nonconformity by securing none but church & Tory tenants'.[72] His fear was that this might be falsely attributed to NWPDA. He reacted swiftly to counter the claims, with a number of refutations appearing in local newspapers.[73] By October 1892 he could claim that 'the editors of the Welsh vernacular press have been compelled to exercise considerable caution.'[74] The apparent success Owen had in unravelling and disproving so many of the 'reckless statements' fuelled a sense within NWPDA that the stage of the Land Question was not the lived experience of rural Wales but instead the columns of the radical press.[75]

In addition to responsive action, the Association made active efforts to propagate its views and 'form a sound public opinion'.[76] The Association had always been able to rely on papers such as the Bangor-based *North Wales Chronicle*, but in 1888 also formed a Publication and Press Sub-Committee to place landowners' responses on a more strategic footing.[77] One of its first activities was to make terms with the proprietors of the *Gwalia* Welsh-language Tory weekly, for special issues on the subject of land. Copies of the same were purchased by the Association and posted out to members' tenants, Owen having requested the details 'of such persons on your estate as you would wish should receive a copy of the special issue of the *Gwalia*'.[78]

Owen's assertive responses in the press and the *Gwalia* special edition expressed a confidence in the landowner position, underpinned by a massive evidence-gathering exercise. Owen wrote to members in December 1887 with a proposal to:

> organise a full & complete investigation into the subject, with a view to bringing before the public a fair and complete statement of the case from the

landowners' standpoint and to contradict the misrepresentations and incorrect statements which have been made.[79]

The proposal was accompanied by a list of questions relating to the management and character of estates, tenancy agreements, rents and improvements. In addition to these wide-ranging membership surveys, Owen directly targeted individuals who could provide reliable information on key issues. In June 1889, for example, he wrote to Owen Slaney Wynn (d. 1908), recently retired chief agent on the sprawling Wynnstay estates, to request details of Sir Watkin Williams-Wynn's gifts and leases of chapel sites, to refute allegations that Welsh landowners charged exorbitant fees for the same.[80] The Association adopted a fact-based approach to countering both generic and case-specific allegations.

Owen also argued that 'it is very desirable that small pamphlets should be issued by the Association frequently, in both languages'.[81] The recognition of the need to engage with the debate through the medium of Welsh was essential, and by 1892 Owen could assert that 'a good deal of literature has been printed in Welsh and circulated amongst the tenant farmers'.[82] In 1889 the Association published *The Land Question in Wales*, with 1,500 copies printed in Welsh and 1,011 in English.[83] The work was split into two parts, the first featuring a series of letters published in *Y Faner* about a speech made by Gee at Criccieth in May 1888, and the second an account of the so-called 'Cae-Einion Farce'. The publication was heavily reliant on the Welsh-speaking Gwynfryn land agent and NWPDA member Walter Jones. His letters challenged Gee to 'prove that one tenant in a thousand in Wales has been wronged by his landlord', arguing that estates and country houses made essential economic contributions to their communities, especially through the employment of 'stonemasons, carpenters, slaters, plasterers, labourers, keepers, coachmen, gardeners, woodmen &c.'.[84] The second part dealt with the allegation that David Evans, the sitting tenant at Cae-Einion, a farm on the Gwynfryn estate, was ejected from his holding on account of his political allegiance and involvement in the tithe disturbances.[85] The publication mockingly referred to this episode as 'an experiment of being held up to the world as a tenant farmer enduring the oppression commonly reputed to be generally exercised by landowners'.[86] On exiting the farm, Evans had organised a public sale of his stock, which was appropriated by leading reformers including Tom Ellis and Michael D. Jones who delivered speeches 'posing as heaven-born deliverers of an oppressed tenantry'.[87] The land agent's careful explanation of the circumstances and deconstruction of the allegations succeeded, in the view of the Association, in denigrating a potentially potent narrative of martyrdom to mere farce.

In addition to the continuous barrage of newspaper coverage, in 1887 *Cymru Fydd* and the Liberal Federations of north and south Wales sponsored the publication of two popular pamphlets which comprehensively outlined the rationale for reform, decrying 'the great evils flowing from the present land system' and the 'spirit of domination' which prevailed on landed estates.[88] Owen warned that 'Adfyfr's' *Landlordism in Wales* 'contains the most vile and misleading statements' and urged that it should be formally answered.[89] Owen's research was put to excellent use in the publication which followed. He drafted a proposal focusing on the 'system of tenure and occupation of land', dealing with the operation of estates, the contribution of landowners to society and relationships with tenants.[90] It promoted a positive image, highlighting significant landowner investment in agricultural improvement, the building of new churches, chapels, schools, infirmaries and other public amenities, while also outlining the funding that the gentry provided for *eisteddfodau*, agricultural societies and charitable causes. It discussed the 'great services of landlords to the community', in the spheres of law and order, administration and politics, and the encouragement and stimulus they provided to local trade, including through direct employment on their estates. The Association employed J. E. Vincent (1857–1909), a barrister on the north Wales circuit and a prominent journalist, to formalise the written response which followed.[91] Since September 1887 Vincent had authored a series of detailed articles for *The Times* on the subject of Welsh politics, with a particular focus on land issues.[92] Armed with Owen's draft and the significant body of evidence accumulated by the Association, Vincent compiled *Tenancy in Wales: A Reply to 'Landlordism in Wales'* (1889) 'to expose the flagrant inconsistency and culpable vagueness of the charges which "Adfyfr" has lamented'.[93] Owen believed this reply to be 'trenchant and complete'. It articulated the landowner response to the Land Question with great clarity, dismantling 'Adfyfr's' 'vague stories of tyrannous oppression' and providing a template for the Association's mantra for the years to come.[94] It challenged allegations on insecurity of tenure, oppressive agreements, excessive and exorbitant rents, inadequate compensation for improvements, damage by game, politically motivated evictions, absenteeism and religious antagonism.[95] Vincent's case included references to the significant number of native gentry who still presided over their hereditary estates within the Welsh countryside. It evidenced huge landowner investments in building repairs, drainage schemes, road construction and industrial initiatives; outlined rent reductions and abatements made during the ongoing depression; concluded that since the politically motivated ejections associated with the 1859 and 1868 elections, evictions had been 'phenomenally rare'; listed the significant funding and support for local chapel building by a largely Anglican landowner class; and asserted that 'fixity of tenure already exists to all intents and purposes', pointing to the large number of tenant families who had lived on individual estates for generations. Vincent also challenged the basis of the landowner–tenant relationship as a financial contract driven exclusively by pounds, shillings and pence:

> Welsh landowners, as a body, have never yet regarded land from the commercial point of view; they acknowledge that under the existing system the ownership of land carries with it certain privileges, which involve certain corresponding responsibilities.[96]

This was an attempt to correct the narrative of profound cultural, religious and political division, and related allegations of alienation, anglicisation, hostility and oppression which characterised radical denouncements of landlordism. Vincent argued that 'differences of language, religion or politics have no practical influence on the relation of landowner and tenant in Wales' and insisted that the introduction of a Land Court administering the 'three Fs' would fundamentally undermine the ability of landowners to support their tenantry, local communities, society and the economy in the traditional fashion.[97] Copies were sent to 'all landowners in Wales; the tenants of Association members; leading land agitators; and all the leading papers of the day'.[98]

THE ESTABLISHMENT OF THE WELSH LAND COMMISSION

Alongside the battle within Wales, conducted through newspapers and pamphlets, and from political platform and pulpit, radical parliamentarians also succeeded in keeping the agitation alive with regular attempts to introduce a Welsh Land Bill to the Commons. A long speech by Tom Ellis in Parliament in March 1892 – the most articulate and piercing portrayal of the Welsh Land Question to date – succeeded in grabbing the attention of Gladstone, who endorsed a 'thorough, searching, impartial and dispassionate inquiry'.[99] The Association became so confident in its position that in April 1892 it resolved to approach the sitting Tory government to request the appointment of a Royal Commission to 'inquire into the relations between landowners and tenants in Wales'.[100] This appeal was rejected by the Board of Agriculture.[101] The general election later that year returned a thin majority for Gladstone, assisted by a massive Liberal triumph in Wales. Addressing a large crowd at Cwmllan on the slopes of Snowdon in September 1892, Gladstone adopted Ellis' indictment, drawing negative comparisons between English and Welsh landowners and pledging to establish a Royal Commission as the centrepiece of a historic speech on 'Justice to Wales'.[102] A similar tactic had previously been employed in Ireland with the appointment of the Devon (1843–5) and Bessborough (1880–1) commissions. Although the Welsh Commission was not actually secured until December 1892 and was only officially appointed in March 1893 – largely because of incessant pressure from Ellis, David Lloyd George (1863–1945), J. Herbert Lewis (1858–1933) and Sam Evans (1859–1918) – Gladstone's interjection transformed the Welsh Land Question.[103] In the words of George Owen, it 'produced an electrical effect'.[104] The Association was incensed with Gladstone's assessment of the issue, railing that 'the question created by the Welsh vernacular press at the outset, and taken up by a few irresponsible and unscrupulous agitators, has now been raised in a definite and meaningful fashion by the Prime Minister'.[105] Lord Penrhyn complained:

> One would naturally infer from that speech that the whole country was seething with discontent, and that the farmers would be eager to ventilate their grievances on the first opportunity. But that had not been the case, and the whole agitation was got up by the advanced section of a political party, following the example of Ireland.[106]

Owen characteristically sprang into action, initiating a tenacious flurry of correspondence with Gladstone's secretary (which was published across the Welsh and English press) disputing the evidence underpinning the Prime Minister's assertions.[107] Owen asked members to send him 'materials of unquestionable authenticity for the formulation of an answer to the serious charge made by Gladstone against Welsh landowners', and with the guidance of Vincent produced a detailed response for publication in *The Times*.[108]

From September 1892 the Association 'engaged with unremitting zeal in the task of preparing evidence for the Commission', more than matching the disjointed efforts initiated by the Welsh radical press and Liberal Federation.[109] During this period, Owen's organisational abilities came to the fore as he managed the articulation of a clear, coordinated and compelling landowner response, to nullify the potential threat of the enquiry. In October 1892 he wrote to members warning that it was a 'very serious crisis for Welsh landowners', producing a lengthy list of questions based on the content of Ellis' parliamentary speech, including enquiries on acreages, rentals, abatements, tenancy agreements, revaluations, the nature of farms, evictions, improvements and the duration of tenants' connection with estates.[110] The responses from estate owners were tabulated and published in another volume entitled *The Land Question in Wales*.[111]

By the time the Commission was appointed in March 1893, the Association was well-prepared, believing its case to be 'practically impregnable'.[112] Owen asserted that 'the landowners of North Wales look forward to this conflict with calm confidence; they are nonetheless fully alive to its serious character'.[113] Special efforts were made to stress that the Association was not only fighting for landowners, but also for tenant farmers and the whole estates system, despite external efforts to pitch the Commission as a battle between landowners and tenants.[114] If preparations among north Wales landowners were advanced, the same could not be said for their counterparts in the south. Expanding the Association to cover all of Wales had been discussed from the time of establishment, and was strongly advocated by Lord Sudeley across autumn 1892.[115] However, an all-Wales scheme was never advanced and 'south Wales set to work at the eleventh hour to form a similar organisation'.[116] Owen was invited to address and advise the inaugural meeting of the South Wales Property Defence Association, organised by Lord Emlyn, with the Earl of Cawdor, Earl of Dunraven and 'about 20 other leading gentlemen' in attendance.[117] Owen reported that he had 'explained to them thoroughly what had been done in the north & they all seemed exceedingly anxious to commence now to do likewise' for the south.

The Commission's broad terms of reference were 'to inquire into the conditions and circumstances under which land in Wales and Monmouthshire is held, occupied and cultivated'. The Association was aggrieved with the appointment of commissioners, believing the balance to be skewed against its interests.[118] NWPDA also pushed hard to allow for cross-examination of witnesses by counsel – even offering to pay for counsel to represent the 'opposition' – but was ultimately unsuccessful.[119] The Association's belief that the make-up of the Commission was stacked against landowners' interests is summarised by Owen's letter to members in March 1893:

> I am desired to draw your serious attention to the need for immediate action and to indicate to you the points to which attention must be specially directed by each and every landowner in Wales unless judgement is to be allowed to go by default against.[120]

He held the opinion that it was the duty of all members to address the Commission; 'everything depends upon landowners, their agents and their tenants', he remarked.[121] The Association provided members with copies of the syllabus, together with an incredibly detailed 'guide with suggestions as to answering the queries', formulated by Vincent.[122] Another simplified version was produced by the Association for tenant farmers.[123]

The Commission sat between May 1893 and December 1895, taking evidence across Wales, and in 1896 produced an immensely detailed and wide-ranging report.[124] Throughout this period the Association employed Vincent, 'who has a good colloquial knowledge of Welsh', to attend all of the sittings to 'watch the interests of landowners' as counsel.[125] It also employed Owen Slaney Wynn, former chief agent of Wynnstay, to act as advisor on agricultural affairs.[126] George Owen prepared evidence on a vast scale, attending most of the north Wales sittings in person and fully briefing landowner witnesses.[127] He was determined that 'no single misstatement will be permitted to remain unchallenged', and armed with his impressive body of evidence, was able to disprove many general accusations on the spot.[128] On other occasions he followed up on allegations with requests for further information; for example, after Gee gave evidence alleging that landowners did not look after the welfare of their farm labourers by keeping their cottages in repair, he wrote to members for information to refute the claim.[129] The Association also employed clerks to make full shorthand notes of each day's proceedings, which were sent out to members so that they were speedily and fully notified of any particular claim relating to their estate which they might want to refute.[130]

Though Owen expressed occasional frustration at the lack of persistent landowner engagement with the work of the Commission, many NWPDA members attended sittings and provided thorough and forthright contributions.[131] Lord Penrhyn's evidence was particularly significant in that it promoted the assertion that the agitation was a product of the radical press, and included the submission of the Association's comprehensive file of newspaper cuttings and translations as evidence.[132] The Association pursued a narrative that its case was based on evidence, facts and statistics, in opposition to the hearsay, refutable and isolated examples offered by those seeking reform.[133] Lord Stanley's criticism that 'this is not a tenant coming forward to complain, it is some meddling outsider; what does he know about it?' embodied a broader line of attack that the agitation did not exist in the farming communities of rural Wales, but was instead the product of politically motivated radicals.[134] Indeed, remarkably few tenant farmers came forward to give evidence.[135] Allegations abounded that this was because they feared the implications of giving public statements against their landlords, though as the secretary of the Commission, D. Lleufer Thomas, stated: 'the tenant farmers [. . .] were not organised on anything like the same scale as the landowners'.[136] Owen was conscious of this weakness, correctly referring to 'a split between the two leading agitators in north Wales' – namely Gee and the more radical Pan Jones – which poisoned the land reform movement.[137] Delivering his annual report in 1892, Owen commented that 'at present it is difficult to trace what the Welsh Land League is doing; to all appearance, the organisation seems to have become defunct'; and the following year he concluded that 'the Welsh Land League was an absolute and complete failure'.[138] Whereas NWPDA succeeded in navigating landowners through the Commission with impressive preparedness, organisation and collective urgency, tenant farmers were poorly represented by the vestiges of the Land League consumed within the Liberal Federation. This contrasts sharply with the success of the Irish Land League.

CONCLUSION: LANDED ESTATES IN WELSH SOCIETY AT THE TURN OF THE TWENTIETH CENTURY

The composition of the Commission meant that it was always likely to advise in favour of reform; the majority *Report* included critical conclusions on the existing system of landowner–tenant relations, with yearly tenancy agreements targeted for especial condemnation. Significantly, the recommendations of the majority also included the establishment of a Land Court. However, for what was supposed to be the defining opportunity for the *gwerin* of Wales to dismantle the structure on which rested the centuries-old power of the gentry, the Commission being 'the very *raison d'être*' of Tom Ellis' political career, it failed to deliver a killer blow.[139] It is true that it generated widespread consensus on a raft of necessary changes in agricultural practice. The proceedings also shone a light on the troubling political evictions which had followed the 1859 and 1868 elections, which landowners struggled to justify, and it did allow individual examples of tenant grievance to be aired in public.[140] However, despite meticulous and excitable coverage in the Welsh press, the Commission did not deliver that stream of sensational allegation and overpowering revelation of landowner tyranny and oppression that some agitators had envisioned. Evidence of deep-seated antagonism between landowner and tenant simply did not materialise. Owen tentatively concluded that 'the general impression [is] that the landowners have made a very much better case so far than was anticipated and that the enemy are greatly disappointed'.[141] Lord Penrhyn's evidence was reported under the headline 'Great Landlords Vindicated', aligning with Matthew Cragoe's conclusion that 'the landowners emerged remarkably well from the Commission's investigation'.[142] 'Even the Welsh popularists themselves admit in their confidential moments, this precious Commission resulted in something like a triumph for the squires', narrated one commentator.[143]

Speaking to NWPDA members in October 1894, Lord Penrhyn affirmed that the Association 'has been of very great value to landowners generally [and] the want of such an organisation as ours would have placed the landowners at a serious disadvantage'.[144] However, its work had put a terrible strain on George Owen, who described his time during the sitting of the Commission as 'arduous' and 'anxious'.[145] He had acted with a tremendous sense of responsibility throughout, commenting that he had 'practically represented the majority of leading north Wales landowners'. Alongside Vincent, Owen was crucial to the success of the operation. He very sadly committed suicide in the build-up to the 1895 general election, in which he was acting as agent to the Tory candidate for Caernarfonshire, H. J. Ellis Nanney.[146]

By the time the Commission reported in 1896, the Conservatives were back in office and the agricultural depression had waned, scuppering attempts to introduce the recommended Land Court and depriving the Welsh Land Question of much of its impetus. Unlike Ireland and Scotland, Wales was not to have its own distinctive legislative reform on the issue of land during the nineteenth century. However, the campaign for separate treatment for Wales, coupled with a sense of inherent inequality and division between landowners and the *gwerin*, continued to characterise Welsh radical-nonconformist politics. Members of NWPDA were among the last generation of Welsh estate owners who occupied pivotal positions in Welsh society based on their ownership of land. Writing in the 1920s, Herbert M. Vaughan asserted that the 'far-reaching power of the Welsh gentry has now been completely broken'; 'as an influential class, the old squirarchy has been practically wiped out'.[147] Nonetheless, it was neither the Welsh Land Question, nor the Royal Commission to which it gave rise, which orchestrated this demise. Instead, changes in local government, the impacts of the First World War, heavy taxation and loss in income led to the sale, break-up and diminishment of Welsh estates on a massive scale, allowing thousands of former tenants to become freehold farmers in their own right across the early decades of the twentieth century.[148]

NOTES

1. The quote is from *Baner ac Amserau Cymru* [hereafter *BAC*], 24 November 1886 (translated in J. E. Vincent, *The Land Question in North Wales* (London, 1896), p. 15). I am grateful to my colleague Dr Lowri Ann Rees for her comments on an early draft of this article. Most newspaper articles referenced in this article are sourced from *Welsh Newspapers Online*: https://newspapers.library.wales/.
2. Bangor University Archives and Special Collections [hereafter BUASC], Penrhyn PFA/18/322 and Flintshire Record Office, D/NA/1283 are examples of the printed invitation to landowners. See also *North Wales Chronicle* [hereafter *NWC*], 18 December 1886, p. 5; *Cambrian News*, 17 December 1886, p. 5. In October 1886, a similar meeting had taken place in Chester in response to the tithe disturbances.
3. D. W. Howell, *Land and People in Nineteenth-Century Wales* (London, 1977), p. 152. See also J. Graham Jones, 'Michael Davitt, David Lloyd George and T. E. Ellis: The Welsh experience, 1886', *Welsh History Review* [hereafter *WHR*], 18:3 (1997), pp. 450–82.
4. For earlier examples, see S. Roberts, *Diosg Farm: A Sketch of its History* (Newtown, 1854); idem, *Farmer Careful of Cilhaul Uchaf* (2nd edn, Conwy, 1881); J. Gwynfor Jones, 'Sir John Wynn of Gwydir and his tenants: The Dolwyddelan and Llysfaen disputes', *WHR*, 11:1 (June, 1982), pp. 1–30; D. J. V. Jones, *Rebecca's Children: A Study of Rural Society, Crime and Protest* (Oxford, 1989), pp. 45–98; B. Phillips, *Peterwell: The History of a Mansion and Its Infamous Squire* (Lampeter, 1997); L. Ann Rees, 'Paternalism and rural protest: The Rebecca riots and the landed interest of south-west Wales', *Agricultural History Review*, 59:1 (June, 2011), pp. 36–60.
5. Howell, *Land and People*, p. 152.
6. K. O. Morgan, 'Gladstone and Wales', *WHR*, 1:1 (1960), pp. 65–82; idem, 'Liberals, Nationalists and Mr Gladstone', *Transactions of the Honourable Society of Cymmrodorion* (1960), pp. 36–52.
7. H. Richard, *Letters and Essays on Wales* (London, 1884), esp. pp. 105–24; I. Gwynedd Jones, *Explorations and Explanations: Essays in the Social History of Victorian Wales* (Llandysul, 1981); K. O. Morgan, *Wales in British Politics, 1868–1922* (Oxford, 1991), pp. 1–27; M. Cragoe, *Culture, Politics and National Identity in Wales, 1832–1886* (Oxford, 2004), pp. 142–72.
8. P. Morgan, 'The *Gwerin* of Wales – Myth and reality', in I. Hume and W. T. R. Pryce (eds), *The Welsh and Their Country* (Llandysul, 1986), pp. 134–52; P. O'Leary, 'The languages of patriotism in Wales,

1840–1880', in G. H. Jenkins (ed.), *The Welsh Language and its Social Domains, 1801–1911* (Cardiff, 2000), pp. 533–60.
9. H. M. Vaughan, *The South Wales Squires* (London, 1926), pp. 154–5.
10. See Richard, *Letters*, p. 120.
11. Morgan, *Wales in British Politics*, pp. 53–5; P. J. Perry (ed.), *British Agriculture 1875–1914* (London, 1973).
12. A comprehensive and longer-term account of the origins of the 'History of the Welsh Land Question, 1755–1892' is provided in D. Ll. Thomas, *Welsh Land Commission: A Digest of Its Report* (London, 1896), chapter 3.
13. Jones, 'Welsh experience, 1886', p. 471. For the political influence of BAC, see Cragoe, *Culture, Politics and National Identity*, pp. 210–12.
14. *BAC*, 24 November 1886 (translated in Vincent, *Land Question*, p. 15).
15. The most complete and recent study is S. E. Jones' PhD thesis, 'Hanes y degwm yng Nghymru yn ystod y bedwaredd ganrif ar bymtheg: gyda sylw arbennig i Ryfel y Degwm' (Bangor University, 2017).
16. Howell, *Land and People*, pp. 54–7.
17. Thomas, *Land Commission*, pp. 97–103; D. W. Howell, 'The Land Question in nineteenth-century Wales, Ireland and Scotland: A comparative study', *Agricultural History Review*, 61:1 (2013), pp. 96–101; Vincent, *Land Question*, pp. 11–16. This was the framework for David Lloyd George's public entry to politics: J. Graham Jones, 'Lloyd George's Diary for 1886 and 1887', *Caernarvonshire Historical Society Transactions* [hereafter *CHST*], 70 (2009), pp. 66–83; 71 (2010), pp. 47–62. The League was later rebranded the 'Welsh Land, Commercial and Labour League' and by c. 1891 appears to have been absorbed into the Liberal Federations of north and south Wales.
18. Morgan, *Wales in British Politics*, pp. 72–5; Jones, 'Welsh experience, 1886', pp. 450–82. For Ellis' perspective on the Land Question, see his *Speeches and Addresses* (Wrexham, 1912), pp. 119–39, 227–72.
19. Morgan, *Wales in British Politics*, pp. 28–165; W. Griffith, 'Devolutionist tendencies in Wales, 1885–1914', in D. Tanner, C. Williams, W. Griffith and A. Edwards (eds), *Debating Nationhood and Governance in Britain, 1885–1945: Perspectives from the 'Four Nations'* (Manchester, 2006), pp. 89–117.
20. M. Cragoe, '"A contemptible mimic of the Irish": The Land Question in Victorian Wales', in M. Cragoe and P. Readman (eds), *The Land Question in Britain, 1750–1950* (2010), pp. 92–108; Howell, 'Land Question', pp. 83–110.
21. Cragoe, 'A contemptible mimic', p. 92. See also Jones, 'Welsh experience, 1886', pp. 450–82; Howell, 'Land Question', pp. 83–110; P. Jones-Evans, 'Evan Pan Jones – Land reformer', *WHR*, 4:2 (1968), pp. 143–59.
22. BUASC, Penrhyn PFA/9/8(1).
23. *Cambrian News*, 15 January 1886, p. 4.

24. Vincent, *Land Question*, p. 5. For the response of Irish landowners, see L. Perry Curtis, 'Landed responses to the Irish Land War, 1879–87', *Éire-Ireland*, 38:3–4 (Fall–Winter, 2003), pp. 134–88.
25. BUASC, Penrhyn PFA/18/32. The newspaper report was from the *Denbighshire Free Press*, 30 October 1886.
26. *South Wales Daily News*, 14 December 1886, p. 2.
27. S. Evans, '"Between two interests": Pennant A. Lloyd's agency of the Penrhyn estate, 1860–77', in L. Ann Rees, C. Reilly and A. Tindley (eds), *The Land Agent, 1700–1920* (Edinburgh, 2018), pp. 184–201 (quote p. 187). See also R. Merfyn Jones, *The North Wales Quarrymen, 1874–1922* (Cardiff, 1981).
28. 'Brogyntyn estate and family records', *National Library of Wales* [hereafter *NLW*], online: https://archives.library.wales/index.php/brogyntyn-estate-and-family-records-2 [accessed 9 November 2019].
29. 'Ormsby-Gore (Baron Harlech)', *NUI Galway Landed Estates Database*, online: http://landedestates.nuigalway.ie/LandedEstates/jsp/family-show.jsp?id=291 and http://landedestates.nuigalway.ie/LandedEstates/jsp/estate-show.jsp?id=183 [accessed 9 November 2019].
30. NLW, Voelas & Cefnamwlch EC 4–5. North Wales loosely defined as the historical counties of Anglesey, Caernarfon, Denbigh, Flint, Merioneth and Montgomery.
31. BUASC, Penrhyn PFA/9/8(5).
32. *Royal Commission on Land in Wales and Monmouthshire* [hereafter *RCLWM*], HMSO (London, 1896), Vol. II, pp. 32–7; Vol. IV, pp. 796–812; BUASC, Penrhyn PFA/18/322.
33. Ibid., PFA/18/320. There was a recognition that the name of the Association, especially the 'property defence' element, was an obstacle to recruitment.
34. For a rough guide to the size of the estates, see B. Ll. James, 'The great landowners of Wales in 1873', *National Library of Wales Journal*, 14:3 (1965–6), pp. 301–17.
35. Taylor managed the Downing, Penbedw, Talacre, Caerwys Hall and Hanmer estates, as well as the lands of Lady Vivian in Anglesey; Birch was agent for Llannerch, Gwysaney, Wigfair and Soughton; whereas Powell had previously administered estates in Montgomeryshire.
36. The best analysis of the gentry's use of the Welsh language is R. J. Moore-Colyer, 'Landowners, farmers and language in the nineteenth century', in Jenkins, *Welsh Language*, pp. 505–32. For the Mostyn family's attachment to Welsh heritage, see S. Evans, 'Inventing the Bosworth tradition: Richard ap Hywel, the "King's Hole" and the Mostyn family image in the nineteenth century', *WHR*, 29:2 (December, 2018), pp. 218–53. See also the biographies of NWPDA members and their families in https://biography.wales/.
37. BUASC, Penrhyn PFA/18/263.

38. Howell, *Land and People* remains the best overarching study of landed estates in nineteenth-century Wales. For good regional case studies, see M. Cragoe, *An Anglican Aristocracy: The Moral Economy of the Landed Estate in Carmarthenshire, 1832–1895* (Oxford, 1996); R. J. Colyer, 'The gentry and the county in nineteenth-century Cardiganshire', *WHR*, 10 (1981), pp. 497–535; M. A. Griffiths, 'Agricultural development in South Wales, 1830–75', *Morgannwg*, 27 (1973), pp. 10–24.
39. BUASC, Penrhyn PFA/18/322.
40. Vincent, *Land Question*, pp. 41–3. See also NLW, Voelas & Cefnamwlch EC 4–5.
41. BUASC, Penrhyn PFA/18/322.
42. J. E. Vincent, *Tenancy in Wales: A Reply to 'Landlordism in Wales' by Adfyfr in two parts: Part 1 – Adfyfr Answered; Part 2 – The case for landowners* (1889), p. 7; Vincent, *Land Question*, p. 10.
43. BUASC, Penrhyn PFA/9/8(3); 18/322.
44. Howell, *Land and People*, p. 149.
45. A. G. Jones, *Press, Politics and Society: A History of Journalism in Wales* (Cardiff, 1993), pp. 170–6. Jones overplays the Association's hostility towards the Welsh language.
46. Vincent, *Tenancy in Wales*, pp. 77, 82.
47. E. Bristow, 'The Liberty and Property Defence League and individualism', *Historical Journal*, 18:4 (1975), pp. 761–89.
48. BUASC, Penrhyn PFA/18/315. See also NLW, Voelas & Cefnamwlch EC 4–5.
49. Vincent, *Land Question*, pp. 2, 114. In 1887 W. E. Sackville-West said that he did not 'believe the Irish grievances exist in Wales': *North Wales Express* [hereafter *NWE*], 2 September 1887, p. 8. For a full comparative analysis, see Howell, 'Land Question'.
50. BUASC, Penrhyn PFA/18/315.
51. Ibid.
52. Full biographical details are provided in *NWE*, 16 October 1891, p. 6; *Carnarvonshire and Denbigh Herald*, 12 July 1895, p. 5; *NWC*, 13 July 1895, p. 3.
53. This was the endorsement of W. E. Sackville-West (23 March 1887): BUASC, Penrhyn PFA/18/315.
54. Ibid.
55. For example, see his invitation to Henry Platt of Gorddinog: Conwy Archives, CD6/4/2/10.
56. NLW, Voelas & Cefnamwlch EC 7–9, 12.
57. For example, see *NWC*, 21 January 1888, p. 8.
58. BUASC, Penrhyn PFA/18/315.
59. Vincent, *Land Question*, p. 10; letter inserted in BUASC, X/JC/21.
60. Cragoe, *Culture, Politics and National Identity*, p. 213. See also Jones, *Press, Politics and Society*, p. 3.

61. Ibid., pp. 152–3; Cragoe, *Culture, Politics and National Identity*, pp. 210–13.
62. Vincent, *Tenancy in Wales*, pp. 65–6. A good selection of articles is reproduced in Vincent, *Land Question*, pp. 14–31.
63. BUASC, Penrhyn PFA/18/315.
64. Ibid., PFA/9/8(1). See also NLW, Picton Castle 4829 (transcribed in Jones, *Press, Politics and Society*, pp. 171–2).
65. BUASC, Penrhyn PFA/18/315.
66. Ibid., PFA/9/8(1). Examples of these from *Y Genedl Gymreig*, 1 February 1888; *BAC*, 1 February 1888; *Liverpool Daily Courier*, 9 February 1888; and *Y Werin*, 11 February 1888 can be found in NLW, Voelas & Cefnamwlch EC 16–18 and BUASC, Penrhyn PFA/18/315. Further examples are available at BUASC, Penrhyn PFA/17/101; 18/318–19 and Conwy Archives, CD6/4/2/10.
67. Examples of translations from *BAC* relating to the Duke of Westminster's estate at Halkyn can be found in Flintshire Record Office, D/GR/1169.
68. Translation of *Y Werin*, 11 February 1882, p. 2 in BUASC, Penrhyn PFA/18/315.
69. BUASC, Penrhyn PFA/9/8(1); NLW, Voelas & Cefnamwlch EC 20–21.
70. *NWE*, 29 July 1887, p. 8; 5 August 1887, p. 5; 2 September 1887, p. 8; 9 September 1887, p. 7.
71. NLW, Voelas & Cefnamwlch EC 4–5. Examples include *NWE*, 10 May 1889, p. 6; 15 November 1889, p. 7; *Flintshire Observer*, 1 October 1891, p. 5; *NWC*, 4 January 1890, p. 8; 28 October 1893, p. 5.
72. BUASC, Penrhyn PFA/18/316.
73. *NWC*, 7 November 1889; *Carnarvon & Denbigh Herald*, 8 November 1889: BUASC, Penrhyn PFA/18/316.
74. Letter inserted in BUASC, X/JC/21. See also Jones, *Press, Politics and Society*, p. 176.
75. Vincent, *Land Question*, p. 38.
76. NLW, Voelas & Cefnamwlch EC 4–5.
77. Ibid., EC 18.
78. Ibid., EC 19; BUASC, Penrhyn PFA/18/315.
79. NLW, Voelas & Cefnamwlch EC 12.
80. Denbighshire Archives, DD/WY/9161.
81. BUASC, Penrhyn PFA/9/8(1).
82. Ibid., PFA/9/8(2). The Welsh-language title for NWPDA was given as 'Cymdeithas Amddiffyniad Eiddo yn Ngogledd Cymru'.
83. Ibid., PFA/9/8(1). The work was published in Welsh as *Pwngc y Tir yn Nghymru* (1889). Welsh and English copies are available at BUASC, X/JC 21 CAE.
84. *The Land Question in Wales* (1889), pp. 9–24 (quotes pp. 15–17).
85. Ibid., pp. 24–53.
86. Ibid., p. 53.

87. Ibid., p. 41.
88. These were R. A. Jones, *The Land Question and a Land Bill, with special reference to Wales* (1887), quotes pp. 59, 70; and T. J. Hughes ('Adfyfr'), *Landlordism in Wales* (1887), published in Welsh as *Landlordiaeth yn Nghymru* (1887).
89. BUASC, Penrhyn PFA/18/315.
90. Ibid.
91. G. Le G. Norgate and M. Pottle (rev.), 'James Edmund Vincent (1857–1909)', *Oxford Dictionary of National Biography*, online: https://doi.org/10.1093/ref:odnb/36662 [accessed 10 November 2019].
92. These are reproduced in [J. E. Vincent], *Letters from Wales* (London, 1889).
93. Vincent, *Tenancy in Wales*, p. 10. Published in Welsh as *Tenantiaeth yn Nghymru: Atebiad i 'Dir-arglwyddiaeth yn Nghymru' gan Adfyfr*. Welsh and English copies are available at BUASC, X/JC 21 VIN. The Association printed 1,012 copies of the publication in English and a further 2,486 in Welsh, at a total cost of £138 12s. 9d.: BUASC, Penrhyn PFA/9/8(1).
94. Vincent, *Tenancy in Wales*, p. 5.
95. Ibid., pp. 8–53.
96. Vincent, *Land Question*, p. 235.
97. Ibid., pp. 237–8.
98. BUASC, Penrhyn PFA/9/8(1). It was also advertised in the local press 'to be had of all booksellers' or from Owen at the cost of 6d.: *The Cambrian News*, 25 October 1889, p. 1; 8 November 1889, p. 3; *NWC*, 2 November 1889, p. 4.
99. *House of Commons Debates*, 16 March 1892, Vol. 2, cc. 961–1026: https://api.parliament.uk/historic-hansard/commons/1892/mar/16/tenure-of-land-wales-bill-no-27 [accessed 23 January 2020]. Gladstone's son had inherited the substantial Hawarden Castle estate in Flintshire in 1874.
100. BUASC, Penrhyn PFA/9/8(2).
101. Ibid., PFA/8/10; Vincent, *Land Question*, pp. 42–3.
102. C. J. Williams, 'Gladstone, Lloyd George and the Gladstone rock', *CHST*, 60 (1999), pp. 55–75.
103. For a comprehensive analysis of this period, see J. Graham Jones, 'Select Committee or Royal Commission?: Wales and "The Welsh Land Question", 1892', *WHR*, 17:2 (December, 1994), pp. 205–29.
104. G. Owen, 'The land agitation in Wales', *The Liberty Review* (April, 1893): BUASC, Penrhyn PFA/20/97.
105. BUASC, Penrhyn PFA/16/39. See also ibid., PFA/9/8(3).
106. *House of Lords Debates*, 23 March 1893, Vol. 10, cc. 849–54: https://api.parliament.uk/historic-hansard/lords/1893/mar/23/question-observations [accessed 23 January 2020].
107. Copies of the letters are in BUASC, Penrhyn PFA/16/36; 16/39. See also *NWC*, 21 January 1893, pp. 6–7.

108. BUASC, Penrhyn PFA/16/39; 18/320.
109. Ibid., PFA/9/8(3); 18/320.
110. Letter inserted in BUASC, X/JC/21. See also BUASC, Penrhyn PFA/9/8(3); 18/320.
111. *The Land Question in Wales: Being a survey of the evidence collected in view of the appointment of a Royal Commission and suggestions for the collection of further evidence; together with a review of some of the main aspects of the question* (1892), available at BUASC X/JC 21.
112. BUASC, Penrhyn PFA/9/8(3).
113. G. Owen, 'The land agitation in Wales': BUASC, Penrhyn PFA/20/97.
114. For example, *Y Genedl Gymreig*, 31 January 1893.
115. BUASC, Penrhyn PFA/18/320; I am grateful to Mary Oldham (ISWE Doctoral Researcher) for providing a transcript of an additional letter dated 4 November 1892, in the possession of the current Lord Sudeley.
116. NLW, Voelas & Cefnamwlch EC 28.
117. BUASC, Penrhyn PFA/18/320.
118. For a list of commissioners with biographical details, see Thomas, *Land Commission*, pp. 2–9.
119. Vincent, *Land Question*, chapter 4; *House of Lords Debates*, 23 March 1893, Vol. 10, cc. 849–54.
120. BUASC, Penrhyn PFA/18/320.
121. Ibid.
122. Ibid., PFA/9/9; NLW, Voelas & Cefnamwlch EC 34–35. An example of a response to this is ibid., EC 23.
123. Ibid., EC 42.
124. *Royal Commission on Land in Wales and Monmouthshire* [hereafter *RCLWM*]: *Minutes of Evidence (vols. I–V), Report (vol. VI) and Appendices (vol. VII)*, HMSO (London, 1896). Summarised in Thomas, *Land Commission*, with articles on historical subjects covered by the *Report* later appearing in J. Rhys and D. Brynmor-Jones, *The Welsh People* (New York, 1900).
125. There is a suggestion that the NWPDA's preferred candidate for this role was Edward Carson (1854–1935), the Solicitor General for Ireland, who had significant experience as a barrister during the Irish Land War: BUASC, Penrhyn PFA/18/320. Vincent also served as secretary to the South Wales Property Defence Association.
126. NLW, Voelas & Cefnamwlch EC 28.
127. *RCLWM*, Vol. II, pp. 32–7; Vol. IV, pp. 796–812; Thomas, *Land Commission*, p. 14.
128. BUASC, Penrhyn PFA/18/320.
129. NLW, Voelas & Cefnamwlch EC 30.
130. BUASC, Penrhyn PFA/8/10. There is a complete run of these proceedings in the library at Gwysaney Hall, Flintshire.

131. Full lists and indexes of witnesses are provided in *RCLWM*, Vol. V, pp. 701–27; Vol. VII, pp. 486–507.
132. *RCLWM*, Vol. IV, pp. 224–46; Vincent, *Land Question*, pp. 10–33. Owen arranged the publication of a special supplement to *NWC* featuring a full report of the evidence, with six hundred copies distributed to landowners. See also E. Douglas Pennant, 'Landlordism: The Second Lord Penrhyn and the Royal Commission on Land in Wales and Monmouthshire', *CHST*, 57 (1996), pp. 101–24.
133. Vincent, *Land Question*, p. 86.
134. Ibid., p. 87.
135. Ibid., p. 84.
136. Thomas, *Land Commission*, p. 14.
137. BUASC, Penrhyn PFA/9/8(1).
138. Ibid., PFA/9/8(2); G. Owen, 'The land agitation in Wales', *The Liberty Review* (April, 1893): BUASC, Penrhyn PFA/20/97.
139. Jones, 'Select Committee', p. 222.
140. Vincent, *Land Question*, pp. 156–7. For the evictions, see M. Cragoe, 'The anatomy of an eviction campaign: The General Election of 1868 in Wales and its aftermath', *Rural History*, 9 (1998), pp. 177–93; I. Gwynedd Jones, 'Merioneth politics in mid-nineteenth century: The politics of a rural economy', *Journal of the Merioneth Historical and Record Society*, 5 (1965–8), pp. 273–334.
141. NLW, Voelas & Cefnamwlch EC 28.
142. *Montgomery County Times*, 21 October 1893, p. 3; Cragoe, 'Contemptible mimic', p. 103.
143. A. G. Bradley, *Highways and Byways in North Wales* (London, 1901), pp. 113–15.
144. BUASC, Penrhyn PFA/18/322.
145. NLW, Voelas & Cefnamwlch EC 28.
146. *Carnarvonshire and Denbigh Herald*, 12 July 1895, p. 5; *NWC*, 13 July 1895, p. 3. Owen was succeeded by Charles A. Jones. NWPDA continued to operate and was active during the Great Penrhyn Quarry Strike, 1900–3.
147. Vaughan, *South Wales Squires*, pp. 3–4. This includes a comprehensive analysis of the Land Question and Commission from a landowner perspective at pp. 153–212.
148. J. Davies, 'The end of the great estates and the rise of freehold farming in Wales', *WHR*, 7:2 (December, 1974), pp. 186–212.

13

Under Pressure? The Cawdor Estates and their Responses to Agricultural Depression, Land Reform and Land Crisis

John E. Davies

INTRODUCTION

THE CAWDOR ESTATE IN south-west Wales was the third-largest estate in the country, after those of Wynnstay and Powis Castle, and the nineteenth largest estate in the UK.[1] Its owners, the Campbells of Cawdor in Scotland, acquired part of the estate when Alexander Campbell (d. 1697) married Elizabeth Lort (d. 1714), the co-heiress of Stackpole Court, Pembrokeshire, in 1689.[2] Just over a century after their move to Stackpole, John Campbell, 1st Baron Cawdor (1755–1821) was bequeathed the Golden Grove estate in Carmarthenshire by his friend John Vaughan (c. 1752–1804).[3] Golden Grove was by far the largest estate in the county, and together with the Stackpole estate gave the family over 50,000 acres, and huge amounts of patronage in south-west Wales. At its zenith in the mid-nineteenth century, the Welsh Cawdor estates had almost 1,300 agricultural tenants. The lords Cawdor were also lords of twenty-two manors, sixteen of which were in Carmarthenshire, giving them substantial control over half of that county.[4] Additionally, the ancestral home at Cawdor Castle was the centre of a 50,000-acre agricultural estate, mostly in Nairnshire, giving the family significant influence even though they were largely absentee landlords. However, despite this seemingly entrenched position of power, the last quarter of the nineteenth century saw the erosion of both their political and economic status. This chapter will consider the reaction of the estate, its agents and its tenants to the decline in agriculture, the rise in agitation for land reform in the last quarter of the nineteenth century and the subsequent loss of confidence in landed wealth which resulted in a land crisis in the first two decades of the twentieth century.

AGRICULTURAL DEPRESSION AND THE CAWDOR RESPONSE

The Cawdor properties were overwhelmingly agricultural. The Nairnshire estate generated an annual rental income of between £8,000 and £10,000 from the 1870s onwards, the Stackpole estate a rental of £10,000 and the Golden Grove estate a rental of around £20,000 per annum, with an additional yearly mineral rental income of around £2,000–3,000.[5] Most of the farms practised mixed farming and generally ranged from 50 to 150 acres in extent. However, two areas in Wales stand out from this general picture. In the Castlemartin hundred of south Pembrokeshire, many of the principal Cawdor tenants farmed relatively large holdings, often well in excess of 200 acres, and while some were mixed farms the emphasis was on wheat production. The area had much in common with the cereal-growing areas of England: 'the farmers of Castlemartin differed very much from those of other Welsh districts, not only in their manner of farming, but in their style of living, which approximated to that of prosperous agriculturalists in the English counties [they] ... farm highly, employ more labour in consequence, and live in a better way than farmers from other districts. In past times when corn-growing paid, high farming also paid, but these bad times tell more heavily against them.'[6] The Golden Grove estate also had its wheat-growing area of larger farms, particularly in the Tywi valley.[7] These farmers did not fit the 'peasant mentality' model of Welsh farmers discussed by David Howell.[8] But from the mid-1870s, as corn-growing farms they were finding it increasingly difficult to make ends meet, as much cheaper imported wheat undermined their ability to sell, their relative lack of diversity in farming contributing to the predicament.[9] George Williams,[10] an outspoken Cawdor tenant farmer of 230 acres in the Castlemartin area stated to the Welsh Land Commission in the 1890s, that many farmers had been struggling from the mid-1870s, and that the Cawdor estate had responded too slowly to the effects of the agricultural depression. However, the head agent of the estate, Thomas Mousley, was conscious that depression was hitting the tenants. In 1879 he wrote that:

> they [the farmers] must have experienced great losses over the last 3–4 years, owing to the bad seasons and the low prices of corn but, of course, nothing compared to the English farmers ... [although] ... I fear there are several on this Estate [Stackpole] who will find it very difficult to struggle thro' another year, unless we get most unexpected favorable [sic] changes immediately.[11]

Mousley's acknowledgement of struggling farmers going back three to four years indicates an awareness of looming depression, and that he was also cognisant of struggling farmers much earlier than he publicly acknowledged. This seems to vindicate George Williams' view that the estate was slow in responding to tenants' financial problems, but also that Mousley was reluctant to respond to tenants' complaints until it became an absolute imperative to do so. He was, after all, employed to ensure his master's interests were maintained.[12] Nevertheless, Williams was not alone in his criticism of his landlord. Tenants on other estates became increasingly vocal over their predicament. At the 1877 Llanboidy Agricultural Show Dinner, a Mr Lewis stated that landlords needed to help their tenants, by giving them reductions in rent of 50 per cent.[13] However, the local press reported that on the Angle estate, which was adjacent to Stackpole property, the landlord, Richard Mirehouse, had raised the rents 'of nearly all his tenants' in April 1879.[14]

From the late 1870s, rumour of tenant discontent occasionally surfaced. In July 1879, a story of a 'tenant combination' on the Stackpole estate reached the second earl, though Mousley insisted he had not heard of any such combination.[15] Agitation by struggling farmers is next mentioned in 1882, when the agent refers to a 'Farmer Grievance' pamphlet circulating in the Stackpole area. He dismissed this, concluding, 'It originated, probably, with one obscure mischievous Person. And that will be the extent of its influence. It would be most unwise to take any notice of such rubbish.'[16] Three years later and again on the Stackpole estate at Castlemartin, tenant farmers spearheaded a movement for rent reductions, demands which were echoed throughout Wales. A short-lived Pembrokeshire Tenant-Farmers' Association held its first meeting in November 1885, and many of its members, its chairman and its secretary were prosperous farmers on the Stackpole estate. The Association's brief was simple, namely to apply to landlords as a combination 'for a substantial reduction of rent on account of the present agricultural depression'.[17] However, their intention to approach landlords as a body was pre-empted by the promise of temporary reductions offered by many landlords for the following year, including on the Cawdor estates. In October 1885, the second earl's correspondence with Lord Dynevor shows him to have been keen initially to give a 20 per cent temporary abatement to all his tenants from early 1886. Although Lord Cawdor's response was generous, Dynevor was alarmed. As the largest estate in south-west Wales, the Cawdor estate could absorb the losses that such a rebate would entail, whereas other, much smaller estates, could not. Lord Dynevor foresaw that if many of the smaller proprietors tried to match the lead given by Cawdor, they would fail, close or sell their houses and move away, thereby inflicting permanent economic damage to the area. This does, however, seem to be an overreaction by Dynevor.[18] Smaller landowners may have struggled, but none seem to have failed at this time, and in any case they did not necessarily follow the example set by Cawdor. It was Cawdor's agent, Mousley, who had the final say: he persuaded his master to give more modest abatements of rent in the region of 10 per cent, but that the estate should pay the tithe (for a long time a source of contention, especially with the largely nonconformist tenantry), which was calculated as 7.5 per cent of a farmer's outgoings. Usually the estate expected the tenant to pay the tithe, with Cawdor's heir, Lord Emlyn remarking in 1889 that it was a legally binding payment and that he was totally opposed to it being paid by the estate.[19] However, it may well be that by paying the tithe from this date, the estate had in mind the prominent tithe agitations in north Wales, which were increasingly mirrored in a number of outbreaks in south-west Wales between 1886 and 1892.[20] An anti-tithe meeting held at Solva, Pembrokeshire, in 1886 sent greetings and sympathy to 'our brethren in North Wales in their righteous opposition to an unholy tax', before resolving to form a Solva branch of the Welsh Anti-Tithe League. This proposal was seconded by Reverend G. Thomas, who added that farmers of the district should form a branch of the Welsh Land League, which was carried 'nem. con.'.[21] The League demanded the 'Three Fs' for Welsh farmers, along the lines of those established in Ireland after the Irish Land Act of 1881: fair rents, security of tenure and compensation for improvements.

Mousley also voiced caution regarding the 1885 decision on abatements: 'what dare we promise, just on the eve of an Election? Any promise of allowance out of Rents made now, would certainly be called "undue influence".'[22] In both the 1837 election (when there were accusations of excessive coercion by the then agent, Richard Williams) and the 1868 election (when Mousley had made overtly political evictions), the estate's public image had been tarnished. Since then the Cawdors had been highly sensitive to further public disapproval.[23] In the same letter, Mousley also wrote of farmers' meetings in both Carmarthenshire and Pembrokeshire: 'I hear that the farmers in the Cwmamman Country have had a meeting. This is unfortunate as the movement should have emanated from the Landlords.'[24] The press also reported a Carmarthenshire Tenant-Farmers' Association, which held its first meeting in January 1886 in St Clears.[25] No Cawdor tenant was mentioned as being in attendance, and the area was distinctly lacking in Cawdor property, but the establishment of such an association, in an area adjacent to the county border with Pembrokeshire, is an indication that such associations were spreading as agricultural depression took hold, and landlords were seen to be doing little to help. Interestingly, the area included many of the farms belonging to W. R. H. Powell (1819–89) of Maesgwynne, a Liberal landowner who was looked upon as a friend by many radicals.[26]

The depression eased somewhat in 1890, and landowners, including Cawdor, began to reduce their general abatements.[27] However, it was a short respite, as a general economic depression set in from 1892. Farmers, barely recovering from the earlier economic downturn, were hit more severely and this time it was not just arable farmers who were affected.[28] The Pembrokeshire Tenant-Farmers' Association, which had gone into abeyance after abatements were granted in 1886, was reconvened. On 7 November 1891, a meeting of over seventy farmers took place in Pembroke, many being Cawdor tenants from the Castlemartin area, and with George Williams voted unanimously as chairman, agreed to send a petition to their landlords seeking permanent reductions in rent. Interestingly, no mention of other grievances and objectives, such as the 'Three Fs', featured in the petition.[29] The second Earl Cawdor was the only landowner to respond to the petition in any length. He realised the farmers were in difficulties and was prepared to meet with his own tenants, 'but would have nothing to do with a general public movement'. This response was reiterated by the other handful of landlords who returned the petition.[30] Throughout the nineteenth century, the Cawdors had refused to meet with any combination of their tenants, so Cawdor's ambiguous answer probably meant he, or rather Mousley, would meet with tenants individually on rent audit day to discuss their situation.[31] The Cawdors' belief in the free contract between landlord and tenant extended to relief of financial difficulties, and thus help was afforded to individual farmers who declared a problem.[32] The Association also invited landlords to attend its meetings, but all refused, many stating they would have nothing to do with tenant combinations.[33]

The Pembrokeshire meeting was widely reported, and a debate ensued in the Welsh press which partly influenced Gladstone's decision to establish a Royal Commission on Land in Wales, which he first announced in a speech at Cwm-llan in September 1892. The radical *Cardiff Times* wrote that the Pembrokeshire farmers' meeting was the first of a series to be held throughout Wales 'for the purpose of combining to secure permanent reductions of rents and to redress other grievances under which tenants have so long and patiently lain'.[34] The Tory *Western*

Mail, meanwhile, stated that 'while the meeting showed great respect for landowners and the relationship they had with their tenants, it feared that farmers may be dragged into demanding changes which were being proposed by Welsh agitators (along the lines of the Irish agitations) intent upon fomenting division between the two classes which have so much in common'.[35] However, the Pembrokeshire Tenant-Farmers' Association seems not to have been intent on any radical solution, George Williams stating that 'they did not want to become violent or antagonistic to the landlords'.[36] Just after the meeting, Mousley wrote:

> From what I hear, I'm afraid that our tenants on this Estate [Stackpole] are intending to make a formal application to Your Lordship for definite & immediate assistance. This morning I have had Roch of Longstone & [George] Williams of Hayston both with the same tale, that they cannot go on without substantial help. They each owe considerable arrears ... & neither of them has any money ... I fear that 10 per cent; in addition to the tithe, allowed next February rent days, may not be sufficient. I think we ought to consider seriously whether we should not commence the New Year with a general reduction of expenditure all round.[37]

Mousley, like his master, refused to be interviewed, even by the landlord-supporting *Western Mail*, though he did state to the paper that he had no truck with meeting the farmers 'publicly' or in combination. In private he wrote that although tenants were struggling, he believed some were well able to pay, but were being deliberately awkward.[38]

The Cawdor Castle estate in Scotland saw similar tenant complaints regarding financial struggles in the last quarter of the nineteenth century, although it is not clear how severely the depression hit this mixed-farming area, with soils and climate unsuitable for wheat growing. In 1879 Mousley commented to Cawdor:

> I am really glad to hear that Mr Stables [the factor] is able to think so lightly of the Agricultural depression. And I hope he may not have cause to find that there is something more serious about it than Newspapers reports.[39]

Two years later, William Stables wrote to his master, who was away yachting in the Mediterranean:

> Your Lordship may have seen by the Newspapers that there have been in the South of Scotland, in Aberdeen and even in Rosshire [sic] many meetings of Farmers to complain of Agricultural distress & the consequent necessity of a deduction of Rents – which in a good many cases has been granted – there has been no meeting in the 'Province of Moray' i.e. Moray & Nairn shires & I don't hear of any *Movement* or talk of getting up one of these Meetings in this district – And if it should be I don't think many of the Cawdor Tenants

will join in the demonstration – unless Brackla perhaps – If he does I will offer to take the farm off his hands as I have no fear of letting a better Tenant and a rise of rent. In a fortnight I will have a Rent collection & will be surprised if it be not as good as hitherto & don't expect to have any complaints of Rents being too high.[40]

As in Wales, it took several years of struggle before tenant farmers combined to react to the depression. In November 1887, the Morayshire Farmers' Club circulated its resolution, to demand a large reduction in rent, fixity of rent, rearrangement of the contracts between landlords and tenants, and longer leases, to various farmers' clubs and agricultural societies in the north-east and north of Scotland, seeking their opinion and support. It is significant that this resolution came after the Crofters Holdings Act of 1886, which 'breached the sacred rights of private property'. The tenant farmers of the north-east region may have been hoping to have the Act's provisions extended to their area.[41] Thirty-six societies responded, including the Nairnshire Farmers' Club, which included many Cawdor tenants. Only the Monquhitter Agricultural Association, Aberdeenshire, disapproved of the report in its entirety. Five clubs said the proposed 33 per cent rent reduction was inadequate and wanted to see 50 per cent reductions, while three associations said they wanted to see a land court established.[42] The clubs and societies that responded to the resolution were traditional farmers' clubs, and by the late-nineteenth century were mostly under the influence of landlords and their agents. The Nairnshire Farmers' Club was one such club. Like the Moray club, it had been established at the end of the eighteenth century and was composed of landlords and substantial tenants, with Lord Cawdor as its president. However, at its special meeting to adopt the Morayshire Farmers' Club report, Robert Fraser, the Cawdor tenant of Brackla farm, referred to in Stables' letter above, was voted chairman, in the absence of the secretary, Ian Brodie of Brodie Castle, who had a prior engagement.[43] In his chairman's speech, Fraser gave his full support to the Morayshire farmers, stating that:

> over a series of years ... tenant farmers had had great difficulties ... [but] it had now come to a climax, and that the present rents were impossible [and] unless a most violent change took place within a short time he did not suppose there would be a farm in Scotland [that] could pay a sixpence of rent for they were all very near financial ruin.[44]

In 1894 the Cawdor factor, John Robertson, painted a very different picture: that the Cawdor Castle estate had not suffered any significant financial hardship up to that time despite the depression.[45] One of the principal tenants of the estate seems to corroborate Robertson's statement. The tenant of Delnies claimed that 'there had not been depression in Nairnshire to the same extent as in other parts of Scotland', and that 1879 had been one of his best years for the grain harvest, thanks in no small part due to the much fairer weather that year.[46] He also believed the lack of severe depression was in part because the estates in the county had been exceptionally well managed.[47] However, the majority of tenants experienced hardship, and the estate gave a 20 per cent rebate from 1886 (to coincide with the provisions made for Welsh tenants). Other landlords in the Nairn-Moray area gave similar reductions, all on temporary arrangements. The Kilravock estate tenants, neighbouring the Cawdor estate, thanked their landlord for the 'very handsome' 20 per cent reduction 'while regretting that even 20% ... is nothing like what would be required in the present very depressed condition of agriculture'.[48] Six years later, Robertson could report that 'my rent collection for these times were good' and that 'The Highland Cattle & Clydesdales [sales] are doing well' – neither an indication of struggling farmers. Nevertheless, just a few weeks later he wrote that 'as your Lordship says the farmers are suffering this year badly and perhaps by next rent day, if means can be devised, an allowance of some sort may be necessary'.[49]

THE EFFECTS OF DEPRESSION ON ESTATE INCOME

The exceptionally well-kept estate rentals record arrears, allowances and permanent adjustments to rents. Arrears were expected to be gradually paid off, though on occasion they were written off entirely by the agent if he considered they would never be repaid; allowances were the temporary rebates on rents which were taken from estate income; and adjustments were usually permanent reductions or in a few cases increases (usually where the estate had spent on improvements) in rent. From the rentals and the estate correspondence, there is no evidence that the Cawdor estates had to sell farm properties in the late 1880s to assuage the effects of the depression. The estate had always bought and sold land to consolidate its holdings, but nothing is out of the ordinary with regard to land transactions during the advancement of the depression, either in Wales or Scotland, with one exception: the urban holdings in Llanelli, and more particularly in Carmarthen, were reduced significantly. There is nothing in the archive to indicate why they preferred to sell urban rather than rural property, though it may be the latter was

Table 13.1 Stackpole Court Estate: income and expenditure in £[53]

Year	Rental	Arrears	Allowances granted	Estate improvements
1876	13,710	2	0	3,622
1886	13,721	302	1,868	2,052
1891	13,748	241	18	1,753
1894	12,903	955	1,168	1,322

Table 13.2 Golden Grove Estate: income and expenditure in £[54]

Year	Rental	Arrears	Allowances granted	Estate improvements
1878	22,199	653	0	4,642
1887	23,120	685	2,732	2,276
1888	23,117	514	2,750	2,408
1894	21,899	1,565	1,706	2,555

deemed more profitable than the former.[50] In Carmarthen they disposed of 68 of their 111 properties between 1875 and 1899, while in Llanelli they sold 17 of their 48 town dwellings in the same period.[51] If sales and purchases of farms are considered, purchases exceed sales throughout the 1870s and 1880s. Only in the mid-1890s did buying and selling decline to almost nothing.[52]

The rentals of the estates in both Scotland and Wales remained relatively stable through the depression years, even when allowances are taken into consideration. In Wales, Mousley managed this by cutting back drastically on estate improvements and other works, for which a yearly budget had been set in 1863 of £8,000.

The Cawdor Castle estate factor's accounts show a more varied relationship between income, arrears, allowances and estate improvements.[55] Arrears and allowances were relatively small, while the sums spent on improvements do not decline as the depression deepened. This may have been offset by annual timber sales, which added considerably to estate income.[56]

Robertson explained to the Royal Commission on Agricultural Depression that 'The rents had been met very well [and] small farms did quite as well as the larger ones.' However, he admits to a 7 per cent fall in the estate rental since he took on the role of factor in 1886, though it is uncertain if this was due to the decline in agriculture or because Robertson had 'almost re-arranged the whole estate' in his seven years as factor. Expenditure on improvements at Cawdor amounted to around £2,400 annually under Robertson's management, from a rental of around £10,000 (or about 25–30 per cent per annum), and this was maintained throughout the depression years. Tenants' holdings had been

Table 13.3 Cawdor Castle Estate: income and expenditure in £[58]

Year	Rental	Timber sales	Arrears	Allowances granted	Estate improvements	Remittances to Cawdor's account
1876	9,657	8,683	0	519	3,730	4,350
1880	9,555	2,235	0	0	1,693	5,200
1886	10,298	1,223	496	278	2,574	2,000
1889	10,166	2,054	85	632	2,391	2,801
1894	9,998	1,453	263	84	3,475	3,001
1897	9,846	2,023	137	339	2,017	3,001

maintained free of interest to the tenant, as well as abatements of 20 per cent. At the same sitting, a Cawdor tenant asserted that Nairnshire landlords 'had met the depression fairly', and that improvements had been going on as much as the properties could bear.[57]

In Robertson's 'Fifty Years of Agriculture' on the Cawdor Castle estate, he wrote that the relative lack of depression there was in part due to there being no rent increases over the previous fifty years and partly to the policy of refusing to lease farms upon 'public competition' (which tended to raise rents) and instead filling any vacant farm with the representatives of old tenants or the tenants of other holdings on the estate rather than outsiders.[59] Both of these policies were also in place on the Welsh estates, although the last general rent increase there was thirty years before, rather than fifty.[60] The Stackpole and Cawdor Castle estates had similar-sized rentals. Yet the difference between arrears and the allowances granted is stark (see Tables 1 and 3). The limited extent of those granted at Cawdor Castle seems to confirm Robertson's statement that the estate suffered very little during the depression. The difference was most likely due to the more diverse farming carried out in Scotland.

LAND REFORM AND THE CAWDOR ESTATES

At the same time, landowners were contending with financial difficulties imposed by depression in agriculture, and demanded by an increasingly vocal tenantry, the political demands for land reform, particularly among Welsh radicals, became 'a burning issue with strong national overtones'.[61] Demands for fundamental land reform after the model of the Irish Land Act of 1881 came from the likes of Thomas Gee and Tom Ellis in Wales.[62] In Scotland, towards the end of the century there were attempts to extend the Crofters Holdings Act of 1886 to other areas, while in 1908 calls for a land court and allotments in Scotland were opposed by the third Earl Cawdor in the House of Lords. In one of his last debates, he stated that such a move would destroy the land tenure system in Scotland, which was fundamentally the same as that in Wales, where 'tenants and landlords were bound together by ties of generations' in a voluntary contract between the two parties, and having, fundamentally, the same outlook.[63]

The question of Irish Home Rule and Gladstone's dependence on Irish members for a majority in the Commons, as well as pressure from Welsh radical Liberals for land reform, induced Gladstone to establish Royal Commissions on Land in Wales and into Agricultural Depression in the UK in the early 1890s.[64] The Welsh Land Commission sat for three years and published its final *Report* in 1896. As the Commission dragged on, Welsh landowners became fearful of its findings, since it was perceived that the Commissioners were biased towards the tenant farmers. Indeed, one of the Commissioners was John Morgan Griffiths, a nonconformist tenant farmer from the Castlemartin area.[65] In December 1886, north Walian landowners had established a North Wales Property Defence Association as a response to the establishment of the Welsh Land League and tithe agitations which were then disturbing the peace. A number of Denbighshire and Flintshire tenant farmers had joined the Lancashire Tenant-Farmers' Association, one of the largest and more radical groups.[66] However, in the south it was not until the Land Commission had been appointed that the Landowners' Association of South Wales was established. The inaugural meeting in 1893 was organised by Lord Emlyn, who formed part of the committee alongside the second Earl Cawdor.[67] Both the north and south Wales landowners' associations used the services of the barrister and *Times* journalist J. E. Vincent, who became the secretary of the south Wales group.[68] The establishment of the landowners' associations is an indication that they were beginning to feel insecure in their role as undisputed leaders in rural society. The tenants, motivated by years of seemingly endless agricultural depression, had demanded changes in the relationship between themselves and their landlords. The latter felt a need to combine their forces, something they denied to their tenants.

However, as far as the Cawdor estate was concerned, the Welsh Land Commission exonerated it from the evils of landlordism as espoused in the radical press. In fact, the Cawdor estate was singled out by no less a figure than the radical Liberal leader of Carmarthenshire County Council, Gwilym Evans, who stated that 'the [Cawdor] tenants are so situated that practically I do not believe that any land court or any recommendations that might be made by the Commission could to any extent affect the tenants to their advantage'.[69] Perhaps the only serious complaint the Commission could direct at the Cawdor estate was that of having an English-speaking chief agent. Mousley explained this away, however, by stating that the estate used under- or sub-agents who were Welsh speakers in order to communicate with the tenantry. Interestingly, the Commission did not refer to the political evictions which had taken place on the Cawdor estate in the aftermath of the 1868 election.[70]

The reversal in agricultural fortunes as a result of the challenges posed by the opening of overseas supply markets proved long term and lasted long into the twentieth century. For the most part, central government did not help the sector, and in 1921, with the repeal of the Corn Production Act, agriculture was once again left to compete with the cheaper international market. Confidence in land as a stable source of wealth had begun to wane in the 1880s with the onset of the depression and demands for land reform.[71] To these developments was added a significant change in political attitudes to the landed classes as successive Liberal governments began to view them as a major source of tax revenue. Legislation extending death duties and income tax to land and rents derived therefrom were introduced by Liberals. Interestingly, while these were not unsurprisingly criticised by the Tories, they were never subsequently reversed when they came to power. After the First World War 'the value of land had doubled', reaching a brief pinnacle in 1921 before the bubble burst. Nevertheless, landowners did not reap the benefit of the rise in value since at the same time 'income from land had been halved', the result of new taxations. While land prices remained high, many landowners sought better financial investments elsewhere and sold their holdings. Land had never been a good investment and without its accompanying social and political prestige, largely removed since the last two decades of the nineteenth century, there was no reason not to sell.[72] In 1920–1 the Cawdor estate sold some two hundred lots in outlying areas in both Pembrokeshire and Carmarthenshire and raised £84,264.[73] However, the Cawdors needed the money, not for reinvestment as many landlords did, but in order to pay multiple death duties, which had been introduced as part of the Finance Act of 1894.[74] Emlyn wrote to the second earl that he believed around £100,000 would be needed in the event of the earl's death, as a result of the new Act, 'for the whole estate [Scotland and Wales] which would be very difficult to meet & would mean shutting up everything & every place for a time'.[75] Four years later, the second earl died, followed by the third earl in 1911 and the fourth earl in 1914. Death duties amounting to over £100,000 were required after the third earl's death. In 1921 the estate's agent, Col. Ralph Campbell, a younger son of the third earl, pessimistically stated to the Scottish tenants that 'only by working harder and longer would the estate (both in Scotland and Wales) survive, especially as the worst was yet to come'.[76]

CONCLUSION

The Cawdor estates in both Wales and Scotland largely survived the decline in agriculture and the demands of the land reformers. However, politically they lost most of their power to a more democratic age. During the agricultural depression they responded slowly to farmers' pleas, partly because their agents' role was to protect the income of the estates for the benefit of their masters, so they tended to prevaricate before relenting to rebates and reductions, hoping that better times would soon return. The Cawdors were not alone in this 'waiting game', and criticisms by tenant farmers were justifiable. When they did offer assistance, many farmers, although grateful, believed it to be too little, too late. The Land Question agitations were passed over with little trouble for the Cawdor estates, except for an undermining of their confidence in land, although they were well organised to counter any adversity from the Land Commissioners, who found little fault with the larger estates, including the Welsh Cawdor estates. The Scottish estate had less land agitation to contend with, and probably less severe depression. Hence, it too survived the times, despite Col. Campbell's remarks.[77]

NOTES

1. J. Bateman, *The Great Landowners of Britain and Ireland* (London, 1873).
2. For a detailed study of the Welsh Cawdor estates, see J. E. Davies, *The Changing Fortunes of a British Aristocratic family: The Campbells of Cawdor and Their Welsh Estates* (Suffolk, 2019).
3. Although Vaughan relatives were numerous, John Vaughan deemed them to be too insubstantial to become owners of the Golden Grove estate.
4. For instance as lords of the manor, they held mineral rights over most of the Llanelli anthracite field. See Davies, *The Changing Fortunes*, chapter 4.
5. The Scottish estate had a regular income from forestry of around £2,000 per annum during the same period: Carmarthenshire Record Office [hereafter CRO], CAW 3/1/4/1.
6. *Western Mail*, 11 November 1891, 'The situation in Pembrokeshire'. The writer continued that when Lord Cawdor was out hunting a gentleman remarked, 'Dear me what a lot of country squires you have here.' 'Squires!' replied his lordship, 'There are none at all: they are all my tenants.'

7. The Tywi Valley, along with the Castlemartin area, were often linked with the Vale of Glamorgan as the prime wheat-growing areas in Wales. See, for instance, the *Cardiff Times*, 14 June 1879, report on Cowbridge Farmers' Club.
8. D. W. Howell, *Land and People in Nineteenth Century Wales* (London, 1978), pp. 91, 151.
9. E. J. T. Collins (ed.), 'The Great Depression', in *The Agrarian History of England & Wales* (Cambridge, 2011), Vol. vii, p. 148: 'The depression it can be reasoned, was the measure of the failure of the arable sector to reshape its production function and to switch to alternative products.'
10. George Williams of Hayston farm. He employed five 'farm servants' in 1891 but this had reduced to three in 1901. He claimed his family had been Stackpole estate tenants for over two hundred years. In 1883 Williams had been hauled before magistrates, who referred to him as an 'obstinate farmer' for allowing his pigs to roam on the highway. He refused to pay a fine and the case was sent up to the assizes. Thus, Williams was unafraid of confronting authority – contradicting somewhat T. J. Hughes' argument that all tenant farmers were fearful of speaking out in case of reprisals.
11. CRO, Cawdor box 142: Mousley to Cawdor, 28 July 1879. The agent continued, 'I never saw anything more Melancholy than the general appearance of *all* the agricultural Crops in the English Counties through which I passed last week. The Corn that was in ear, seemed to have heads of about ½ their proper size. Scarcely any hay gathered – And very few promising looking Green crops. I saw nothing nearly so good as Your Lordships Crops at this place [Stackpole].'
12. Mousley could almost be accused of following Mr James Pigg (agent): 'Mar cousin Deavilboger always said that ne man is fit to be called a farmer what isn't a good grumbler . . . Robert S. Surtees, *Hillingdon Hall or, The Cockney Squire* (1845)!
13. *South Wales Daily News*, 15 September 1877. However, his statement was followed by 'laughter'. Llanboidy was at the heart of the Liberal landowner Powell of Masegwynne's estate.
14. *South Wales Daily News*, 14 April 1879. The Angle estate was 3,456 acres in extent and may have been one of the smaller Welsh estates that drew criticism from the Land Commission for being unwilling/unable to give much help to tenants struggling during the depression years.
15. Perhaps Cawdor was a little perturbed. A newly formed Warwickshire Tenant-farmers' Association was widely reported in the Welsh press in March 1879. The *Cardiff Times*, 15 March 1879, reported the meeting, to which landlords and agents had not been invited, as 'Farmers versus landlords'. Over three hundred farmers attended.
16. CRO, Cawdor box 157, Mousley to Cawdor, 7 July 1882.
17. *Pembrokeshire Herald*, 20 November 1885.

18. CRO, Dynevor 155/7, Correspondence between lords Dynevor and Cawdor, November 1885.
19. *Carmarthen Journal*, 1 February 1889. Emlyn stated that anti-tithe agitators would be as well to advise people not to pay for a leg of mutton or Welsh cheese, than not pay the tithe, which was part of the agreement farmers signed upon taking a tenancy.
20. Whitland saw the first tithe distress sales in south-west Wales in 1887. See *South Wales Daily News*, 9 December 1887.
21. *Pembrokeshire Herald*, 10 September 1886. The short-lived Welsh Land League was founded in 1886, in Rhyl, by Thomas Gee.
22. CRO, Cawdor box 157, Mousley to Cawdor, 28 October 1885. The General Election took place 24 November–18 December 1885.
23. In February 1898, when Lord Emlyn was put forward by the Unionists as parliamentary candidate for Wiltshire, his position as chair of the GWR and the fact that he allowed a day off to GWR workers to vote, was raised by Liberals with long memories as Emlyn trying to influence the vote (which, however, he lost).
24. Cwmamman is a mainly hilly area of smallish farms and sheep runs: CRO, Cawdor box 157: Mousley to Cawdor, 28 October 1885.
25. *Cardiff Times*, 9 January 1886, 'Land agitation in Carmarthenshire'.
26. Powell defeated Emlyn in the 1885 election. A Liberal election pamphlet stated Powell won because he was in touch with farmers concerning the land question in Carmarthenshire: 'The desire of a land court or its equivalent has been over and over again most emphatically expressed by an overwhelming majority of the Carmarthenshire peasants', *Land Commission Report*, p. 173.
27. CRO, Cawdor box 158, Mousley to Cawdor, 1 March 1890: 'I have finished a wonderfully good collection of rents – All cheerfully paid.'
28. P. J. Perry, 'Where was the "Great Depression"? A Geography of Agricultural Bankruptcy in Late Victorian England and Wales', *Agricultural History Review* [hereafter *AgHR*], 20:1 (1972), p. 42.
29. *Western Mail*, 13 November 1891. Mr Gibbs of Hodgeson, Lamphey, 'a well-known Radical, who holds advanced views on the Land Question', was instrumental in establishing the earlier incarnation of the Association, but refused to be involved with the 1891 Association (he thought it was a 'rope of sand'), since he believed nothing effective would happen until the establishment of a nationwide 'Farmers' Union of League'.
30. *Western Mail*, 2 December 1891, and *Pembrokeshire Herald*, 18 December 1891. Thirty-two circulars were sent out.
31. CRO, Cawdor box 158, Tom Mousley (junior) to George Williams, 24 November 1891: 'that lord Cawdor declines to receive a "deputation of his Tenants"'.
32. A. R. Jones, *The Land Question and a Land Bill* (Wrexham, 1887), writing for the North Wales Liberal Federation, stated that 'the freedom is all on the part of the landlord and none is on the part of the tenant', p. 24.

33. *Pembrokeshire Herald*, 18 December 1891. At the same time, in Pembrokeshire, the National Labour Federation was attempting to organise agricultural labourers, under the leadership of Robert Hazell, in demands for higher wages and better working conditions. See the *Western Mail*, 16 November 1891, for an interview with Hazell, who had organised the Pembroke Dock Labourers' Union and a failed strike at the Hook colliery, Pembrokeshire.
34. *Cardiff Times*, 21 November 1891. The paper does not specify other grievances, but high on the agenda would have been compensation for unexhausted improvements and a land court.
35. *Western Mail*, 11 November 1891: the paper continued, 'There are men, especially in West Wales who are ever eager for a pretext to set class against class.'
36. Ibid. The Pembrokeshire association was founded about a year before a similar association was established in Lancashire. In both counties the farms were relatively large, with well-off tenants in predominantly wheat-growing areas. See A. Mutch, *Rural Life in S.W. Lancashire, 1840–1914* (Lancaster, 1988) and the same author's 'Farmers' organizations and the agricultural depression in Lancashire, 1890–1900', *AgHR*, 31 (1983).
37. CRO, Cawdor box 158, Mousley to Cawdor, 22 November 1892.
38. CRO, Cawdor box 157, Moulsey to Cawdor, 1 March 1882. The agent wrote that the Carmarthenshire rents had been paid, but the 'Stackpole Estate Men are behind, and most of these could pay if they choose'.
39. CRO, Cawdor box 142: Mousley to Cawdor, 28 July 1879.
40. CRO, Cawdor/Scotland/02: Stables to Cawdor, 27 December 1881. Brackla farm was one of the larger properties on the estate, and Fraser the tenant was a long-standing outspoken thorn in the side of Stables' agency.
41. The nineteen-year lease was usual: T. M. Devine, *The Scottish Clearances* (London, 2018), p. 343. The Cawdor estate held over 3,000 acres in Inverness-shire, and one or two crofting tenants invoked the terms of the Act in the 1890s.
42. CRO, Cawdor (Scotland) 2: Report of the Standing Committee of the Morayshire Farmers' Club on the Subject of Agricultural Depression with Abstract of Replies received from Agricultural Associations of Scotland and resolutions adopted by the Club, 1888.
43. It is not certain whether any landlords attended this meeting.
44. *Northern Scot and Moray and Nairn Express*, 24 December 1887.
45. *Falkirk Herald & Linlithgow Journal*, 27 March 1895, 'Fifty years of agriculture'.
46. For Wales, 1879 was a notoriously wet season, flooding destroying crops and livestock.
47. *Aberdeen Journal*, 17 August 1894, report of the Royal Commission on Agriculture sitting at Nairn, 16 August 1894.

48. *The Highland News*, 17 March 1888. The tenant, one Arres Mather, owned farms in Inverness-shire and Cromarty, as well as Ireland. He said he paid £2,483 in rent for his Scottish farms, so he was hardly a typical tenant farmer.
49. CRO, Cawdor/Scotland/03: Robertson to Cawdor, 13 March 1895; CRO, Cawdor/Scotland/03: Robertson to Cawdor, 3 April 1895.
50. See Davies, *The Changing Fortunes*, pp. 25–6.
51. The Llanelli properties were nearly all small dwellings, while the Carmarthen properties included many of the most substantial buildings in the town, including several public houses.
52. See Davies, *The Changing Fortunes*, pp. 25–6.
53. CRO, Cawdor boxes 262–70: Stackpole Court estate rentals.
54. CRO, Cawdor boxes, 261–5, Golden Grove estate rentals.
55. That is, the accounts of the factor, the usual Scottish term for land agent.
56. The Golden Grove and Stackpole estates sold timber but not regularly, and from the mid-nineteenth century very little when compared with the Cawdor Castle estate.
57. *Aberdeen Journal*, 17 August 1894, report of the Royal Commission on Agriculture sitting at Nairn, 16 August 1894.
58. CRO, Cawdor/Scotland/02, estate factory accounts, 1863–1900.
59. *Falkirk Herald & Linlithgow Journal*, 27 March 1895, 'Fifty years of agriculture'.
60. *Land Commission Report*, Qu. 28,637 & Qu. 40,628, p. 291. At the Commission, Mousley stated that the odd rent raised had been incurred since 1863, though only 'seldom' and cases with real grounds to do so, for instance when improvements had been made at the estate's expense.
61. D. W. Howell, 'The Land Question in nineteenth century Wales, Ireland and Scotland: A comparative study', *AgHR*, 61:1 (2013), p. 85.
62. Ibid., pp. 85–92; A. Taylor, 'Richard Cobden, J. E. Thorold Rogers and Henry George', in M. Cragoe and P. Readman (eds), *The Land Question in Britain, 1750–1950* (London, 2010), chapter 8.
63. Davies, *The Changing Fortunes*, p. 230. A land court was established in Scotland in 1912 as part of the Small Holdings (Scotland) Act of 1911. The third earl had died in February 1911.
64. J. R. Fisher refers to Royal Commissions as 'the standard substitute for action', in J. Thirsk (ed.), *The Agrarian History of England and Wales*, Vol. vii, pt.1, chapter 4 Agrarian Politics, p. 325. Gladstone effectively used the Land Commission to delay Welsh demands for land reform, until he had (he hoped) established Home Rule in Ireland.
65. Morgan farmed Penally Court farm, Solva. It was 440 acres in 1881 and he employed three men and two boys as farm workers as well as his own two sons.

66. It was established in 1879 and had Liberal MP William Smith as its chairman.
67. *The Times*, 23 May 1893, refers to a joint meeting of both the north and south Wales associations taking place on 23 May, two months after the first sitting of the Land Commission.
68. Vincent was born in Bethesda and was Welsh speaking. In 1886 *The Times* sent him to north Wales to cover the tithe wars. In 1887 he republished his reports as *Letters from Wales*. He also published *Tenancy in Wales*, a response to Adfyfr's *Landlordism in Wales*. In 1896 he published *The Land Question in North Wales*, and the following year *The Land Question in South Wales*. These last two volumes were landowners' defence against some of the findings of the Land Commission's Report, which had been published in 1896; S. Evans, '"The battle of the Welsh nation against landlordism": The response of the North Wales Property Defence Association to the Welsh Land Question, c. 1886–1896'. See Bangor University Archives and Special Collections, Penrhyn PFA/18/320. I would like to thank Shaun Evans for this reference.
69. Royal Commission on Land in Wales and Monmouth, Vol. iii, Qs 38, 970–1. At the Pembrokeshire Tenant-Farmers' Association meeting of 7 November, Mr Vaughan of East farm stated he would 'rather starve under earl Cawdor than live under some [other landlord]'.
70. See Davies, *The Changing Fortunes*, pp. 78–80; Cragoe, *Anglican Aristocracy*, pp. 171–82.
71. J. Beckett and M. Turner, 'The Land Question and the burden of ownership', *AgHR*, 55:2 (2007), p. 273.
72. J. Davies, 'The end of the great estates and the rise of freehold farming in Wales', *Welsh History Review*, 7:2 (1974), p. 195. See J. Beckett and M. Turner, 'End of the old order? F. M. L. Thompson, the Land Question, and the burden of ownership in England, c. 1880–c. 1925' and F. M. L. Thompson, 'The land market, 1880–1925: A reappraisal reappraised', both in *AgHR*, 55:2 (2007), pp. 269–300.
73. There is no evidence that they sold on any scale in Scotland.
74. D. Cannadine, *The Decline and Fall of the British Aristocracy* (London, 1990).
75. CRO, Cawdor box 156, Emlyn to Cawdor, 9 September 1894.
76. *Aberdeen Journal*, 20 August 1921, 'The coming of age of Earl Cawdor'.
77. For the ultimate demise of the Welsh estates, see Davies, *The Changing Fortunes*, chapter 9.

14

From Landlord to Rentier: The Wealth Management Practices of Irish Landlords, 1903–1933

Tony McCarthy

INTRODUCTION

THE OPENING YEARS OF the twentieth century saw a concerted effort by the British government to bring to an end the hitherto intractable Irish land question. The introduction of the Irish Land Act 1903, better known as the Wyndham Land Act after its creator, George Wyndham, Chief Secretary for Ireland (1900–5), and its subsequent amending legislation, the Irish Land Act 1909 (the Birrell Land Act), while not concluding, did contribute significantly to the resolution of the problem.[1] By the time these two Acts had run their course in 1919, over 70 per cent (9.2 million acres) of the agricultural land of Ireland, representing 256,735 holdings, had been sold to their former tenants, creating a new peasant proprietor class, at a cost of £82.2 million.[2]

The Irish Land Act 1903 achieved what many saw as an impossible feat, namely, how to incentivise landlords to sell their estates while at the same time encouraging tenants to buy their holdings. Wyndham managed this through a combination of complicated legislative measures, deft financial engineering, winning over a somewhat reluctant Treasury and gaining the support of landlord and tenant representatives both in and outside of Parliament. It was a significant political achievement and merited George Wyndham much credit at the time.

One of the changes wrought by the legislation was the creation of a small rentier class of former landlords who were now faced with the challenge of living off the proceeds of the sale of their estates and providing for future generations of their families. Until now this aspect of Irish land reform history has been neglected. By studying the financial records of four former landed families, the author has, for the first time, been able to construct a detailed picture of how these families went about investing the sale proceeds and their attempts to protect these for future generations. This chapter sets out the findings of this research, explains the financial workings of the 1903 Act and how these impacted on the prices paid for estates, and finally, examines the wealth management practices adopted by landlords who availed of the provisions of the two Acts. A knowledge of this previously unexplored aspect of landlord life in the early twentieth century is important in terms of gaining a more holistic understanding of how they dealt with the sales of their estates and their family fortunes thereafter. The chapter also provides a partial framework to address the question as to whether landlords were better off selling their lands and living off the proceeds or whether they would have been better holding onto their estates and continuing to live off the rents derived therefrom, albeit in a rapidly changing political environment.

THE WYNDHAM LAND ACT 1903

The position of Irish landlords at the start of the twentieth century was financially precarious. Addressing the House of Commons in March 1903, George Wyndham painted a picture of Irish agriculture as one of stasis and chaos in which, 'The landlords of Ireland being financially ruined; the tenants are being morally ruined' and 'agriculture starved of capital and industry.'[3] In 'A policy for Ireland', a paper prepared by Wyndham for the then Prime Minister Arthur Balfour in 1902, he pointed out that, 'The landlord will not sell if a sale involves a material loss of gross income and the tenant won't buy if [the] annuity is greater than rent or future rent.'[4] Wyndham argued that the absence of commercial bank lending meant that there was little chance of normal land purchase transactions occurring. The situation was one of almost complete paralysis, with landlords facing further state-dictated rent reductions and inevitable financial ruin and tenants facing an uncertain and despondent future. A further complication existed in the level of indebtedness of Irish landlords. Addressing this point, Wyndham observed: 'I am afraid, the majority of Irish estates are somewhat heavily indebted', which meant that landlords were subject to 'paramount interests' and were in many cases 'caretakers' for these lenders. A sale in such cases meant the landlord 'walking into the workhouse'.[5]

The provisions of the Irish Land Act 1903 were constructed by Wyndham to address the conflicting demands of landlords and tenants and can be seen as an attempt by him to provide the former with a dignified exit from their precarious predicament. Whether the motivation for the legislation was to solve the Irish question, further his own personal political career, repay past loyalties to their former 'garrison in Ireland' or as a test case for similar situations that might well have arisen in other parts of Britain, gives rise to a number of intriguing questions but ones that must be left for another forum. While not without its critics, the popularity of the Act with landlords can be seen from the fact that within one year of its enactment applications to sell totalled £19 million while only £4.2 million had been advanced by the Land Commission, which was charged with administering all transactions under the 1903 Act.[6]

That this was so was due very much to the generous terms of the Act whereby landlords, at least in the initial years, were paid sums of between twenty-three and twenty-six times the annual rents received from their estates. In addition, they received a further sum, called 'the Bonus', of 12 per cent of the gross sales proceeds. An important feature of the Bonus was that unlike the sales proceeds, which were paid net of any outstanding mortgages, it was paid directly to the landlord and was therefore 'ring-fenced' from lenders with claims on the estate. This was attractive to the many heavily indebted landlords. The fact that sales proceeds were paid in cash, unlike land bonds, as was the practice with previous land purchase Acts, added to the Act's attraction. In embracing the opportunity to sell their estates, many landlords were for the first time entering into a world that could, on occasion, be no less challenging and frightening than the one they were escaping from.

THE INVESTMENT ENVIRONMENT AT THE FIN DE SIÈCLE

The challenge for a landlord who sold his estate under the 1903 Act was how to invest the proceeds in order to maintain his income at a level similar to that previously derived from the estate rentals. According to contemporary commentators and contributions to the parliamentary debates at the time of the Act's introduction, the price provisions of the Act were constructed so that a selling landlord could achieve the same level of net income that he currently derived from his estate, on the assumption that the proceeds along with the Bonus were invested so as to give an annual return of 3.5 per cent per annum.[7] This challenge is best illustrated by looking at a working example of the calculation carried out on behalf of the Bellew estate in Galway in 1904 (see Table 14.1). The report was prepared by the family solicitor.

In preparing the table below (14.1), James Robinson was estimating on behalf of his client, Sir Henry Grattan Bellew, the likely sales proceeds from any future sale and the liabilities that would have to be discharged out of the sales consideration received.

Table 14.1 Bellew estate: initial estimate of sales proceeds, 1904

	£
Proceeds of sale of estate	101,334
Add. Bonus at 12 per cent	12,160
	113,494
Less: Deductions	
– Board of Works annual charges at 25 years purchase	4,011
– Head rent redemptions at 25 years purchase	9,576
– Quit rent reductions at 25 years purchase	825
– Redemption of Tithe rent charges at 22.5 years purchase	5,503
– Loan repayments	11,185
– Lady Bellew's contingent annuity at €500 per annum	14,300
– Estimated costs associated with sale	1,500
Total deductions	46,900
Net sale proceeds	66,594

Source: NLI, Bellew papers, MS 27,290 (2), J. Robinson, solicitor, to Henry Grattan Bellew, 15 November 1904.

Table 14.2 Bellew estate: estimated rental versus investment income, 1904

	£
Annual rents from estate	4,438
Less: Annual deductions	
– Board of Works charges	161
– Head rents	382
– Quit rents	33
– Tithe rent charges	243
– Estimated interest on loans at 5 per cent	560
– Lady Bellew's annuity	500
Total annual deductions	1,879
Annual net income derived from rents	2,559
Estimated annual net income derived from net sale proceeds of £66,594 at 3.5 per cent per annum	2,330

Source: NLI, Bellew papers, MS 27,290 (2), J. Robinson, solicitor, to Henry Grattan Bellew, 15 November 1904.

Table 14.2 sets out Lord Bellew's annual income and estimates the level of investment income he might expect from the net proceeds of sale, £66,594, if invested at 3.5 per cent per annum. The investment income of £2,330 compares reasonably closely to the net rental income (£2,559) derived from his estate, particularly when taking account of the fact that one of the annual charges on the estate was £500 payable to his wife. This example highlights how Lord Bellew would not suffer any significant reduction in his income following a sale of his estate.

Similar estimations to that carried out on behalf of Lord Bellew appear to have been undertaken by many other estates. Critical to achieving the desired outcome was the generation of an annual investment return of 3.5 per cent, and this chapter examines how the investment environment might have afforded this opportunity. In interpreting investment environments in the opening decades of the twentieth century it is necessary to divide them into three distinct periods: before the Great War (1860–1914), during the war (1914–18) and the post-war years (1919–33). Each of these time frames had very distinct features and characteristics which had significant consequences for investors.

THE PRE-WAR YEARS, 1860–1914

Investment environments thrive on economic and political stability. The pre-war period from 1860 to 1914 was, apart from the Franco-Prussian War (1870–1) and the Boer War (1899–1902), largely devoid of any major international conflict, and saw great economic growth both domestically and internationally spurred on by major investment in transport infrastructure and an absence of any significant corporate collapses, except that of the City of Glasgow Bank in 1878 and the near collapse of Barings Bank in 1890 as a result of poor investments in South America. It was also a period when the world economic order was stable, albeit the tectonic plates had moved so that Britain's hegemony was being challenged by both Germany and the United States of America. Coupled with these underpinnings was the almost total absence of inflation since the end of the Napoleonic Wars in 1815. Investment markets thrive in such conditions, and not surprisingly activity on the London Stock Exchange reflected this.

London in the pre-war years was very much the epicentre of the global financial world. The American economist, C. A. Conant, observed in 1904 that 'Great Britain easily leads the world in the volume of her stock exchange business'.[8] Similarly, R. M. Bauer, a member of the New York Stock Exchange, noted in 1911 that 'The London Stock Exchange is the only really international market in the world. Its interests branch over all parts of our globe.'[9] Indicative of the increasing activity was the growth in the value of securities traded on the exchange. In 1853 the value of securities quoted on the London Stock Exchange was £1,215 million. By 1903 this figure had reached

£7,000 million and by 1913 it had reached £9,550 million.[10] This growth in stock market investment led in 1909 to the former Prime Minister, Arthur Balfour, observing that: 'the bulk of the great fortunes are now in a highly liquid state ... They do not consist of huge landed estates, vast parks and castles, and all the rest of it.'[11] Reflective of this was the breakdown of Britain's wealth whereby in 1850, 39 per cent of national wealth was in the form of financial securities and 61 per cent in land and buildings, whereas in 1912 these figures were reversed, with 64 per cent of wealth held in securities and 36 per cent in land.[12] An important aspect of investment behaviour in the period was the unparalleled growth in overseas investments. In 1850, 7 per cent of traded securities represented overseas shares and government bonds; by 1870 this figure had reached 14 per cent. On the eve of war in 1913, 32 per cent of all securities traded on the London Stock Exchange were international. At no time before or since has any country had so much exposure to international investments.[13] This development provided investors with great diversity of opportunity in terms of the geography, industry and level of returns but also brought with it higher levels of risk. The dangers associated with investment in Mexican railway stocks and Paraguayan guano harvesting ventures have been well exposed in literary works such as Trollope's *The Way We Live Now* and Follet's *A Dangerous Fortune*, which highlight the precarious and indeed devious nature of many such investments.[14]

A further change that occurred in the period was the nature of the securities traded. The Appendix highlights these changes. Of note was the shift in trading from government and municipal bonds to corporate shares and bonds. In 1853, 76 per cent of all securities quoted on the London Stock Exchange were government or municipal bonds and 24 per cent corporate securities. By 1913 only 35 per cent of stocks quoted were government or municipal bonds, whereas 65 per cent were corporate securities.[15] Again, as with the increased availability of international investment opportunities, the greater availability of corporate securities represented a two-sided coin in that while they gave greater choice to investors, they also increased the risk profile in that corporate risk is almost always higher than sovereign risk.

For investors seeking to generate returns such as those sought by Lord Bellew in the above illustration, there were ample opportunities in quoted securities. Some examples best illustrate this (see Table 14.3).

The above example shows that in all but the case of the British 2.5 per cent CONSOL, a rate of return greater than 3.5 per cent could be earned by investing in various forms of quoted Dominion bonds,

Table 14.3 Sample sovereign bond prices on 12 January 1910

Stock	Traded price £ s. d.	Yield Per cent
British 2.5 per cent CONSOL	82 10 00	3.03
Canadian 4 per cent stock	100 00 00	4.00
Cape of Good Hope 4 per cent stock	102 00 00	3.92
Indian 3.5 per cent stock	96 05 00	3.64
Western Australian 3.5 per cent stock	98 00 00	3.57

Source: *Irish Independent*, 12 January 1910.

Table 14.4 Realised rates of return on quoted railway securities, 1870–1913

Region	Equity per cent	Debentures per cent
United Kingdom	4.33	3.74
Eastern Europe	2.58	5.33
Western Europe	6.31	5.28
India	4.97	3.65
United States	8.41	6.03
Latin America	8.43	5.33

Source: Edelstein, 'Foreign investment, accumulation and empire, 1860–1914', p. 198.

which while not explicitly so, were effectively guaranteed by the British Treasury.[16] For investors willing to take on a higher level of risk and invest in railway stocks, the level of return could have been even higher, as Table 14.4 highlights.

For those landlords fortunate to have availed of the Wyndham Act or its amending legislation, the Birrell Land Act 1909, and who received their sale proceeds in the period 1903–14, the benign investment environment in quoted securities would have afforded them ample opportunity to generate annual incomes at a rate in excess of the 3.5 per cent benchmark return suggested by Wyndham in introducing the Act.

A notable feature of the investment portfolios examined here is the absence of property as an investment asset. Modern portfolio investment theory would suggest that to achieve a balance in terms of diverse asset classes, a long-term investment portfolio should include a considerable property element to provide capital protection, income and a means of protecting the portfolio from the effects of inflation. However, property, either commercial or residential, in the opening decades of the twentieth century was not regarded as attractive an investment as it is today, and this may well account for its absence from the investment portfolios examined. Commercial properties tended to be let on long leases of over one hundred years and without the benefit of rent review clauses. As such, they were seen as the equivalent of a government bond and were regarded as quasi-gilts without the backing of a sovereign guarantee.[17] Rental yields on property at the turn of the century are not readily available but research carried out by a group from Nottingham University provides an indication that they ranged from 4.5 to 6.5 per cent.[18] While clearly more attractive than yields in the region of 4 per cent derived from quoted government securities, the owning of property had its risks in terms of recalcitrant tenants and a need to maintain property. Such risks were all too familiar to those former landlords who had just sold their own properties under the Wyndham Act.

Likewise, with buy-to-let residential property the early years of the twentieth century experienced what contemporary commentators referred to as the 'Edwardian housing slump'.[19] Between 1903 and 1915 the price of private housing in London fell by over 36 per cent.[20] In Dublin the situation was only slightly better in that prices declined by 25 per cent in the period 1900 to 1911.[21] Whether it was these circumstances, a fixation with guaranteed income, an unwillingness to re-engage with tenants or a no to low-risk strategy, landlords seeking to invest showed no inclination to purchase investment property.

THE WAR YEARS, 1914–1918

Investment markets were not prepared for the outbreak of war in August 1914. Hartley Withers observed in 1915 that 'It came upon us like a thunderbolt from a clear sky.'[22] The economist, Professor William Kirkaldy, wrote in 1915 that 'the outbreak of war took the financial world by surprise'.[23] Many historians have placed the First World War in the context of the emerging struggle for economic supremacy among the major European powers and saw it as an inevitable consequence of such power plays; financial markets did not, nor one suspects did investors, such as former Irish landlords who had sold their estates under the Wyndham Land Act.

The outbreak of war engendered great fear and uncertainty among investors, and for former Irish landlords who held investment portfolios it would have been a stressful time. These fears would have been fuelled greatly by the suspension of stock exchange activities throughout the world. Fears of a major fall in the value of securities resulted in a rush to liquidate share and bond portfolios by individuals and institutional investors. To prevent this, stock exchanges and bourses across the world suspended dealing and effectively closed on the commencement of war in August 1914. The New York Stock Exchange remained closed until late December 1914 and London until 4 January 1915.[24] When exchanges did eventually reopen, the trade in securities had changed from the pre-war days. The price of securities such as government bonds was impacted by news from the Front. A military reverse or victory could send values crashing or spiralling.

In Britain, the war had a dramatic effect on the government's finances. In 1913 Britain's unfunded short-term debt stood at just £31.5 million; by 1919 this figure had risen to £7,100 million.[25] Prior to the outbreak of war, Britain's annual defence budget totalled £50 million, whereas during the war it reached £5 million per day.[26] Although the revenue generated from taxes trebled, it still only accounted for 28 per cent of total public spending.[27] To make up the difference the government was forced to borrow. It did this in two ways. Firstly, by borrowing from other nations, principally the USA. In so doing, it altered its status as the world's largest creditor to become its biggest debtor. As the twentieth century unfolded, this change of status would be seen as a seminal event in the decline of the British empire. The second means was by issuing what were known as War Bonds. Massive advertising campaigns were run throughout the war appealing for people to support their empire. Full-page advertisements like that shown in Figure 14.1 were run seeking support for War Loan Bonds and these were heavily subscribed. As the review of the portfolios covered later in this chapter makes clear, Irish landlords were not slow in responding to the call to buy War Bonds. An indication of the support for such issues can be gauged from the fact that in 1913 it was estimated that one million people in Britain and Ireland held Stock Exchange traded securities, whereas by 1918 over 13 million people held securities principally because of the purchase of War Loan Stock.[28]

Apart from the patriotic sense of duty that the purchase of such stocks imbued, they also provided an annual yield of 5 per cent that was well in excess of that available before the outbreak of war.

From an investment perspective the war introduced another invidious and pernicious influence that had a major effect on those living on fixed incomes from their portfolios – inflation. For people who had not seen the effects of inflation on the purchasing power of incomes in their lifetimes it would have been a major shock. In the period of the Great War and its immediate aftermath (1915–20), inflation in Britain and Ireland totalled 63.7 per cent. For those living on fixed incomes this

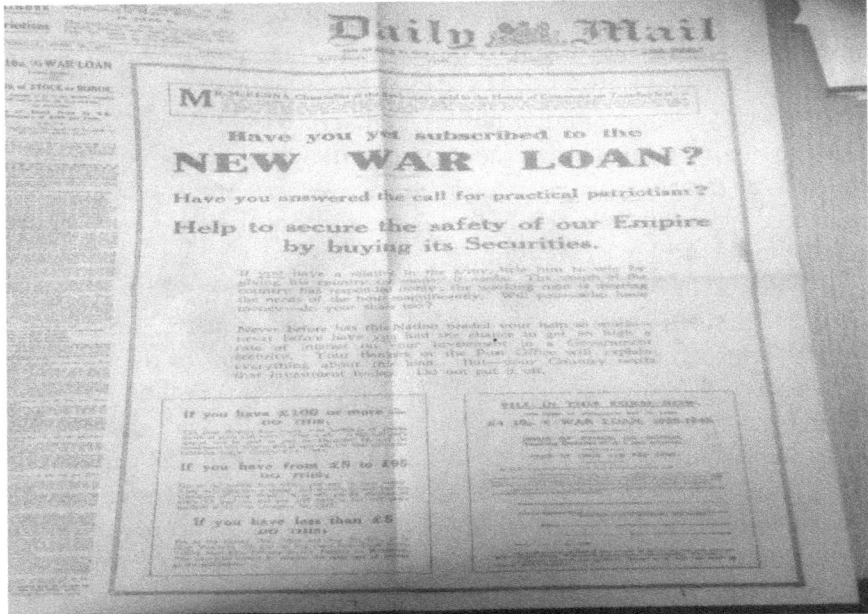

Figure 14.1 Advertisement for War Loan Stock from *Daily Mail*, 26 June 1915.

would have represented a very significant deterioration in their standard of living.

THE POST-WAR YEARS, 1919–33

The post-war years in Britain and Ireland were difficult from an economic perspective. Demobilisation resulting in high unemployment, the problems associated with transitioning a war economy to a peacetime one, depressed demand caused by countries trying to come to terms with enormous war debts, and the political paralysis that followed the conflagration of Europe all contributed. Consequently, most of Europe was economically moribund and a severe deflationary cycle took hold. In the years 1921–33, cumulative deflation reached over 45 per cent in Britain, resulting in total economic stagnation.[29] In the German Weimar Republic the economic position was, by several orders of magnitude, worse.

For investors, however, the period up to October 1929 was benign. Deflation meant that those individuals who had fixed incomes benefited from the increase in purchasing power of their incomes. This was coupled with a near ten-year increase in the value of government bonds, which rose by 26.7 per cent in the years 1920–30. For those lucky enough to hold ordinary shares, they would in the years 1920–8 have seen significant increases in the value of their portfolios. The London Stock Exchange ordinary share index showed a 61 per cent increase in nominal values. In addition, the dividend yield on equities averaged 5 per cent per annum during the period, ensuring a good income flow. For those holding US equities the gains would have been even greater. Even allowing for the Great Stock Market Crash of 1929, UK equities showed an increase in value of over 18 per cent between 1920 and 1933.[30]

For those landlords who held large cash balances, good returns were also available. Due to the British government's efforts to protect the value of sterling by maintaining the gold standard, deposit rates were maintained at high levels and averaged close to 5 per cent until 1931, when the standard was abandoned and sterling was allowed to float.

The benign investment environment came to a sudden and dramatic end in October 1929, when the value of shares on US stock markets plummeted. Between October 1929 and the end of 1933, US stock markets lost 62.7 per cent of their value and the London Stock Exchange fell 14.4 per cent. The attendant spate of US banking failures and more significantly the inappropriate measures taken by regulatory authorities precipitated the Great Depression, causing economic misery throughout the world. For investors it was a time of financial terror and in many cases ruin as people and institutions sought to liquidate whatever remained of their fortunes. It was in this world that Irish landlords who sold their estates in the opening years of the twentieth century found themselves as they embarked on their new life as rentiers.

THE WEALTH MANAGEMENT PRACTICES OF IRISH LANDLORDS, 1903–1933

The four landlords whose financial records underpin the study upon which this chapter is based represent a range of estate sizes.[31] The Dopping Hepenstal estate in Wicklow (£10,039) and the Coolgreany estate in Wexford (£61,503) would be categorised as small, the Clonbrock estate in east Galway (£213,000) as medium, and the Leinster estate in Kildare and Carlow (£766,647) was the largest estate sold under the 1903 Act. While all four examples exhibit particular and idiosyncratic behaviours, there are enough common traits to infer that the wealth management practices applied were likely to be representative of a wider population. Key among these were the preoccupation with income-producing securities such as sovereign-backed bonds, corporate debentures and, in the case of the Leinster estate, private mortgages. Apart from the mortgages in the case of the Leinster estate, all the investments were made in securities traded on the London Stock Exchange and to a far lesser extent the Dublin Stock Exchange. The focus on income- generating securities meant that there was little room for any inflation-protecting assets such as ordinary shares or investment property. As will be shown later, this was a serious and in some cases fatal flaw in the construction of many investment portfolios. Another trait common to all four portfolios examined was the speed with which the funds were committed. In the case of the vast Leinster estate, the sales proceeds of £766,647 (£84 million in present value) were after charges of £101,940 (head rents, quit rents, Board of Works loan repayments, family charges, etc.) fully invested within twelve months.[32] Some of the Clonbrock proceeds were even invested prior to receipt, as Lord Clonbrock sought to avail of a provision of the 1909 Land Act whereby sales which were agreed but the funds not yet paid over could have them invested in certain prescribed securities pending payment.[33] On the instructions of the trustees of the Brookes estate in Coolgreany, the full net sales proceeds were invested within days of receipts via the trustees' Dublin stockbrokers.[34] Similarly, in the case of the sale of the Dopping Hepenstal Wicklow estate in August 1914, investments were being made within days, in stocks, by the family's stockbrokers.[35] The rapidity with which the funds were invested may well signify a desire to get the funds working as quickly as possible for their owners but also may have been a means of removing any temptation to use them for personal expenditure.

It is noticeable also in the portfolios examined that after allowing for various charges and legal costs the full net proceeds were invested. In this respect the four portfolios may not be wholly representative of the wider picture in that there is clear anecdotal evidence that in certain instances some proceeds were expended on personal luxuries such as motor cars and house improvements. For instance, the Marquis of Sligo, who sold almost his entire estate under the Wyndham Act, spent a considerable portion of the proceeds renovating Westport House and installing heating and electricity to light and heat the twelve bathrooms he added.[36] Similarly, the Butlers of Ormonde spent a significant sum on the electrification of Kilkenny Castle.[37] Mark Bence Jones tells the story of how his uncle Reginald purchased a Mercedes limousine with silver flower vases in the passenger compartment following the sale of his estate.[38]

The use of family trust-type arrangements in all but one of the portfolios points to the fact that trustees were conscious of the fact that the investments had to be protected for future generations. In the case of the Leinster estate, such a mechanism was to provide some form of protection from the profligate seventh duke, Edward Fitzgerald, who succeeded to the title on the death of his brother, Maurice, in 1922. Even the existence of a family trust did not prevent the wayward duke disposing of his life interest in the estate to the financier Henry Mallably Deeley in 1919.[39] Similarly, the existence of a family trust afforded some protection against the family patriarch, Sir George Brooke, who despite an annual income of £1,000 from the trust and further sums from his family's wine business found them insufficient to fund his lifestyle and in February 1911 was forced to sell his Somerton residence in Dublin's Castleknock to pay off mounting debts.[40] In the case of the Clonbrock estate, the family papers show that the 4th Baron Clonbrock was very familiar with the use of family trust structures prior to the sale and proceeded to establish a number of such, all with specific purposes in mind. As with their previous estates, the family patriarchs were given life interests and not full beneficial ownership of the assets, in an effort to protect the investments for future generations of the families.[41]

In terms of investment strategies, the outlier of the four portfolios examined was most certainly the Leinster estate. Table 14.5 summarises the portfolio in June 1905 and shows that 90.72 per cent of it was invested in five personal mortgages.[42] While the granting of mortgages by rich individuals was not uncommon at the time, the scale of the Leinster loans was unusual, particularly at a time when most lending institutions such as banks and life assurance companies were withdrawing from the mortgage market due to falling land values. While the mortgages would have been secured on land belonging to the borrowers, it would still have been legally cumbersome to enforce the security. Why such an approach was adopted is unclear, particularly given the many, more secure stock exchange-quoted investment options offering similar if not higher rates of return. Quite apart from risk-reward arguments, the concentration of investment in a single asset class or indeed individual, such as Lord Tankerville who accounted for 44.83 per cent of the portfolio, is difficult to understand. On the death of the sixth duke in 1922, the valuation of the portfolio prepared for probate valuation purposes showed that the mortgage element had decreased from just over 90 per cent in 1905 to a still high but more manageable 46.5 per cent (£314,449), whereas quoted securities accounted for 54.5 per cent (£361,226).[43]

The Clonbrock family records afford further insight into the investment strategies and practices of the time. The 4th Baron Clonbrock,

Table 14.5 Leinster Estate application of sales proceeds at July 1905

Security type	£ s. d.	%
Invested in mortgages		
– Loan to Lord Tankerville @ 3.5%	298,000 00 00	44.83%
– Loan to Mr Duncombe Shafto @ 3.75%	82,500 00 00	12.41%
– Loan to Col. Henry Denison @ 3.75%	59,000 00 00	8.88%
– Loan to Lord Fitzwilliam @ 3.75%	41,000 00 00	6.17%
– Loan to Lord Hastings @ 3.5%	122,500 00 00	18.43%
	603,000 00 00	90.72%
Stocks purchased		
– Dublin Corporation 3.25%	9,225 01 00	1.39%
– Belfast City 3% stock	8,635 11 00	1.30%
– Belfast Corporation 3.5% stock	10,125 08 06	1.52%
– Bank of Ireland 11.5% stock	6,213 16 05	0.93%
– Natal inscribed 3.5% stock	3,960 19 11	0.60%
– Midland Great Western Railway of Ireland 5% stock	7,872 18 00	1.18%
– Great Southern & Western Railway 4% Guar. Stock	1,910 02 03	0.29%
– Caledonia Railway 4% stock	5,883 11 00	0.89%
– Bristol Corporation 3.5% stock	3,035 13 06	0.46%
– Lagos 3.5% inscribed stock	2,898 16 00	0.44%
– Cape 3.5% stock	1,945 01 00	0.29%
	61,706 18 07	9.28%
Total value of investments made	664,706 18 07	100.00%

Source: Public Record Office of Northern Ireland [hereafter PRONI], Leinster estate papers, D.3078/2/15/10, Statement of application of funds, July 1905.

Luke Dillon, was an already experienced investor by the time he sold his estate in 1914. He was a trustee of a number of family trusts and was diligent in recording information such as dates of purchases and sales of securities, dividend receipts and so on. Both he and, following his death in 1917, his son Robert, the 5th Baron Clonbrock, maintained excellent records of their investment portfolios. It is clear from letters in the family archive that Luke Dillon regularly sought advice from people he would have regarded as well connected to the financial markets, such as Christopher Digges La Touche, a prominent Dublin banker.[44]

The similarity of the investments across the various trust portfolios also displays a consistency in the strategy being adopted. As with all the other family portfolios examined, there is a focus on income-yielding quoted securities, with no evidence of any inflation-protecting investments such as ordinary shares. Unfortunately, such a diligent and professional approach could not protect the portfolios from the vicissitudes of

Table 14.6 Breakdown of Clonbrock portfolio by investment category, as at 12 May 1917

Security	Valuation £	Valuation %
International Bonds	109,150	51.54%
War Loan Stock	41,552	19.62%
UK Corporate & Treasury Bonds	33,697	15.91%
Irish Stocks	10,420	4.92%
Irish Land Bonds	11,133	5.26%
Ordinary Shares	5,828	2.75%
Total	211,780	100.00%

Source: This table has been derived from an analysis of the various Clonbrock portfolios at the time of the fourth baron's death in May 1917.

Table 14.7 Coolgreany estate trust investment portfolio, December 1904

Security	Purchase price £	Investment amount £ s. d.
Canadian Pacific Railway 4% Pref Stock	102.87	10,390 12 03
New South Wales 3.5% 1924 Stock	96.37	7,730 01 00
Grand Trunk Railway Co. 4% Debenture stock	107.94	9,811 17 06
Cape of Good Hope 4% 1916/36 Stock	104.37	8,370 01 00
Ontario & Quebec Railway 5% Debenture stock	136.62	2,760 01 09
Cape of Good Hope 4% 1916/36 Stock	104.75	5,250 01 00
Fishguard & Rosslare Railway Co. 3.5% Guar. Stock	101.06	7,919 12 06
Balance uninvested – Cash		3,805 10 09
Total portfolio		56,037 17 09

Source: Hamilton papers (in private possession).

life, as the relatively close deaths of father (1917) and son (1926) meant that over quarter of the value of the portfolios went in the payment of Death Duties – £54,210 within twelve years of the sale of the estate.

The Coolgreany estate trust, which was administered by its trustees Lord Monck and Charles Hamilton, land agent of the Leinster estate, shows a similar focus on income-producing securities as the Clonbrock trusts. As Table 14.7 illustrates, there is a significantly higher concentration of railway stocks (55 per cent) compared to any of the other portfolios examined. While no records were available of the portfolio post-1904, had it remained as constituted the impact on capital value would have been catastrophic as the value of railway stocks declined significantly, and were in many cases wiped out as the century progressed due to falling passenger numbers and a reduction in freight traffic due to competition from road transport.

The Dopping Hepenstal investment records show a less nuanced approach to investing than the three other portfolios in that it is more opportunistic or *ad hoc* in style. Some of this may have been accounted for by the relatively small sum involved, £10,000, but more likely it was Colonel Dopping Hepenstal's personal preference. Receiving £10,000 for the sale of his Wicklow estate, he deferred making any investments until March 1915, and then invested the full amount in 3.5 per cent War Loan Stock. While this commitment may have been for patriotic reasons, it most certainly was done without any regard to the investment risks involved in that had Britain been defeated it would have been highly unlikely that Germany would have repaid such loans and thus the stock would have been worthless. The family archive contains many newspaper clippings dealing with advice regarding investment in particular stocks. It also contains 'tip sheets' received from a number of brokers in the UK and addressed to Colonel Dopping Hepenstal proposing specific investments. The papers also contain many contract notes for the purchase and sale of stocks such as the Malaysia-based Brieh Rubber Estate Limited and Sablas (North Borneo) Rubber Limited. Another difference was that Dopping Hepenstal was dealing in ordinary shares as opposed to debentures or bonds and that he tended to hold these shares for relatively short periods. In 1918 the records show him cashing in his portfolio. This coincides with his leaving Ireland and moving to London.

INVESTMENT PERFORMANCE

The measuring and assessing of investment performance require a benchmark or other reference point. In the case of an investment portfolio, the benchmark is usually the investment objectives set by the owner of the fund when setting it up. These objectives might include protecting the capital value, obtaining a specified level of capital growth or generating a particular level of income from the portfolio. While there is nothing in any of the family papers examined that sets out precisely these objectives, it is a reasonable assumption, based on the structure of the portfolios, that the key objectives were capital protection and income generation.

With regard to income generation, if the benchmark for the portfolios was to generate a level of income that was at least equivalent to the net incomes from their former estates, then it is clear that at least up to 1918

Table 14.8 Estimated surplus of annual investment income over net rental income for four estates, 1904–18

Estate	Annual gross rents £	Annual estate costs £	Annual net rents £	Annual investment income £	Surplus investment income £
Leinster estate	32,220	11,277	20,943	23,720	2,777
Clonbrock estate	9,861	3,532	6,329	8,036	1,707
Dopping Hepenstal estate	480	150	330	350	20
Coolgreany estate	2,735	957	1,778	2,100	322

Source: The data used in compiling this table has been extracted by the author from the family papers of the four estates examined, 1904–18.

this objective would have been not only achieved but exceeded. Table 14.8 compares the estimated annual incomes from the four portfolios with the net rents that were derived from the estates immediately prior to their sale. Certain caveats need to be entered in interpreting this data, such as the aforementioned negative impact on the purchasing power of these incomes caused by war-driven inflation. In contrast, the operation of the judicial rent review process brought in by the Irish Land Act 1881 would have resulted in substantially lower rents than those cited below.[45]

The absence of point-in-time valuations makes it difficult to be precise regarding how the portfolios performed in terms of capital appreciation or depreciation. Fortunately for this study, the deaths of patriarchs in the case of the Leinster and Clonbrock estates afford some comparative valuations. With regard to the Leinster estate, when the sixth duke died in 1922 the portfolio was valued at £675,668, compared to £664,707 in July 1905.[46] Allowing for the extraction of an average annual income of £25,574 (the estate pre-sale annual net rental income) derived from this, means that the portfolio increased in value by £10,951, which was principally accounted for by the increased interest charged on mortgages from 3.5 per cent in 1905 to 5.5 per cent in 1922, albeit on a lower capital sum advanced.[47] Based on the quoted securities element of the portfolio in February 1922 (see Table 14.9), there was no scope for any long-term capital appreciation. On the contrary, the conversion of War Loan Bonds from 5 per cent to 3.5 per cent stock in 1932 had a significant detrimental effect on their value, the continuing bear market in bonds in general and the almost total annihilation of railway stocks in the late 1920s and 1930s meaning that the value of the portfolio, if left as it was in 1922, would have decreased significantly as the century

Table 14.9 Leinster Estate quoted securities portfolio at 8 February 1922

Security type	Valuation £	Percentage %
War Loan Stock	124,994	34.60%
UK Gov. Bonds	81,528	22.57%
UK Municipal Bonds	29,875	8.27%
Railway Stocks	68,565	18.98%
Overseas Bonds	48,982	13.56%
Corporate Bonds	7,282	2.02%
Total	361,226	100.00%

Source: PRONI, Leinster estate papers, D3078/1/3, Portfolio valuation at 8 February 1922.

progressed.[48] On the assumption that the mortgages making up that side of the portfolio (i.e. £314,449) were honoured, this would have provided at least some form of capital protection to the overall estate. The Leinster estate, however, was fortunate in one respect; despite the profligacy of the 7th duke, the fact that he lived until he was eighty-four (d. 1976) meant that it was spared the impact of death duties for many years.

In the case of the Clonbrock estate, we are afforded three distinct valuations. At the time of the sale of the estate in 1914, a total of £212,000 was invested. In May 1917, on the death of the fourth baron the value of the portfolios for probate purposes was £199,534.[49] Whether the decline of £12,466 was all attributable to capital decline or income demands it is impossible to say, but it would not be surprising if it were the former, as the price of many stocks declined as a result of the war.[50] On the death of the fifth baron in 1926, the portfolio was valued at £153,384, representing a decline of £46,150 compared to the 1917 valuation, due principally to the death duties payable on the death of the fourth baron.

CONCLUSION

The experience of the estates examined in this chapter contrasts with that of American plutocrat, William Rockefeller. In his *America's Sixty Great Families*, Ferdinand Lundberg relates how Rockefeller left $50,000,000 in 1922, stipulating that a portion of income be divided among four children and fourteen grandchildren and that the principal itself be reserved for his great-grandchildren. From 1922 to 1937, the children and grandchildren drew income of $9,514,834 from the estate, which increased in value by $13,947,361 in the fifteen-year period. Lundberg stated that it was expected that upwards of fifty great-grandchildren were likely to inherit an estate valued at between $75,000,000 and $100,000,000 after the payment of income to children and grandchildren.[51] The value of the estate ultimately turned out to be $102,000,000 before taxes when finally liquidated.[52] The difference between the Rockefeller portfolio and those of many Irish landlords was that while their portfolios consisted mainly of fixed-interest securities, the Rockefeller portfolio was made up principally of direct equities and in particular holdings in various US oil companies and the Amalgamated Copper Mining Company which he had founded in the late 1890s. Despite the 1929 stock market crash, these companies continued to prosper, providing investment returns significantly more than inflation, and do so to this day.

Irish landlords who sold their estates in the opening decades of the twentieth century could indeed be said to have lived in 'interesting times'. Following a near century of relative economic stability, the first three decades of the twentieth century were both volatile and traumatic, encompassing periods of stability (1900–14), global economic and political turmoil (1914–20), deflation (1920–7), the near collapse of the world's financial system (1929–30) and the Great Depression (1930–5). Those landlords who relied on the then conventional investment wisdoms with portfolios dominated by fixed-income securities with little scope for capital appreciation fared badly in such an unpredictable economic environment that saw many family fortunes decimated. The absence of any known great fortunes emanating from this period provides some support to this contention.

APPENDIX

Table 14.10 Value of securities on the London Stock Exchange, 1853–1920

	1853 £m	%	1893 £m	%	1903 £m	%	1913 £m	%	1920 £m	%
Government/Municipal stocks										
- British Government stock	853.6	70.24%	901.6	18.40%	1,102.2	15.79%	1290.1	13.51%	5753.2	34.71%
- Colonial Government stocks	69.7	5.74%	1,031.5	21.05%	1,411.4	20.23%	2034.4	21.30%	3094.7	18.67%
- Total Government / Municipal Stocks	923.3	75.98%	1,933.1	39.46%	2,513.6	36.02%	3,324.5	34.81%	8,847.9	53.38%
Corporate Stocks										
- UK Railway stocks	193.7	15.94%	854.8	17.45%	1,104.6	15.83%	1217.3	12.75%	1259.5	7.60%
- Overseas railway stocks	31.3	2.58%	1,564.2	31.93%	1,977.8	28.34%	2929.8	30.68%	3888.4	23.46%
- Financial stocks	13.1	1.08%	199.5	4.07%	440.5	6.31%	609.1	6.38%	715	4.31%
- Utility stocks	24.5	2.02%	140.3	2.86%	200.1	2.87%	435.8	4.56%	465.7	2.81%
- Industrial stocks	21.9	1.80%	172.6	3.52%	690.9	9.90%	917.6	9.61%	1269.9	7.66%
- Resource stocks	7.4	0.61%	34.6	0.71%	50.8	0.73%	116.4	1.22%	129.8	0.78%
- Other stocks										
Total corporate stocks	291.9	24.02%	2,966.0	60.54%	4,464.7	63.98%	6,226.0	65.19%	7,728.3	46.62%
Total nominal value of quoted securities	1,215.2	100.00%	4,899.1	100.00%	6,978.3	100.00%	9,550.5	100.00%	16,576.2	100.00%

Source: The data used in the above table was extrapolated by the author from Ranald Michie, *The London Stock Exchange: a history* (Oxford, 2004), p. 88.

NOTES

1. The Irish Land Act 1903 [3 Ed. VII, c. 37.] (14 August 1903) [hereafter the Wyndham Act 1903 or the 1903 Act]; The Irish Land Act, 1909 [9 Ed. VII, c. 42] (3 December 1909).
2. *Report of the Irish Land Commission for the year from 1 Apr. 1934 to 31 Mar. 1935* (Dublin, 1936), p. 10.
3. *Hansard 4*, cxx, 186 (25 March 1903).
4. British Library [hereafter BL], Arthur Balfour Papers, Add. MS 49804/77, 'A policy for Ireland'.
5. In using these phrases, Wyndham was referring to situations where estates were so indebted that should they be sold and the debts paid off, and landlords would be left with no capital, no income, no home and no means of support. In such instances, landlords would be better off not selling, in that they would have a roof over their head and some means of surviving.
6. *Interim report of the estates commissioners for the period from 1st November 1903, to 31st December 1904*, 50, [Cd. 2471], H.C. 1905, xxii, 177.
7. National Library of Ireland [hereafter NLI], Bellew Papers, MS 27290 (2), James Robinson to Sir Henry Bellew, January 1912.
8. C. A. Conant, *Wall Street and the Country: A Study of Recent Financial Tendencies* (New York, 1904), p. 147.
9. London Stock Exchange, General purposes minutes, 15 May 1911, quoted in Ranald Michie, *The London Stock Exchange – A History* (Oxford, 2004), p. 70.
10. See Appendix.
11. David Cannadine, *The Decline and Fall of the British Aristocracy* (London, 1990), p. 91.
12. Michie, *The London Stock Exchange*, p. 71.
13. M. Edelstein, 'Foreign investment, accumulation and empire, 1860–1914', in R. Floud and P. Johnson (eds), *The Cambridge Economic History of Modern Britain, Vol. ii, Economic Maturity, 1860–1939* (Cambridge, 2010), p. 191.
14. Anthony Trollope, *The Way We Live Now* (London, 2001 edn) and Ken Follett, *A Dangerous Fortune* (New York, 1993).
15. Michie, *The London Stock Exchange*, p. 88.
16. Dominion bonds were issued by British colonies or protectorates around the world. They were generally issued to finance capital projects such as railway or road building. These bonds were not guaranteed by the Treasury, but it would have been unthinkable to allow a default in payment as it would have undermined the whole principle of self-funding colonies and required direct intervention by the British government. As such, investors assumed that these bonds were guaranteed by the British Treasury.
17. Tim Harvard, *Investment Property Valuation Today* (London, 2014), p. 10.

18. http://www.blackwellpublishing.com/content/BPL_Images/Content_store/Sample_Chapter/9781405135559/9781405135559_4_004.pdf [accessed 9 September 2016].
19. Luke Samy, 'Indices of house prices and rent prices of residential property in London, 1895–1939', University of Oxford, Discussion papers in *Economic and Social History*, 134 (April, 2015), p. 9.
20. Ibid., p. 30.
21. Ronan Lyons [Department of economics, TCD], *A housing price index for Dublin 1900–2014*, Presentation to the Irish Quantitative History Group, Trinity College Dublin, January 2015. Slide 30.
22. Hartley Withers, *War and Lombard Street* (London, 1915), p. 1.
23. A. W. Kirkaldy, *Credit, Industry and the War* (London, 1915), p. 245.
24. Michie, *London Stock Exchange*, p. 145.
25. Ibid., p. 165.
26. J. S. Gordon, *The Great Game – A History of Wall Street* (London, 1999), p. 207.
27. Michie, *The London Stock Exchange*, p. 174.
28. Gordon, *The Great Game*, p. 207.
29. Inflation calculator; http://inflation.stephenmorley.org/ [accessed 21 September 2016].
30. The performance figures quoted in this section are drawn from the *Barclays Equity Gilt study 2016*. This study, which has been published annually since 1955, is the definitive work used by investment managers to benchmark their performances over the years. It provides statistics showing the performance of equities and gilts markets since 1900.
31. Tony McCarthy, 'From landlord to rentier: The Wyndham Land Act 1903 and its economic consequences for Irish landlords 1903–1933', unpublished PhD thesis (Maynooth University, 2017).
32. Bank of England inflation calculator: http://www.bankofengland.co.uk/education/Pages/resources/inflationtools/calculator/index1.aspx accessed 20.40 [accessed 8 November 2016].
33. NLI, Clonbrock papers, MS 35,721.5, Statement explaining meaning of election to take Land Stock or cash for purchase money and probable results of such election, 11 March 1910.
34. Hamilton papers (in private possession), Contract notes 19 December 1904 from Bruce, Symes and Williams, Stockbrokers of 37 Dame Street, Dublin.
35. NLI, Dopping Hepenstal papers, MS 35,873.2, Various contract notes from Barton, Copland & Hamilton, Stockbrokers.
36. M. Bence Jones, *Twilight of the Ascendancy* (London, 1987), p. 117.
37. Terence Dooley, *The Decline of the Big House in Ireland* (Dublin, 2001), p. 35.
38. Ibid., p. 118.
39. Henry Mallaby-Deeley (1863–1937) was a wealthy London-based financier who famously acquired the Duke of Bedford's Covent Garden estate for

£2.75 million in 1913: see *The Sphere*, 27 December 1913. He was elected MP for Harrow in 1910 and held a seat until 1923. He was knighted in 1922. Under a resettlement of the Leinster estate in 1919, it was provided that if Edward FitzGerald succeeded to the dukedom that Mallaby-Deeley would acquire Edward's life interest in the estate. On the death of Maurice, the sixth duke, in 1922, Mallaby-Deeley stepped into Edward's shoes and became entitled to his life interest in the estate. For a fuller account of this transaction, see Terence Dooley, *Decline and Fall of the Dukes of Leinster 1872–1948: Love, War, Debt and Madness* (Dublin, 2014), pp. 196–210.
40. Pauric J. Dempsey, 'Brooks, George (1849–1926)', *Dictionary of Irish Biography*, Vol. 1 (Cambridge, 2009), pp. 871–2.
41. A life interest in an investment trust means that the beneficiary has a right to any income generated by the trust but does not actually have any rights to the capital.
42. A mortgage is a loan secured on land or property charging a fixed rate of interest for a specified loan term.
43. McCarthy, 'From landlord to rentier'.
44. NLI, Clonbrock papers, MS 35,816.8, Undated handwritten note by Lord Clonbrock.
45. Judicial rents were introduced under Section 8 of the Land Law (Ireland) Act 1881. Under the terms of this section, any tenant or landlord (it was virtually always the tenant) who was dissatisfied with the rent he was paying could apply to the Land Court to have it reviewed. Once adjudicated on, the rent was fixed for a period of fifteen years, and this was known as a first-term rent. After fifteen years, the process could be repeated and the revised rent set for a further fifteen years (second-term rent). On expiry of the second period, a further review could be undertaken, and the rent fixed for another fifteen-year period (third-term rent). While the reviews could in theory lead to an upward rent review, the reality was that virtually all such reviews resulted in downwards revisions. Frederick Bailey, in *The Irish Land Acts* published in 1917, calculates the average rent reductions across the country because of the judicial rent review process as follows: first-term reviews −20.7 per cent., second-term reviews −19.3 per cent, third-term reviews −9.2 per cent (p. 20). In practical terms, this meant that a rent of say £100 00s. 00d. immediately prior to the first review in 1881 would have fallen to £79 6s. 6d., in 1896 it would have further reduced to £64 0s. 0d. and by 1911 it would be down to £58 2s. 2d.
46. McCarthy, 'From landlord to rentier', pp. 228–9.
47. Ibid., p. 229.
48. In June 1932, the British government announced that it was going to redeem the 5 per cent War Loan Stock at par on 1 December 1932. Under the terms of the measure announced by Neville Chamberlain, Chancellor of the Exchequer, on 30 June 1932, holders of the 5 per cent War Loan Stock would have their holdings redeemed at par value on 1 December

1932, or if they wished they could convert to a newly issued 3½ per cent War Loan Stock that was to be issued. The background to the move by the chancellor was that in the wake of Britain abandoning the gold standard in September 1931, interest rates fell dramatically from around 6 per cent to 2.5 per cent by June 1932. British bank deposit interest rates were ½ per cent (*The Times*, 2 June 1932). Newly issued British treasury bonds were being issued at close to 3 per cent. In such an environment, the 5 per cent interest being paid on the £2 billion overhang of outstanding War Loan Stock was extremely costly for the British government and it decided to act. Introducing the measure, Mr Chamberlain stated: 'The War Loan at 5 per cent was out of relation with the yield of other Government securities and moreover, that the maintenance of the old war time rate attaching to so vast a body of stock and hanging like a cloud over the capital market was a source of depression and hindrance to the expansion of trade' (*The Times*, 1 July 1932). *The Times* opined, 'The scheme which is a financial operation of unparalleled magnitude and will annually save £30 million gross and £23 million net, was received with enthusiasm when announced by Mr Chamberlain and Lord Hailsham in Parliament last evening' (*The Times*, 1 July 1932). From the government's perspective the scheme was a massive success, with holders of £1,921 million worth (out of a total of £2,087 million) of 5 per cent War Loan Stock converting to the new 3½ per cent issue: see Charles Poor Kindleberger, *A Financial History of Western Europe* (London, 1985), p. 388. For holders of the stock, however, it meant a 30 per cent reduction in the income previously received.
49. McCarthy, 'From landlord to rentier', pp. 228–9.
50. Ibid., p. 222.
51. Ferdinand Lundberg, *America's Sixty Great Families* (New York, 1938), p. 49.
52. *New York Times*, 5 August 1937.

Index

Abercorn, dukes of, 215, 227, 228
Aberdeen, 29–30, 290, 291
Absenteeism, 82, 192, 245, 270, 285
Access
  commons, 3, 137–41, 149–50
  importance of land access in Ireland, 113–14, 115
  public access, 3, 7, 10, 137–8, 139–41, 149, 150
  rights of way, 138
  rights to roam, 141
Achavandra, 30, 31, 32, 36, 37–8
Act of Union (Ireland: 1800), 6, 13
Act of Union (Scotland: 1707), 8
Acts of Union (Wales: 1536–43), 12, 191
Adam, James, 58
Adam, R. J., 31
Adamson, Gregor, 56, 57
Aghada, 164
Agrarian agitation
  Ireland, 6, 9, 12–15, 115–27, 192–3, 238, 242–4
  Northern Ireland, 220–1
  press representations, 10, 221, 259, 260, 265–72, 274–6, 287, 289–90
  Scotland, 6, 8, 9, 242–4, 290–2
  Wales, 9, 10–11, 192–3, 242, 259–61, 264–76, 287–90, 294–5
Agricultural colleges, 228
Agricultural depression, 6, 9, 11, 17, 103, 114, 164, 191, 196, 214–15, 242, 260, 265, 271, 276, 286–94
Agricultural Holdings Act (1906), 190, 198, 200
Agricultural Holdings Act (1908), 200
Agricultural Holdings Act (1923), 200
Agricultural Holdings Act (1948), 201–2
Agricultural Holdings Act (1986), 204, 205

Agricultural Holdings (England) Act (1875), 190, 194–5
Agricultural Holdings (England) Acts (1883–1900), 190, 193, 195–8, 200
Agricultural Land Commission, 201
Agricultural Land Tribunals, 201, 202, 203, 204, 205
Agricultural Law Association, 204
Agricultural Revolution, 8, 35
Agricultural Tenancies Act (1995), 204
Agriculture
  arable farming, 35, 37, 38–9, 40–1, 43, 286
  cattle farming, 40, 49, 59–60, 125, 227
  Common Agricultural Policy, 17, 205
  Congested Districts Board assistance schemes, 249
  crofting, 8, 9, 48, 57, 98–9, 172–86
  crop rotation, 35, 38–9
  declining economic role, 17, 242
  direct farming by landowners, 226–8, 230
  England, 3, 27, 38, 39–41, 103, 286
  farm sizes, 114–15
  grazing, 36, 38, 39–40, 43, 60, 114, 120–1, 137, 143–4, 185
  and improvement *see* improvement
  international competition, 296
  Ireland, 13, 114–15, 125, 249, 304
  legislation, 190–206
  mechanisation, 3
  mixed farming, 35, 183, 286, 290
  modernisation and reform, 8, 27–9, 34
  Northern Ireland, 226–8
  productivity levels, 27, 51, 115, 183
  role of 'Great Men', 27, 40–1
  Scotland, 8, 27–43, 48–51, 57–61, 249, 286, 290–4

Agriculture *(cont.)*
  seasonal labour, 29
  sheep farming, 8, 28, 35–6, 39–41, 43, 48–51, 57–61
  smallholdings, 3, 98, 157–63, 172–86
  tax advantages, 227
  Wales, 190–206, 260, 286–90, 292–4
Agriculture Act (1947), 201–2
Agriculture Act (1958), 202–3
Agriculture Act (2020), 204
Aiken, Frank, 129, 218
Aird of Tong, 58
Alexander, Sir Claud, of Ballochmyle, 180
America, 31, 32, 34, 41, 72, 101, 145, 162, 307, 311, 313, 320–1
American Civil War, 101
Angle estate, 287
Anglesey, 262, 263
Anglican church, 11, 16, 191, 212, 260, 271
Anglicisation, 11–12, 260, 271
Anglo Celt, 162
Anglo-Irish ascendancy, 4, 117
Anglo-Irish Treaty, 121, 122
Anglo-Irish Truce, 121, 122, 124
Anne, Queen, 144
Annesley family, 215
Annexed Estates Board, 33–4
Anti-imperialism, 95, 96, 102
Anti-Tithe League, 260, 288
Antrim, 212, 216–17, 220–1, 223, 226, 227, 229
Antrim, William Randal McDonnell, 6th earl, 214, 223, 227, 228, 229
Arable farming, 35, 37, 38–9, 40–1, 43, 286
Arbitration, 175–6, 190–1, 193–5, 198, 200, 202–5
Ardrahan, 162
Argyll, George Campbell, 8th duke, 16, 34, 100, 245, 246
Argyll, John Campbell, 5th duke, 57
Armagh, 215, 216, 221
Armstrong, Henry, 56
Armstrong family, 215
Arran, 182, 184, 185
Ashbourne Act (1885), 214–15, 261
Ashby Park, 149
Ashridge estate, 142, 145
Ashtown estate, 117

Association of Seaboard Proprietors in Scotland, 244
Atholl, John Stewart-Murray, 7th duke, 248
Atkinson, Adam, 39–40
Auld, Alexander, 181
Auld, William, 181–2
Ayrshire, 52, 174, 179–83, 185

Balfour, Arthur, 304, 308
Ballingarry, 164
Ballycumber, 165
Ballylinan, 164
Ballymoney, 221
Ballysaggartmore, 165
Balnagowan, 40, 41
Baner ac Amserau Cymru see *Faner*
Bank collapses, 307, 313
Bank of Scotland, 52
Bannerman, Sir Henry Campbell, 197
Barclay, James, 196
Barings Bank, 307
Baron's Court estate, 227
Barry, Tom, 117–18
Barton estate, 165
Barvas, 52, 58, 59, 60, 62
Bateman, John, 9, 240
Battle of the Braes, 101
Bauer, R. M., 307
Beamish estate, 165
Beaumont-Nesbitt, Edward, 119–27
Beaumont-Nesbitt, Frederick, 120
Beaumont-Nesbitt, Wilfrid, 120–1
Bell, William, 263
Bellew, Sir Henry Grattan, 305–7
Bellew, Richard, 159
Bellew estate, 305–7
Belmore, Somerset Lowry-Corry, 4th earl, 215
Berkhampsted Common, 140, 142
Bessborough Commission, 212, 245, 246, 272
Big Houses see country houses
Bingham, Tom, Lord, 71
Birch, Richard, 263
Birrell Act (1909), 14, 215, 303, 309, 314
Black Act (1723), 138
Blackie, John Stuart, 98
Board of Agriculture, 34–5, 271
Board of Agriculture for Scotland (BoAS), 106, 173, 175–85
Board of Trade, 73–7, 78, 79

INDEX

Bodnant estate, 263
Bodrhyddan estate, 263
Boer War, 96, 106, 307
Boglands, 226
Boland, Patrick, 129
Bolshevism, 116
Bookham Common, 142
Border Leicester sheep, 40
Boston, George Irby, Lord, 262
Boston Guardian, 197
Boswell, George, 40
Boundary Commission, 221
Bounties, 53
Boycotts, 15
Boyd, R. N., 221
Box Hill, 142
BP, 77–8
Braegrudie, 31–2
Brexit, 17
Bristol Mercury, 195
British Empire, 2, 211, 213, 311
Brodie, Ian, 291
Brogyntyn estate, 262, 263
Brook, Sir Norman, 78, 80
Brooke, Basil, Viscount Brookeborough, 14, 229
Brooke, Sir George, 315
Brooke, Sir Victor, 215, 226
Broughton, Urban, 145, 146
Brown, John, 180
Brown, Robert, 51, 56, 63
Brownstown, 168
Buccleuch, John Montagu Douglas Scott, 7th duke, 177
Buchanan, Robert, 97
Bulgaria, 96, 101
Bull, Phillip, 211
Burke, James, 118
Burke's British Husbandry, 41
Butlers of Ormonde, 314
Butt, Isaac, 115
Byrne, Joseph, 122

Cae-Einion farm, 269
Caernarfonshire, 192, 262, 263, 266, 276
Caithness, 29–30, 31, 32, 35, 95, 96, 106
Caledon, earls of, 215, 227
Calman Report, 82
Cameron, Donald, of Lochiel, 248
Cameron, Ewen, 175, 176, 177, 178, 183

Campbell, David, 36
Campbell, Ralph, 296–7
Cambeltown, 57
Cannadine, David, 7
Capahanagh, 161
Capitalism, 8, 98, 241
Car parking, 145–6
Cardiff Times, 289–90
Cardiganshire, 192
Carlow, 164, 313
Carloway, 54, 58
Carlyle, Thomas, 100
Carmarthenshire, 192, 285–6, 288–9, 292–3, 296
Carmarthenshire Tenant-Farmers' Association, 288
Carnarvon *see* Caernarfonshire
Carragher, Thomas, 124–5
Carrington, Charles Wynn, Earl, 197
Carrington, Robert Wynn, 144
Castleconnell, 164
Castlemartin, 286–7, 289, 295
Catholic Defenders, 13
Catholic Emancipation, 12
Catholicism, 12, 119, 221
Cattle farming, 40, 49, 59–60, 125, 227
Cavan, 162, 163, 215
Cawdor, Frederick Campbell, 3rd earl, 294–5, 296–7
Cawdor, Hugh Campbell, 4th earl, 296
Cawdor, John Campbell, 1st baron, 285
Cawdor, John Campbell, 2nd earl, 16, 273, 287–9, 296
Cawdor Castle estate, 285–6, 290–2, 293–4
Cawdor estates, 285–97
Central Association of Agricultural Valuers, 204
Ceylon, 49, 55, 63
Chambers, Robert, 177–8
Channing, Francis, 196
Chaplin, Henry, 196
Charitable landowners, 5, 10, 141–2, 145–50
Charter of the Forest, 143, 150
Chartism, 9, 10, 97, 98, 99, 140
Chartist Land Plan, 99
Chertsey Abbey, 143
Chester, 259, 261, 263
Cheviot hills, 40

Cheviot sheep, 40
Chichester-Clark, James, 14
Chirk estate, 262
Churchill, Winston, 106
City of Glasgow Bank, 307
City of London Corporation, 141
Civil war *see* American Civil War; Irish Civil War
Clan chiefs, 51
Clare, 114, 160–1
Clark, Gavin Brown, 3, 95–107, 261
Clark, Gemma, 121
Climate change, 7
Clonakilty, 165
Clonbrock, Luke Dillon, 4th baron, 314, 315–16, 320
Clonbrock, Robert Dillon, 5th baron, 316, 320
Clonbrock estate, 313–17, 319, 320
Cloncurry estate, 117
Clondoogan, 166
Coast Protection Act (1949), 76, 79
Coast Protection Bill (1929), 76
Coastal erosion, 75
Cobden, Richard, 16
Cockburn, Patrick, 51, 52, 61
Coke, Thomas, of Holkham, 38
Colebrooke Park, 229
Collective action, 15–16, 238–9, 243–4, 247–51, 259–77
College of Physicians (Ireland), 166
Colonialism, 8, 27–8, 33, 35, 42, 63, 118
Combe, Malcolm, 184
Commission on Scottish Devolution, 82
Commissioners of Crown Lands, 75–81
Commissioners of Education (Ireland), 166
Common Agricultural Policy (CAP), 18, 205
Commons
 access, 3, 137–41, 149–50
 common rights, 137–8, 141, 149
 cultivation, 3, 137, 143
 customary use, 137–8, 149, 150
 enclosure, 3, 9, 11, 138–41, 144, 149–50
 England, 3, 9, 39–40, 136–51
 grazing, 39–40, 137, 143–4
 legislation, 138, 140
 preservation, 3, 136–51
 sport and leisure uses, 142, 144, 145–6
 Wales, 11
Commons Preservation Society, 140–1, 150
Commons Registration Act (1965), 138
Community Empowerment Act (2015), 9
Community landownership, 7, 9
Compensation
 for burning of country houses, 121–2, 126–7
 for damage by game, 198, 200, 261, 270
 for disturbance, 180, 198, 202
 for landowners on nationalisation of land, 103–4, 105
 for loss of common rights, 138
 and small landholding settlements, 180–1
 for tenant improvements, 13, 173, 192–6, 200, 202, 204, 247, 261, 270, 288
Compulsory purchase, 117, 211–30; *see also* land redistribution
Conacre system, 114
Conant, C. A., 307
Concentration of ownership, 213, 240, 251
Congested Districts Boards
 Ireland, 217, 249
 Scotland, 99, 176, 178, 249
Conlon, Patrick, 221
Connor, John, 120
Conolly, Edward, 168
Conservative party, 9, 95, 145, 196, 243, 248–9, 262, 264, 276, 296
Controlled flooding, 40–1
Convention of Scottish Local Authorities, 82
Coogan, Eamonn, 123, 126, 127
Cookham Common, 142
Coolgreany estate, 313–15, 317–18, 319
Cooper's Hill, 136–7
Coote, William, 220
Coote estate, 164
Cork, 117, 163, 164, 165
Cork Examiner, 160, 162, 165
Corn Laws, 9, 296
Cornwallis-West, W., 264
Corporate securities, 308, 313
Cosgrave, W. T., 118, 123–4, 128

INDEX

Country houses
  burning of, 117, 121–3, 126–7, 130
  income required to maintain, 218, 225, 228, 230
  Ireland, 117, 121–3, 126–7, 130, 213, 218, 225, 314
  Northern Ireland, 213, 214, 225, 228, 229–30
  renovations and improvements, 314
  and tourism, 229–30
  Wales, 10, 269
  see also estates
County Agricultural Executives, 201, 202, 203
County surveys, 35, 40–1
Court of Chancery, 140
Coventry Evening Telegraph, 149
Cox, Patrick, 122–3, 129
Cragoe, Matthew, 10, 12, 190, 276
Craig, Alexander, 58, 61
Crawford, Sharman, 167–8
Crofter MPs, 95, 96, 98–9, 106
Crofters Holdings (Scotland) Act (1886), 8, 9, 172, 175, 178, 192, 243, 248, 261, 291, 294
Crofters (Scotland) Act (1955), 173, 184
Crofters (Scotland) Act (1993), 173
Crofting, 8, 9, 48, 57, 98–9, 172–86
Crop rotation, 35, 38–9
Crown estate, 71–86, 244
Crown Estate Act (1956), 77
Crown Estate Act (1961), 77, 80–1, 83, 84, 85, 86
Crown Estate Commissioners, 72, 77, 82–3
Crown Estate Scotland, 72, 83–6
Crown Lands Act (1866), 73–4, 80
Crown Lands Act (1927), 75–6, 79, 80
Culley brothers, 40–1
Culmaily Farm, 27–31, 35–43
Cumann na mBan, 122–3
Cumann na nGaedheal, 118, 125–6, 128
Cunliffe, Sir Robert, 264
Cunningham, Roseanna, 82
Currency values, 313
Curteis, Herbert, 160
Custom, 6, 137–8, 149, 150, 192, 198
Cymru Fydd movement, 15, 199, 261, 270

Dáil Éireann, 116–17, 118, 120, 124, 126, 129
Dáil land courts, 117
Damage to Property (Compensation) Act, 126–7
Davitt, Michael, 3, 13, 15, 97, 115, 242, 261
De Valera, Éamon, 128
Death duties, 296, 317, 320
Debt, 8, 49, 51–2, 56, 61–3, 216, 242, 304–5
Decline of the Big House in Ireland (Dooley), 117
Deeley, Henry Mallably, 315
Deer Forest Commission, 247–8
Defence of Property in Ireland Mansion House Group, 244
Deflation, 312, 321
Defoe, Daniel, 33
Demesnes, 114, 117, 119–30, 218
Democracy, 7, 14, 17, 99, 101, 245
Democratic Society, 98
Denbigh, Rudolph Feilding, 8th earl, 263
Denbighshire, 261, 263, 267, 295
Department of Agriculture (DoA), 182, 183, 184, 185
Devine, T. M., 55, 59, 62, 63
Devolution, 2, 17, 72, 81–6, 190, 203–5
Devon Commission, 272
Devoy, John, 115–16
Dicey, A. V., 71
Dickens, Charles, 240
Diggers (1649), 137
Diggers (2010s activist group), 136–7
Dinas Oleu, 142
Disestablishment movement, 11, 15, 191, 260
Dispossession, 6, 8, 28, 30–2, 36, 43, 50–1, 59, 115; *see also* evictions
Dispute resolution, 117, 190–1, 193–5, 198, 200, 202–5
Dissolution of the monasteries, 143
Distilling, 49, 55–7
Diversification, 228–30, 248
Dobbs family, 216
Domestic service, 249
Donegal, 114, 117, 227
Dooley, Terence, 117, 211, 218, 225
Dopping-Hepenstal, M. E., 318
Dopping Hepenstal estate, 313–14, 318, 319

Down, 212, 215, 216, 221, 227
Downing estate, 263
Drimnagh, 165
Dual ownership, 13, 175
Dublin, 102, 125, 157, 158, 166, 168, 192, 242, 248, 250, 310, 315
Dublin Evening Mail, 166
Dublin Stock Exchange, 314
Dublin Weekly Register, 160
Dufferin, Frederick Hamilton-Temple-Blackwood, 1st marquess, 238, 246–7
Dunleath, Henry Mulholland, Baron, 215
Dunne, Francis, 168
Dunraven, Windham Wyndham-Quin, 4th earl, 16, 273
Dunrobin, 30, 36
Dyvenor, Arthur Rice, Lord, 287–8

Easter Rising, 120
Eclectic Society, 98
Economic depression, 6, 242, 246, 289, 313, 321; *see also* agricultural depression
Economic growth, 307
Economic restructuring, 2, 6, 7–8
Edinburgh, 34, 61, 63, 96, 98, 244
Education, 191, 199, 228, 238, 239, 240
Edward VIII, 147–8
Edwardian housing slump, 310
Egan, Liam, 122
Egham, 143–4, 146–7
Egham Enclosure Act (1814), 146
Eisteddfodau, 263, 270
Electricity, 129–30, 314
Ellice, Edward, of Invergarry, 247
Ellis, Tom, 10, 191–3, 196, 259, 260, 269, 271–3, 275, 294
Ellis-Nanney, H. J., 263, 276
Emergency Committee of the Orange Institution, 15
Emergency labour, 15
Emigration
 financial assistance for, 48, 50, 62–3, 247
 Ireland, 116, 128
 Scotland, 31, 32, 48, 50, 55, 62–3, 247
 see also migration
Emlyn, Frederick Campbell, Lord, 16, 273, 288, 296

Employment
 domestic, 249
 on estates, 8, 29–30, 42–3, 53, 119, 120, 269, 270
 in fishing, 42, 53
 industrial, 8, 29–30, 249
 Ireland, 119, 158, 163
 labour migration, 29, 42–3, 116
 public works scheme, 158, 163
 Scotland, 8, 29–30, 42–3, 53
 seasonal labour, 29, 116
 strikes, 120
 unemployment, 116, 312
 Wales, 269, 270
Enclosure
 commons, 3, 9, 11, 138–41, 144, 149–50
 England, 3, 9, 138–41, 144, 149–50, 241
 legislation, 3, 138, 139–40, 144, 146
 resistance to, 138–9, 150–1
 Wales, 11
 waste lands, 3
England
 agriculture, 3, 27, 38, 39–41, 103, 286
 arable farming, 40–1, 286
 Chartism, 9, 98, 99, 140
 commons, 3, 9, 39–40, 136–51
 Corn Laws, 9, 296
 Crown estate, 71–2
 disparate nature of land reform campaigns, 3, 9–10
 enclosure, 3, 9, 138–41, 144, 149–50, 241
 foreshore management, 71–2
 game laws, 3, 9
 housing, 9, 10, 136, 310
 land values, 243
 landlord responses, 237
 landlord–tenant relations, 16, 103, 190, 241
 Magna Carta, 136–7, 143–5, 149
 national identity, 6–7
 National Trust, 5, 10, 139, 141–2, 145–50
 People's Budget, 9, 243
 poverty, 9, 142
 press, 145–6, 148–9, 195, 197, 272
 sheep farming, 39–41
 smallholdings, 3
 taxation, 9, 10

English Votes for English Laws (EVEL), 17
Enlightenment, 8, 33
Enniskillen, Lowry Cole, 4th earl, 215
Ennistymon, 160
Epping Forest, 140, 141, 150
Erasmus Smith Schools, 166
Estates
  break-up and sale, 7, 10, 51–2, 119, 214–17, 224, 238, 276–7, 296, 303–5
  country houses, 4, 10, 117, 121–3, 126–7, 130, 213, 214, 218, 225, 228–30, 269, 314
  demesnes, 114, 117, 119–30, 218
  designed landscapes, 4
  employment, 8, 29–30, 42–3, 53, 119, 120, 269, 270
  gardens, 222, 223, 228–9
  home farms, 36, 218, 224
  improvement *see* improvement
  industry, 4, 29–30, 42, 55–7, 262, 271
  Ireland, 117–27, 213–19, 238, 262, 303–5, 313–18
  management, 5, 8, 17, 27–43, 48–64, 228, 240, 245–6
  in more than one nation, 4, 6, 213, 216, 239, 262
  Northern Ireland, 213–30
  parks, 4, 140, 226, 229
  Scotland, 8, 27–43, 48–64, 241, 246, 285–6, 290–2, 293–4
  social function, 4–5, 213, 260, 270
  and social status, 3–4, 7, 213–14, 217, 239, 243, 245, 276, 296
  sport and leisure uses, 4, 102, 103, 229–30
  and tourism, 229–30
  Wales, 10, 11, 12, 193–4, 259–77, 285–97
European Union, 17
Evangelical Christianity, 48
Evans, David, 269
Evans, Gwilym, 295
Evans, O. Lloyd, 263
Evans, Sam, 272
Evelyn, John, 141
Evictions
  Ireland, 160, 163–9
  political evictions, 11, 269, 270–1, 275, 288, 296
  press coverage, 165, 166, 168

Scotland, 6, 8, 28, 30–2, 36, 43, 48, 50–1, 59, 101–2
Wales, 11, 191–2, 269, 270–1, 275, 288, 296
see also dispossession
Excise Act (1823), 55–6

Fabian Society, 96
Factors, 4, 28–32, 35–6, 54–5, 58, 60, 61, 246, 290–3; *see also* land agents
Faenol estate, 263, 268
Fair rents, 173, 202, 261, 288
Fairhaven, Cara Rogers, Lady, 144–5, 148
Falconer, Cosmo, 36, 37
Family trusts, 314–16
Famines
  Ireland, 2, 115, 157–69, 213–14, 241, 249
  Scotland, 36, 62, 175, 249
Faner, 10, 260, 267, 269
Farm Business Tenancies, 204
Farmer's Magazine, 33
Farmer's Monthly Visitor, 41
Farming *see* agriculture
Farrer, Thomas, 73–7, 78, 81, 83, 85, 86
Fenian movement, 12, 115
Ferguson, John, 15
Fermanagh, 215, 226, 229
Feudalism, 104, 140
Fianna Fáil, 128–9, 218
Finnebrogue estate, 227
Firewood, 137, 138, 149
First International, 96, 100–1
First World War, 104, 106, 114, 116, 119–20, 176–7, 180, 276, 310–12
Fish-curing, 42–3, 53, 55
Fishing, 42–3, 49, 50–1, 52–5, 57, 62, 72, 74, 247
Fixity of tenure *see* security of tenure
Flax, 29–30, 43
Flintshire, 263, 295
Flooding, 18, 33, 40–1, 143, 147
Follett, Ken, 308
Food production, 18, 104
Footpaths, 141
Foreshore licences, 74, 77
Foreshore management, 71–86, 244
Forestry Commission, 228
Forests, 4, 18, 143, 228, 247–8
Forfeited Estates Commission, 8, 33

Foster, Gavin, 121
Fuel, 137, 138, 149
Franco-Prussian War, 307
Franklin, Steven, 144
Fraser, Lewis, 121, 123
Fraser, Robert, 291
Fraser-Mackintosh, Charles, 95, 102
Free trade, 53, 103, 194
Freedom of contract, 194, 265, 289
Freedom of cropping, 198, 200
Freedom of sale, 247, 261
French Revolution, 6, 15
Fry, Michael, 43

Gaelic language, 34, 98, 241
Galway, 117, 157, 158, 161, 162, 164, 305–7, 313
Game damage, 192, 198, 200, 261, 270
Game laws, 3, 9
Gardens, 141, 214, 229
Gee, Thomas, 10, 260, 261, 267, 269, 274, 275, 294
Genedl Gymreig, 267
General Enclosure Acts, 139–40
George III, 71
George, Henry, 14, 16, 99–100, 102, 104–5
Geraghty, Matthew, 120, 123, 129
Geraghty, Patrick, 122
German, Kieran, 56, 57
Germany, 307, 312, 318
Gerrard estate, 164
Gilliland, James, 182
Gilliland, Thomas D., 182
Ginnell, Laurence, 116, 120
Gladstone, W. E., 10, 193, 196, 214, 238, 242, 245, 259, 261, 271–2, 289, 295
Glasgow, 57, 60, 96, 99, 102, 242
Glenarm estate, 214, 229–30
Globalisation, 14
Gloucester Citizen, 148
Glynllifon estate, 262
Gold standard, 313
Golden Grove estate, 263, 285–6, 293
Golspie, 30, 36
Good Templar, 96
Gorry, P. J., 129
Gosford, earls of, 215
Government bonds, 308, 310, 311, 312–13
Government debt, 311, 312

Government of Ireland Act (1920), 217, 218–19, 220
Government of Wales Act (1998), 190, 203–4
Graham, Robert, 55, 62, t63
Grant, James, 42
Grassmillees, 174, 179–83, 185
Gray, Malcolm, 49, 57
Grazing, 36, 38, 39–40, 43, 60, 114, 120–1, 137, 143–4, 185
Great Bernera, 59
Great Depression, 313, 321
Great Famine, 2, 115, 157–69, 213–14, 241, 249
Great Landowners of Britain and Ireland (Bateman), 9, 240
Great Stock Market Crash, 313, 321
Greenmount Agricultural College, Antrim, 228
Gregory, William, 157–60, 166, 168, 169
Gregory clause, 2, 157–69
Grey, Sir George, 163
Griffith, W. D. W., 263, 266, 267
Griffiths, John Morgan, 295
Grogan, George, 146–7
Guerilla Days in Ireland (Barry), 117–18
Gwalia, 268
Gwerin society, 11–12, 259–60, 275, 276
Gwynfryn estate, 263, 269

Halkyn estate, 263
Hamilton, Charles, 317
Hampstead Heath, 140, 150
Hansard, 158, 196–9
Hare, John, 202
Harlech, William Ormsby-Gore, Lord, 16, 262
Harmsworth, Leicester, 95, 96
Hart, Peter, 117
Health, 104
Helmsdale, 42
Henderson, George, 221, 222–3
Henderson, John, 35
Henry III, 143
Hickey, William, 126
Hicks, Sir William Joynson, 221
Highland Agricultural Society, 34
Highland Clearances, 6, 8, 28, 30–2, 36, 43, 50–1, 56, 59, 101–2, 175, 179, 241

Highland Exceptionalism, 28, 177
Highland Land Law Reform Association, 96, 101
Highland Property Association, 247–8, 251
Highland Roads and Bridges Commission, 48
Highlands and Islands Enterprise, 82
Hill, Octavia, 141–2
Hillsborough Castle, 227
Hindhead Common, 142
Historicism, 9, 177, 179, 242, 245–6
Hoare, Gurney, 140
Hogan, Patrick, 118, 121, 123–6, 129
Hogan Act *see* Land Act (1923)
Home farms, 36, 218, 224;
  see also demesnes
Home Rule
  federal Home Rule, 102
  Ireland, 13, 98, 115, 119, 120, 212, 295
  Scotland, 95
  Wales, 194, 196, 197, 198–9, 261
  see also devolution
Horse racing, 144
House of Commons, 6, 17, 76, 83, 157–60, 163, 167–8, 192, 196–9, 203, 240, 249
House of Lords, 6, 74, 197, 218, 240, 242, 245, 249, 265, 294–5
Housing
  buy-to-let properties, 310
  Edwardian housing slump, 310
  England, 9, 10, 136, 310
  Ireland, 165–6, 168–9, 310
  land for construction of, 182
  levelling of, 165–6, 168–9
  living conditions, 104
  protests against developments, 136
  reforms, 9
  right to buy, 16
  Scotland, 182
  social housing, 16
Howell, David W., 12, 190, 259, 265, 286
Howkins, Alun, 139
Hoyle, Richard, 5
Hughes, T. Jones, 231
Hughes, William, 33
Hunter, James, 28, 48, 50, 55, 57, 59, 62–3, 177
Hunter, Robert, 141–2

Ide Hill, 142
Imperial Parliament, 219, 220, 221
Imperialism *see* anti-imperialism; British Empire; colonialism
Improvement
  compensation for, 13, 173, 192–6, 200, 202, 204, 247, 261, 270, 288
  Ireland, 238, 248–9
  and landlord–tenant relations, 5, 175–6, 193–4
  and leases, 4, 58
  paid for by landlords, 176, 193–4, 270, 293–4
  resistance to, 28, 29, 31–3, 43
  Scotland, 2, 27–43, 58, 175–6, 248–9
  supporters of, 33–6
  by tenants, 13, 58, 103, 173, 175, 192–6, 200, 202, 204, 247, 261, 270, 288
Income tax, 227, 296
India, 9, 61, 96, 245, 246
Individualism, 98, 100
Industrial Revolution, 17
Industry
  distilling, 49, 55–7
  diversification, 8
  employment, 8, 29–30, 249
  on estates, 4, 29–30, 42, 55–7, 262, 271
  industrialisation, 4, 7, 17, 238, 241
  kelping, 2, 49–50, 51, 57, 244
  lands acquired with profits from, 4, 145, 241, 263–4
  manufacturing, 4, 33
  mining and quarrying, 4, 181, 229, 262, 264
  Scotland, 8, 29–30, 42, 55–7, 229, 244
  steel industry, 229, 264
  textile production, 29–30, 217
  training schemes, 249
  Wales, 262, 264, 271
Inequality, 9, 106, 114, 245, 276
Inflation, 307, 309, 311–12, 319
Infrastructure, 181, 194, 229, 247, 248–9, 307
Inheritance, 4, 5, 99, 159, 182, 263
Institutional landowners, 5, 166
International Magna Carta Day Association, 144
International Working Men's Association, 96, 100–1

Invershin, 40
Inverness, 247
Inverugie, 32
Investment, 51, 100, 103, 105, 194, 248, 270–1, 296, 303–21
Investment property, 309–10, 314
Ireland
  agrarian agitation, 6, 9, 13–15, 115–27, 192–3, 238, 242–4
  agriculture, 13, 114–15, 125, 249, 304
  Anglo-Irish ascendancy, 4, 117
  Anglo-Irish Treaty, 121, 122
  Ashbourne Act, 214–15, 261
  Bessborough Commission, 212, 245, 246, 272
  Big Houses, 117, 121–3, 126–7, 130, 213, 214, 218, 225, 314
  Birrell Act, 14, 215, 303, 309, 314
  cattle farming, 125
  Civil War, 114, 117, 121–4
  concentration of ownership, 213, 240
  Congested Districts Board, 217, 249
  Crown estate, 71
  Dáil Éireann, 116–17, 118, 120, 124, 126, 129
  Dáil land courts, 117
  demesne lands, 114, 117, 119–30, 218
  Devon Commission, 272
  Easter Rising, 120
  electrification, 129–30, 314
  emigration, 116, 128
  employment, 119, 158, 163
  estates, 117–27, 213–19, 238, 262, 303–5, 313–18
  evictions, 160, 163–9
  foreshore management, 71
  Government of Ireland Act, 217, 218–19, 220
  Great Famine, 2, 115, 157–69, 213–14, 241, 249
  Gregory clause, 2, 157–69
  Home Rule, 13, 98, 115, 119, 120, 212, 295
  housing, 165–6, 168–9, 310
  improvement, 238, 248–9
  Irish Convention, 114, 217, 218, 220, 222
  Irish Republican Army (IRA), 113, 117–18, 122–5, 128–9
  labour movement, 116, 120
Land Act (1881), 192, 214, 243, 247, 261, 288, 294, 319
Land Act (1923), 13, 117, 118, 123–4, 126, 128, 217–18, 222–3
Land Act (1933), 129
Land Commission, 114, 117, 127, 128, 129, 130, 218, 224, 261, 305
land hunger, 113–14, 121, 230
Land League, 6, 14–15, 102, 115, 125, 261, 275
land redistribution, 2–3, 13–14, 113–30, 211–19, 225, 230, 243, 303–5
land values, 243
Land War, 6, 115, 116, 119, 261
landlord defence associations, 15, 244, 247, 248, 261
landlord responses, 14–15, 237–8, 242, 244–51, 261
landlord–tenant relations, 6, 12–15, 103, 115–27, 163–9, 241
leases, 159–60, 167–8
Mitchelstown massacre, 192
national identity, 6–7, 16
nationalism, 4, 12, 115–25, 128–30, 211–12, 242
partition, 2, 217
Plan of Campaign, 6, 14, 15
plantations, 4, 118, 121
Poor Law Bill, 157–69
poverty, 157–69
press, 160, 162, 163, 165, 166, 168, 221
Public Safety (Emergency Powers), Act, 118, 122, 126
relief committees, 161–3, 167
Return of owners of land of one acre and upwards, 212–13, 214
smallholdings, 157–63
unionism, 119–20, 122
untenanted land, 114, 117, 217–18, 225
War of Independence, 113–14, 117, 123, 124–5, 130
workhouses, 157–61, 164–6, 168–9
Wyndham Act, 2, 14, 115, 119, 214, 215–16, 224, 227, 303–5, 309, 314
see also Northern Ireland
Irish Civil War, 114, 117, 121–4
Irish Convention, 114, 217, 218, 220, 222

Irish Grants Committee, 121–2, 123
Irish Land Commission, 114, 117, 127, 128, 129, 130, 218, 224, 261, 305
Irish Land Committee, 15
Irish Land League, 6, 15, 102, 115, 125, 261, 275
Irish Legal and Patriotic Union, 15
Irish Parliamentary Party, 115
Irish Republican Army (IRA), 113, 117–18, 122–5, 128–9
Irish Times, 221
Italy, 101

Jacobite Risings, 8, 33
Jenkins, Philip, 12
John, King, 136, 143
Johnston, Thomas, 95
Jones, Brynmor, 197, 198–9
Jones, Christopher (Sr), 120–1, 123–7
Jones, Christopher (Jr), 122, 129, 130
Jones, E. Pan, 15, 261, 275
Jones, Ernest, 98, 99
Jones, J. Graham, 190, 191, 192, 196
Jones, J. Gwynfor, 12
Jones, Lloyd, 97
Jones, Mark Bence, 314
Jones, Michael D., 259, 269
Jones, Walter, 263, 269
Judicial rent reviews, 13, 197, 204, 319

Kames, Henry Home, Lord, 33, 35
Kelping, 2, 49–50, 51, 57, 244
Kelsterton estate, 263
Kenyon, Lloyd, Lord, 197, 198
Kerry, 163, 166, 168
Kerry Evening Post, 163
Kiely-Ussher, Arthur, 165
Kildare, 117, 120, 168, 313
Kilkenny, 164–5, 314
Kilkenny Castle, 314
Kilmaine, John Browne, Lord, 164
Kilmallock, 164
Kilmarnock, 96, 97
Kilmorey, earls of, 215, 229
Kilnaleck, 162
Kilravock estate, 292
King's County *see* Offaly
Kingsley, Charles, 100
Kirkaldy, William, 310
Knock, 48, 53, 60, 62

Knox, Thomas, 55, 60, 62, 63
Kyle, Samuel, 223

La Touche, Christopher Digges, 316
Labour migration, 29, 42–3, 116
Labour movement, 106, 116, 120
Labour party, 95, 96, 106, 149; *see also* Northern Ireland Labour Party; Scottish Labour Party
Lairg, 31, 36
Laissez faire approaches, 2, 49–50, 184, 194
Lalor, James Fintan, 12, 115
Lancashire Tenant-Farmers' Association, 295
Land Act (1881), 192, 214, 243, 247, 261, 288, 294, 319
Land Act (1903) *see* Wyndham Act
Land Act (1909) *see* Birrell Act
Land Act (1923), 13, 117, 118, 123–4, 126, 128, 217–18, 222–3
Land Act (1933), 129
Land agents, 4, 11, 16–17, 28–32, 164–5, 180, 193, 241, 244–6, 262–3, 268–9, 274, 286–96
Land agitation *see* agrarian agitation; landlord–tenant relations; protest
Land and the People, The (Clark), 103, 105
Land Campaign, 9
Land Commission *see* Irish Land Commission; Scottish Land Commission; Welsh Land Commission
Land Corporation of Ireland, 15
Land courts
  Dáil land courts, 117
  proposed Welsh Land Court, 190, 192, 194–7, 201, 205, 271, 275, 276
  Scottish Land Court, 175–6, 181
Land for the Many report, 149
Land for the people (Dooley), 211
Land hunger, 113–14, 121, 230
Land League *see* Irish Land League; Welsh Land League
Land nationalisation, 96–107
Land Nationalisation (Wallace), 100
Land Nationalisation Society, 102–3, 105
Land Plan, 9
Land Question in Wales, The (NWPDA, 1889), 269

Land Question in Wales, The (NWPDA, 1892), 273
Land reclamation, 32–3, 38
Land redistribution
  impacts upon landlords, 2–3, 13–14, 18, 214, 218, 225–30, 303–21
  Ireland, 2–3, 13–14, 113–30, 211–19, 225, 230, 243, 303–5
  Northern Ireland, 2, 14, 211–30
  Scotland, 8–9, 243
Land Reform (Scotland) Act (2003), 9, 172, 173
Land Reform (Scotland) Act (2016), 9, 172
Land restoration, 99–100, 105
Land Revenue Acts, 73–4, 75
Land settlement schemes, 174–85
Land Settlement (Scotland) Act (1919), 8, 172–3, 177, 179–80
Land valuation, 103, 193, 196, 243, 296
Land War, 6, 115, 116, 119, 261
Landed elites, 3–4, 6, 7, 13–14, 16, 99–101, 117, 191, 213–30, 237–51, 259–77
Landlord–tenant relations
  dispute resolution, 117, 190–1, 193–5, 198, 200, 202–5
  England, 16, 103, 190, 241
  Ireland, 6, 12–15, 103, 115–27, 163–9, 241
  Northern Ireland, 212
  Scotland, 6, 8, 48–51, 55, 103, 175–6, 241, 290–5
  Wales, 10–12, 190–4, 203, 205, 259, 264–77, 286–90, 292–6
Landlordism in Wales ('Adfyfr'), 270
Landlords
  absenteeism, 82, 192, 245, 270, 285
  collective action, 15–16, 238–9, 243–4, 247–51, 259–77
  conceptions of property, 239–43
  debt, 8, 49, 51–2, 56, 61–3, 216, 242, 304–5
  declining power of, 7, 10, 13–14, 237–43, 249–51, 276
  defence associations, 15–16, 237–8, 244, 247–8, 251, 259–77, 295
  direct farming, 226–8, 230
  impacts of land redistribution upon, 2–3, 13–14, 18, 214, 218, 225–30, 303–21
  improvements paid for by, 176, 193–4, 270, 293–4
  political lobbying, 15, 238, 244, 246–7
  press representations, 17, 238, 247, 249, 260, 264–72, 275–6, 287, 289–90, 295
  relations with tenants *see* landlord–tenant relations
  reputation, 11, 169, 245, 250, 251, 265–76, 288
  responses to land reform, 14–16, 237–51, 259–77, 285–97
  wealth management, 303–21
Landscape design, 4
Lansdowne, Henry Petty-Fitzmaurice, 5th marquess, 218, 238
Laois, 164, 168
Larson, Ruth, 5
Leases
  commercial properties, 310
  competitive bidding for, 50, 294
  and improvement, 4, 58
  Ireland, 159–60, 167–8
  Scotland, 50, 58, 247, 294
Leblanc process, 50
Lefevre, George Shaw, 140–1
Leinster, Edward Fitzgerald, 7th duke, 315, 320
Leinster, Maurice Fitzgerald, 6th duke, 315, 319
Leinster estate, 313–16, 319–20
Leinster Leader, 119
Leisure, 4, 72, 74, 102, 103, 142, 144, 145–6, 229–30, 243
Leitrim, 262
Leneman, Leah, 176, 178, 181, 183
Leslie, Sir John, 117
Lewis, 2, 48–64, 177–8
Lewis, J. Herbert, 272
Liberal Federations, 96, 270, 272, 275
Liberal party, 9, 10, 95, 142, 172, 175, 190, 196–7, 242–3, 245, 247, 259, 264, 271–2, 296
Liberty and Property Defence League, 265
Limerick, 161, 164
Limerick and Clare Examiner, 168
Lincoln, Abraham, 101
Linen, 29–30, 217
Lissan estate, 215, 228, 229
Little Bernera, 59
Liverpool Mercury, 197

Livingstone, David Naismith, 181
Llanelli, 292–3
Llewellyn, Sir John, 198
Lloyd George, David, 10, 144, 243, 272
Loans, 15, 52, 121–2, 222
Lobbying, 15, 238, 244, 246–7
Local government, 6, 14, 213, 276
Loch, George, 244
Loch, James, 28–9, 32, 34, 37–9, 42, 56
Lochs parish, 50, 52, 59, 60, 62
London, 61, 96, 97, 100–1, 123, 140–1, 143, 221, 239, 265, 307–8, 310
London Stock Exchange, 307–8, 311, 313, 314
Lort, Elizabeth, 285
Lundberg, Ferdinand, 320–1
Lutyens, Sir Edwin, 146, 147, 150
Luxury goods, 243, 314

McAllister, Thomas, 223–4
Macartney, G. C., 216–17
Macaulay, Donald, 59
MacAskill, John, 50, 62
MacCabe, Alistair, 116
McClintock family, 215
McDonagh, Briony, 5
Macdonald, Donald, 48, 56, 59
MacDonald, James, 41
Macdonald estate, 241
MacFarlane, Donald, 98
McGregor, William, 53–4, 58, 60
McHugh, Edward, 242
McIver, Evander, 246
McIver, Lewis, 59, 61
Mackenzie, Alexander, 102
Mackenzie, William, 61
Mackenzie estate, 2, 48–64
Mackillop, Andrew, 34
McMullan, Henry, 121
Macnaghten, Sir Francis, 216
McNall, Christopher, 203
Macphail, Calum Campbell, 241
McRae, Alexander, 60
Magna Carta, 136–7, 143–5, 149
Magna Carta Commemoration Committee, 144–5, 147
Mahoney, Paschal, 169
Maidenhead Common, 142
Malcolm, George, 247–8
Manchester Martyrs, 98
Manufacturing, 4, 33; *see also* industry

Marine (Scotland) Act (2010), 85
Markievicz, Constance, 116
Marriage, 4, 241, 263
Marshall, Anthony, 39–40
Marx, Karl, 100, 101
Matheson, Sir James, 63
Mauchline, 180–1
Maurice, F. D., 100
Mayo, 113
Meath, 166, 168
Mechanisation, 3
Media *see* press
Meelick, 160–1
Mercers Hospital, 166
Merioneth, 262, 263
Metropolitan Commons Act, 140
Mexico, 124, 308
Meyrick, Sir George, 262
Middle classes, 14, 16, 118, 124, 240
Midland Tribune, 121
Migration, 29, 31, 32, 42–3, 116; *see also* emigration
Milford Haven, 77–81
Military, 33, 34, 39, 49, 50, 119–20, 164, 177, 180–1, 183, 239–40, 312
Military Service Pensions, 122–3, 128, 129
Mill, John Stuart, 14, 100
Mineral rights, 72, 73, 181, 222, 223, 228–9
Mining, 4, 229, 264
Minister of Shipping, 76
Minister of Transport, 76, 77–8, 80
Minister of War Transport, 76
Ministry of Agriculture and Fisheries, 200
Mirehouse, Richard, 287
Mitchell, Joseph, 48–9, 55
Mitchelstown massacre, 192
Mixed farming, 35, 183, 286, 290
Monaghan, 124
Monbiot, George, 1, 16, 149
Monck, Henry, Lord, 317
Monopolies, 7, 9, 54, 59, 78–80, 85, 100–1, 240
Monquhitter Agricultural Association, 291
Montgomery, Hugh de Fellenburg, 219–20
Montgomeryshire, 262
Moore-Colyer, R. J., 12
Moray, 32, 38, 40, 42, 43, 290–2

Morayshire Farmers' Club, 291
Moriarty, Thomas, 163
Morrison brothers, 57
Mortgages, 314, 315–16, 319–20
Morvich, 29–30, 35, 38, 43
Mostyn, Llewellyn Lloyd-Mostyn, Lord, 263
Mott-Radclyffe, Sr C., 203
Mountmellick, 164
Mourne estate, 229
Mousley, Thomas, 286–90, 293, 296
Muirkirk estate, 52
Mulholland, John, 217
Municipal bonds, 308
Murdoch, John, 102

Nannau estate, 262
Nairnshire, 285–6, 290–2, 293–4
Nairnshire Farmers' Club, 291
Napier Commission, 101, 172, 246, 247–8
Napoleonic Wars, 17, 49, 307
Nation, 115
National Footpaths Society, 141
National identities, 6–7, 11–12, 16, 191, 199, 211–12, 259–60
National Liberal Federation, 96
National Trust, 5, 10, 139, 141–2, 145–50
National Trust Act (1907), 142, 146
Nationalisation, 96–107
Nationalism
  Irish, 4, 12, 115–25, 128–30, 211–12, 242
  Welsh, 11, 15, 259–60
Navigation, 72, 73, 74, 76
Ness, 53, 54, 55
New Statistical Account, 33
New York Stock Exchange, 307, 311
Nonconformity, 11–12, 191, 259–60, 265, 268, 276, 288, 295
Norbury, Hector Graham-Toler, 3rd earl, 164
Norfolk, 38
Normanton, Helena, 144, 145
North Wales Chronicle, 268
North Wales Express and Observer, 267, 268
North Wales Property Defence Association, 16, 259, 261–77, 295
Northern Ireland
  agrarian agitation, 220–1
  agriculture, 226–8
  cattle farming, 227
  country houses, 213, 214, 225, 228, 229–30
  Crown estate, 72
  devolved government, 17
  estates, 213–30
  foreshore management, 72
  forestry, 228
  land redistribution, 2, 13–14, 211–30
  landlord–tenant relations, 212
  mineral rights, 222, 223, 228–9
  mining and quarrying, 229
  national identity, 211–12
  Northern Ireland Land Act, 2, 211–12, 214, 222–30
  Northern Ireland Parliament, 220, 221, 222–4
  partition, 2, 217
  Protestantism, 212, 220–1
  textile production, 217
  tourism, 229–30
  Ulster Farmers' Union, 221, 224
  Unbought Tenants' Association, 220–1
  unionism, 212
  untenanted land, 225
  see also Ireland
Northern Ireland Labour Party, 223
Northern Ireland Land Act (1925), 2, 211–12, 214, 222–30
Northern Ireland Parliament, 220, 221, 222–4
Northern Whig, 221
Northumberland, 39–41
Notice periods, 194, 195
Notices to quit, 192, 194, 195, 201, 202, 205
Nottingham Journal, 145–6
Nugent family, 215, 216

O'Connell, Daniel, 12
O'Connell, Morgan J., 168
O'Connor, Emmet, 116
O'Connor, Fergus, 9
O'Connor, John, 128, 129
O'Donnell, Peadar, 124
Offaly, 119–30, 163, 165
Office of Woods and Forests, 71–2, 73–5, 76
O'Halpin, Eunan, 123
O'Higgins, Kevin, 118, 121, 123, 124, 125–6

Old Statistical Account, 32, 36, 37, 41
O'Malley, Ernie, 113–14
On another man's wound (O'Malley), 113
O'Neill, Edward, Lord, 216, 226
O'Neill, Terence, 14
Oranmore and Browne, Geoffrey Browne, Lord, 218, 219, 224
Orkney, Thomas FitzMaurice, 5th earl, 164
O'Shiel, Kevin, 116
Otmoor, 138
Outdoor relief scheme, 158, 161
Overseas investments, 308
Owen, George H. M., 266–70, 272–6
Owen, Robert, 97–8

Paine, Thomas, 98
Paisley, Ian, 221
Paraguay, 308
Parks, 4, 9, 140, 226, 229
Parnell, Charles Stewart, 13, 115
Parry, John, 260
Partition, 2, 217
Pasture, 38, 39, 51, 60, 144; *see also* grazing
Paternalism, 5, 55, 239, 240, 241, 248, 250
Paton, Robert, 180
Peace movement, 95, 96
Peasant proprietorship, 105, 114, 115, 214, 219, 224, 303
Peep O day boys, 13
Pembrokeshire, 285–90, 296
Pembrokeshire Tenant-Farmers' Association, 287, 289–90
Peniarth estate, 263
Penrhos estate, 263
Penrhyn, George Sholto Douglas-Pennant, Lord, 16, 262, 263, 266, 268, 272, 274, 276
Penrhyn estate, 262, 263, 268
People's Budget, 9, 243
Perceval-Maxwell family, 216, 227
Percy, Eustace, Lord, 222
Persse estate, 117
Petitions, 53, 119, 161, 260, 289
Piers, 54–5, 249
Plan of Campaign, 6, 14, 15
Planned towns and villages, 8, 33
Plantations, 4, 118, 121
Plea for the Nationalisation of Land (Clark), 103

Poaching, 138–9
Pochin, H. D., 263, 264
Poland, 101
Poll Tax, 17
Pollock, Hugh, 220
Poor Law Bill, 157–69
Poor Relief Extension Act, 168
Population growth, 50, 51, 62
Portaferry, 215, 216
Ports, 4, 30, 42
Poverty, 9, 11, 40, 48, 62, 63, 142, 157–69, 175, 260–1
Powell, Evan, 263
Powell, W. R. H., 289
Powis Castle, 285
Presbyterian church, 212, 220–1
Press
  coverage of agricultural legislation, 195, 197
  coverage of evictions, 165, 166, 168
  coverage of Poor Law relief, 160, 162, 163
  coverage of Runnymede, 145–6, 148–9
  England, 145–6, 148–9, 195, 197, 272
  Ireland, 160, 162, 163, 165, 166, 168, 221
  landlord defence associations' use of, 238, 247, 249, 266–71
  representations of agitation, 10, 221, 259, 260, 265–72, 274–6, 287, 289–90
  representations of landlords, 17, 238, 247, 249, 260, 264–72, 275–6, 287, 289–90, 295
  Scotland, 247
  Wales, 10, 259, 260, 264–72, 274–6, 287, 289–90, 295
Productivity, 27, 51, 115, 183
Progress, 33, 245
Progress and Poverty (George), 99–100, 104–5
Property Defence Association, 15, 261
Protestantism, 164, 212, 220–1, 238
Protests, 6, 10, 136–7, 138–9, 150–1, 260; *see also* agrarian agitation
Public access *see* access
Public interest, 71–86, 142
Public open spaces, 139–40, 142
Public rivers, 71–2, 73, 76

Public Safety (Emergency Powers), Act, 118, 122, 126
Public trust doctrine, 72, 74
Public works scheme, 158, 163

Quarrying, 4, 181, 229, 262
Queen's County *see* Laois
Quinn, George, 161

Railways, 181, 229, 247, 248–9, 264, 308, 309, 317–18, 319
'Rambling Recollections of an Agitator' (Clark), 97
Rawdon, John, 159
Rawnsley, Hardwicke, 142
Readman, Paul, 10
Rebecca Riots, 11
Recreation rights, 72, 74, 142, 144
Reed, Gabriel, 39
Reed, Ralph, 39
Refugees, 96, 101
Reilly, Ciarán, 121
Relief committees, 161–3, 167
Rent strikes, 15, 214–15, 244
Rents
    abatements, 11, 52, 163, 247, 260, 271, 287–9, 291, 292–4, 304
    arrears and non-payment, 49, 52, 60–1, 163, 164, 201, 290, 292–4
    fair rent, 173, 202, 261, 288
    increases, 5, 182, 192, 193, 200, 287, 292–4
    judicial rent reviews, 13, 197, 204, 319
    negotiation of, 192, 193
    for sheep farms, 59–61
    taxation of, 100, 296
Repeal movement, 13
Reprisals, 117, 122
Reputation, 11, 169, 245, 250, 251, 265–76, 288
Return of owners of land of one acre and upwards, 212–13, 214
Reynolds, John, 168
Reynolds, K. D., 5
Rhiwlas estate, 191, 263
Richard, Henry, 259
Richards, Eric, 29, 41–2, 48, 63
Right to buy, 16, 173
Rights of way, 138
Rights to roam, 141
Roberts, Herbert, 197, 200
Roberts, J. Bryn, 261
Roberts, M. J. D., 139, 141

Roberts, Samuel, 11
Robertson, Henry, 263–4
Robertson, Iain, 177–8
Robertson, John, 291–2, 293
Robinson, James, 305–7
Roche, Edmond, 168
Rockefeller, William, 320–1
Rogart, 31, 32, 36
Rogers, Henry Huttleston, 145
Rogers, James Edwin Thorold, 16
Roscommon, 162, 164, 165
Rose, Hugh, 35
Rosse, William Parsons, 3rd earl, 163
Ross-shire, 30, 40, 61, 63, 290
Rothbury Common, 39–40
Route Tenants' Association, 220–1
Royal Agricultural College, Cirencester, 228
Royal Commission on Agricultural Depression, 293, 295
Royal Commission on Coast Erosion, 75–6, 77
Royal Commission on Land for Wales *see* Welsh Land Commission
Royal Highland and Agricultural Society, 37–8
Royal Institution of Chartered Surveyors, 204
Royal Irish Constabulary (RIC), 116, 122
'rule by the best', 240–1
Runnymede, 136–9, 143–51
Ruskin, John, 100, 142
Russell, John, Lord, 158, 166
Russia, 9
Ruttledge, P. J., 129

Sackville-West, W. E., 263
Salisbury, Robert Gascoyne-Cecil, 3rd marquess, 197
Salt, 2, 50, 53
Sandbach, Samuel, 264
Saville, John, 98
Sayes Court, 141
Scotland
    agrarian agitation, 6, 8, 9, 242–4, 290–2
    agriculture, 8, 27–43, 48–51, 57–61, 249, 286, 290–4
    Annexed Estates Board, 33–4
    arable farming, 35, 37, 38–9, 43
    Board of Agriculture for Scotland, 106, 173, 175–85

INDEX

cattle farming, 49, 59–60
Chartism, 97, 99
Community Empowerment Act, 9
community landownership, 7, 9
concentration of ownership, 240, 251
Congested Districts Board, 99, 176, 178, 249
Crofter MPs, 95, 96, 98–9, 106
Crofters Holdings (Scotland) Act, 8, 9, 172, 175, 178, 192, 243, 248, 261, 291, 294
Crofters (Scotland) Act (1955), 173, 184
Crofters (Scotland) Act (1993), 173
crofting, 8, 9, 48, 57, 98–9, 172–86
Crown estate, 71–2, 81–6, 244
Deer Forest Commission, 247–8
devolved government, 17, 72, 81–6, 251
distilling, 49, 55–7
economic restructuring, 2, 6, 7–8
emigration, 31, 32, 48, 50, 55, 62–3, 247
employment, 8, 29–30, 42–3, 53
Enlightenment, 8, 33
estates, 8, 27–43, 48–64, 241, 246, 285–6, 290–2, 293–4
evictions, 6, 8, 28, 30–2, 36, 43, 48, 50–1, 59, 101–2
famines, 36, 62, 175, 249
fishing, 42–3, 49, 50–1, 52–5, 57, 62, 247
foreshore management, 71–2, 81–6, 244
Forfeited Estates Commission, 8, 33
Gaelic language, 34, 98, 241
Highland Clearances, 6, 8, 28, 30–2, 36, 43, 50–1, 56, 59, 101–2, 175, 179, 241
Highlands and Islands, 6, 8, 9, 27–43, 48–64, 82, 98–9, 101–2, 172–86, 241, 242, 247–9
historiography, 174, 177–9
Home Rule, 95
housing, 182
improvement, 2, 27–43, 58, 175, 248–9
Independence Referendum, 17
industry, 8, 29–30, 42, 55–7, 229, 244
Jacobite Risings, 8, 33

kelping, 2, 49–50, 51, 57, 244
Land Commission, 18
land redistribution, 8–9, 243
Land Reform (Scotland) Act (2003), 9, 172, 173
Land Reform (Scotland) Act (2016), 9, 172
land settlement schemes, 174–85
Land Settlement (Scotland) Act, 8, 172–3, 177, 179–80
land used for sport, 102, 103, 243
land values, 243
landlord defence associations, 244, 247–8, 251
landlord responses, 15, 16, 237–8, 244–51, 290–5
landlord–tenant relations, 6, 8, 48–51, 55, 103, 175–6, 241, 290–5
leases, 50, 58, 247, 294
Lowlands, 8, 27, 28, 172–86
Mackenzie estate, 2, 48–64
Napier Commission, 101, 172, 246, 247–8
national identity, 6–7, 16
planned towns and villages, 8, 33
poverty, 40, 48, 62, 63, 175
Scottish Crown Estate Act, 84–6
Scottish Land Court, 175–6, 181
Scottish Parliament, 17, 72, 81, 83, 86, 251
sheep farming, 8, 28, 35–6, 39–41, 43, 48–51, 57–61
Small Landholders and Agricultural Holdings (Scotland) Act, 173
Small Landholders (Scotland) Act, 172–3, 175–7, 178, 185
small landholdings, 172–86
steel industry, 229
Sutherland estate, 27–43, 56, 244, 246
textile production, 29–30
Scotland Act (1998), 81–2, 85
Scotland Act (2016), 83
Scottish Affairs Committee, 83
Scottish Crown Estate Act (2019), 84–6
Scottish Fisheries Board, 54, 55, 99
Scottish Labour Party, 96
Scottish Land and Property Federation (SLPF), 176
Scottish Land Commission, 18
Scottish Land Court (SLC), 175–6, 181
Scottish Landowners Federation, 251

Scottish National Party (SNP), 17
Scottish Parliament, 17, 72, 81, 83, 86, 251
Scrope, George Poulett, 159
Seabed, 71–86
Seabrooke, W., 202
Seaforth, Francis Mackenzie, Lord, 48, 51, 52, 57
Seasonal labour, 29, 116
Secularism, 95, 97
Security of tenure, 13, 100, 173, 192, 194, 197, 200–4, 261, 270–1, 288
Select Committee on Public Walks, 139
Sellar, Patrick, 28–32, 35–9, 41–3
Shane's Castle, 230
Sheehan, Fr John, 160
Sheep breeding, 40
Sheep farming, 8, 28, 35–6, 39–41, 43, 48–51, 57–61
Sheffield Daily Telegraph, 148
Sinclair, Sir John, 34–5
Sinn Féin, 115, 116–17, 120, 124
Six Essays on Commons Preservtion (Peek), 140
Skeffington, James, 221
Skelbo, 30–1, 37
Skye, 62, 102, 177–8, 241
Slavery, 101, 105, 264
Sligo, 262
Sligo, Henry Browne, 5th marquess, 314
Small landholder identity, 174, 182, 184–5
Small Landholders and Agricultural Holdings (Scotland) Act (1931), 173
Small Landholders (Scotland) Act (1911), 172–3, 175–7, 178, 185
Smallholdings, 3, 98, 157–63, 172–86; *see also* crofting
Smith, Adam, 100
Smith, Augustus, 140
Smith, Elizabeth, 158, 161, 166–7
Smith, Samuel, 196
Smith Commission, 83
Smuggling, 55
Social Democratic Federation, 96, 102
Social engineering, 118
Social housing, 16
Social status, 3–4, 7, 213–14, 217, 239–41, 243, 245, 276, 285, 296
Socialism, 11, 95, 97–8, 100, 106, 124, 245

Soil quality, 30, 32, 35, 38, 40, 43, 185
Soldiers *see* military
Somerville, Sir William, 168
Soup kitchens, 158
South Africa, 96
South Wales Property Defence Association, 16, 273, 295
Spence, Thomas, 140
Spencer, John Poyntz, 5th earl, 140
Spinningdale, 29
Sport, 4, 102, 103, 142, 144, 145–6, 229–30, 243
Spynie Loch, 32–3
Stables, William, 290–1
Stackpole estate, 285–7, 290, 293, 294
Stafford, George Leveson-Gower, 2nd Marquess, 31, 41–2
Standing, Guy, 150
Stanley, Henry, Lord, 263, 274
Staples family, 215, 229
Statutory Small Tenancies (SSTs), 176
Steel industry, 229, 264
Sterling, 313
Stewart, Alexander, 54, 60
Stewart, N. P., 263
Stewart Mackenzie, James Alexander, 48–64
Stewart Mackenzie, Mary, 48–9, 51, 52, 63
Stock markets, 307–14, 317–18, 321
Stornoway, 49, 50, 53, 54, 55–7, 59, 62
Stornoway distillery, 49, 55–7
Strathbrora, 31–2
Strikes, 120; *see also* rent strikes
Strokestown, 162
Succession rights, 204
Sudeley, Charles Hanbury-Tracy, Lord, 262, 273
Sunday Closing (Wales) Act (1881), 191, 199
Super tax, 243
Sustainability, 18, 84
Suther, Francis, 32
Sutherland, Angus, 98–9, 242
Sutherland, Elizabeth Leveson-Gower, Countess, 28, 32, 34, 39
Sutherland, George Sutherland-Leveson-Gower, 3rd duke, 16, 244, 246
Sutherland, Sandy, 31–2
Sutherland estate, 27–43, 56, 244, 246

INDEX 345

Swing Riots, 9
Swords, Mary, 122–3, 128

Tacksmen, 31, 34, 52, 58, 60–1
Talbot, Fanny, 142
Tankerville, George Bennet, Lord, 315
Tariffs, 2, 49–50
Taxation, 9, 16, 99–100, 103–6, 227, 243, 276, 296, 311, 317, 320
Taylor, Helen, 97, 106
Taylor, Isaac, 263
Telford, Thomas, 33
Temperance movement, 95, 96
Tenancy in Wales (Vincent), 270–1
Tenants
  agitation *see* agrarian agitation
  Agricultural Holdings Act Tenancies, 204
  compensation for improvements, 13, 173, 192–6, 200, 202, 204, 247, 261, 270, 288
  eviction of *see* evictions
  Farm Business Tenancies, 204
  improvements by, 13, 58, 103, 173, 175, 192–6, 200, 202, 204, 247, 261, 270, 28
  leases *see* leases
  lotters, 30, 32, 43, 57–9, 62
  notice periods, 194, 195
  notices to quit, 192, 194, 195, 201, 202, 205
  relations with landlords *see* landlord–tenant relations
  rent *see* rents
  restrictions of termination of tenancy, 201
  right to buy, 16, 173
  rights and protections, 8, 13, 172–3, 184, 198, 200–5
  security of tenure, 13, 100, 173, 192, 194, 197, 200–4, 261, 270–1, 288
  sub-tenants, 52, 58, 60–1, 166
  succession rights, 204
  tenancy agreements, 4, 5, 163–4, 192, 193, 195, 265, 269, 270, 275
Tenure of Land (Wales) Bill, 192, 196
Textile production, 29–30, 217
Third Party Determination (TPD), 204–5
Thomas, D. Lleufer, 275
Thomas, T. D., 263
Thompson, F. M. L., 7

Thompson, William, 100
Times, 218, 270, 272, 295
Tipperary, 164
Tiree, 57
Tithe War, 11, 260, 269, 288
Tithes, 10–11, 260, 269, 288, 289, 290
Todd, W. R., 221
Tourism, 229–30
Townshend, Charles 'Turnip', 38
Trade unions, 101
Tranter, Albert Cecil, 144, 147
Trevelyan, G. M., 142, 261
Trinity College Dublin, 166
Trollope, Anthony, 240, 308
Tryweryn Valley, 18
Tuam, 161
Tubberdaly, 119–30
Tullamore, 120, 121, 126, 127
Tullygarvey, 163
Turnly, Francis, 216–17
Tyrone, 215, 221, 227

Uig, 48, 50, 52, 53, 55, 59, 60, 61, 62
Ulster Farmers' Union, 221, 224
Unbought Tenants' Association, 220–1
Underdevelopment, 42
Unemployment, 116, 312
UNESCO World Heritage Status, 18
Unionism, 119–20, 122, 212
United Irish League, 115
United Irishmen, 221
United States *see* America
Untenanted lands, 114, 117, 217–18, 225
Urbanisation, 4, 7, 238
Utopianism, 97

Vaughan, Herbert M., 276
Vaughan, John, 285
Ventry, 163
Vincent, James Edmund, 193, 270–1, 274, 276, 295
Vincent, Nicholas, 144

Wales
  agrarian agitation, 9, 10–11, 192–3, 242, 259–61, 264–76, 287–90, 294–5
  Agricultural Land Tribunal, 201, 202, 203, 204, 205
  agricultural legislation, 190–206
  agricultural tenancy reform consultations, 190, 194, 205–6

INDEX

Wales (*cont.*)
  agriculture, 190–206, 260, 286–90, 292–4
  arable farming, 286
  attempts to introduce Land Bill, 261, 271
  Board of Education, 199
  Cawdor estates, 285–97
  commons, 11
  country houses, 10, 269
  Crown estate, 71–2
  Cymru Fydd movement, 15, 199, 261, 270
  devolved government, 17, 190, 203–5
  disestablishment movement, 11, 15, 191, 260
  eisteddfodau, 263, 270
  employment, 269, 270
  enclosure, 11
  estates, 10, 11, 12, 193–4, 259–77, 285–97
  evictions, 11, 191–2, 269, 270–1, 275, 288, 296
  foreshore management, 71–2
  Government of Wales Act (1998), 190, 203–4
  gwerin society, 11–12, 259–60, 275, 276
  historiography, 11–12
  Home Rule, 194, 196, 197, 198–9, 261
  industry, 262, 264, 271
  Land Commission, 10, 11, 18, 190–7, 205, 262, 271–6, 286, 289, 295–6
  Land League, 260, 261, 266, 267–8, 275, 288, 295
  landlord defence associations, 15–16, 259–77, 295
  landlord responses, 15–16, 237, 259–77, 285–97
  landlord–tenant relations, 10–12, 190–4, 203, 205, 259, 264–77, 286–90, 292–6
  mining and quarrying, 262, 264
  National Assembly, 203–4
  National Trust, 142
  national identity, 6–7, 11–12, 16, 191, 199, 259–60
  nationalism, 11, 15, 259–60
  nonconformity, 11–12, 191, 259–60, 265, 268, 276, 288, 295
  poverty, 11, 260–1
  press, 10, 259, 260, 264–72, 274–6, 287, 289–90, 295
  proposed Land Court, 190, 192, 194–7, 201, 205, 271, 275, 276
  Rebecca Riots, 10–11
  steel industry, 264
  Tenure of Land (Wales) Bill, 192, 196
  Tithe War, 10–11, 260, 269, 288
  Welsh Agricultural Sub-Commission, 201
  Welsh language, 199, 200, 259, 260, 263, 266–9, 274, 296
Walker, Brian, 158, 159
Walker, Graham, 220
Wallace, Alfred Russel, 97–8, 99, 100, 102–5
War Bonds, 311–12, 318, 319
War of Independence, 113–14, 117, 123, 124–5, 130
Waste lands, 3, 9, 32, 37, 98
Water supplies, 181
Waterford, 165
Watkins, Tudor, 203
Wealth management, 303–21
Welsh Agricultural Sub-Commission, 201
Welsh Board of Education, 199
Welsh Intermediate Education Act (1889), 191, 199
Welsh Land Commission, 10, 11, 18, 190–7, 205, 262, 271–6, 286, 289, 295–6
Welsh Land League, 260, 261, 266, 267–8, 275, 288, 295
Welsh language, 199, 200, 259, 260, 263, 266–9, 274, 296
Werin, 267
West Indies, 6, 42
West Lothian Question, 17
Western Mail, 290
Westminster, Hugh Grosvenor, 1st duke, 263
Westport House, 314
Wexford, 164–5, 313
Weybridge, 137
Whiteboy movement, 13
Wicken Fen, 142
Wicklow, 161, 166, 313, 318
Wightman, Andy, 82
William IV, 144
Williams, George, 286–7, 289, 290

Williams, David, 12
Williams, Richard, 288
Williams, Thomas, 203
Williams-Bulkeley, Sir Richard, 262
Williams-Wynn, Sir Watkin, 269
Wimbledon Common, 140, 150
Wind farms, 72
Windsor, 136, 146
Windsor Castle, 143
Winstanley, Gerrard, 137
Withers, Hartley, 310
Women, 5, 262
Wood, James, 221
Woodlands *see* forests
Wool trade, 39
Workhouses, 157–61, 164–6, 168–9

Wyndham, George, 303, 304
Wyndham Act (1903), 2, 14, 115, 119, 214, 215–16, 224, 227, 303–5, 309, 314
Wynn, Owen Slaney, 269, 274
Wynne, W. R. M., 263
Wynne-Finch, C. A., 266
Wynnstay estate, 262, 269, 274, 285

York Buildings Company, 33
Young, William (Galgorm), 217
Young, William (Sutherland estate), 28–33, 35, 36, 39, 41–3
Young Ireland movement, 12, 115

Zapata, Emiliano, 124

EU representative:
Easy Access System Europe
Mustamäe tee 50, 10621 Tallinn, Estonia
Gpsr.requests@easproject.com